THE JOURNEY of MARCEL GROB

A STORY BY PHILIPPE COLLIN AND SÉBASTIEN GOETHALS
BASED UPON PHILIPPE COLLIN'S ORIGINAL IDEA
ART AND COLOR BY SÉBASTIEN GOETHALS

STRALSUND
HAMBURG
MINSK
BELARUS
AMSTERDAM
LONDON
ROTTERDAM
NETHERLANDS
BERLIN
WARSAW
BRUSSELS
ENGLISH CHANNEL
landing
June 6, 1944
BELGIUM
DRESDEN
KIEV
BREST
GERMANY
PARIS
LUXEMBOURG
PRAGUE
KRAKOW
UKRAINE
ALSACE-
LORRAINE
STUTTGART
NANTES
STRASBOURG
SLOVAKIA
FRANCE
KIRCHBERG
MULHOUSE
MUNICH
VIENNA
BRATISLAVA
ZURICH
BERNE
SWITZERLAND
BUDAPEST
HUNGARY
GENEVE
ODESSA
LAKE GARDA
TURIN
MILAN
ZAGREB
RUMANIA
BUCHAREST
CROATIA
BOLOGNA
MARZABOTTO
BELGRADE
MONACO
FLORENCE
SARAJEVO
SERBIA
BLACK SEA
ADRIATIC
SEA
MONTENEGRO
CORSICA
ITALY
BULGARIA
SOFIA
ROME
TIRANA
ISTANBUL
ALBANIA
NAPLES
SARDINIA

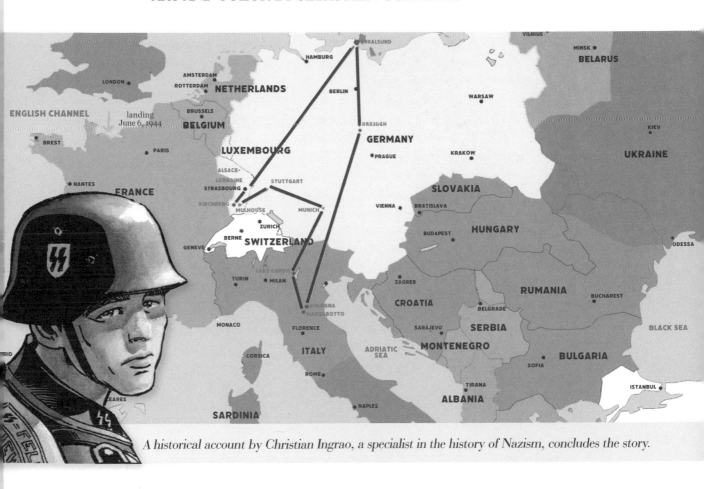

A historical account by Christian Ingrao, a specialist in the history of Nazism, concludes the story.

DEAD RECKONING
Annapolis, Maryland

To all the young people of Europe

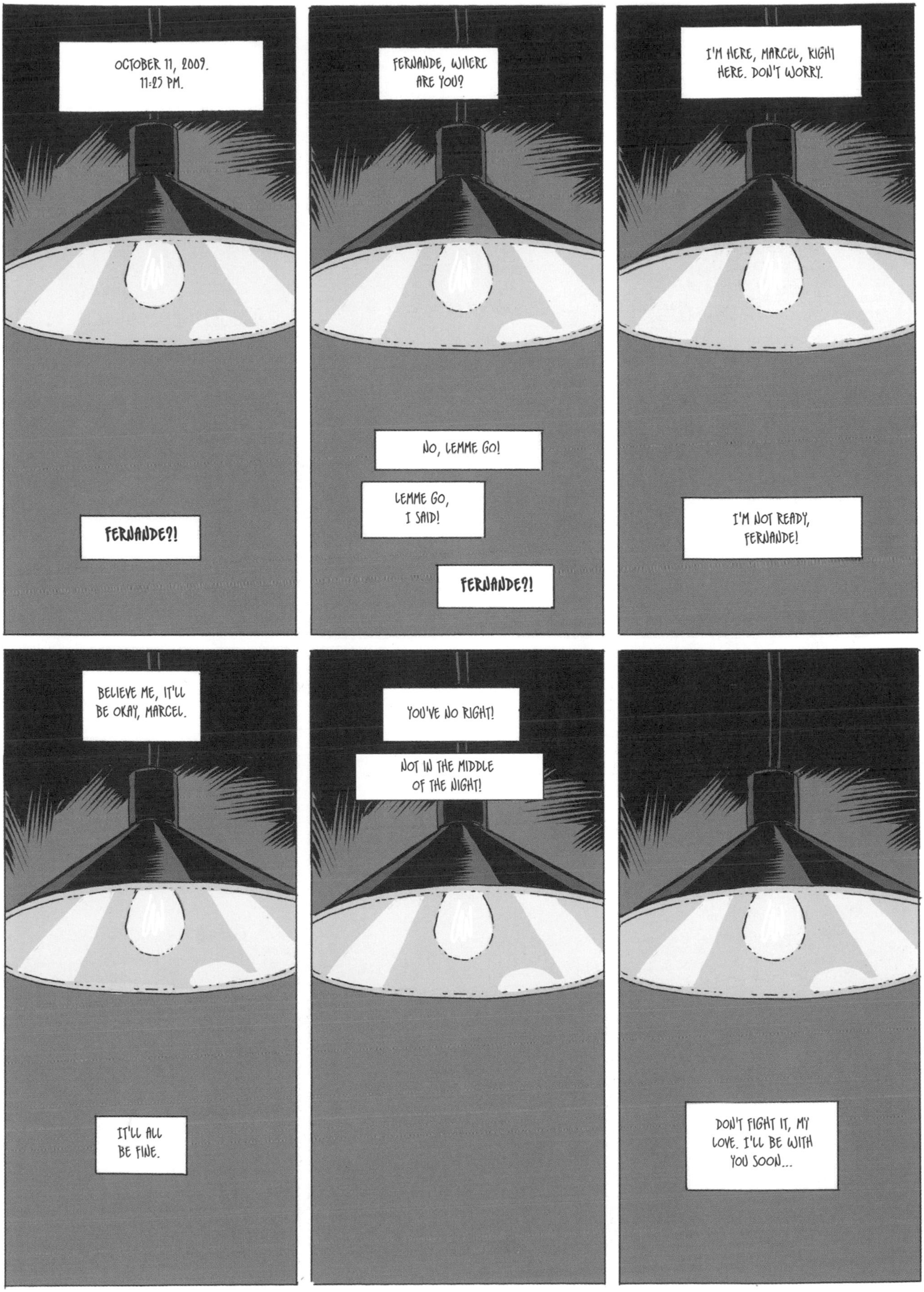
OCTOBER 11, 2009.
11:25 PM.
FERNANDE?!
FERNANDE, WHERE ARE YOU?
NO, LEMME GO!
LEMME GO, I SAID!
FERNANDE?!
I'M HERE, MARCEL, RIGHT HERE. DON'T WORRY.
I'M NOT READY, FERNANDE!
BELIEVE ME, IT'LL BE OKAY, MARCEL.
IT'LL ALL BE FINE.
YOU'VE NO RIGHT!
NOT IN THE MIDDLE OF THE NIGHT!
DON'T FIGHT IT, MY LOVE. I'LL BE WITH YOU SOON...

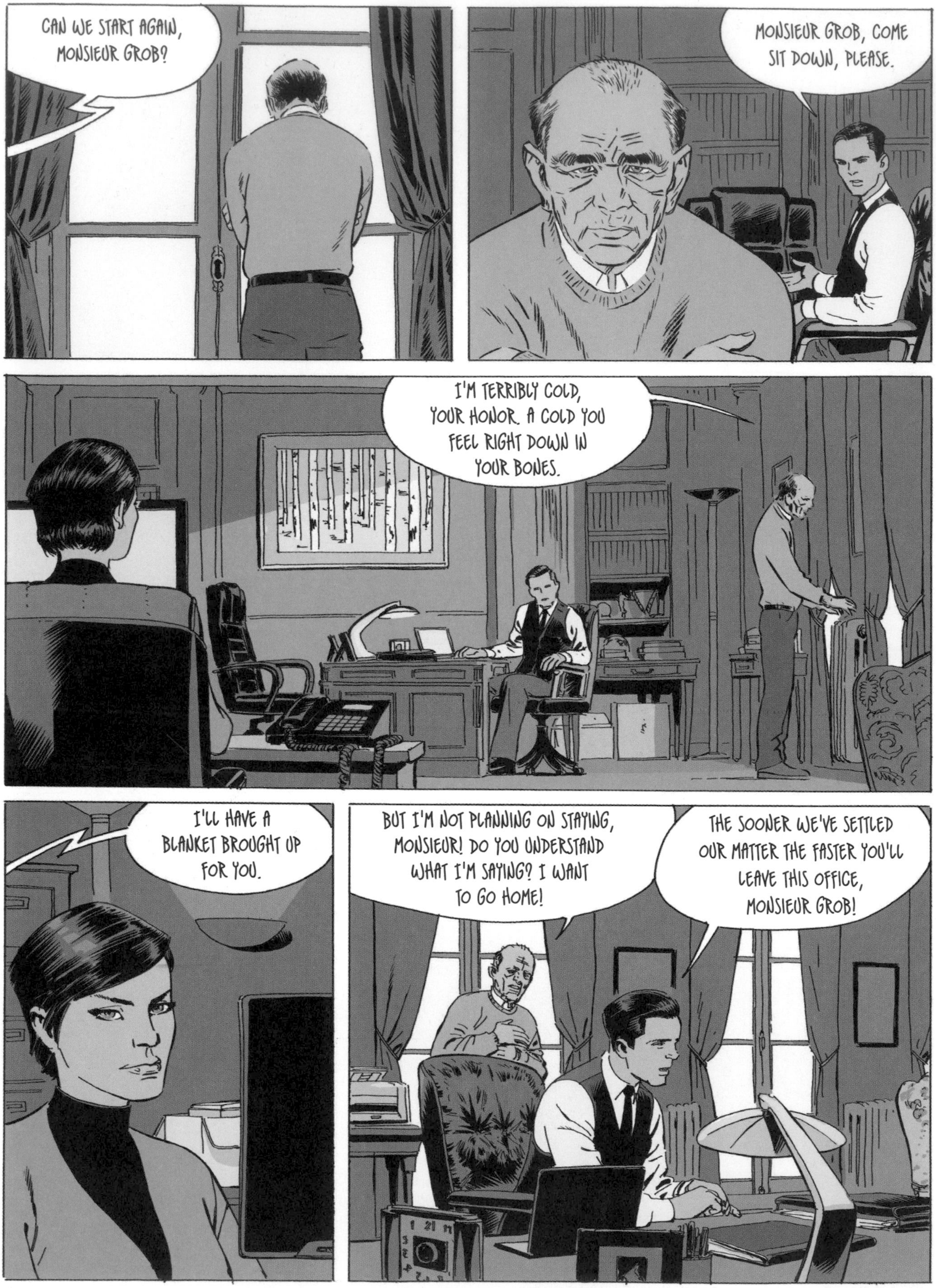
CAN WE START AGAIN, MONSIEUR GROB?
MONSIEUR GROB, COME SIT DOWN, PLEASE.
I'M TERRIBLY COLD, YOUR HONOR. A COLD YOU FEEL RIGHT DOWN IN YOUR BONES.
I'LL HAVE A BLANKET BROUGHT UP FOR YOU.
BUT I'M NOT PLANNING ON STAYING, MONSIEUR! DO YOU UNDERSTAND WHAT I'M SAYING? I WANT TO GO HOME!
THE SOONER WE'VE SETTLED OUR MATTER THE FASTER YOU'LL LEAVE THIS OFFICE, MONSIEUR GROB!

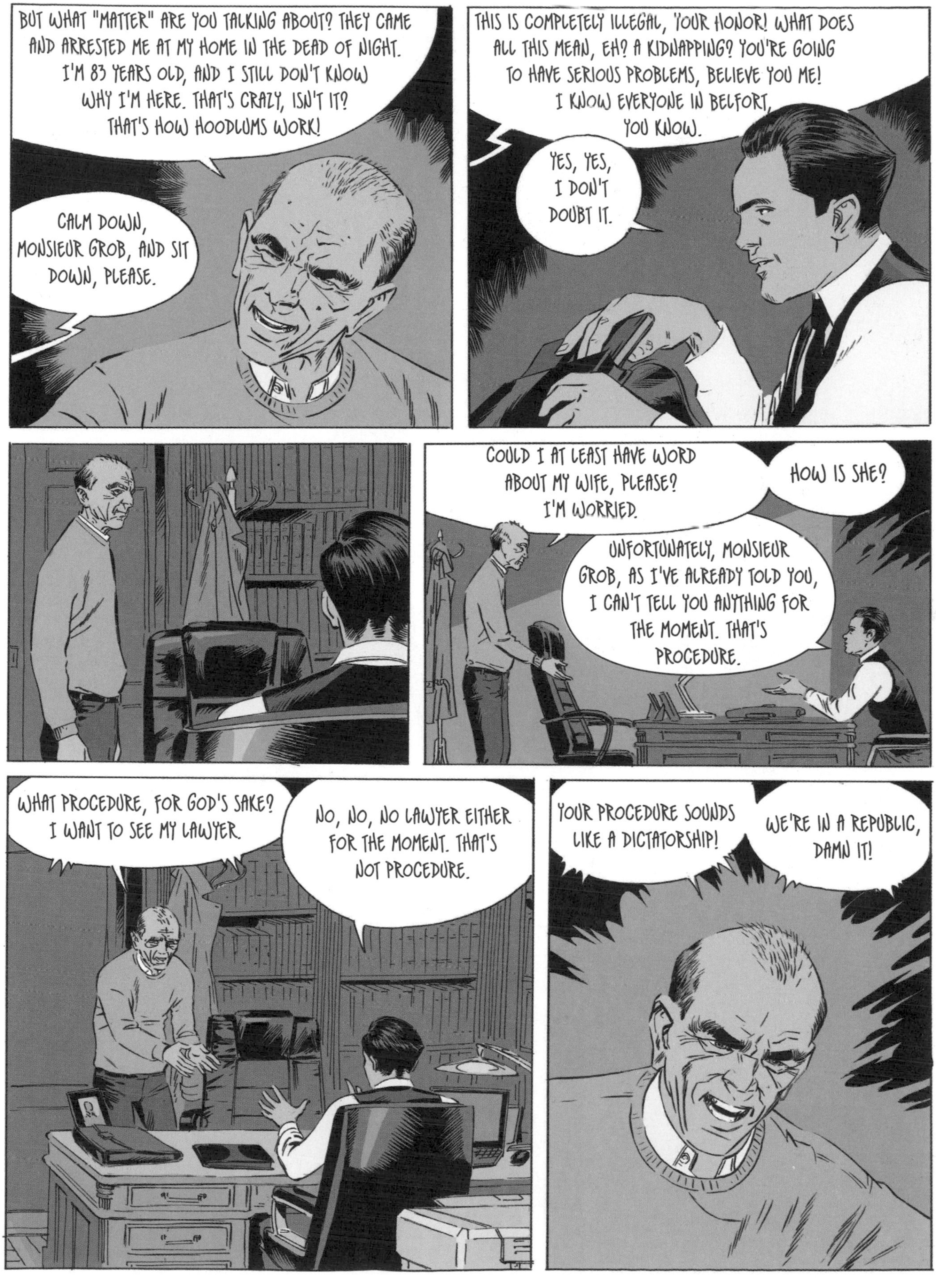

BUT WHAT "MATTER" ARE YOU TALKING ABOUT? THEY CAME AND ARRESTED ME AT MY HOME IN THE DEAD OF NIGHT. I'M 83 YEARS OLD, AND I STILL DON'T KNOW WHY I'M HERE. THAT'S CRAZY, ISN'T IT? THAT'S HOW HOODLUMS WORK!
CALM DOWN, MONSIEUR GROB, AND SIT DOWN, PLEASE.
THIS IS COMPLETELY ILLEGAL, YOUR HONOR! WHAT DOES ALL THIS MEAN, EH? A KIDNAPPING? YOU'RE GOING TO HAVE SERIOUS PROBLEMS, BELIEVE YOU ME! I KNOW EVERYONE IN BELFORT, YOU KNOW.
YES, YES, I DON'T DOUBT IT.
COULD I AT LEAST HAVE WORD ABOUT MY WIFE, PLEASE? I'M WORRIED.
HOW IS SHE?
UNFORTUNATELY, MONSIEUR GROB, AS I'VE ALREADY TOLD YOU, I CAN'T TELL YOU ANYTHING FOR THE MOMENT. THAT'S PROCEDURE.
WHAT PROCEDURE, FOR GOD'S SAKE? I WANT TO SEE MY LAWYER.
NO, NO, NO LAWYER EITHER FOR THE MOMENT. THAT'S NOT PROCEDURE.
YOUR PROCEDURE SOUNDS LIKE A DICTATORSHIP!
WE'RE IN A REPUBLIC, DAMN IT!

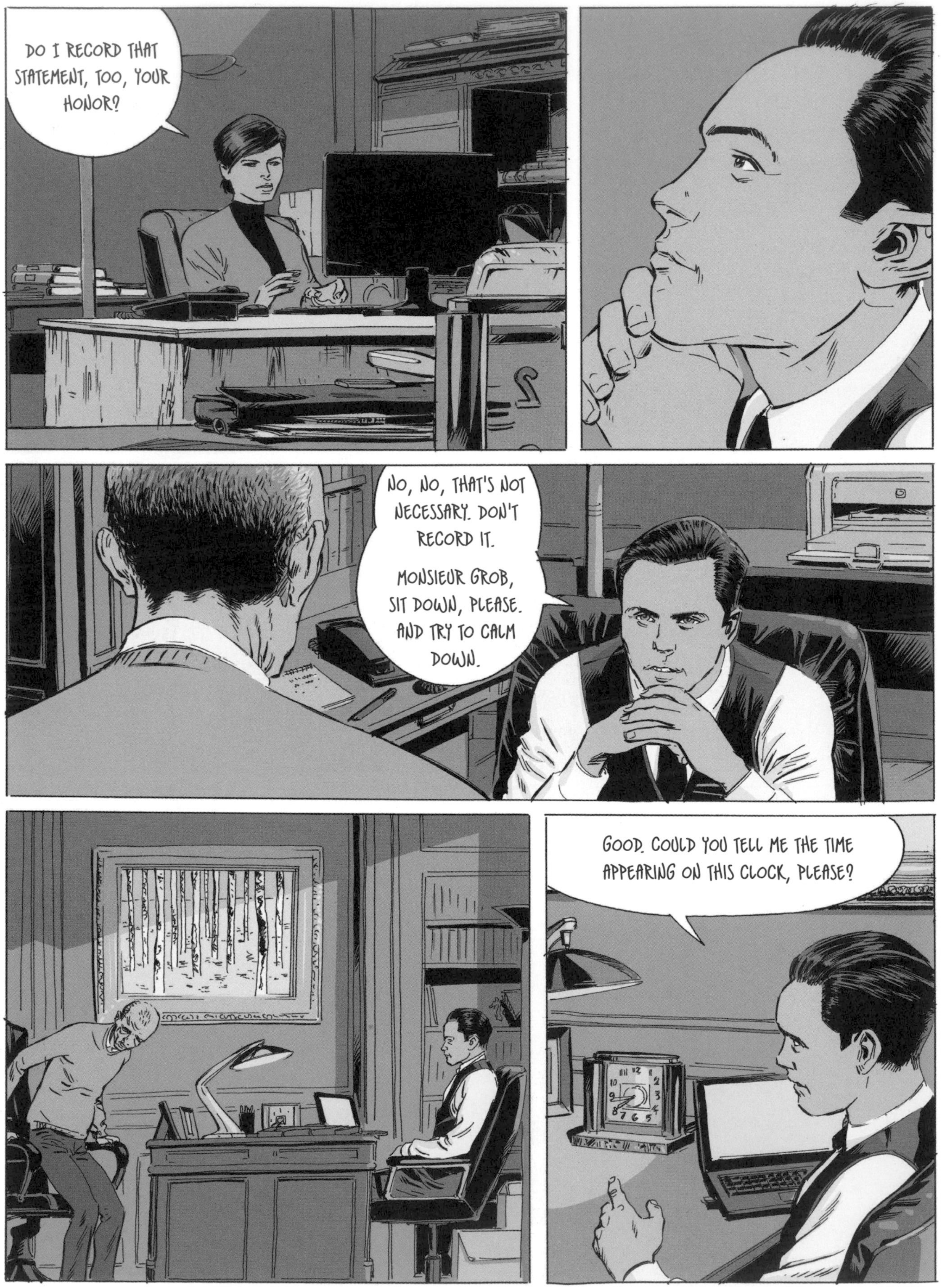
DO I RECORD THAT STATEMENT, TOO, YOUR HONOR?
NO, NO, THAT'S NOT NECESSARY. DON'T RECORD IT.
MONSIEUR GROB, SIT DOWN, PLEASE. AND TRY TO CALM DOWN.
GOOD. COULD YOU TELL ME THE TIME APPEARING ON THIS CLOCK, PLEASE?

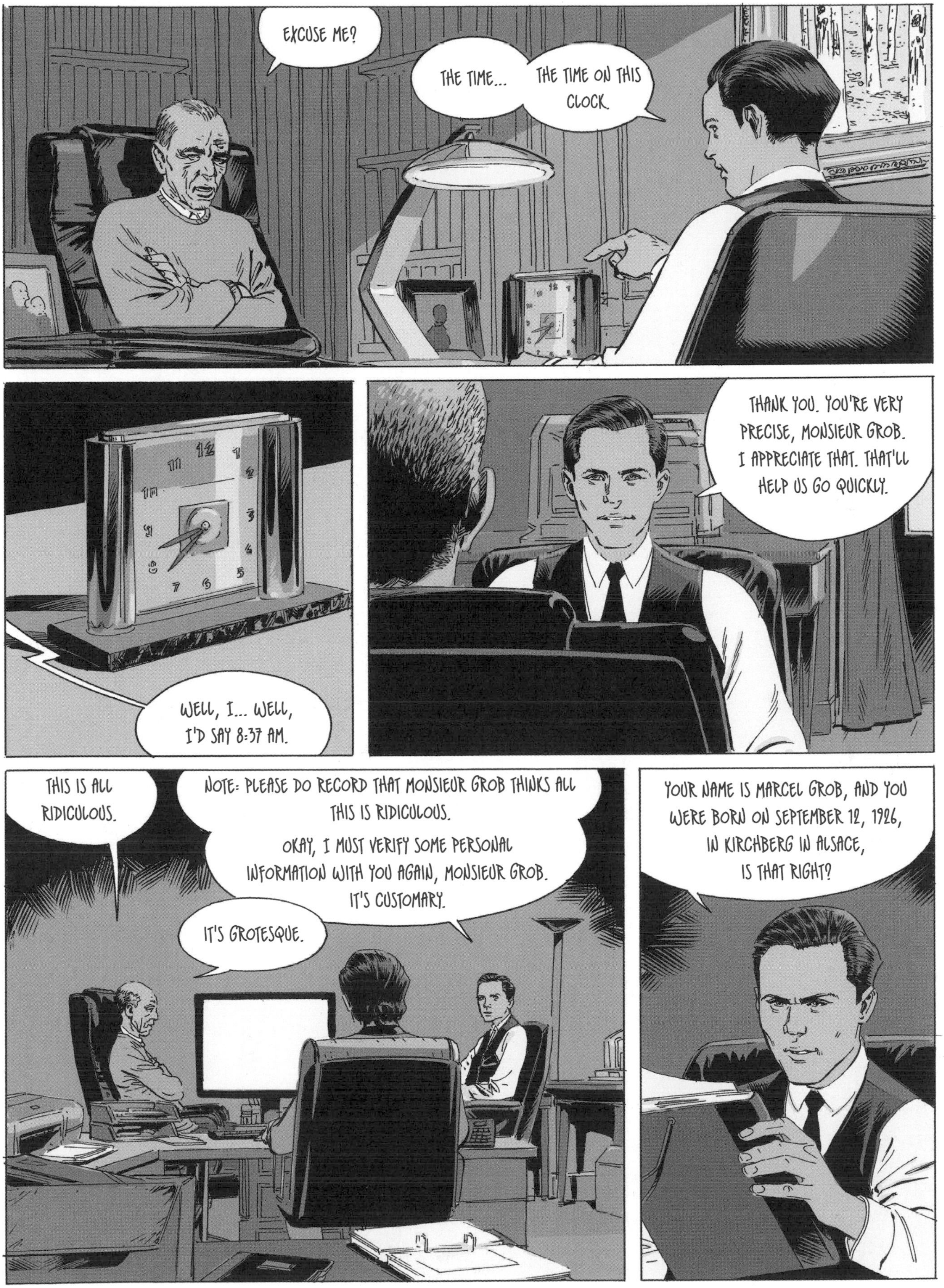
EXCUSE ME?
THE TIME...
THE TIME ON THIS CLOCK.
WELL, I... WELL, I'D SAY 8:37 AM.
THANK YOU. YOU'RE VERY PRECISE, MONSIEUR GROB. I APPRECIATE THAT. THAT'LL HELP US GO QUICKLY.
THIS IS ALL RIDICULOUS.
NOTE: PLEASE DO RECORD THAT MONSIEUR GROB THINKS ALL THIS IS RIDICULOUS.
OKAY, I MUST VERIFY SOME PERSONAL INFORMATION WITH YOU AGAIN, MONSIEUR GROB. IT'S CUSTOMARY.
IT'S GROTESQUE.
YOUR NAME IS MARCEL GROB, AND YOU WERE BORN ON SEPTEMBER 12, 1926, IN KIRCHBERG IN ALSACE, IS THAT RIGHT?

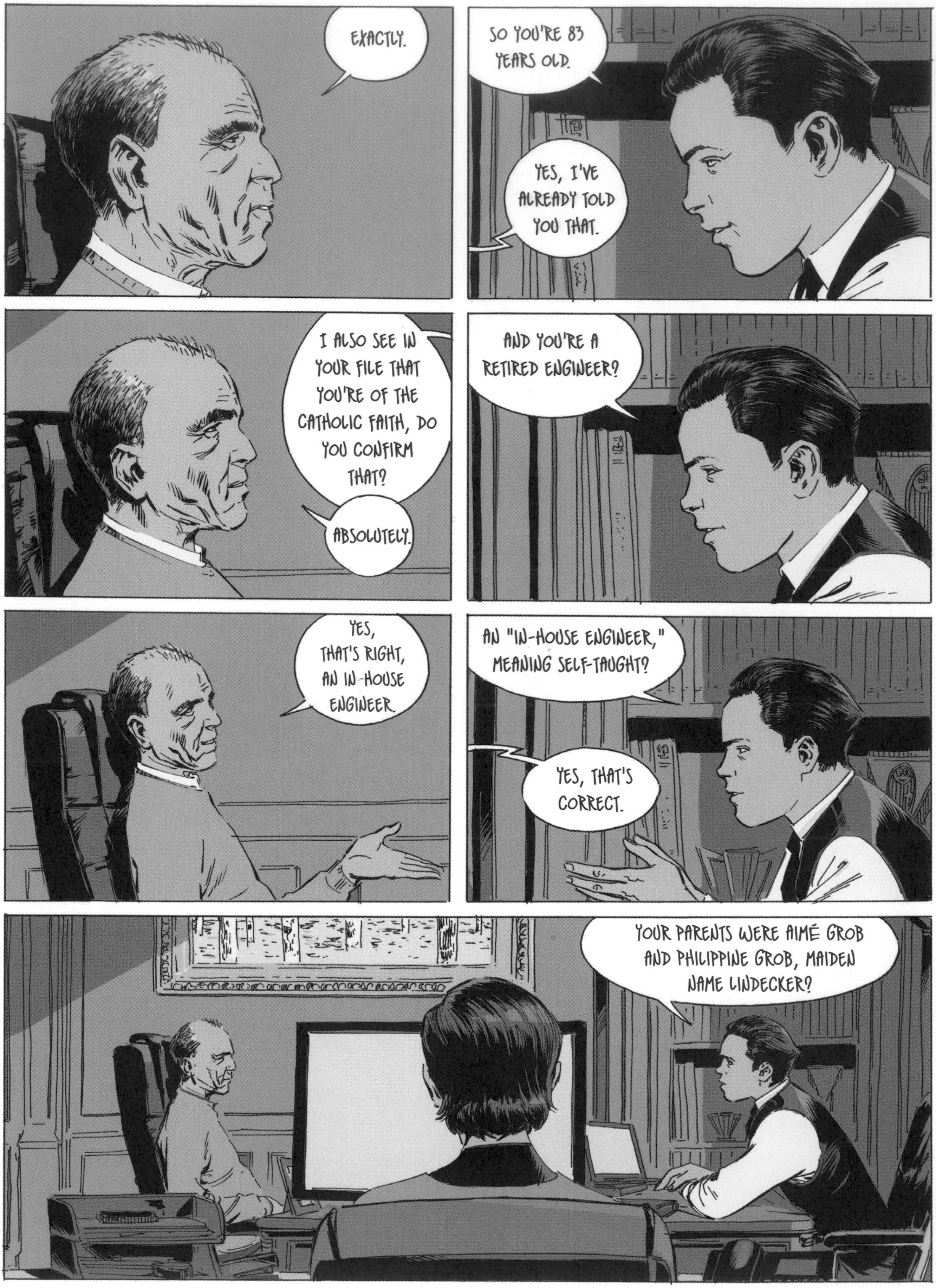
EXACTLY.
SO YOU'RE 83 YEARS OLD.
YES, I'VE ALREADY TOLD YOU THAT.
I ALSO SEE IN YOUR FILE THAT YOU'RE OF THE CATHOLIC FAITH, DO YOU CONFIRM THAT?
ABSOLUTELY.
AND YOU'RE A RETIRED ENGINEER?
YES, THAT'S RIGHT, AN IN-HOUSE ENGINEER.
AN "IN-HOUSE ENGINEER," MEANING SELF-TAUGHT?
YES, THAT'S CORRECT.
YOUR PARENTS WERE AIMÉ GROB AND PHILIPPINE GROB, MAIDEN NAME LINDECKER?

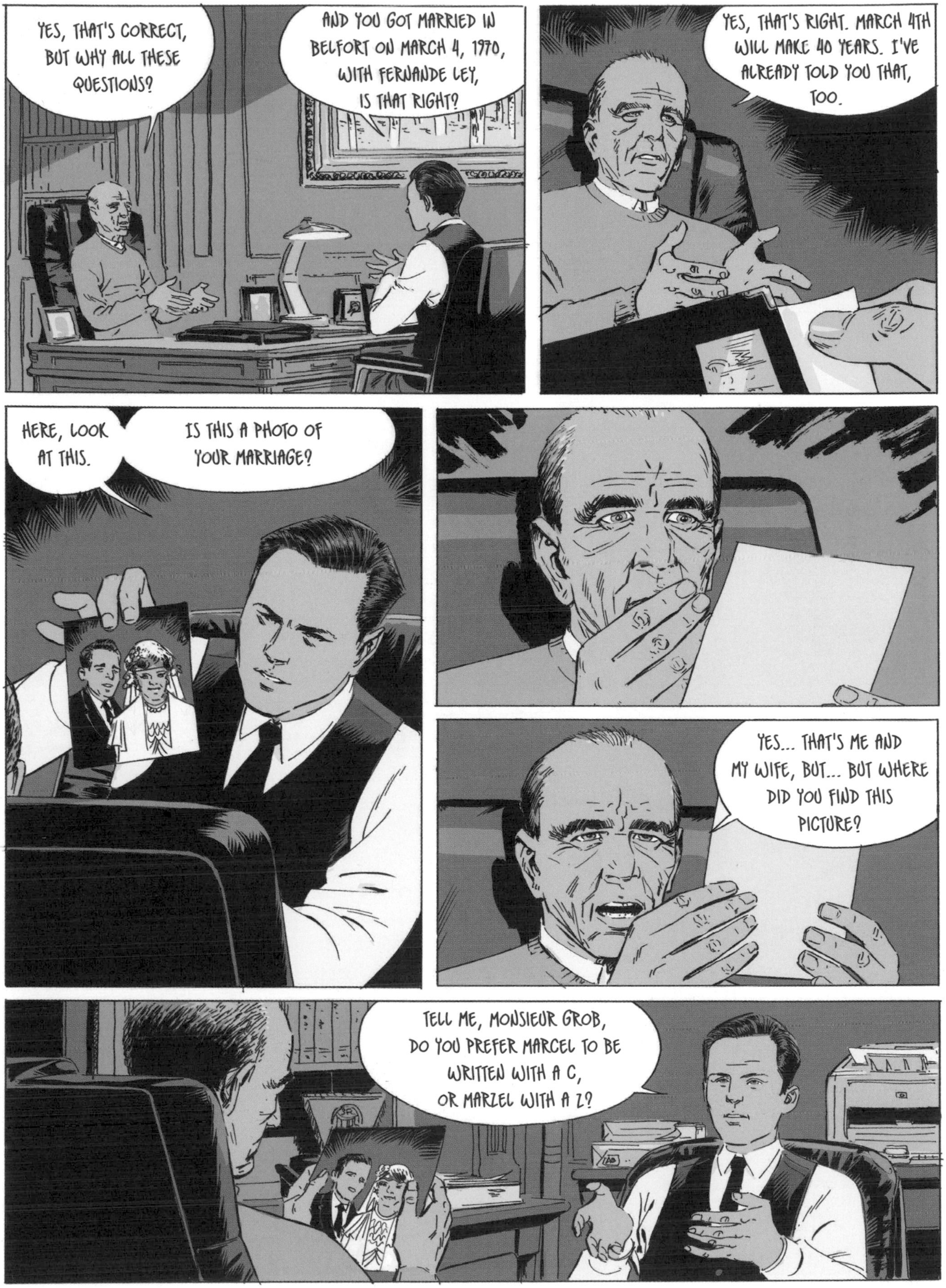
YES, THAT'S CORRECT, BUT WHY ALL THESE QUESTIONS?
AND YOU GOT MARRIED IN BELFORT ON MARCH 4, 1970, WITH FERNANDE LEY, IS THAT RIGHT?
YES, THAT'S RIGHT. MARCH 4TH WILL MAKE 40 YEARS. I'VE ALREADY TOLD YOU THAT, TOO.
HERE, LOOK AT THIS.
IS THIS A PHOTO OF YOUR MARRIAGE?
YES... THAT'S ME AND MY WIFE, BUT... BUT WHERE DID YOU FIND THIS PICTURE?
TELL ME, MONSIEUR GROB, DO YOU PREFER MARCEL TO BE WRITTEN WITH A C, OR MARZEL WITH A Z?

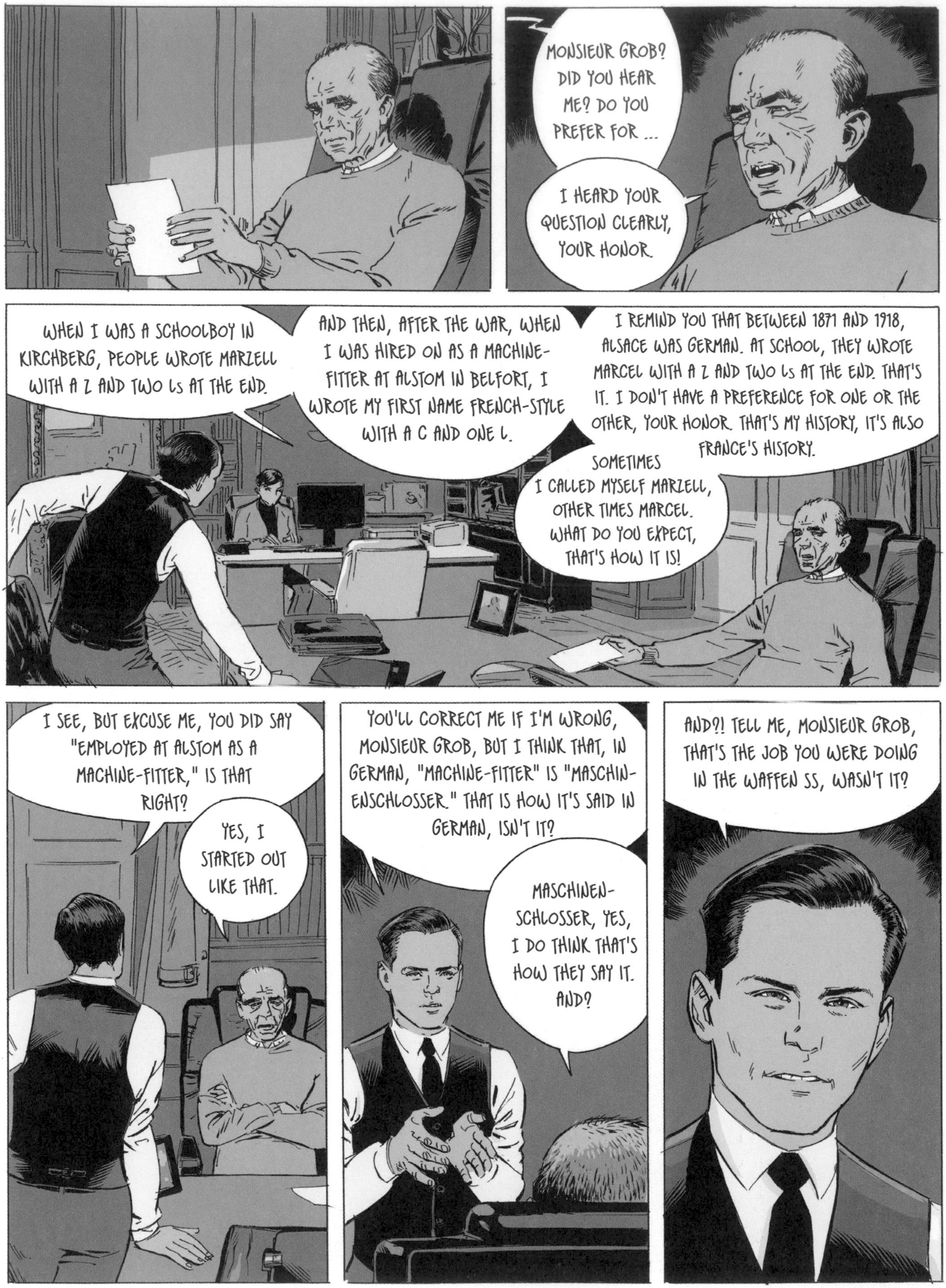
MONSIEUR GROB? DID YOU HEAR ME? DO YOU PREFER FOR ...
I HEARD YOUR QUESTION CLEARLY, YOUR HONOR.
WHEN I WAS A SCHOOLBOY IN KIRCHBERG, PEOPLE WROTE MARZELL WITH A Z AND TWO Ls AT THE END.
AND THEN, AFTER THE WAR, WHEN I WAS HIRED ON AS A MACHINE-FITTER AT ALSTOM IN BELFORT, I WROTE MY FIRST NAME FRENCH-STYLE WITH A C AND ONE L.
I REMIND YOU THAT BETWEEN 1871 AND 1918, ALSACE WAS GERMAN. AT SCHOOL, THEY WROTE MARCEL WITH A Z AND TWO Ls AT THE END. THAT'S IT. I DON'T HAVE A PREFERENCE FOR ONE OR THE OTHER, YOUR HONOR. THAT'S MY HISTORY, IT'S ALSO FRANCE'S HISTORY.
SOMETIMES I CALLED MYSELF MARZELL, OTHER TIMES MARCEL. WHAT DO YOU EXPECT, THAT'S HOW IT IS!
I SEE, BUT EXCUSE ME, YOU DID SAY "EMPLOYED AT ALSTOM AS A MACHINE-FITTER," IS THAT RIGHT?
YES, I STARTED OUT LIKE THAT.
YOU'LL CORRECT ME IF I'M WRONG, MONSIEUR GROB, BUT I THINK THAT, IN GERMAN, "MACHINE-FITTER" IS "MASCHIN-ENSCHLOSSER." THAT IS HOW IT'S SAID IN GERMAN, ISN'T IT?
MASCHINEN-SCHLOSSER, YES, I DO THINK THAT'S HOW THEY SAY IT. AND?
AND?! TELL ME, MONSIEUR GROB, THAT'S THE JOB YOU WERE DOING IN THE WAFFEN SS, WASN'T IT?

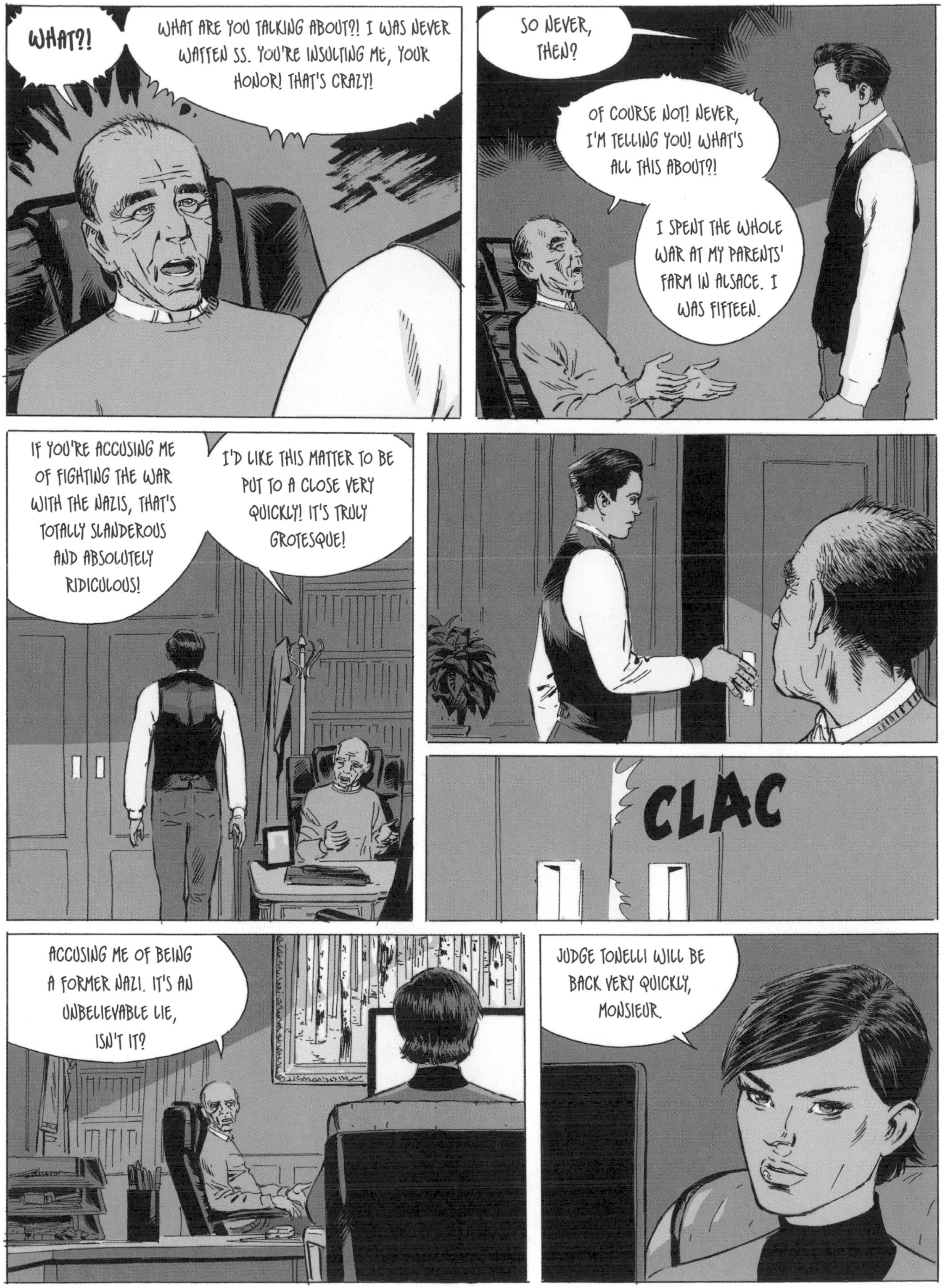
WHAT?!
WHAT ARE YOU TALKING ABOUT?! I WAS NEVER WAFFEN SS. YOU'RE INSULTING ME, YOUR HONOR! THAT'S CRAZY!
SO NEVER, THEN?
OF COURSE NOT! NEVER, I'M TELLING YOU! WHAT'S ALL THIS ABOUT?!
I SPENT THE WHOLE WAR AT MY PARENTS' FARM IN ALSACE. I WAS FIFTEEN.
IF YOU'RE ACCUSING ME OF FIGHTING THE WAR WITH THE NAZIS, THAT'S TOTALLY SLANDEROUS AND ABSOLUTELY RIDICULOUS!
I'D LIKE THIS MATTER TO BE PUT TO A CLOSE VERY QUICKLY! IT'S TRULY GROTESQUE!
CLAC
ACCUSING ME OF BEING A FORMER NAZI. IT'S AN UNBELIEVABLE LIE, ISN'T IT?
JUDGE TONELLI WILL BE BACK VERY QUICKLY, MONSIEUR.

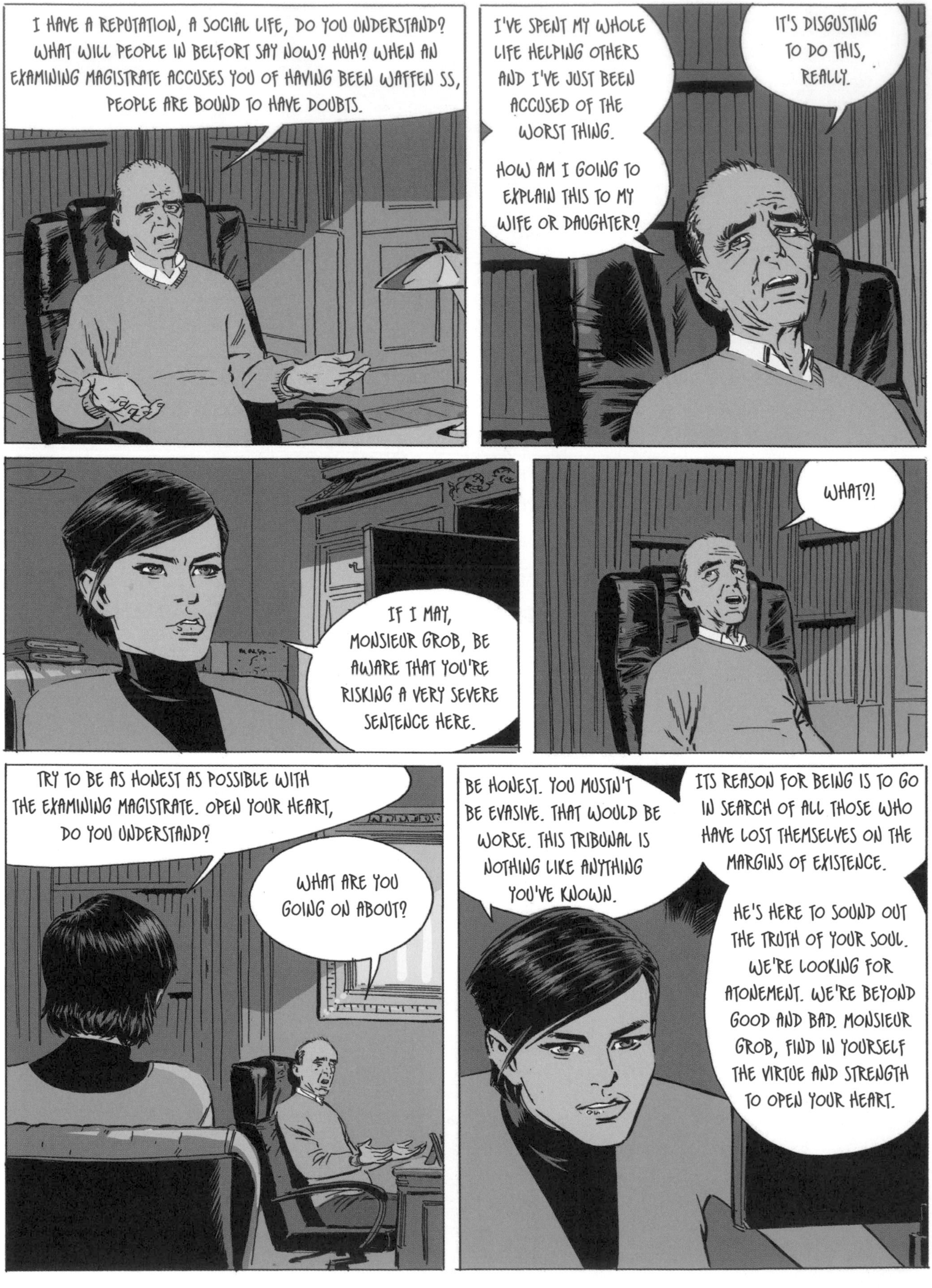
I HAVE A REPUTATION, A SOCIAL LIFE, DO YOU UNDERSTAND? WHAT WILL PEOPLE IN BELFORT SAY NOW? HUH? WHEN AN EXAMINING MAGISTRATE ACCUSES YOU OF HAVING BEEN WAFFEN SS, PEOPLE ARE BOUND TO HAVE DOUBTS.
I'VE SPENT MY WHOLE LIFE HELPING OTHERS AND I'VE JUST BEEN ACCUSED OF THE WORST THING.
HOW AM I GOING TO EXPLAIN THIS TO MY WIFE OR DAUGHTER?
IT'S DISGUSTING TO DO THIS, REALLY.
IF I MAY, MONSIEUR GROB, BE AWARE THAT YOU'RE RISKING A VERY SEVERE SENTENCE HERE.
WHAT?!
TRY TO BE AS HONEST AS POSSIBLE WITH THE EXAMINING MAGISTRATE. OPEN YOUR HEART, DO YOU UNDERSTAND?
WHAT ARE YOU GOING ON ABOUT?
BE HONEST. YOU MUSTN'T BE EVASIVE. THAT WOULD BE WORSE. THIS TRIBUNAL IS NOTHING LIKE ANYTHING YOU'VE KNOWN.
ITS REASON FOR BEING IS TO GO IN SEARCH OF ALL THOSE WHO HAVE LOST THEMSELVES ON THE MARGINS OF EXISTENCE.
HE'S HERE TO SOUND OUT THE TRUTH OF YOUR SOUL. WE'RE LOOKING FOR ATONEMENT. WE'RE BEYOND GOOD AND BAD. MONSIEUR GROB, FIND IN YOURSELF THE VIRTUE AND STRENGTH TO OPEN YOUR HEART.

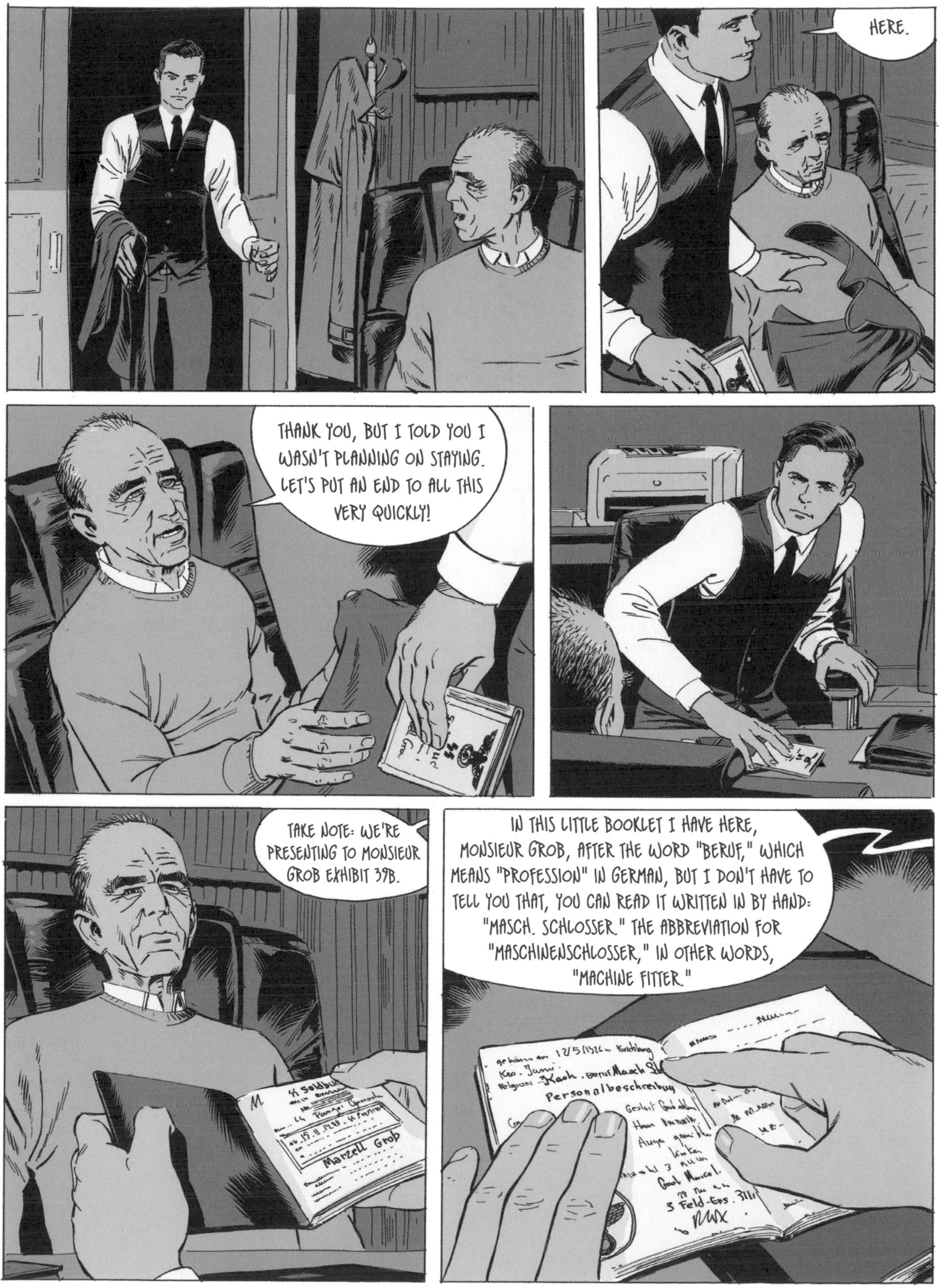
HERE.
THANK YOU, BUT I TOLD YOU I WASN'T PLANNING ON STAYING. LET'S PUT AN END TO ALL THIS VERY QUICKLY!
TAKE NOTE: WE'RE PRESENTING TO MONSIEUR GROB EXHIBIT 39B.
Marzell Grob
IN THIS LITTLE BOOKLET I HAVE HERE, MONSIEUR GROB, AFTER THE WORD "BERUF," WHICH MEANS "PROFESSION" IN GERMAN, BUT I DON'T HAVE TO TELL YOU THAT, YOU CAN READ IT WRITTEN IN BY HAND: "MASCH. SCHLOSSER." THE ABBREVIATION FOR "MASCHINENSCHLOSSER," IN OTHER WORDS, "MACHINE FITTER."
Personalbeschreibung

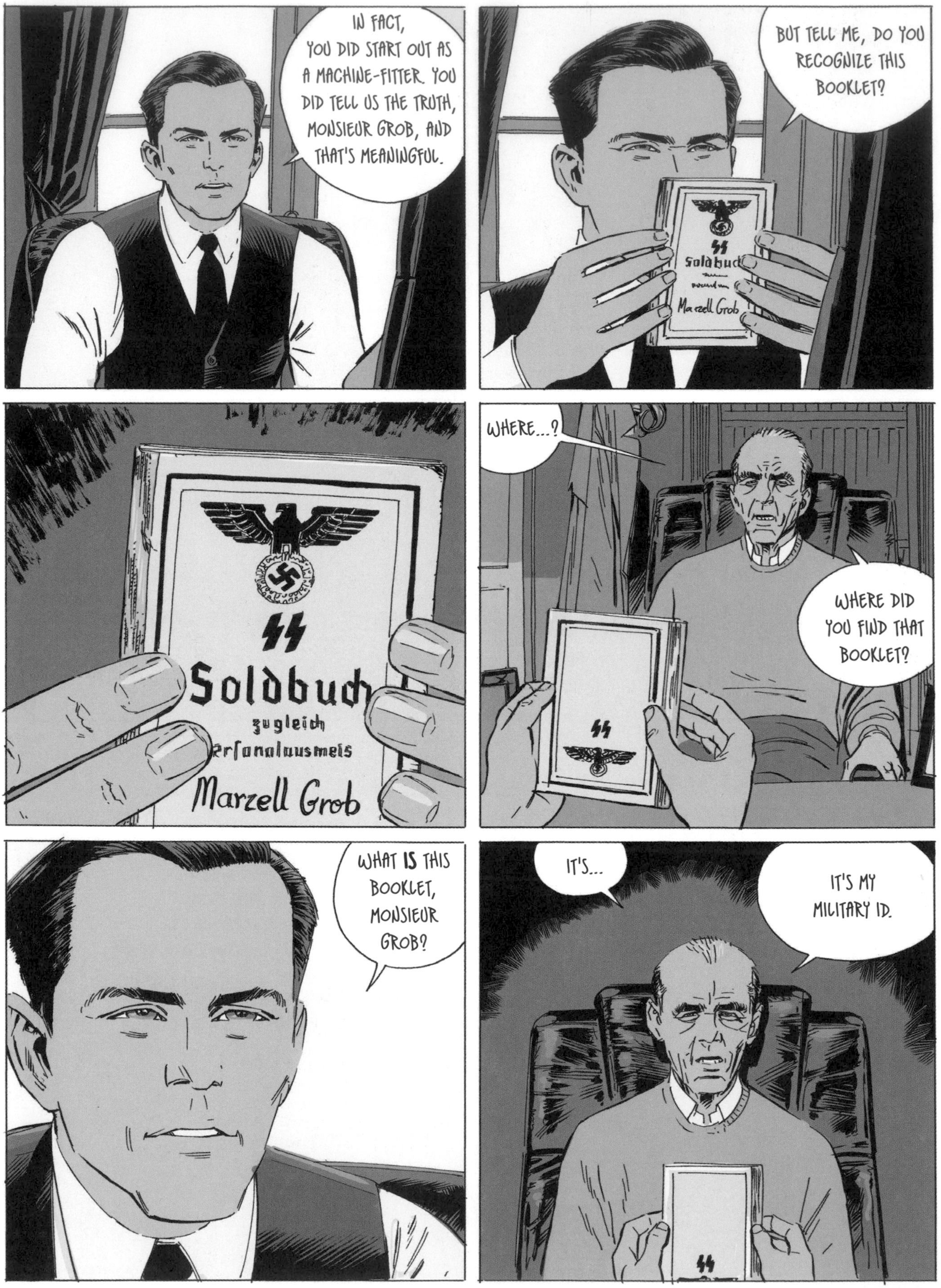
IN FACT, YOU DID START OUT AS A MACHINE-FITTER. YOU DID TELL US THE TRUTH, MONSIEUR GROB, AND THAT'S MEANINGFUL.
BUT TELL ME, DO YOU RECOGNIZE THIS BOOKLET?
Soldbuch
Marzell Grob
Soldbuch
zugleich
Marzell Grob
WHERE...?
WHERE DID YOU FIND THAT BOOKLET?
WHAT IS THIS BOOKLET, MONSIEUR GROB?
IT'S...
IT'S MY MILITARY ID.

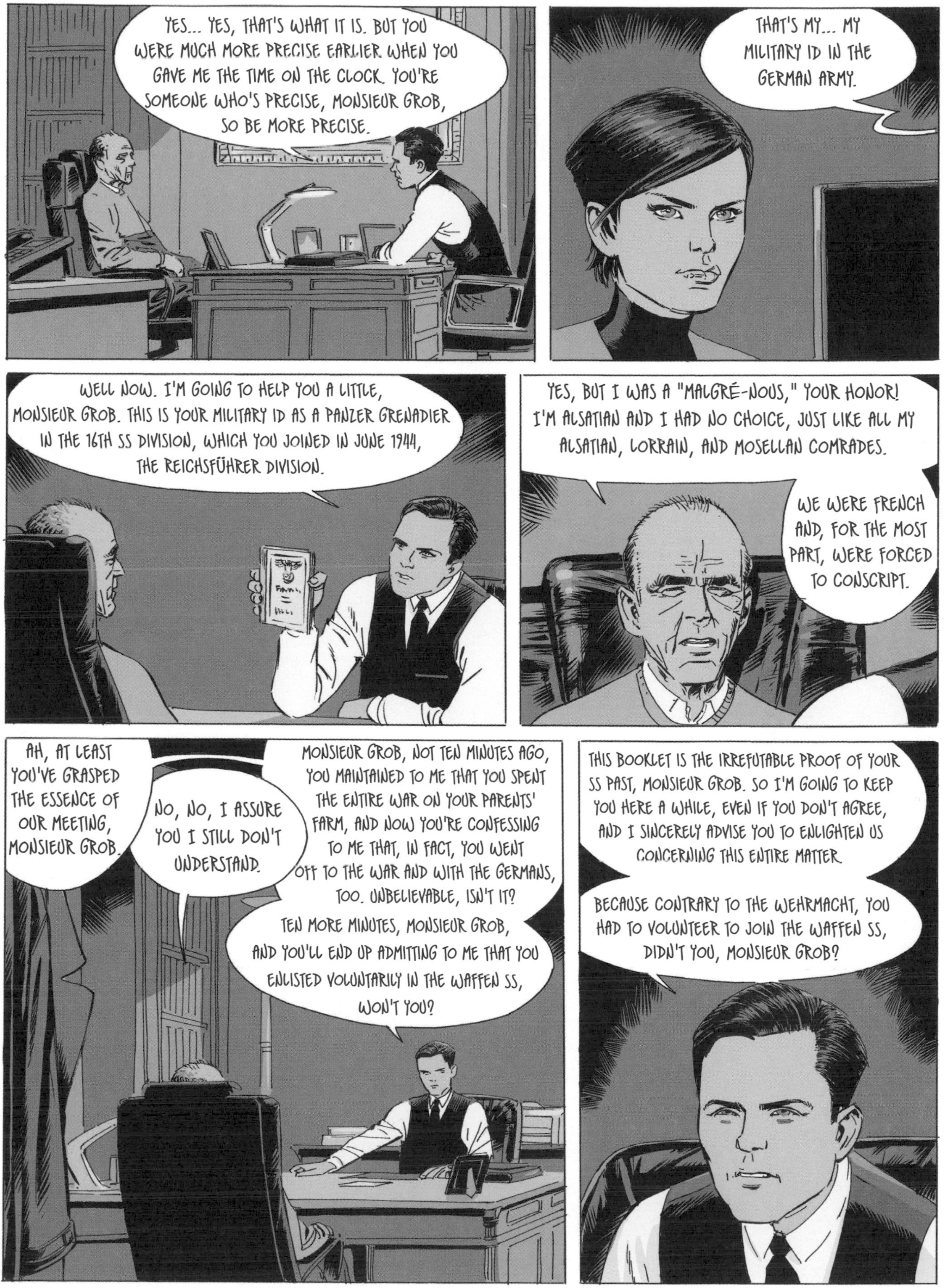
YES... YES, THAT'S WHAT IT IS. BUT YOU WERE MUCH MORE PRECISE EARLIER WHEN YOU GAVE ME THE TIME ON THE CLOCK. YOU'RE SOMEONE WHO'S PRECISE, MONSIEUR GROB, SO BE MORE PRECISE.
THAT'S MY... MY MILITARY ID IN THE GERMAN ARMY.
WELL NOW. I'M GOING TO HELP YOU A LITTLE, MONSIEUR GROB. THIS IS YOUR MILITARY ID AS A PANZER GRENADIER IN THE 16TH SS DIVISION, WHICH YOU JOINED IN JUNE 1944, THE REICHSFÜHRER DIVISION.
YES, BUT I WAS A "MALGRÉ-NOUS," YOUR HONOR! I'M ALSATIAN AND I HAD NO CHOICE, JUST LIKE ALL MY ALSATIAN, LORRAIN, AND MOSELLAN COMRADES.
WE WERE FRENCH AND, FOR THE MOST PART, WERE FORCED TO CONSCRIPT.
AH, AT LEAST YOU'VE GRASPED THE ESSENCE OF OUR MEETING, MONSIEUR GROB.
NO, NO, I ASSURE YOU I STILL DON'T UNDERSTAND.
MONSIEUR GROB, NOT TEN MINUTES AGO, YOU MAINTAINED TO ME THAT YOU SPENT THE ENTIRE WAR ON YOUR PARENTS' FARM, AND NOW YOU'RE CONFESSING TO ME THAT, IN FACT, YOU WENT OFF TO THE WAR AND WITH THE GERMANS, TOO. UNBELIEVABLE, ISN'T IT?
TEN MORE MINUTES, MONSIEUR GROB, AND YOU'LL END UP ADMITTING TO ME THAT YOU ENLISTED VOLUNTARILY IN THE WAFFEN SS, WON'T YOU?
THIS BOOKLET IS THE IRREFUTABLE PROOF OF YOUR SS PAST, MONSIEUR GROB. SO I'M GOING TO KEEP YOU HERE A WHILE, EVEN IF YOU DON'T AGREE, AND I SINCERELY ADVISE YOU TO ENLIGHTEN US CONCERNING THIS ENTIRE MATTER.
BECAUSE CONTRARY TO THE WEHRMACHT, YOU HAD TO VOLUNTEER TO JOIN THE WAFFEN SS, DIDN'T YOU, MONSIEUR GROB?

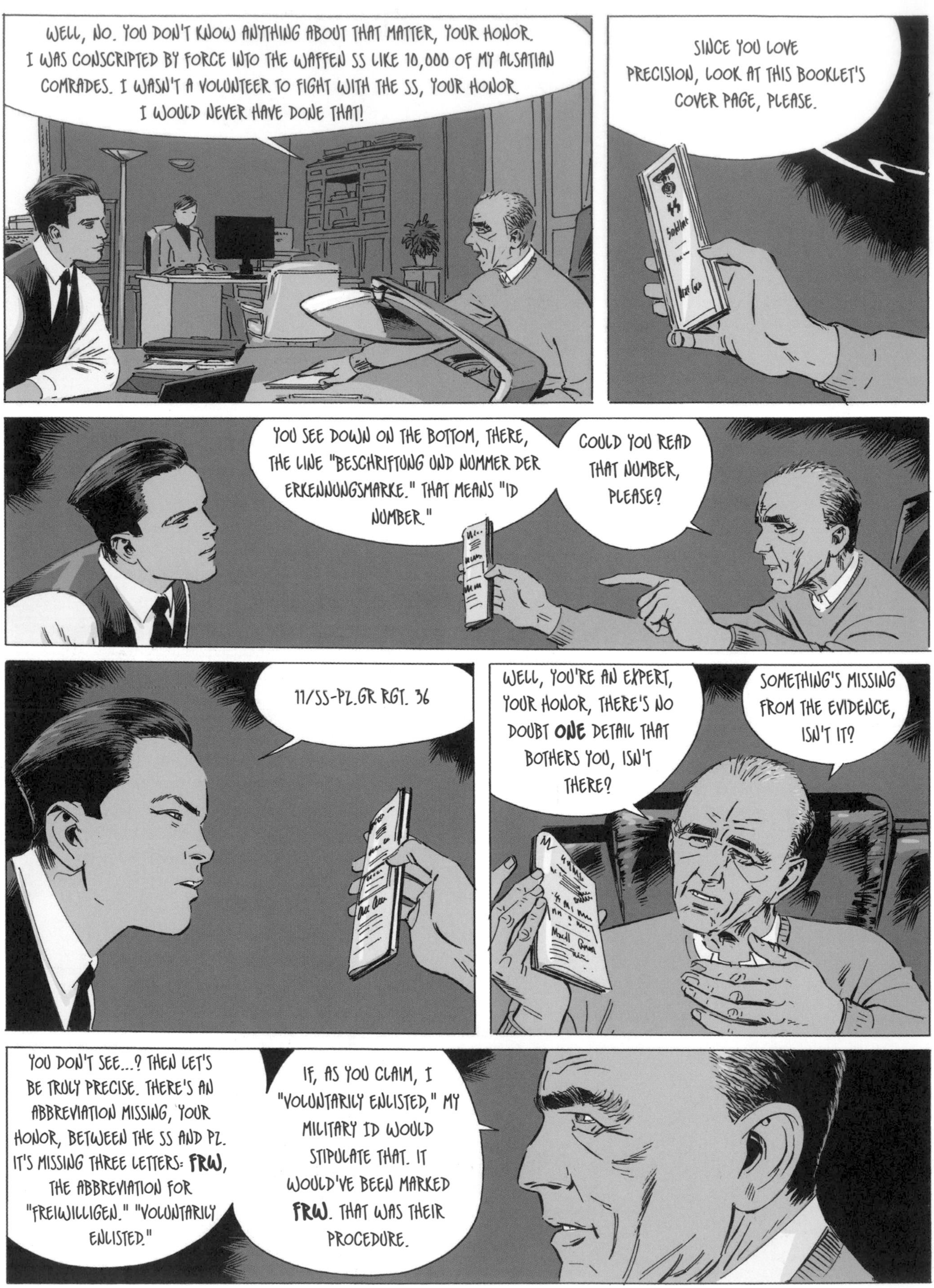
WELL, NO. YOU DON'T KNOW ANYTHING ABOUT THAT MATTER, YOUR HONOR. I WAS CONSCRIPTED BY FORCE INTO THE WAFFEN SS LIKE 10,000 OF MY ALSATIAN COMRADES. I WASN'T A VOLUNTEER TO FIGHT WITH THE SS, YOUR HONOR. I WOULD NEVER HAVE DONE THAT!
SINCE YOU LOVE PRECISION, LOOK AT THIS BOOKLET'S COVER PAGE, PLEASE.
YOU SEE DOWN ON THE BOTTOM, THERE, THE LINE "BESCHRIFTUNG UND NUMMER DER ERKENNUNGSMARKE." THAT MEANS "ID NUMBER."
COULD YOU READ THAT NUMBER, PLEASE?
11/SS-PZ.GR RGT. 36
WELL, YOU'RE AN EXPERT, YOUR HONOR, THERE'S NO DOUBT **ONE** DETAIL THAT BOTHERS YOU, ISN'T THERE?
SOMETHING'S MISSING FROM THE EVIDENCE, ISN'T IT?
YOU DON'T SEE...? THEN LET'S BE TRULY PRECISE. THERE'S AN ABBREVIATION MISSING, YOUR HONOR, BETWEEN THE SS AND PZ. IT'S MISSING THREE LETTERS: **FRW**, THE ABBREVIATION FOR "FREIWILLIGEN." "VOLUNTARILY ENLISTED."
IF, AS YOU CLAIM, I "VOLUNTARILY ENLISTED," MY MILITARY ID WOULD STIPULATE THAT. IT WOULD'VE BEEN MARKED **FRW**. THAT WAS THEIR PROCEDURE.

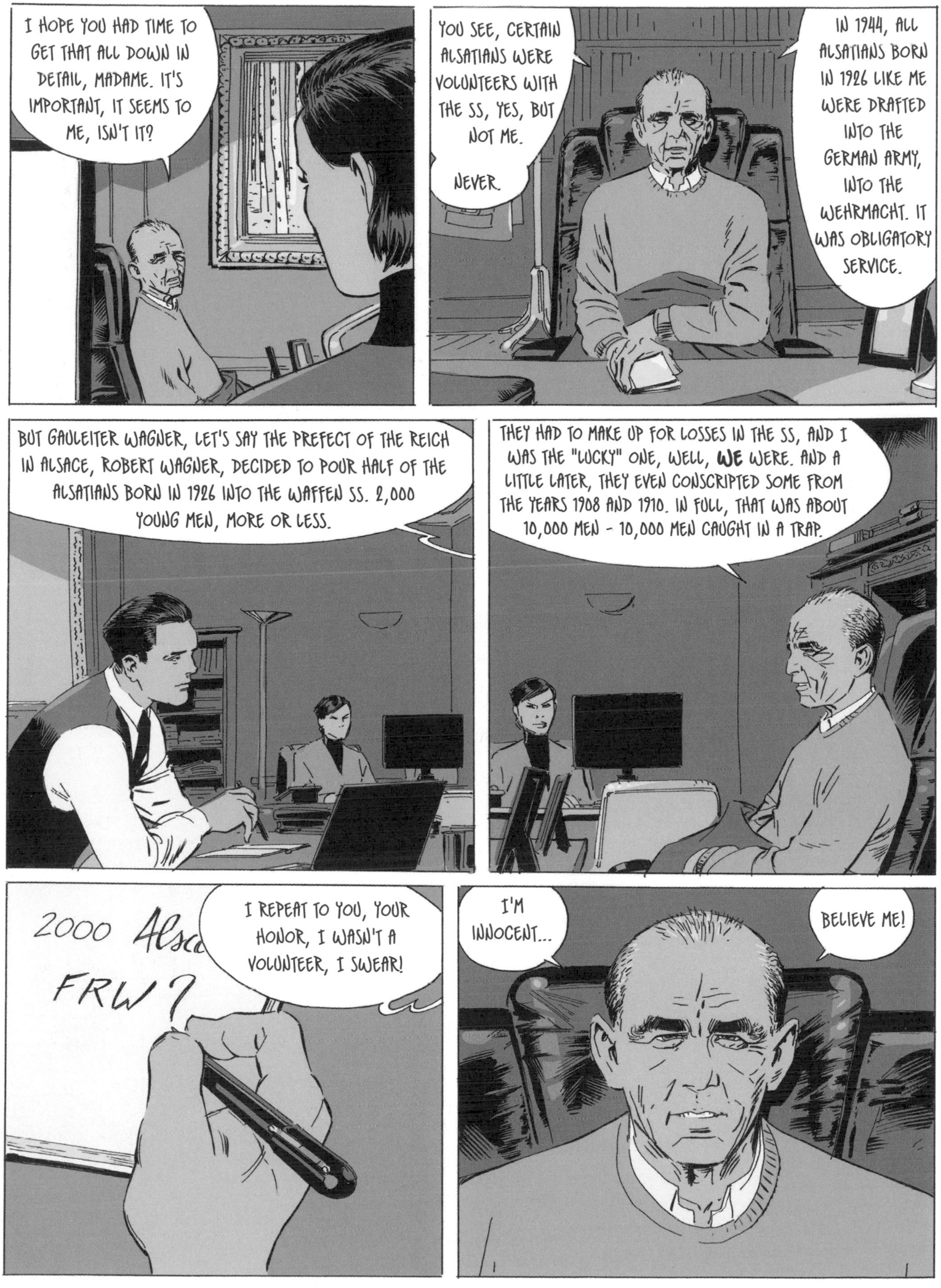
I HOPE YOU HAD TIME TO GET THAT ALL DOWN IN DETAIL, MADAME. IT'S IMPORTANT, IT SEEMS TO ME, ISN'T IT?
YOU SEE, CERTAIN ALSATIANS WERE VOLUNTEERS WITH THE SS, YES, BUT NOT ME.
NEVER.
IN 1944, ALL ALSATIANS BORN IN 1926 LIKE ME WERE DRAFTED INTO THE GERMAN ARMY, INTO THE WEHRMACHT. IT WAS OBLIGATORY SERVICE.
BUT GAULEITER WAGNER, LET'S SAY THE PREFECT OF THE REICH IN ALSACE, ROBERT WAGNER, DECIDED TO POUR HALF OF THE ALSATIANS BORN IN 1926 INTO THE WAFFEN SS. 2,000 YOUNG MEN, MORE OR LESS.
THEY HAD TO MAKE UP FOR LOSSES IN THE SS, AND I WAS THE "LUCKY" ONE, WELL, WE WERE. AND A LITTLE LATER, THEY EVEN CONSCRIPTED SOME FROM THE YEARS 1908 AND 1910. IN FULL, THAT WAS ABOUT 10,000 MEN - 10,000 MEN CAUGHT IN A TRAP.
2000 Alsa
FRW?
I REPEAT TO YOU, YOUR HONOR, I WASN'T A VOLUNTEER, I SWEAR!
I'M INNOCENT...
BELIEVE ME!

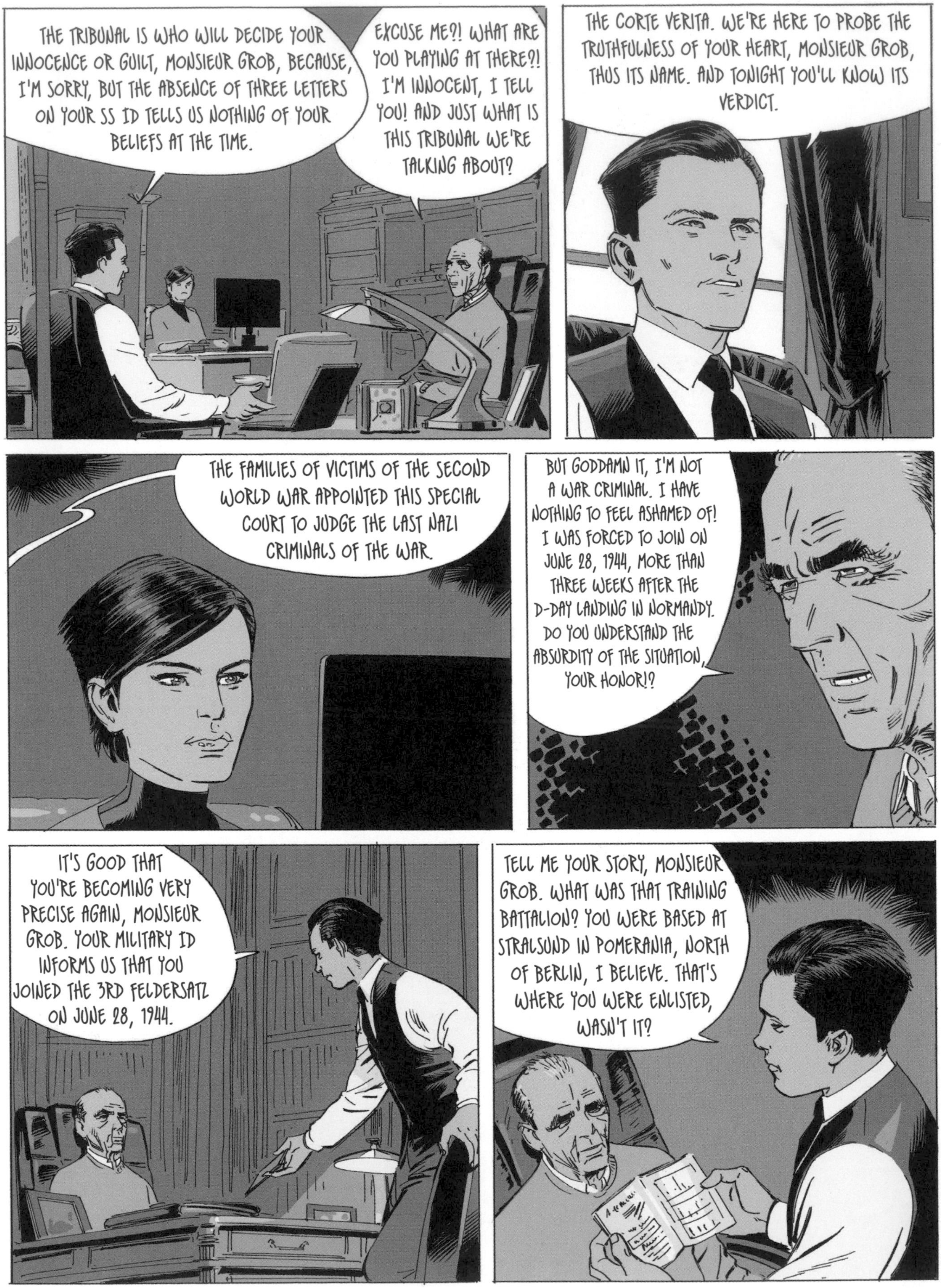
THE TRIBUNAL IS WHO WILL DECIDE YOUR INNOCENCE OR GUILT, MONSIEUR GROB, BECAUSE, I'M SORRY, BUT THE ABSENCE OF THREE LETTERS ON YOUR SS ID TELLS US NOTHING OF YOUR BELIEFS AT THE TIME.
EXCUSE ME?! WHAT ARE YOU PLAYING AT THERE?! I'M INNOCENT, I TELL YOU! AND JUST WHAT IS THIS TRIBUNAL WE'RE TALKING ABOUT?
THE CORTE VERITA. WE'RE HERE TO PROBE THE TRUTHFULNESS OF YOUR HEART, MONSIEUR GROB, THUS ITS NAME. AND TONIGHT YOU'LL KNOW ITS VERDICT.
THE FAMILIES OF VICTIMS OF THE SECOND WORLD WAR APPOINTED THIS SPECIAL COURT TO JUDGE THE LAST NAZI CRIMINALS OF THE WAR.
BUT GODDAMN IT, I'M NOT A WAR CRIMINAL. I HAVE NOTHING TO FEEL ASHAMED OF! I WAS FORCED TO JOIN ON JUNE 28, 1944, MORE THAN THREE WEEKS AFTER THE D-DAY LANDING IN NORMANDY. DO YOU UNDERSTAND THE ABSURDITY OF THE SITUATION, YOUR HONOR!?
IT'S GOOD THAT YOU'RE BECOMING VERY PRECISE AGAIN, MONSIEUR GROB. YOUR MILITARY ID INFORMS US THAT YOU JOINED THE 3RD FELDERSATZ ON JUNE 28, 1944.
TELL ME YOUR STORY, MONSIEUR GROB. WHAT WAS THAT TRAINING BATTALION? YOU WERE BASED AT STRALSUND IN POMERANIA, NORTH OF BERLIN, I BELIEVE. THAT'S WHERE YOU WERE ENLISTED, WASN'T IT?

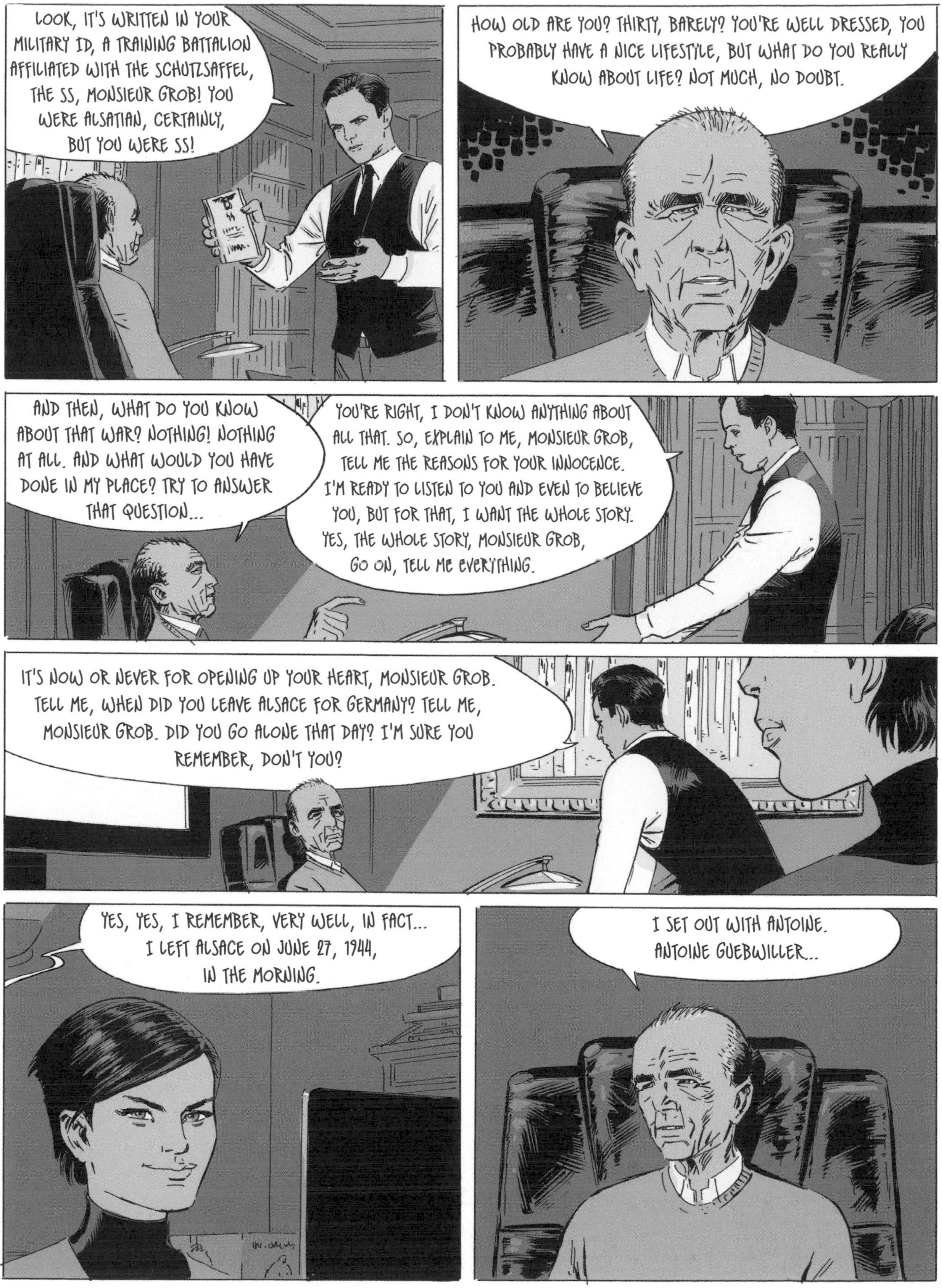
LOOK, IT'S WRITTEN IN YOUR MILITARY ID, A TRAINING BATTALION AFFILIATED WITH THE SCHUTZSAFFEL, THE SS, MONSIEUR GROB! YOU WERE ALSATIAN, CERTAINLY, BUT YOU WERE SS!
HOW OLD ARE YOU? THIRTY, BARELY? YOU'RE WELL DRESSED, YOU PROBABLY HAVE A NICE LIFESTYLE, BUT WHAT DO YOU REALLY KNOW ABOUT LIFE? NOT MUCH, NO DOUBT.
AND THEN, WHAT DO YOU KNOW ABOUT THAT WAR? NOTHING! NOTHING AT ALL. AND WHAT WOULD YOU HAVE DONE IN MY PLACE? TRY TO ANSWER THAT QUESTION...
YOU'RE RIGHT, I DON'T KNOW ANYTHING ABOUT ALL THAT. SO, EXPLAIN TO ME, MONSIEUR GROB, TELL ME THE REASONS FOR YOUR INNOCENCE. I'M READY TO LISTEN TO YOU AND EVEN TO BELIEVE YOU, BUT FOR THAT, I WANT THE WHOLE STORY. YES, THE WHOLE STORY, MONSIEUR GROB, GO ON, TELL ME EVERYTHING.
IT'S NOW OR NEVER FOR OPENING UP YOUR HEART, MONSIEUR GROB. TELL ME, WHEN DID YOU LEAVE ALSACE FOR GERMANY? TELL ME, MONSIEUR GROB. DID YOU GO ALONE THAT DAY? I'M SURE YOU REMEMBER, DON'T YOU?
YES, YES, I REMEMBER, VERY WELL, IN FACT... I LEFT ALSACE ON JUNE 27, 1944, IN THE MORNING.
I SET OUT WITH ANTOINE. ANTOINE GUEBWILLER...

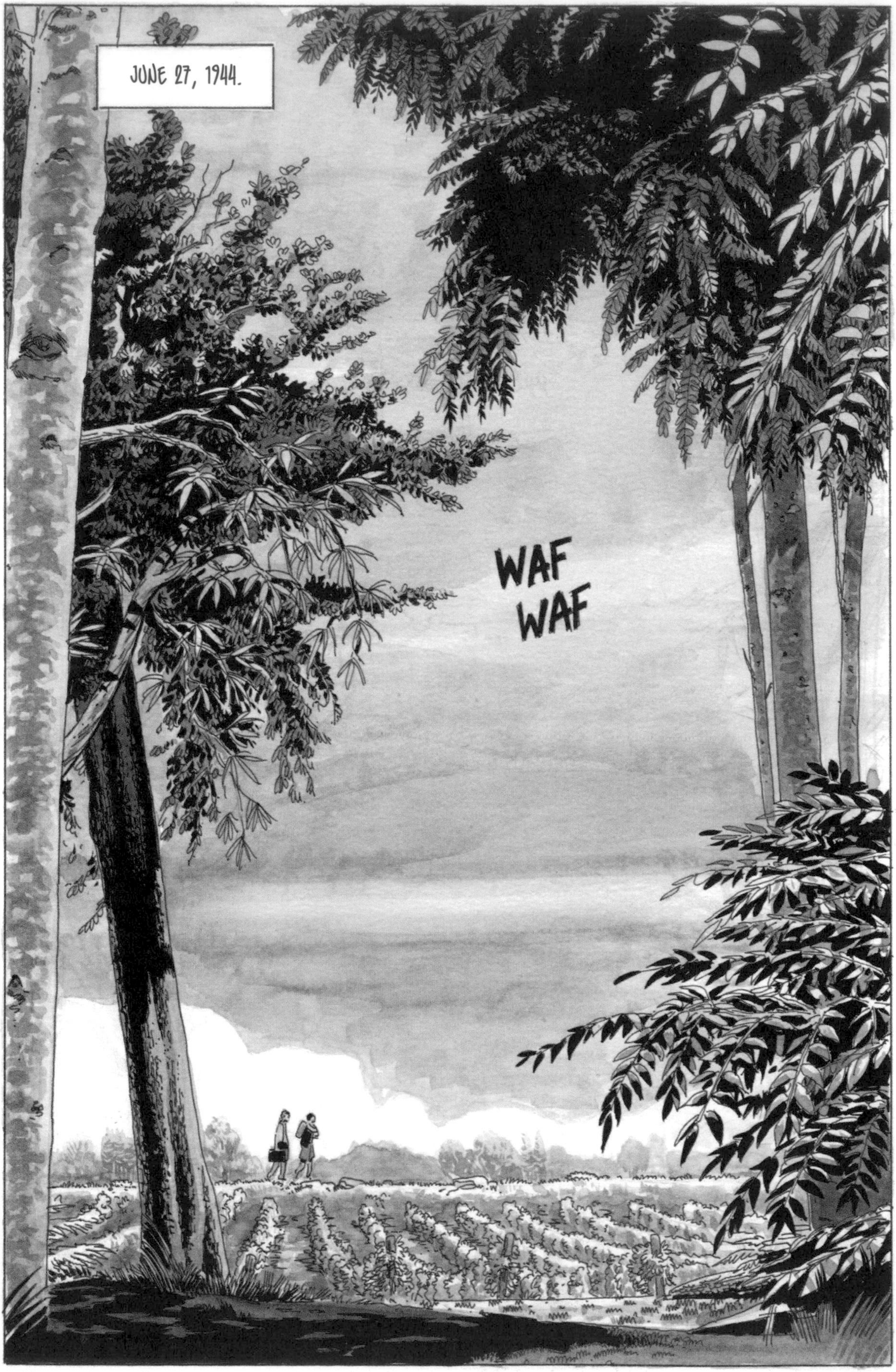
JUNE 27, 1944.
WAF
WAF

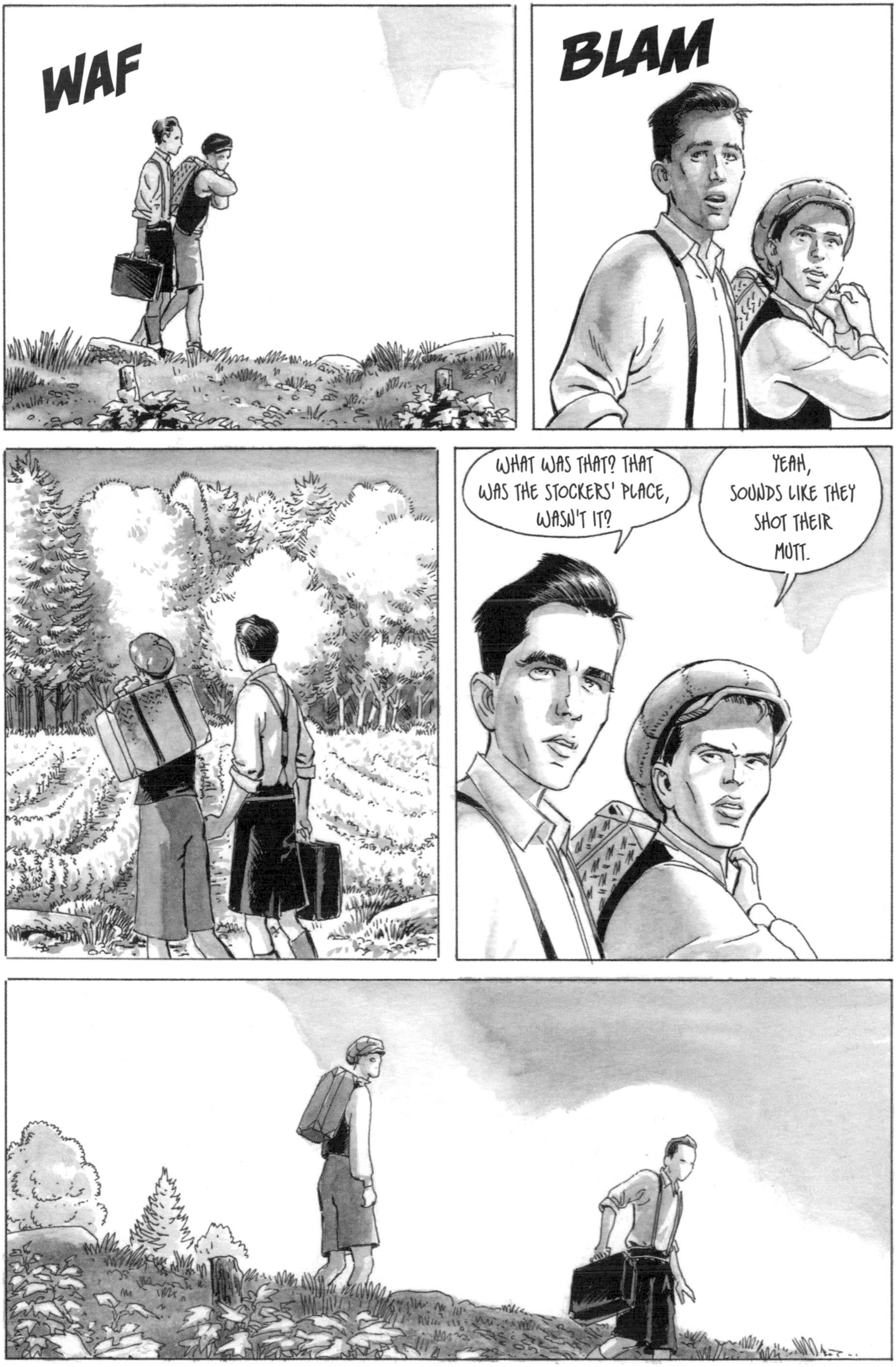
WAF
BLAM
WHAT WAS THAT? THAT WAS THE STOCKERS' PLACE, WASN'T IT?
YEAH, SOUNDS LIKE THEY SHOT THEIR MUTT.

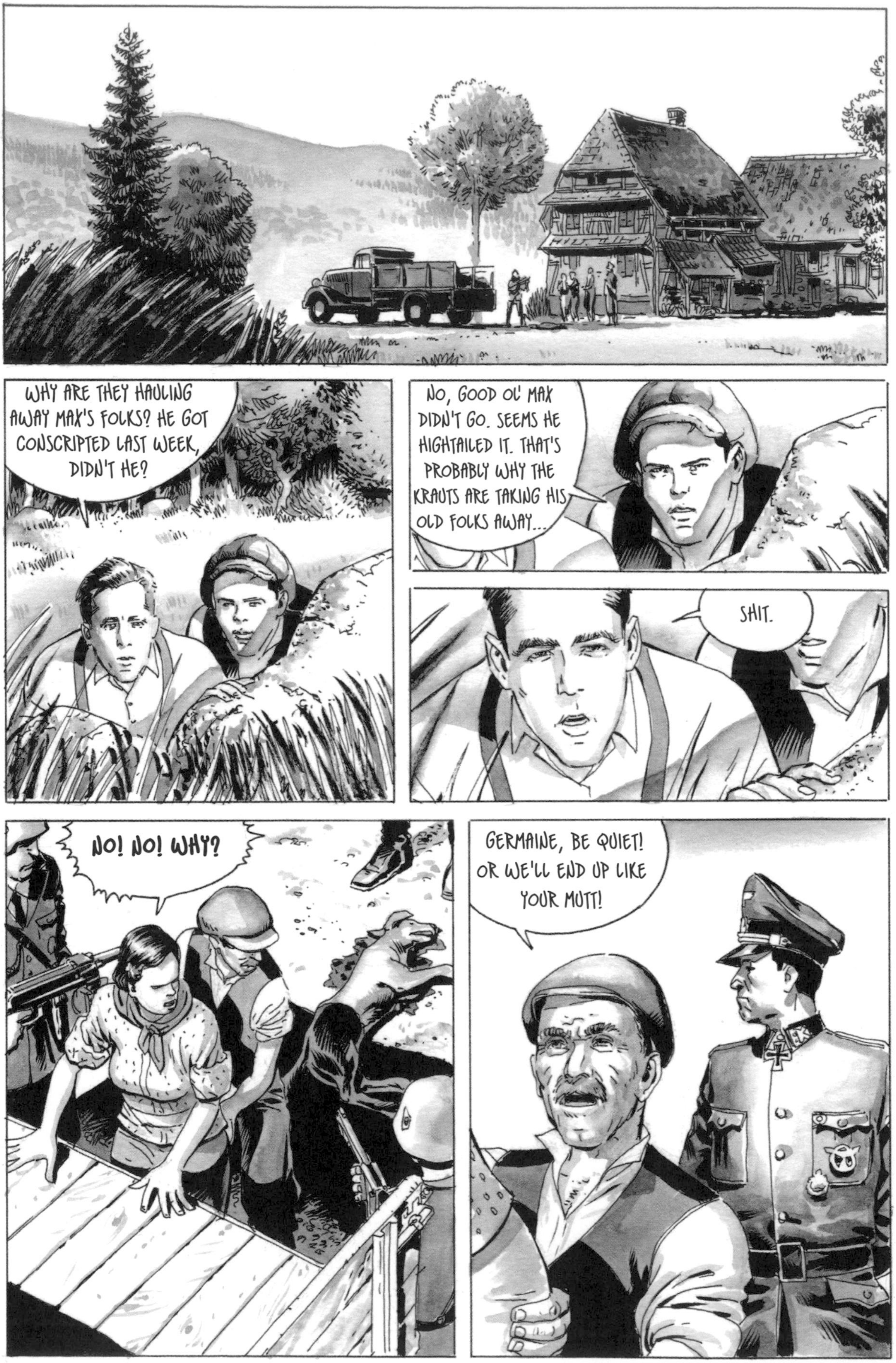
WHY ARE THEY HAULING AWAY MAX'S FOLKS? HE GOT CONSCRIPTED LAST WEEK, DIDN'T HE?
NO, GOOD OL' MAX DIDN'T GO. SEEMS HE HIGHTAILED IT. THAT'S PROBABLY WHY THE KRAUTS ARE TAKING HIS OLD FOLKS AWAY...
SHIT.
NO! NO! WHY?
GERMAINE, BE QUIET! OR WE'LL END UP LIKE YOUR MUTT!

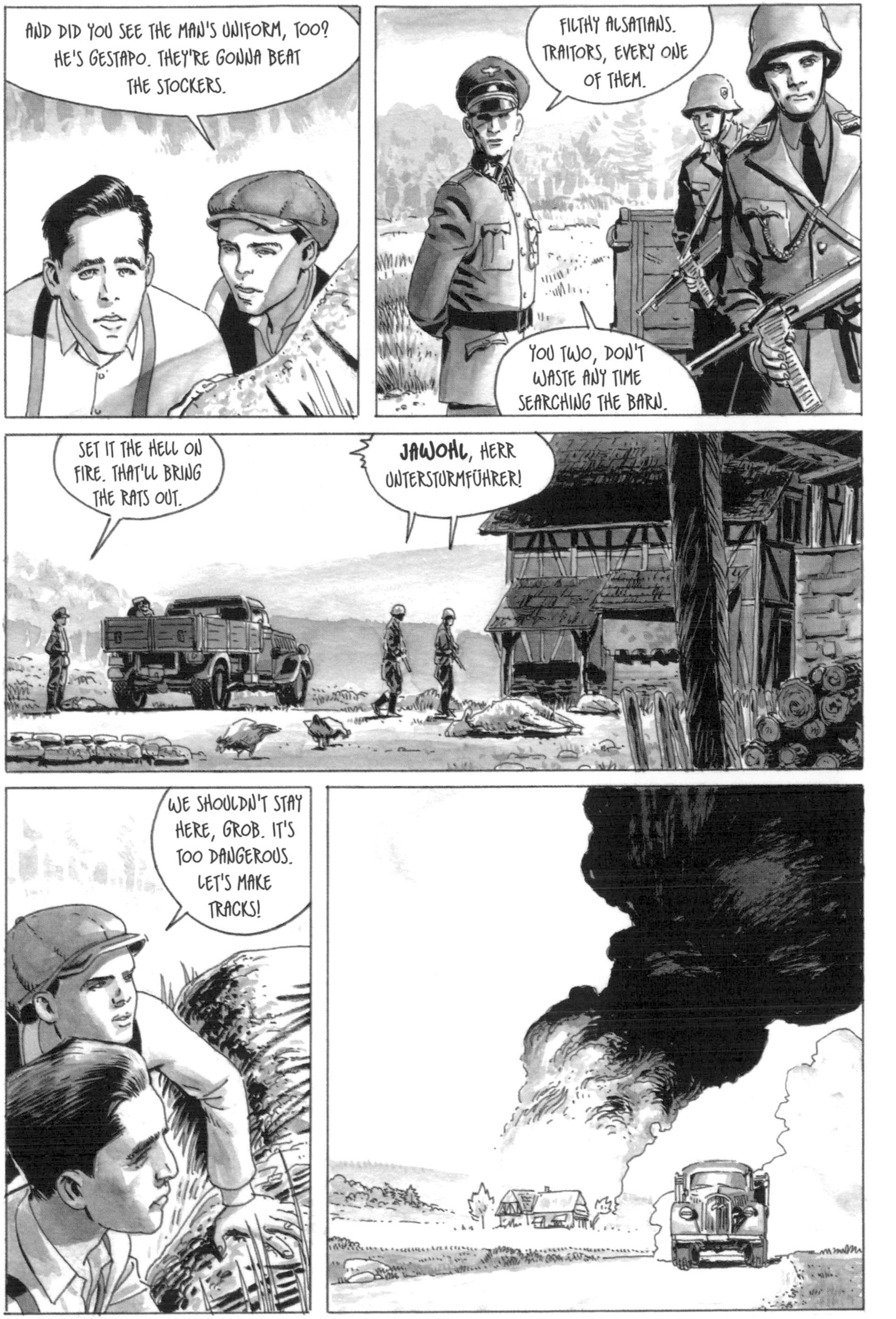

AND DID YOU SEE THE MAN'S UNIFORM, TOO? HE'S GESTAPO. THEY'RE GONNA BEAT THE STOCKERS.
FILTHY ALSATIANS. TRAITORS, EVERY ONE OF THEM.
YOU TWO, DON'T WASTE ANY TIME SEARCHING THE BARN.
SET IT THE HELL ON FIRE. THAT'LL BRING THE RATS OUT.
JAWOHL, HERR UNTERSTURMFÜHRER!
WE SHOULDN'T STAY HERE, GROB. IT'S TOO DANGEROUS. LET'S MAKE TRACKS!

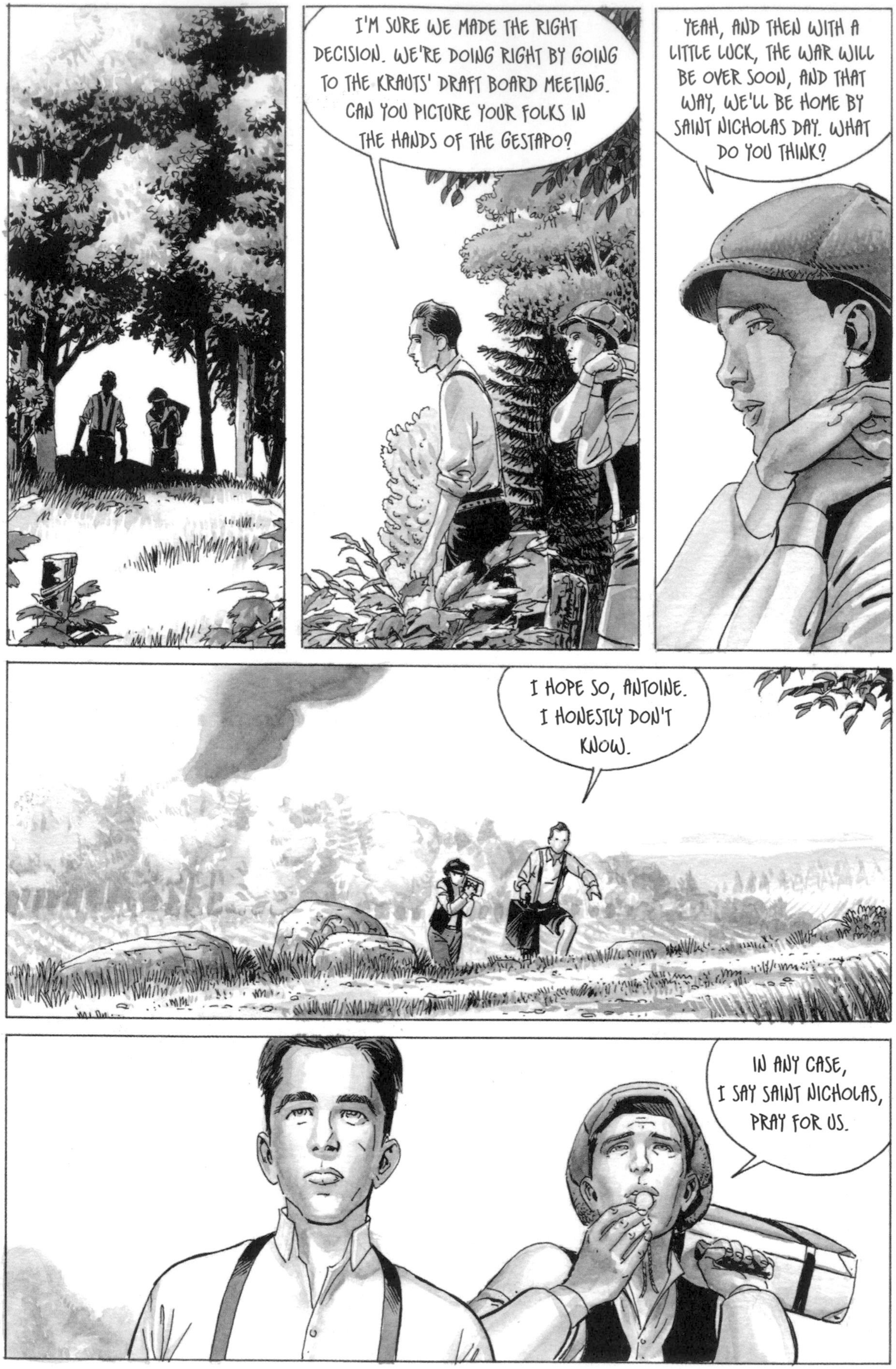
I'M SURE WE MADE THE RIGHT DECISION. WE'RE DOING RIGHT BY GOING TO THE KRAUTS' DRAFT BOARD MEETING. CAN YOU PICTURE YOUR FOLKS IN THE HANDS OF THE GESTAPO?
YEAH, AND THEN WITH A LITTLE LUCK, THE WAR WILL BE OVER SOON, AND THAT WAY, WE'LL BE HOME BY SAINT NICHOLAS DAY. WHAT DO YOU THINK?
I HOPE SO, ANTOINE. I HONESTLY DON'T KNOW.
IN ANY CASE, I SAY SAINT NICHOLAS, PRAY FOR US.

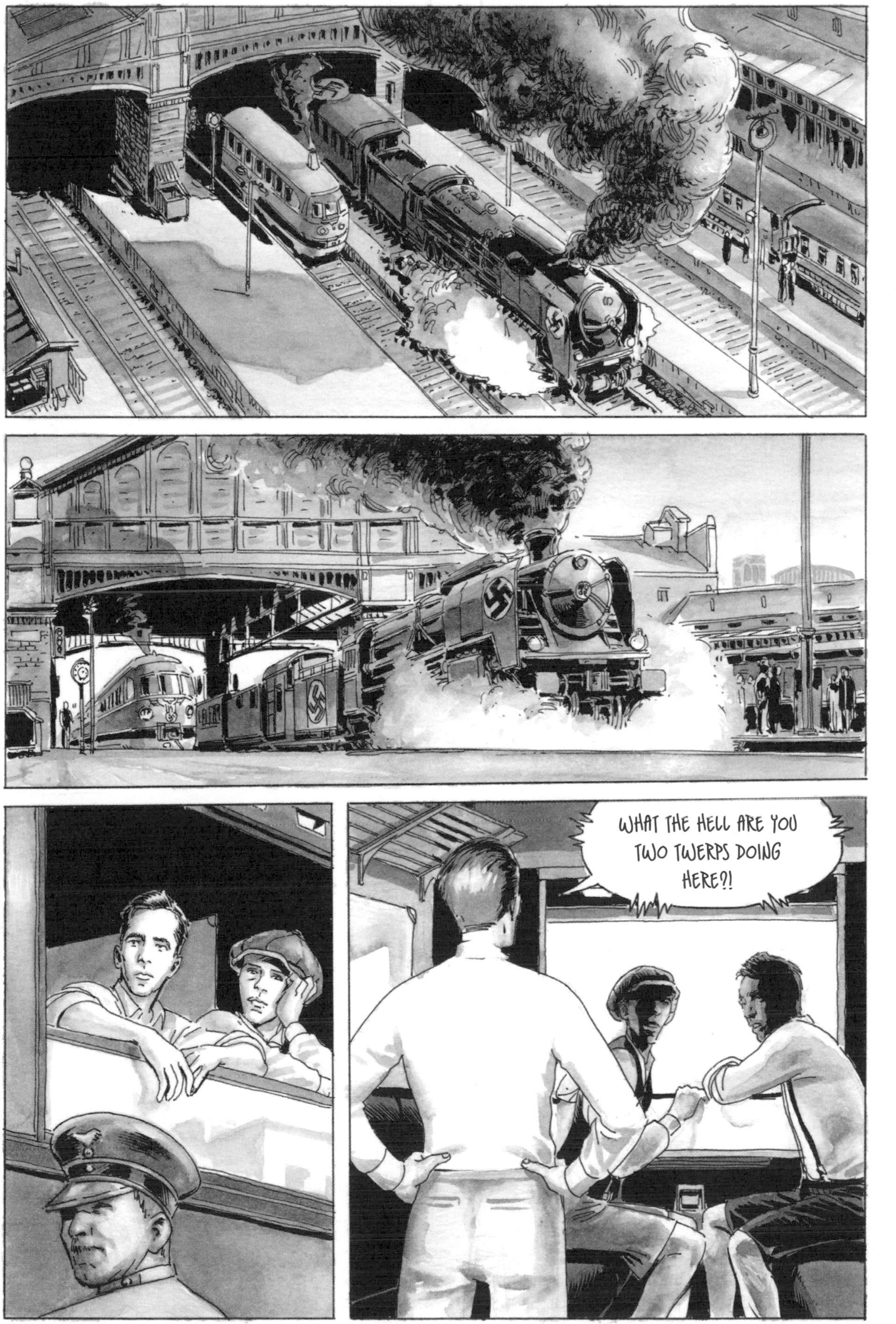
WHAT THE HELL ARE YOU
TWO TWERPS DOING
HERE?!

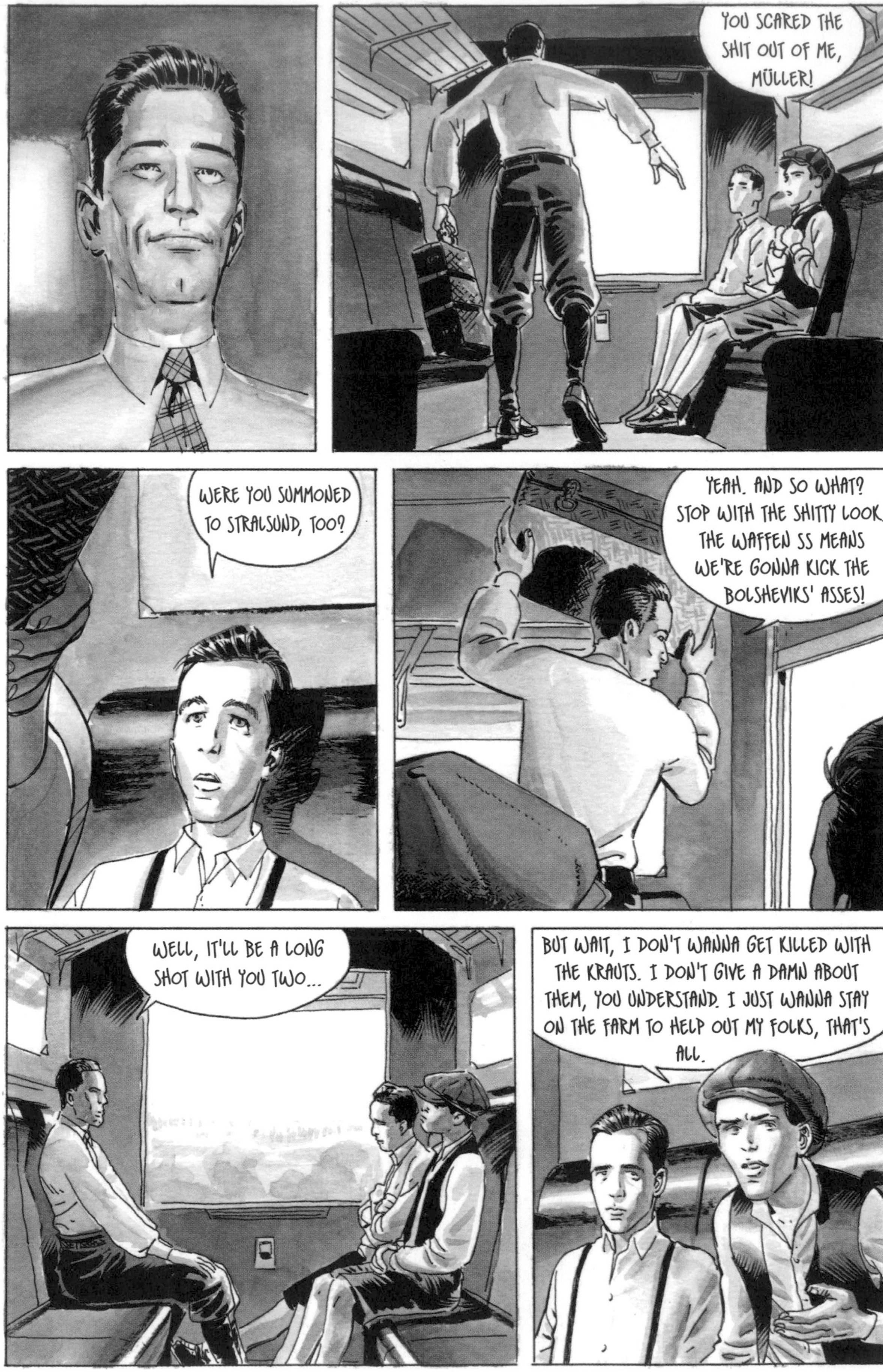
YOU SCARED THE SHIT OUT OF ME, MÜLLER!
WERE YOU SUMMONED TO STRALSUND, TOO?
YEAH. AND SO WHAT? STOP WITH THE SHITTY LOOK. THE WAFFEN SS MEANS WE'RE GONNA KICK THE BOLSHEVIKS' ASSES!
WELL, IT'LL BE A LONG SHOT WITH YOU TWO...
BUT WAIT, I DON'T WANNA GET KILLED WITH THE KRAUTS. I DON'T GIVE A DAMN ABOUT THEM, YOU UNDERSTAND. I JUST WANNA STAY ON THE FARM TO HELP OUT MY FOLKS, THAT'S ALL.

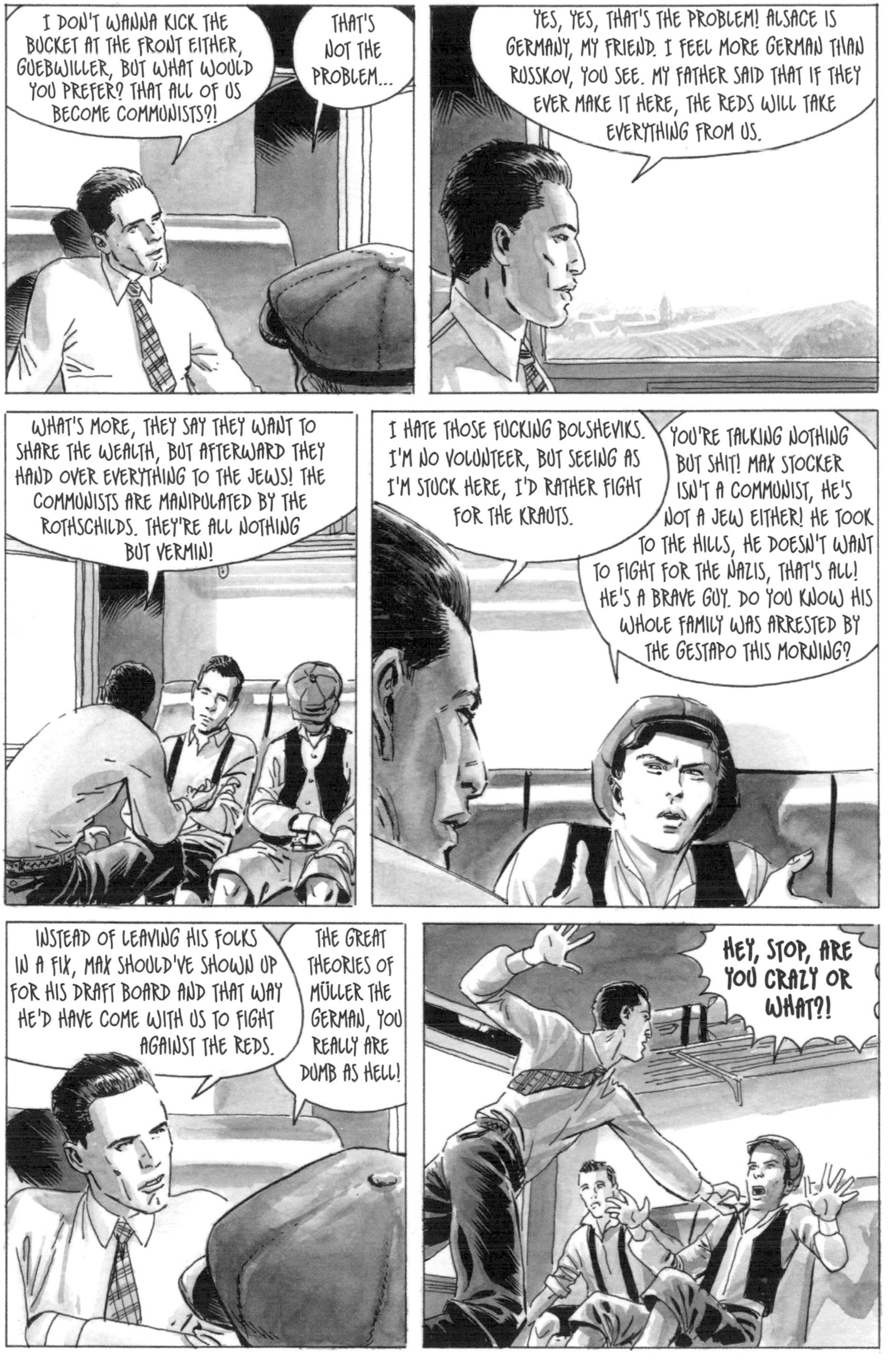
I DON'T WANNA KICK THE BUCKET AT THE FRONT EITHER, GUEBWILLER, BUT WHAT WOULD YOU PREFER? THAT ALL OF US BECOME COMMUNISTS?!
THAT'S NOT THE PROBLEM...
YES, YES, THAT'S THE PROBLEM! ALSACE IS GERMANY, MY FRIEND. I FEEL MORE GERMAN THAN RUSSKOV, YOU SEE. MY FATHER SAID THAT IF THEY EVER MAKE IT HERE, THE REDS WILL TAKE EVERYTHING FROM US.
WHAT'S MORE, THEY SAY THEY WANT TO SHARE THE WEALTH, BUT AFTERWARD THEY HAND OVER EVERYTHING TO THE JEWS! THE COMMUNISTS ARE MANIPULATED BY THE ROTHSCHILDS. THEY'RE ALL NOTHING BUT VERMIN!
I HATE THOSE FUCKING BOLSHEVIKS. I'M NO VOLUNTEER, BUT SEEING AS I'M STUCK HERE, I'D RATHER FIGHT FOR THE KRAUTS.
YOU'RE TALKING NOTHING BUT SHIT! MAX STOCKER ISN'T A COMMUNIST, HE'S NOT A JEW EITHER! HE TOOK TO THE HILLS, HE DOESN'T WANT TO FIGHT FOR THE NAZIS, THAT'S ALL! HE'S A BRAVE GUY. DO YOU KNOW HIS WHOLE FAMILY WAS ARRESTED BY THE GESTAPO THIS MORNING?
INSTEAD OF LEAVING HIS FOLKS IN A FIX, MAX SHOULD'VE SHOWN UP FOR HIS DRAFT BOARD AND THAT WAY HE'D HAVE COME WITH US TO FIGHT AGAINST THE REDS.
THE GREAT THEORIES OF MÜLLER THE GERMAN, YOU REALLY ARE DUMB AS HELL!
HEY, STOP, ARE YOU CRAZY OR WHAT?!

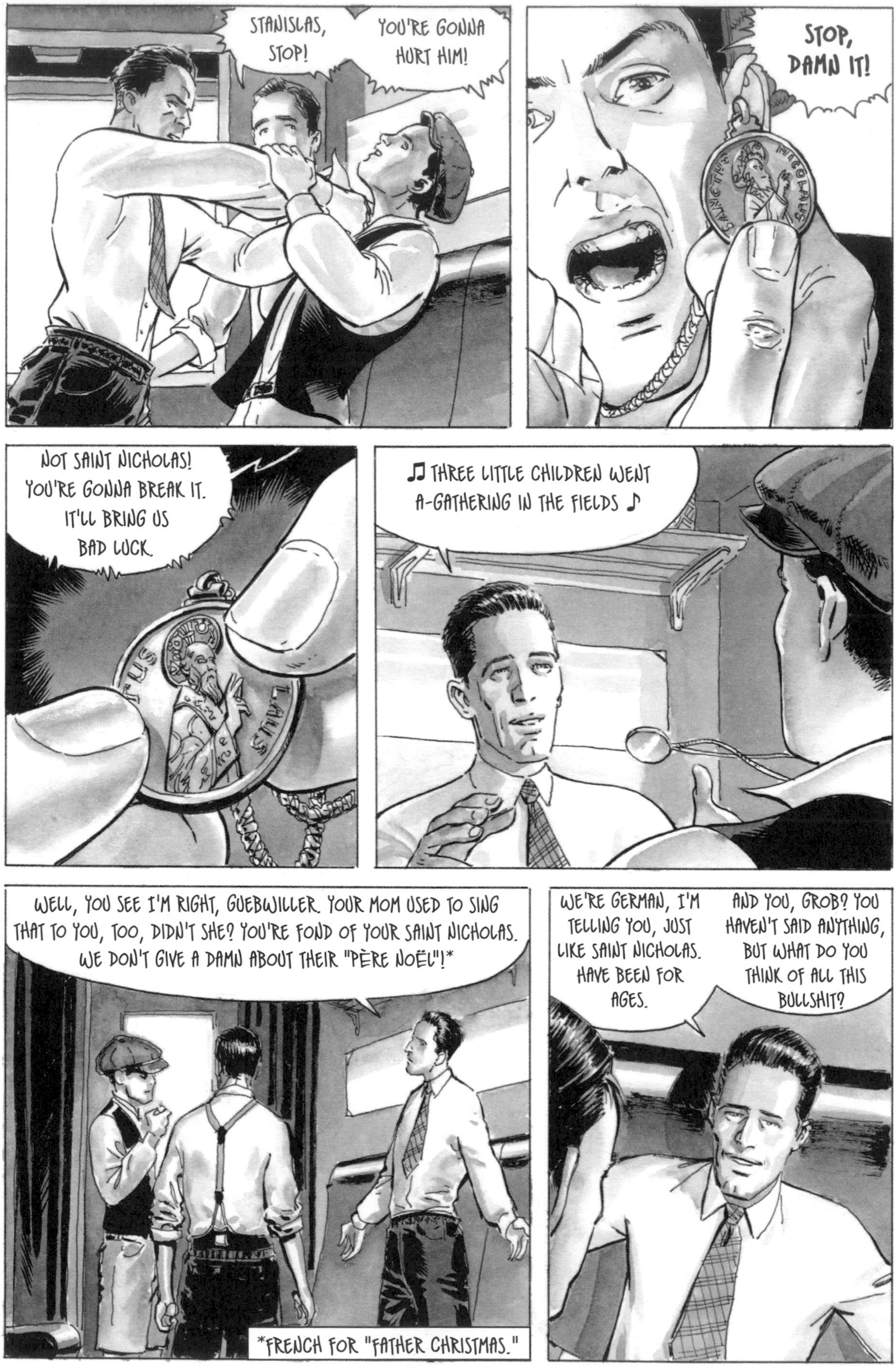
STANISLAS, STOP!
YOU'RE GONNA HURT HIM!
STOP, DAMN IT!
NOT SAINT NICHOLAS! YOU'RE GONNA BREAK IT. IT'LL BRING US BAD LUCK.
♫ THREE LITTLE CHILDREN WENT A-GATHERING IN THE FIELDS ♪
WELL, YOU SEE I'M RIGHT, GUEBWILLER. YOUR MOM USED TO SING THAT TO YOU, TOO, DIDN'T SHE? YOU'RE FOND OF YOUR SAINT NICHOLAS. WE DON'T GIVE A DAMN ABOUT THEIR "PÈRE NOËL"!*
*FRENCH FOR "FATHER CHRISTMAS."
WE'RE GERMAN, I'M TELLING YOU, JUST LIKE SAINT NICHOLAS. HAVE BEEN FOR AGES.
AND YOU, GROB? YOU HAVEN'T SAID ANYTHING, BUT WHAT DO YOU THINK OF ALL THIS BULLSHIT?

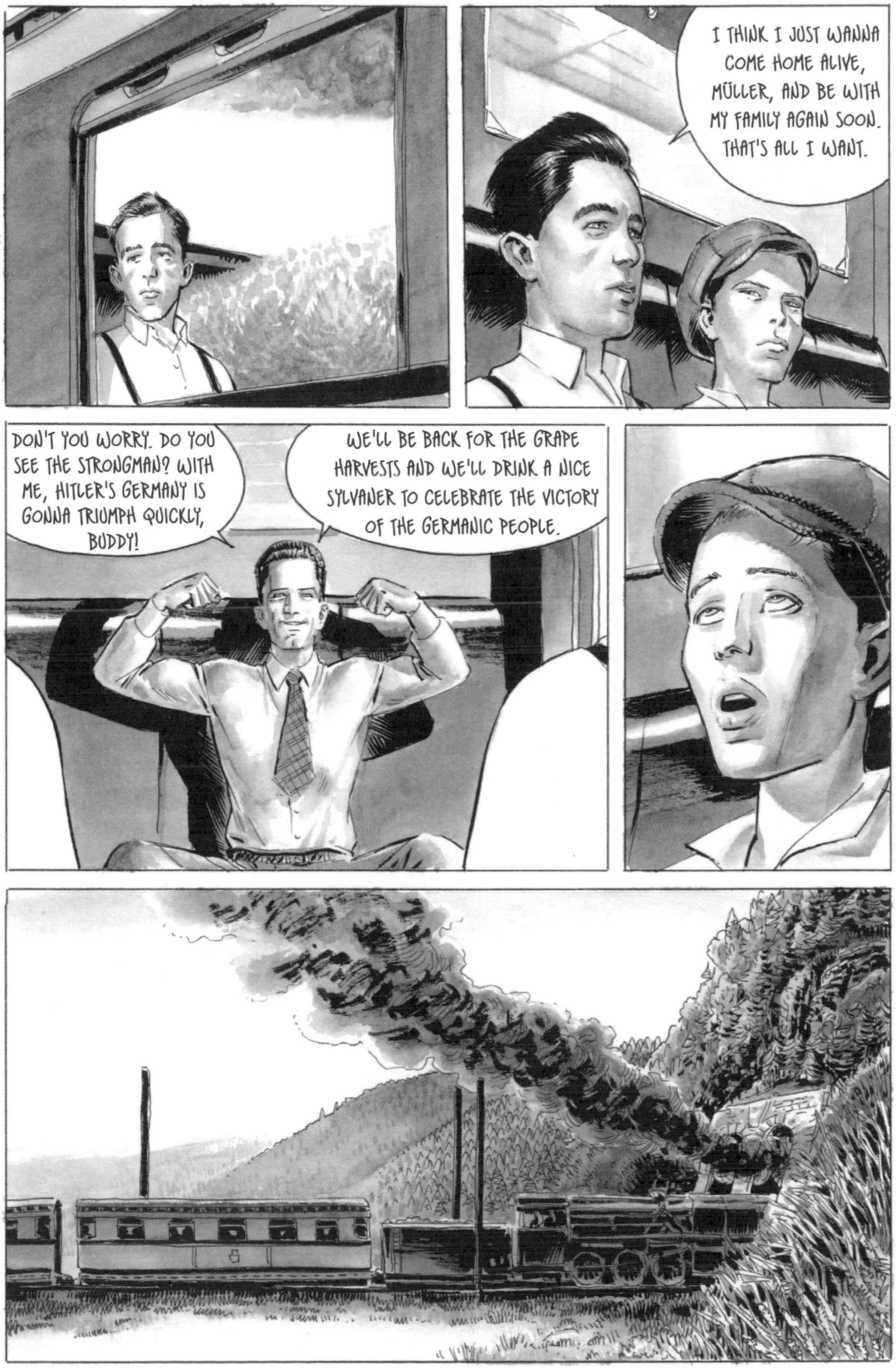
I THINK I JUST WANNA COME HOME ALIVE, MÜLLER, AND BE WITH MY FAMILY AGAIN SOON. THAT'S ALL I WANT.
DON'T YOU WORRY. DO YOU SEE THE STRONGMAN? WITH ME, HITLER'S GERMANY IS GONNA TRIUMPH QUICKLY, BUDDY!
WE'LL BE BACK FOR THE GRAPE HARVESTS AND WE'LL DRINK A NICE SYLVANER TO CELEBRATE THE VICTORY OF THE GERMANIC PEOPLE.

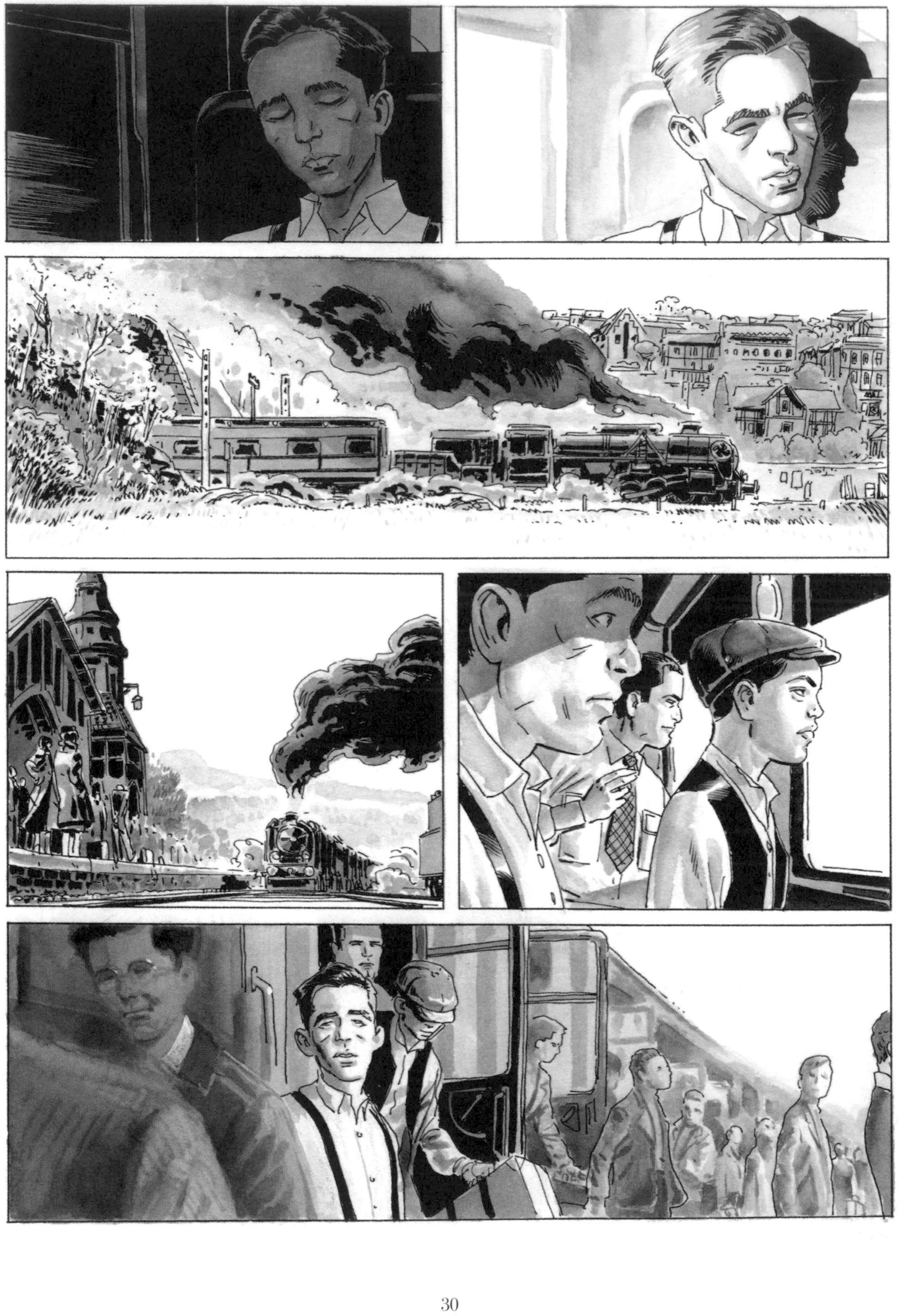

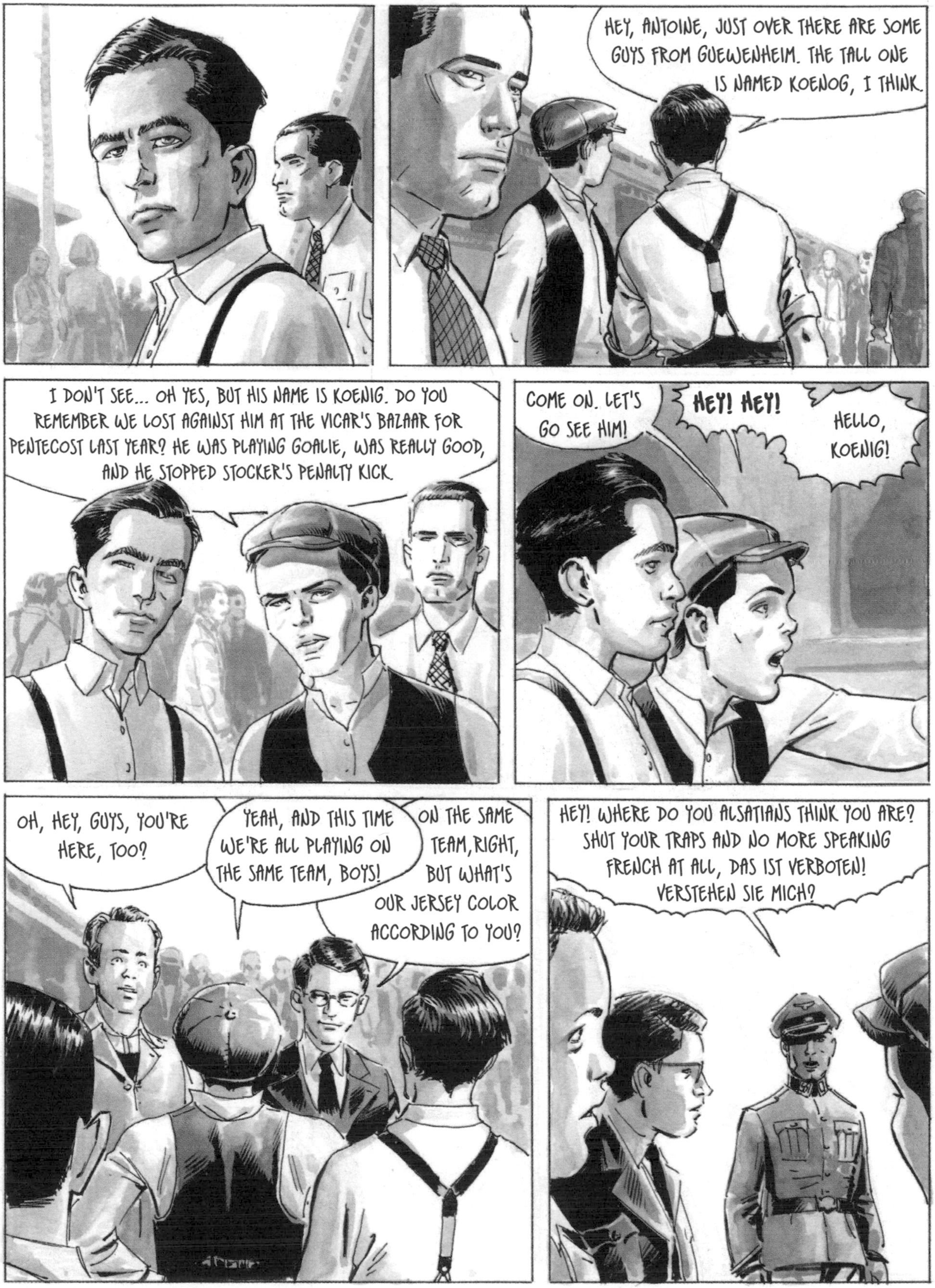
HEY, ANTOINE, JUST OVER THERE ARE SOME GUYS FROM GUEWENHEIM. THE TALL ONE IS NAMED KOENOG, I THINK.
I DON'T SEE... OH YES, BUT HIS NAME IS KOENIG. DO YOU REMEMBER WE LOST AGAINST HIM AT THE VICAR'S BAZAAR FOR PENTECOST LAST YEAR? HE WAS PLAYING GOALIE, WAS REALLY GOOD, AND HE STOPPED STOCKER'S PENALTY KICK.
COME ON. LET'S GO SEE HIM!
HEY! HEY!
HELLO, KOENIG!
OH, HEY, GUYS, YOU'RE HERE, TOO?
YEAH, AND THIS TIME WE'RE ALL PLAYING ON THE SAME TEAM, BOYS!
ON THE SAME TEAM, RIGHT, BUT WHAT'S OUR JERSEY COLOR ACCORDING TO YOU?
HEY! WHERE DO YOU ALSATIANS THINK YOU ARE? SHUT YOUR TRAPS AND NO MORE SPEAKING FRENCH AT ALL, DAS IST VERBOTEN! VERSTEHEN SIE MICH?

TO BE HONEST, GUYS, I DIDN'T THINK THE SEA WOULD BE SO BEAUTIFUL. YOU GET AN EYEFUL FOR FREE.

MY DAD HAS NEVER SEEN THE SEA EITHER. I'LL HAVE TO REMEMBER ALL THIS TO TELL HIM ABOUT IT. THAT'S THE NORTH SEA, RIGHT?

NOT HERE. I THINK THAT'S THE BALTIC SEA, BUT DAMN, IT'S BEAUTIFUL. THIS IS THE FIRST TIME I'VE SEEN THE SEA, TOO, GUYS...

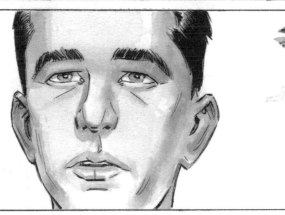

KRANKENHAUS WEST
STRALSUND

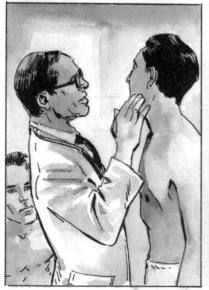

HEY, GROB?! GROB, ARE YOU ASLEEP?

NO, BUT QUIET DOWN OR WE'RE GONNA CATCH HELL!

I CAN'T STOP THINKING ABOUT KIRCHBERG. I'M WORRIED ABOUT MY FOLKS, GROB.

DO YOU THINK THEY BAWLED AFTER WE LEFT?

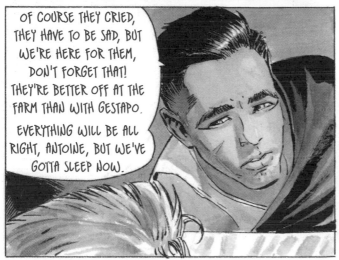

OF COURSE THEY CRIED, THEY HAVE TO BE SAD, BUT WE'RE HERE FOR THEM, DON'T FORGET THAT! THEY'RE BETTER OFF AT THE FARM THAN WITH GESTAPO.

EVERYTHING WILL BE ALL RIGHT, ANTOINE, BUT WE'VE GOTTA SLEEP NOW.

DO YOU THINK WE'RE REALLY GOING TO FIGHT?

I DON'T KNOW.

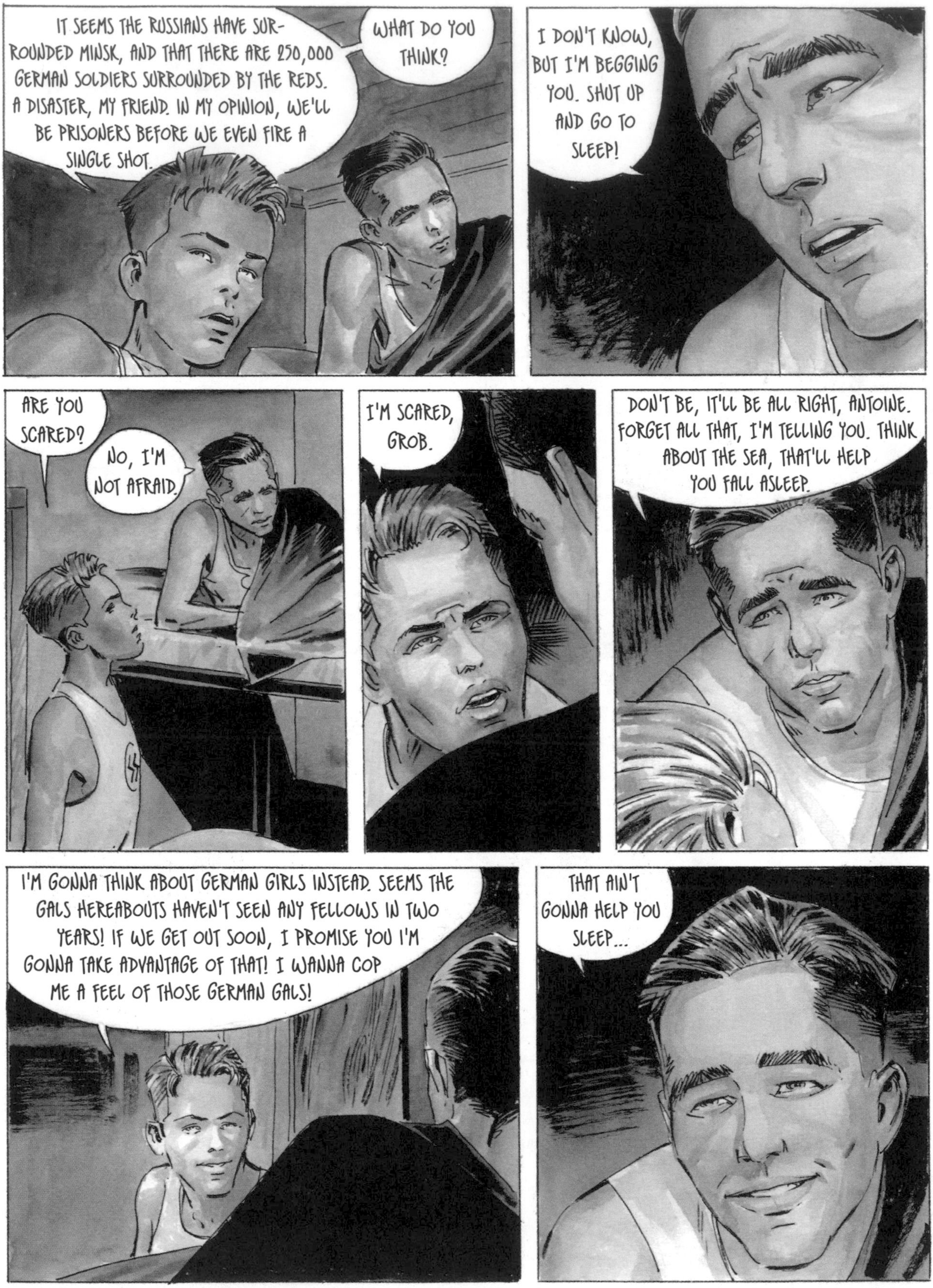
IT SEEMS THE RUSSIANS HAVE SURROUNDED MINSK, AND THAT THERE ARE 250,000 GERMAN SOLDIERS SURROUNDED BY THE REDS. A DISASTER, MY FRIEND. IN MY OPINION, WE'LL BE PRISONERS BEFORE WE EVEN FIRE A SINGLE SHOT.
WHAT DO YOU THINK?
I DON'T KNOW, BUT I'M BEGGING YOU. SHUT UP AND GO TO SLEEP!
ARE YOU SCARED?
NO, I'M NOT AFRAID.
I'M SCARED, GROB.
DON'T BE, IT'LL BE ALL RIGHT, ANTOINE. FORGET ALL THAT, I'M TELLING YOU. THINK ABOUT THE SEA, THAT'LL HELP YOU FALL ASLEEP.
I'M GONNA THINK ABOUT GERMAN GIRLS INSTEAD. SEEMS THE GALS HEREABOUTS HAVEN'T SEEN ANY FELLOWS IN TWO YEARS! IF WE GET OUT SOON, I PROMISE YOU I'M GONNA TAKE ADVANTAGE OF THAT! I WANNA COP ME A FEEL OF THOSE GERMAN GALS!
THAT AIN'T GONNA HELP YOU SLEEP...

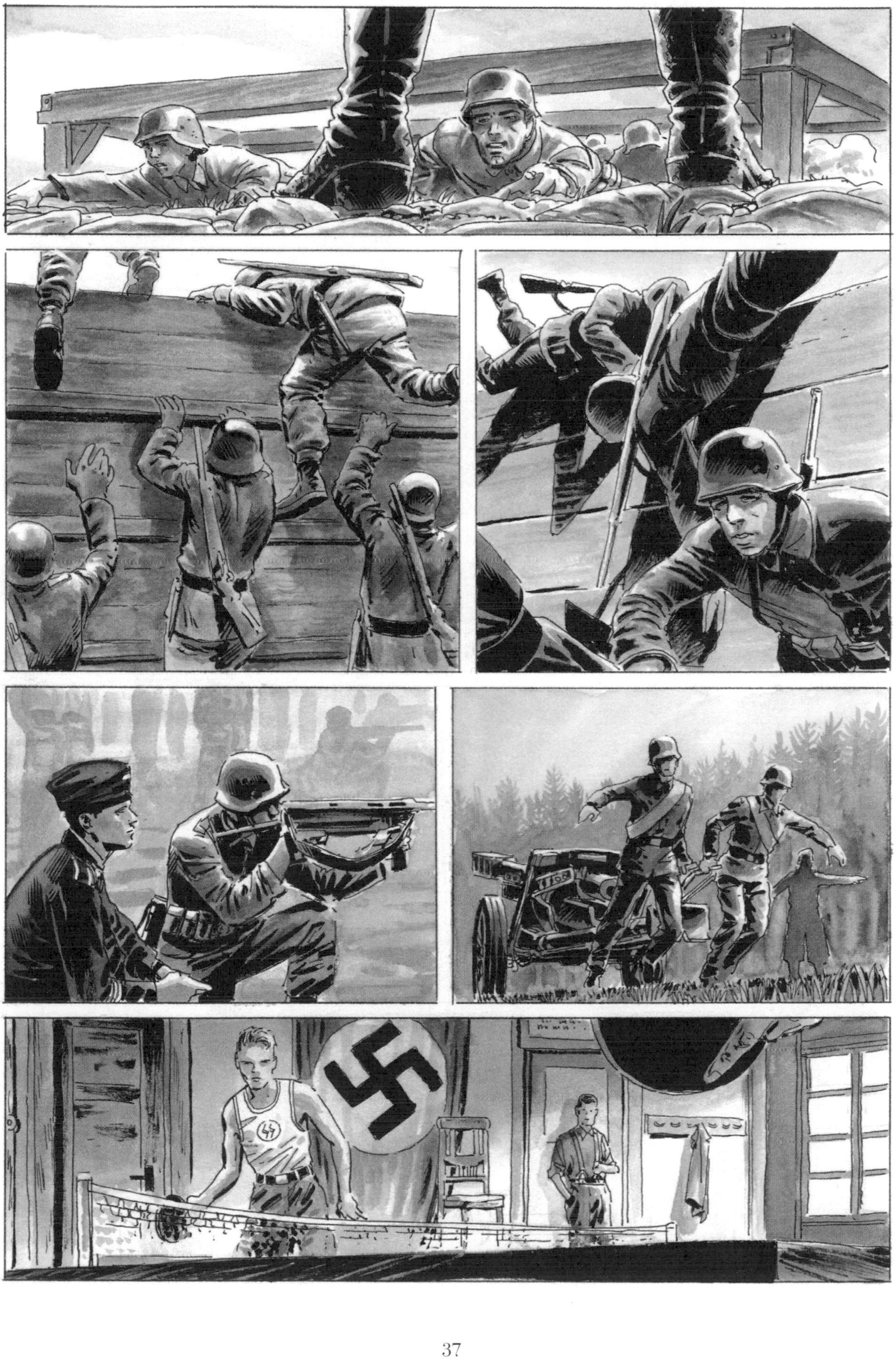

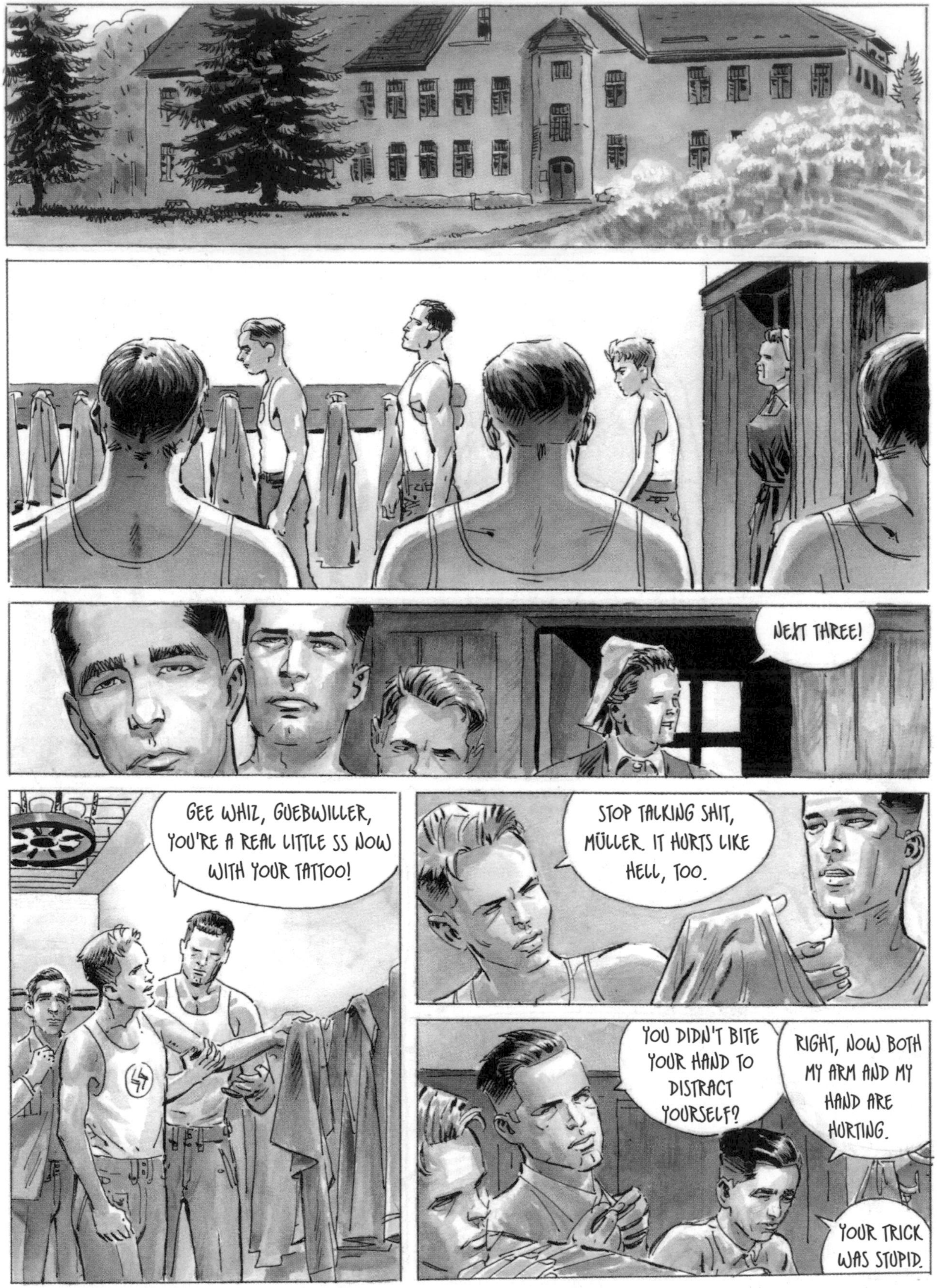
NEXT THREE!
GEE WHIZ, GUEBWILLER, YOU'RE A REAL LITTLE SS NOW WITH YOUR TATTOO!
STOP TALKING SHIT, MÜLLER. IT HURTS LIKE HELL, TOO.
YOU DIDN'T BITE YOUR HAND TO DISTRACT YOURSELF?
RIGHT, NOW BOTH MY ARM AND MY HAND ARE HURTING.
YOUR TRICK WAS STUPID.

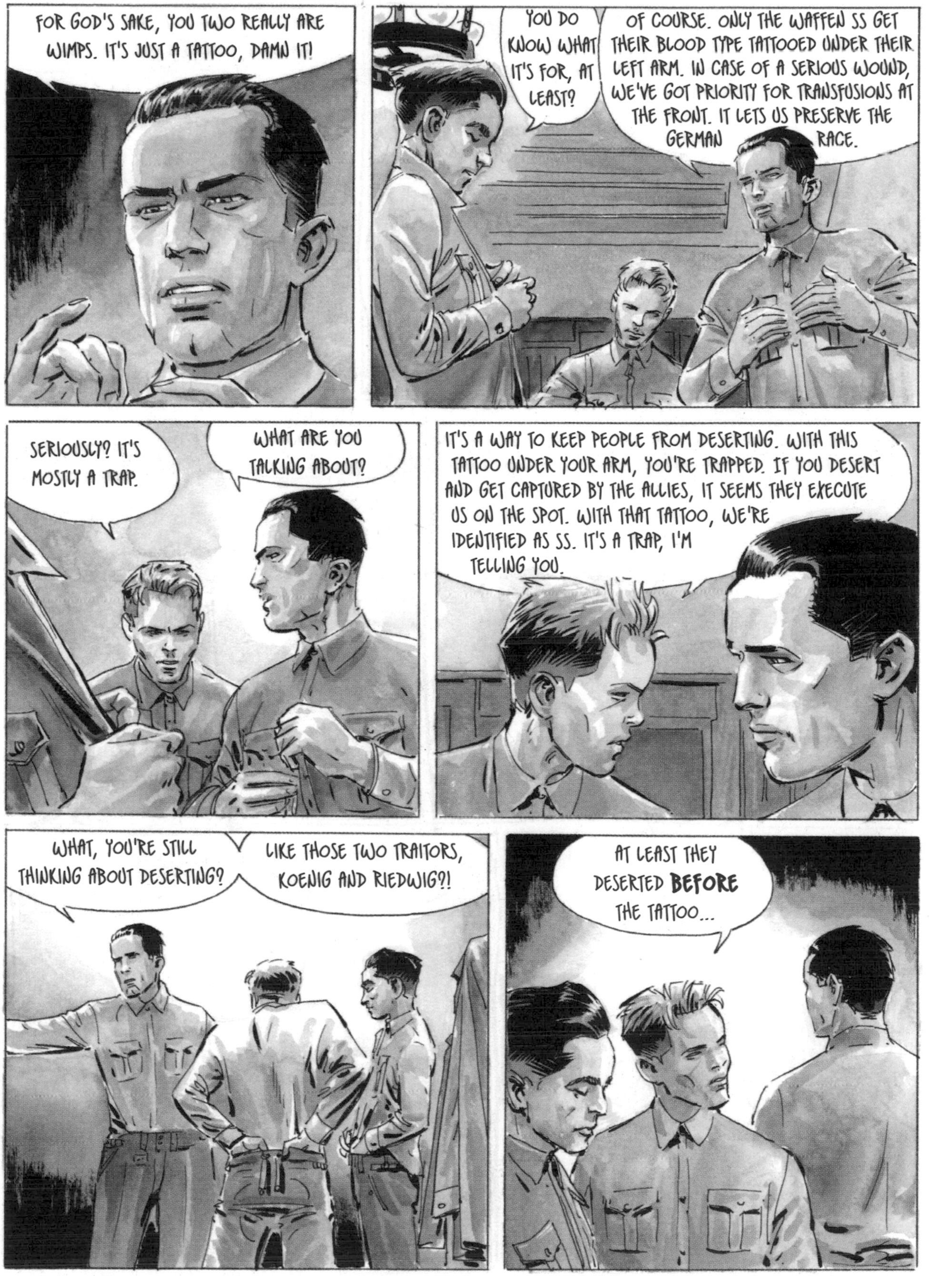
FOR GOD'S SAKE, YOU TWO REALLY ARE WIMPS. IT'S JUST A TATTOO, DAMN IT!
YOU DO KNOW WHAT IT'S FOR, AT LEAST?
OF COURSE. ONLY THE WAFFEN SS GET THEIR BLOOD TYPE TATTOOED UNDER THEIR LEFT ARM. IN CASE OF A SERIOUS WOUND, WE'VE GOT PRIORITY FOR TRANSFUSIONS AT THE FRONT. IT LETS US PRESERVE THE GERMAN RACE.
SERIOUSLY? IT'S MOSTLY A TRAP.
WHAT ARE YOU TALKING ABOUT?
IT'S A WAY TO KEEP PEOPLE FROM DESERTING. WITH THIS TATTOO UNDER YOUR ARM, YOU'RE TRAPPED. IF YOU DESERT AND GET CAPTURED BY THE ALLIES, IT SEEMS THEY EXECUTE US ON THE SPOT. WITH THAT TATTOO, WE'RE IDENTIFIED AS SS. IT'S A TRAP, I'M TELLING YOU.
WHAT, YOU'RE STILL THINKING ABOUT DESERTING?
LIKE THOSE TWO TRAITORS, KOENIG AND RIEDWIG?!
AT LEAST THEY DESERTED **BEFORE** THE TATTOO...

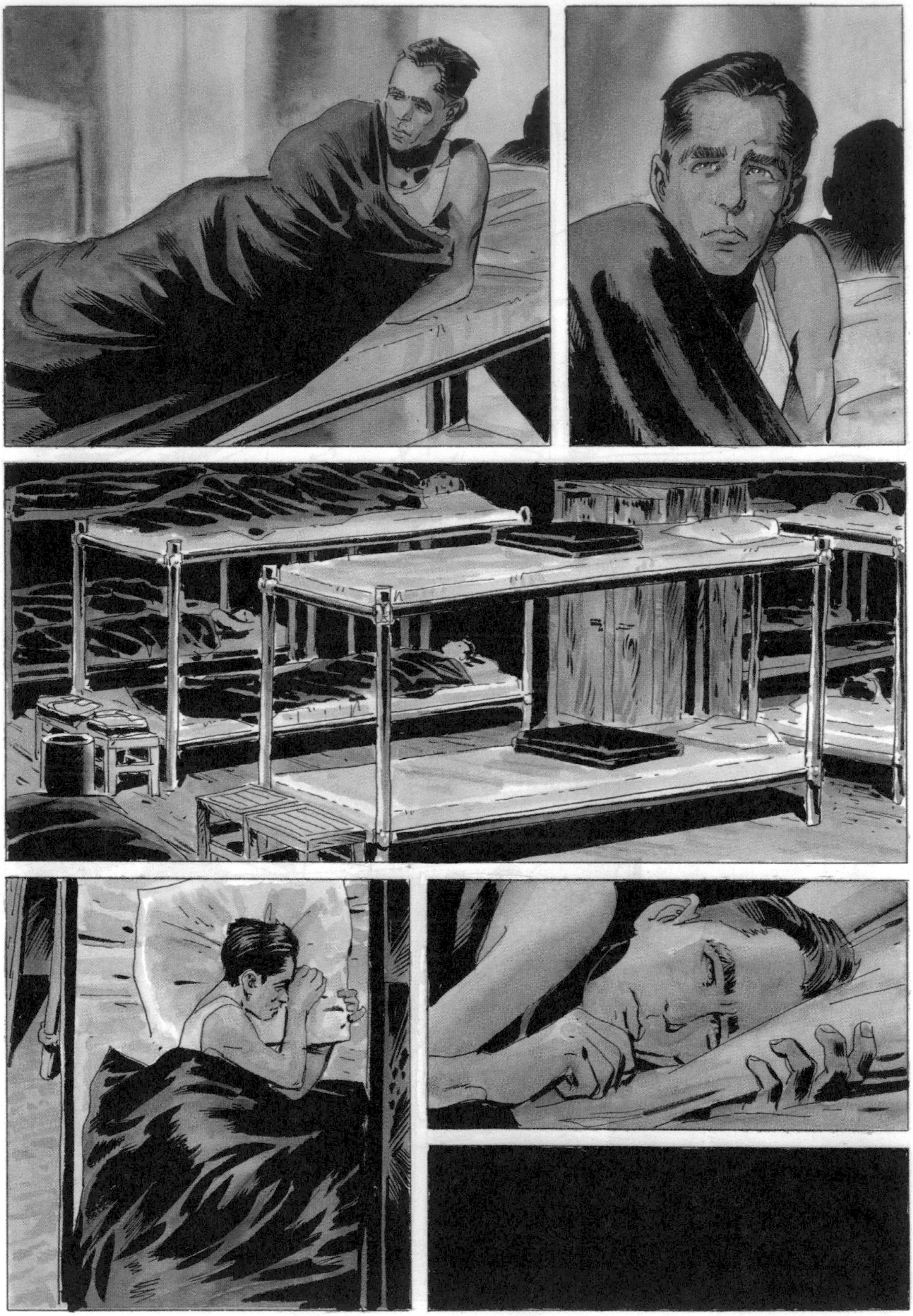

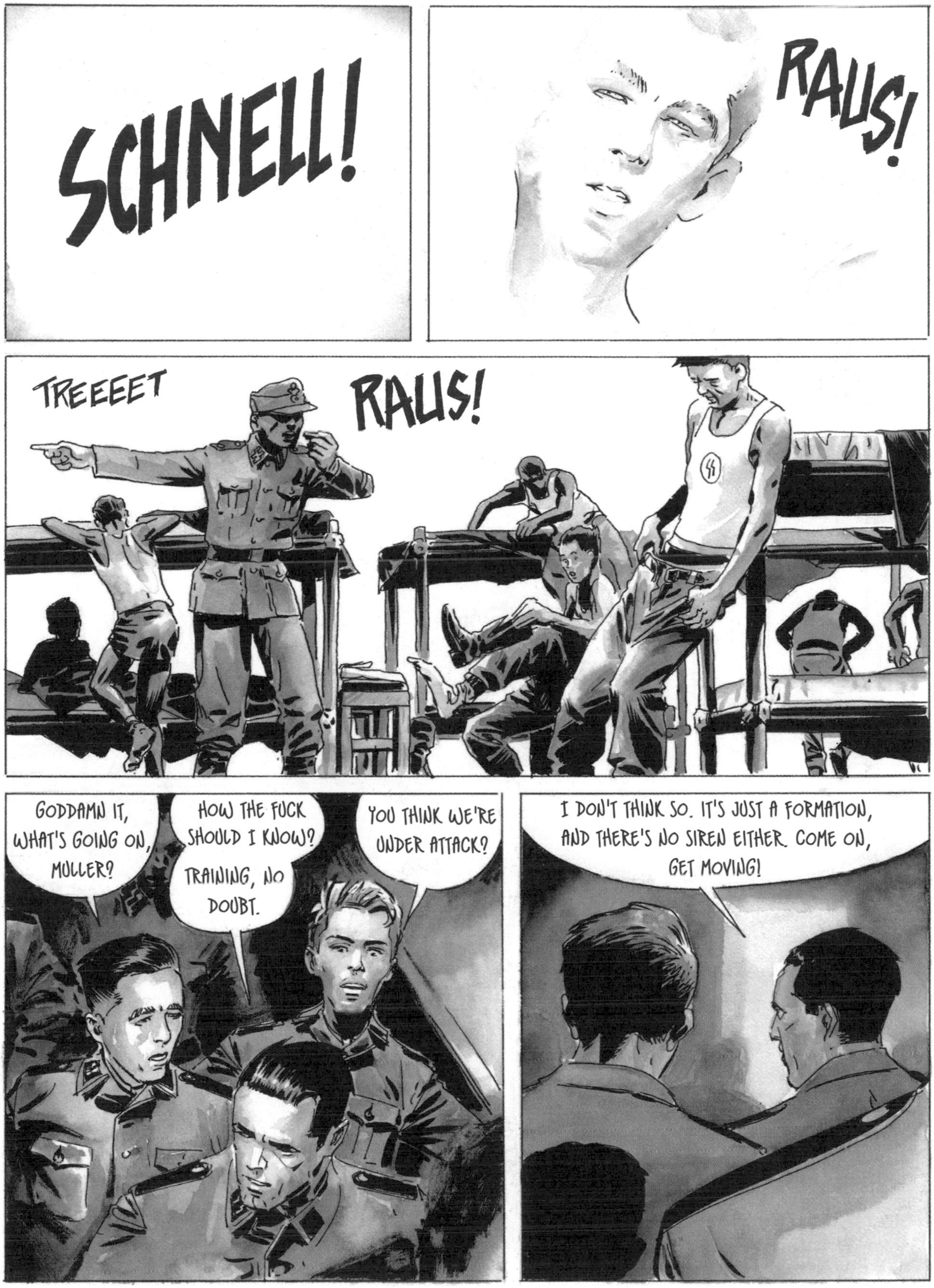
SCHNELL!
RAUS!
TREEEET
RAUS!
GODDAMN IT, WHAT'S GOING ON, MULLER?
HOW THE FUCK SHOULD I KNOW?
TRAINING, NO DOUBT.
YOU THINK WE'RE UNDER ATTACK?
I DON'T THINK SO. IT'S JUST A FORMATION, AND THERE'S NO SIREN EITHER. COME ON, GET MOVING!

OH, SHIT! FUCK!

IT'S KOENIG AND RIEDWIG.

THEY CAPTURED THEM. HOW HORRIBLE...

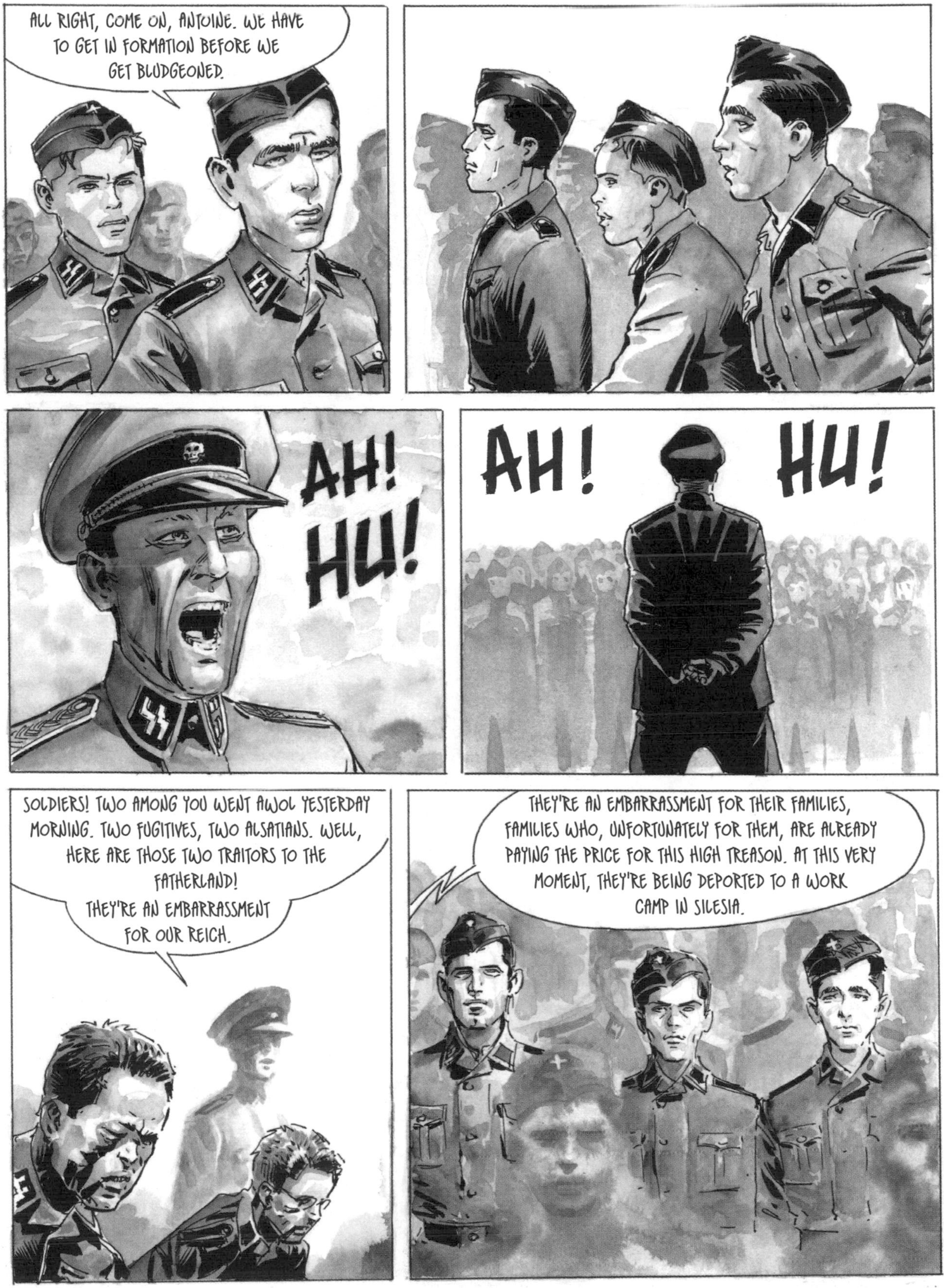
ALL RIGHT, COME ON, ANTOINE. WE HAVE TO GET IN FORMATION BEFORE WE GET BLUDGEONED.
AH! HU!
AH! HU!
SOLDIERS! TWO AMONG YOU WENT AWOL YESTERDAY MORNING. TWO FUGITIVES, TWO ALSATIANS. WELL, HERE ARE THOSE TWO TRAITORS TO THE FATHERLAND!
THEY'RE AN EMBARRASSMENT FOR OUR REICH.
THEY'RE AN EMBARRASSMENT FOR THEIR FAMILIES, FAMILIES WHO, UNFORTUNATELY FOR THEM, ARE ALREADY PAYING THE PRICE FOR THIS HIGH TREASON. AT THIS VERY MOMENT, THEY'RE BEING DEPORTED TO A WORK CAMP IN SILESIA.

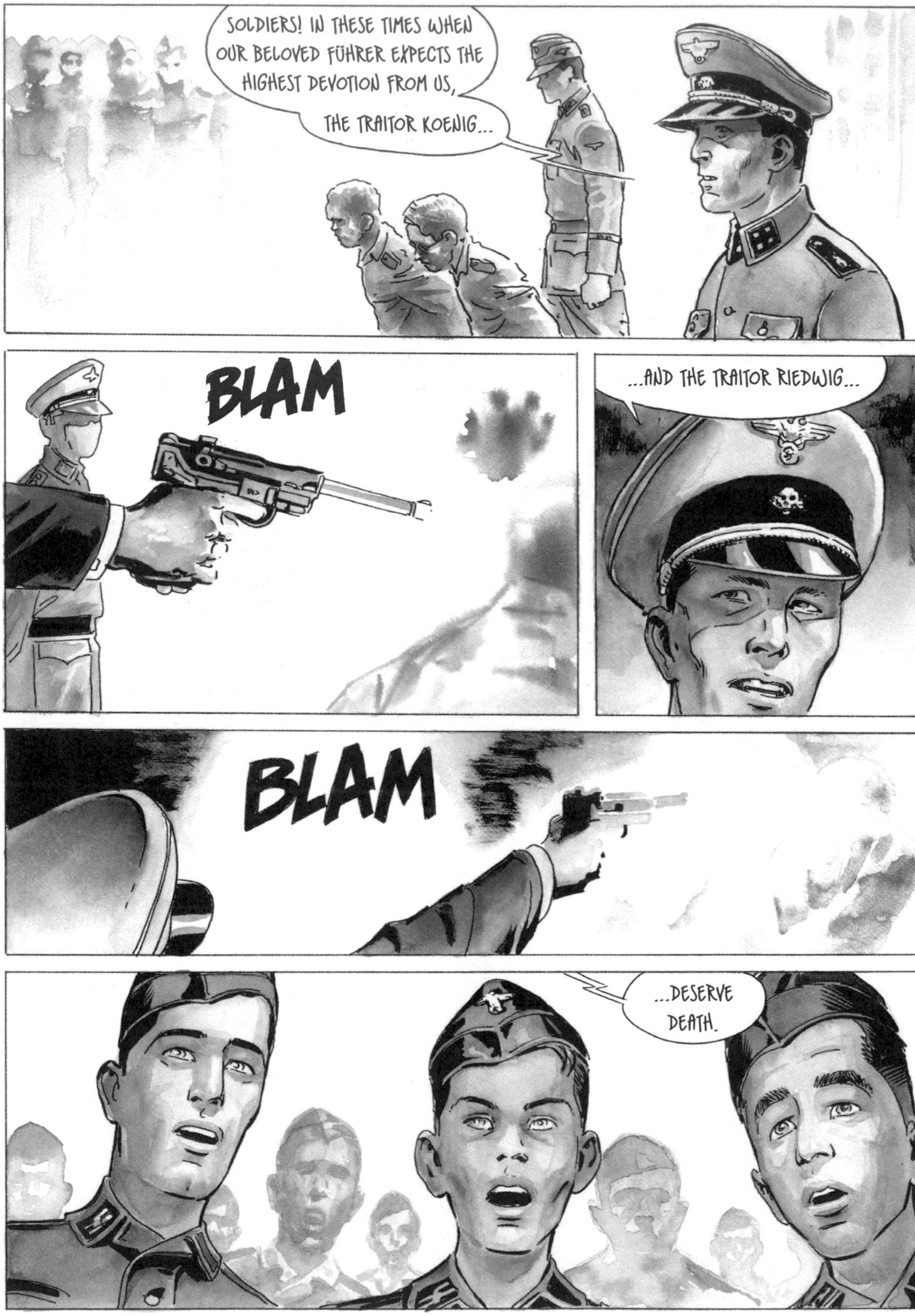
SOLDIERS! IN THESE TIMES WHEN OUR BELOVED FÜHRER EXPECTS THE HIGHEST DEVOTION FROM US,
THE TRAITOR KOENIG...
BLAM
...AND THE TRAITOR RIEDWIG...
BLAM
...DESERVE DEATH.

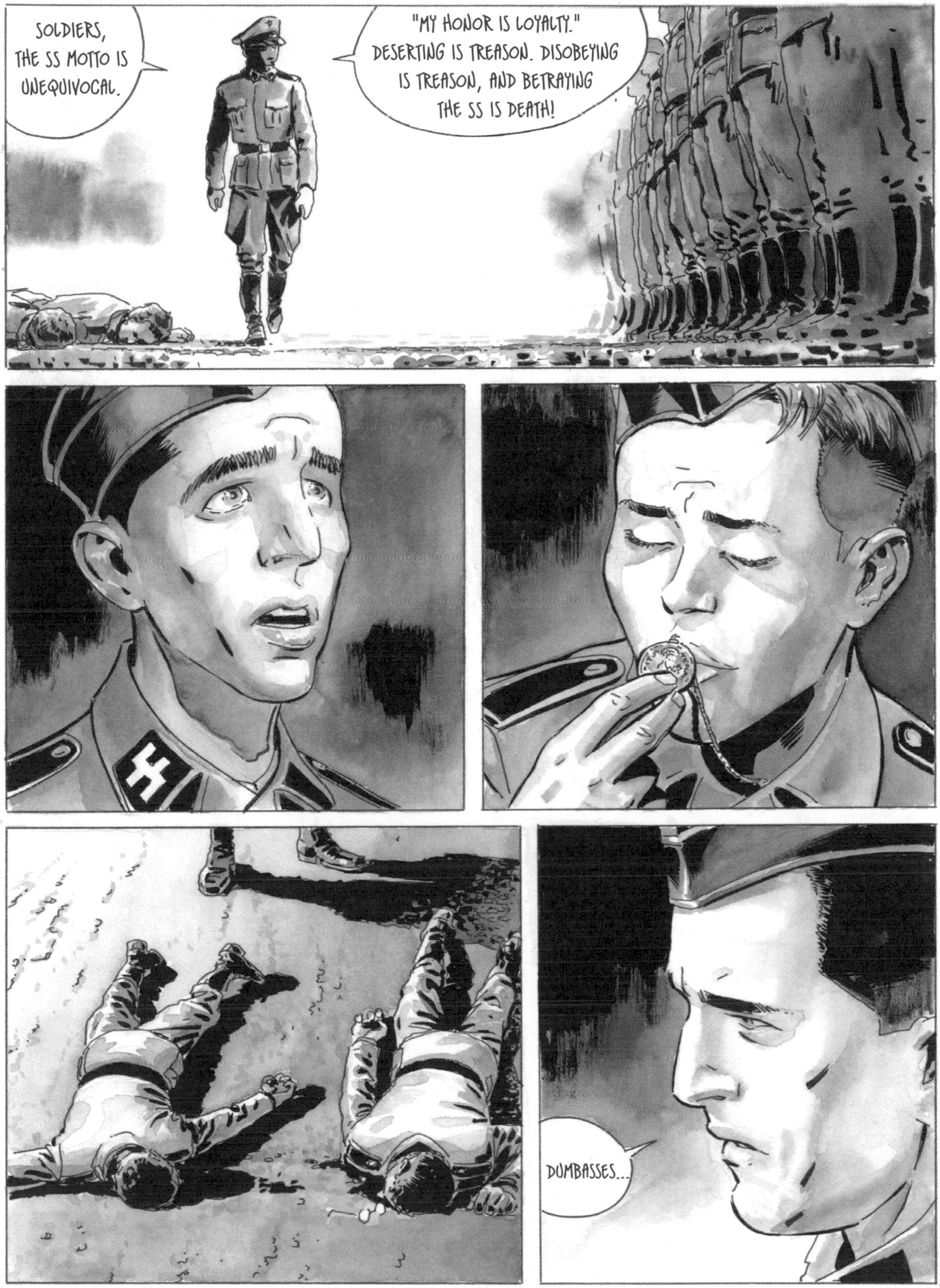
SOLDIERS, THE SS MOTTO IS UNEQUIVOCAL.
"MY HONOR IS LOYALTY." DESERTING IS TREASON. DISOBEYING IS TREASON, AND BETRAYING THE SS IS DEATH!
DUMBASSES...

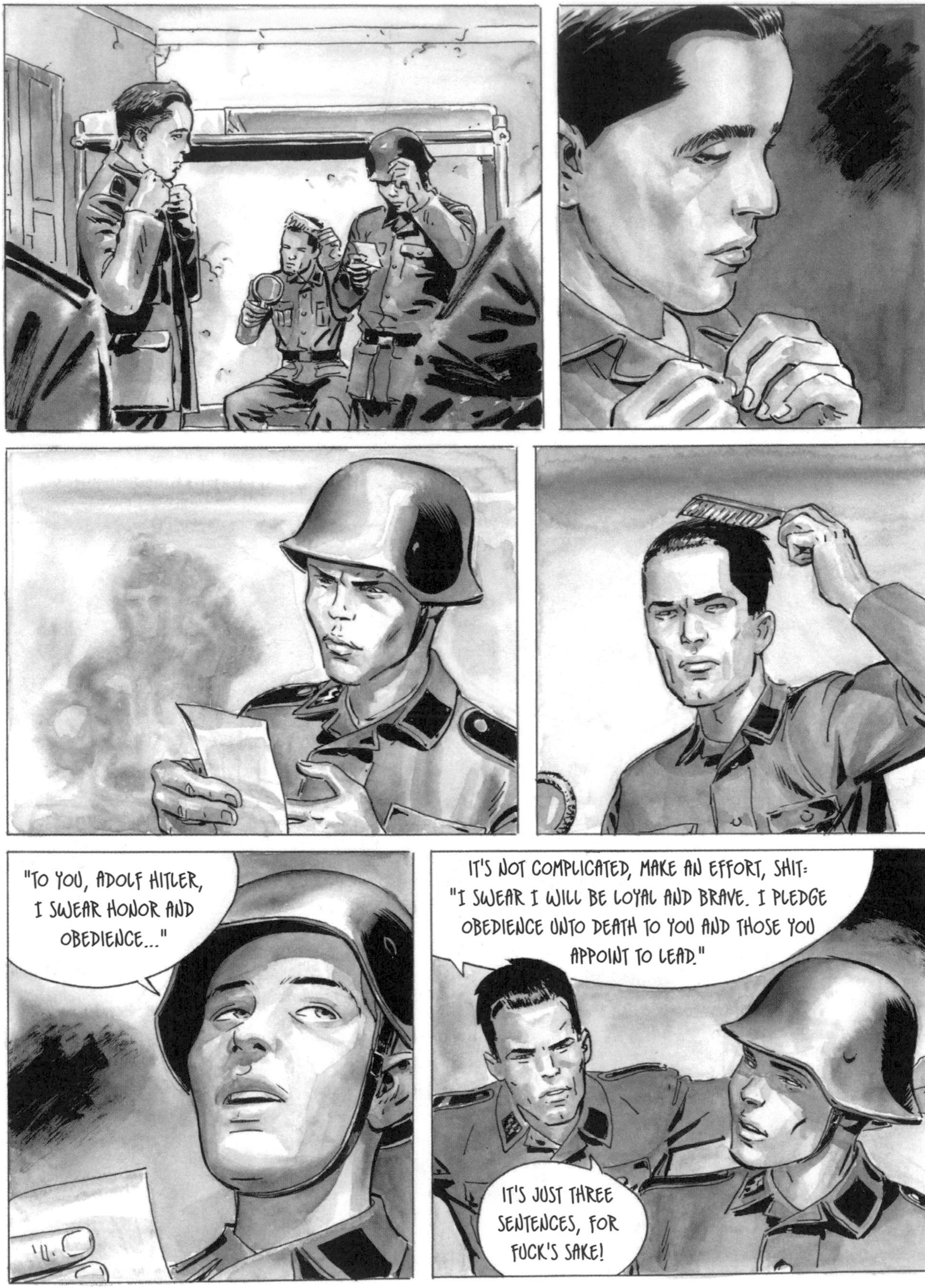
"TO YOU, ADOLF HITLER, I SWEAR HONOR AND OBEDIENCE..."
IT'S NOT COMPLICATED, MAKE AN EFFORT, SHIT: "I SWEAR I WILL BE LOYAL AND BRAVE. I PLEDGE OBEDIENCE UNTO DEATH TO YOU AND THOSE YOU APPOINT TO LEAD."
IT'S JUST THREE SENTENCES, FOR FUCK'S SAKE!

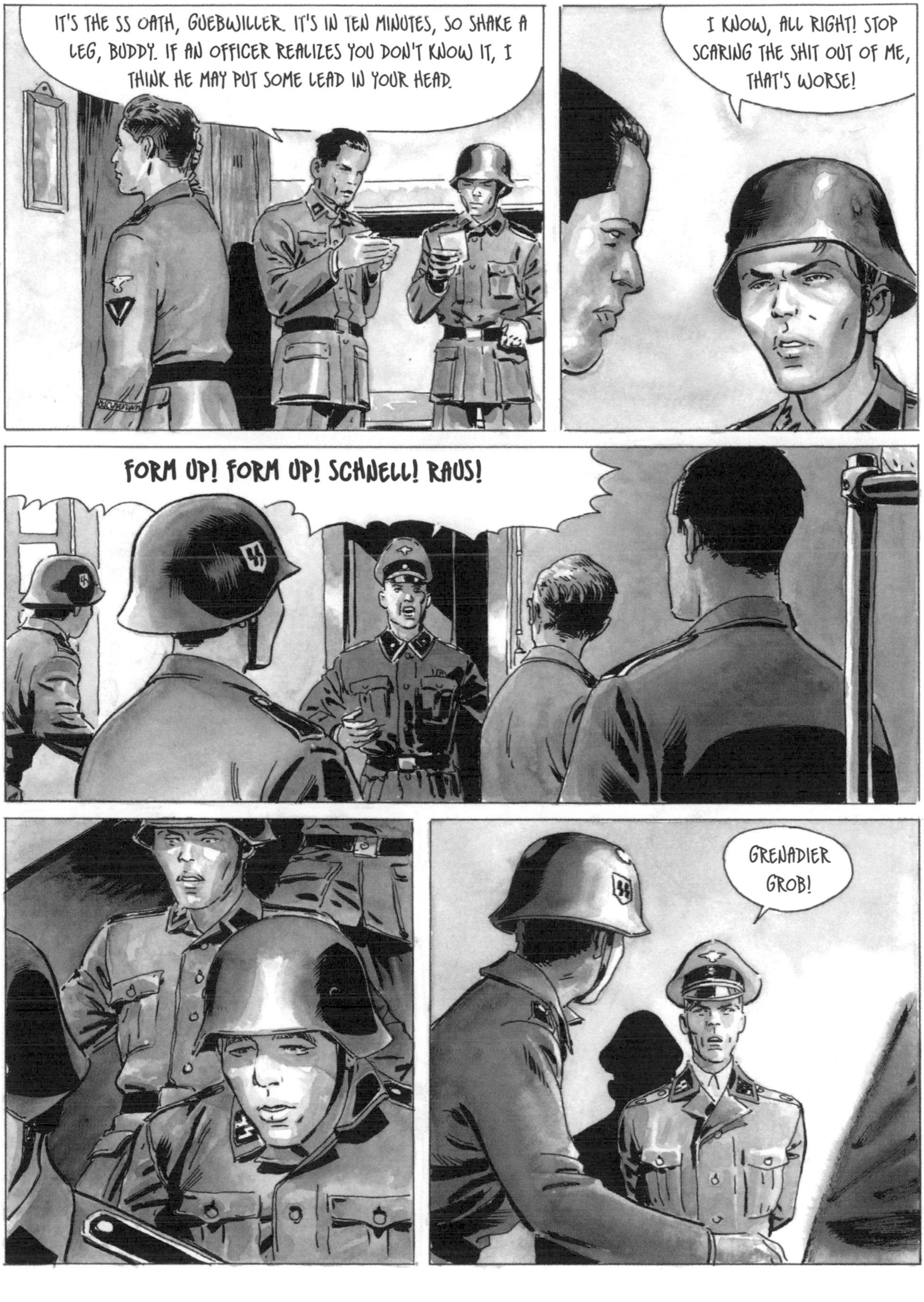
IT'S THE SS OATH, GUEBWILLER. IT'S IN TEN MINUTES, SO SHAKE A LEG, BUDDY. IF AN OFFICER REALIZES YOU DON'T KNOW IT, I THINK HE MAY PUT SOME LEAD IN YOUR HEAD.
I KNOW, ALL RIGHT! STOP SCARING THE SHIT OUT OF ME, THAT'S WORSE!
FORM UP! FORM UP! SCHNELL! RAUS!
GRENADIER GROB!

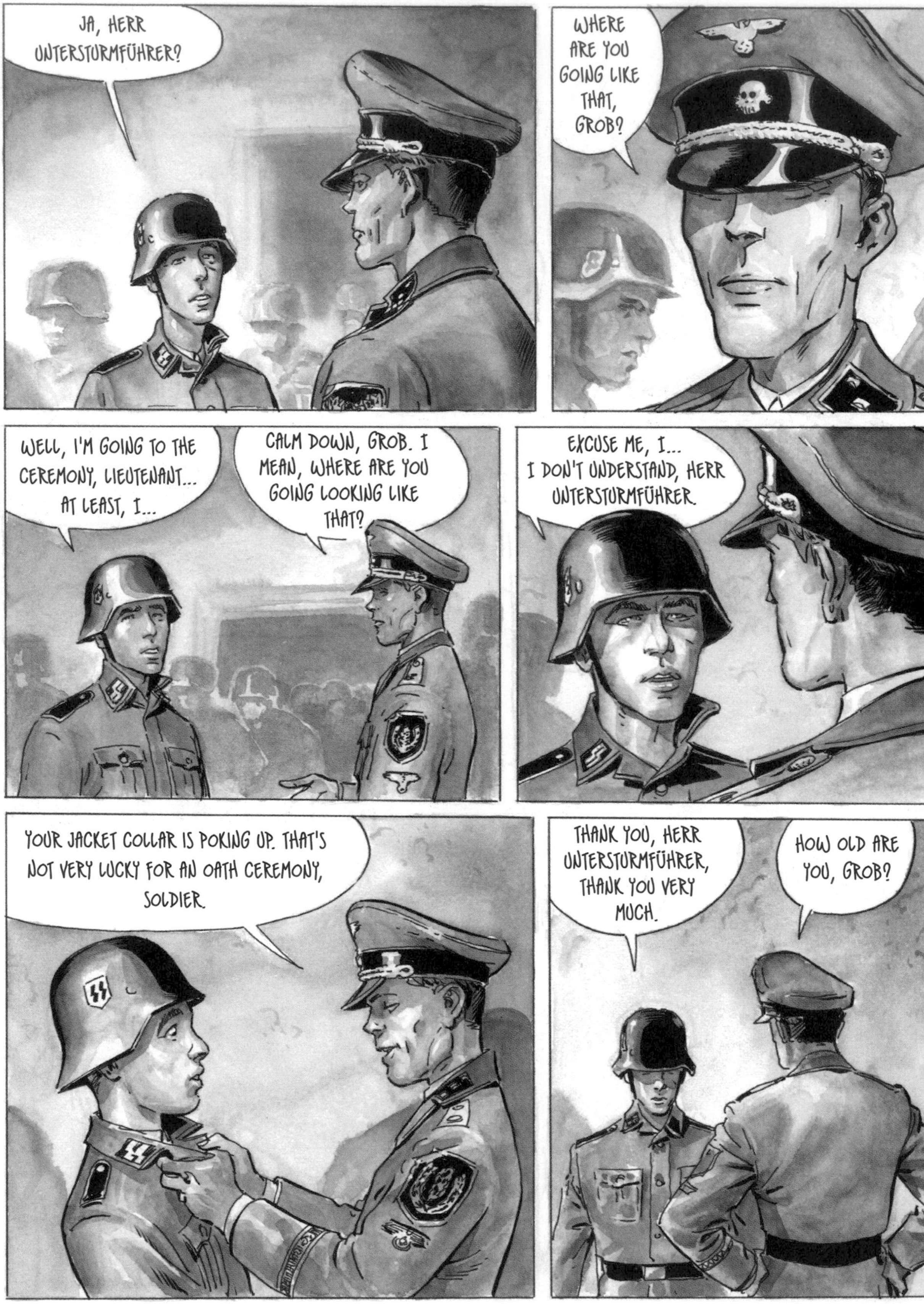
JA, HERR UNTERSTURMFÜHRER?
WHERE ARE YOU GOING LIKE THAT, GROB?
WELL, I'M GOING TO THE CEREMONY, LIEUTENANT... AT LEAST, I...
CALM DOWN, GROB. I MEAN, WHERE ARE YOU GOING LOOKING LIKE THAT?
EXCUSE ME, I... I DON'T UNDERSTAND, HERR UNTERSTURMFÜHRER.
YOUR JACKET COLLAR IS POKING UP. THAT'S NOT VERY LUCKY FOR AN OATH CEREMONY, SOLDIER.
THANK YOU, HERR UNTERSTURMFÜHRER, THANK YOU VERY MUCH.
HOW OLD ARE YOU, GROB?

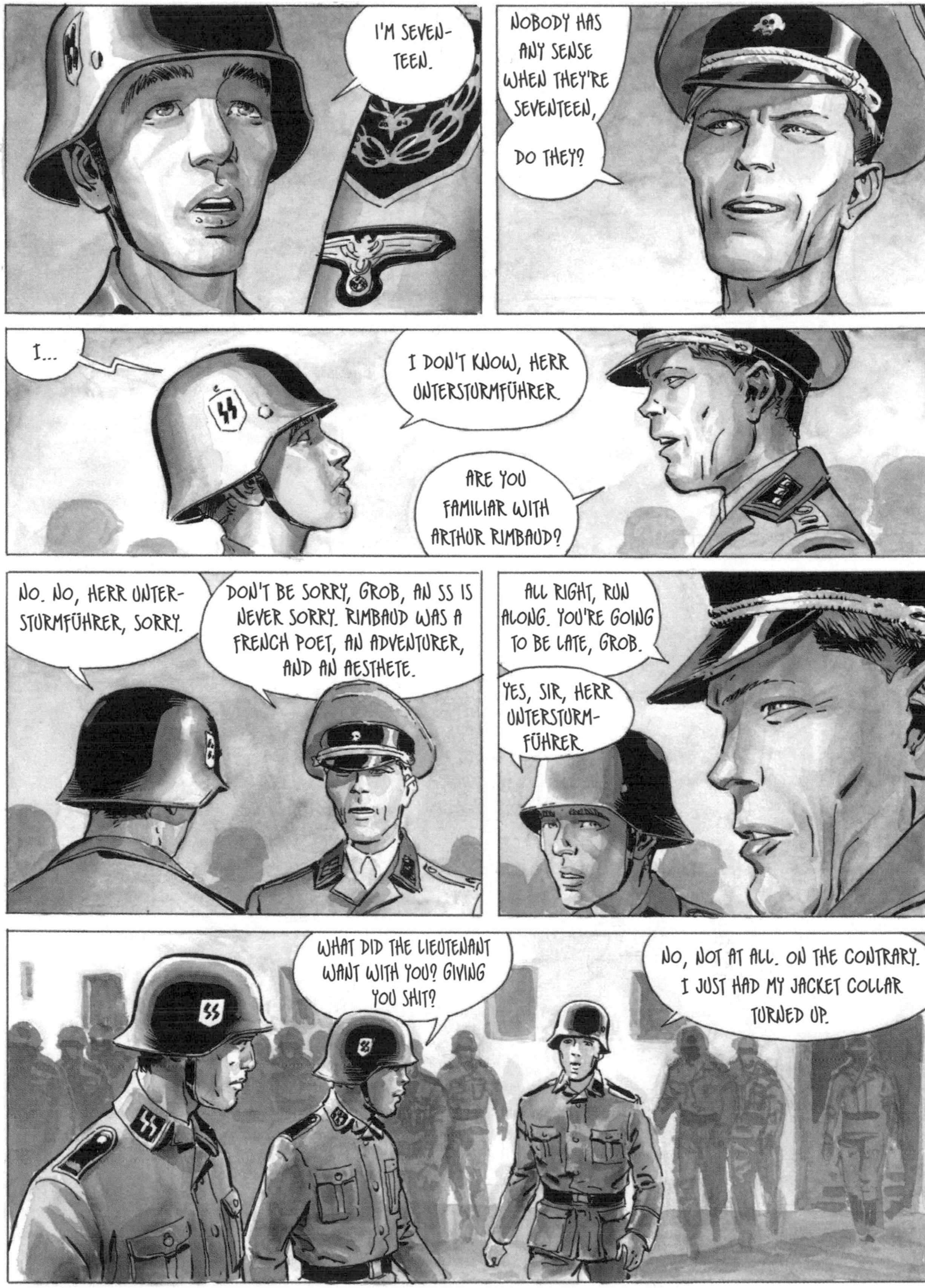
I'M SEVENTEEN.
NOBODY HAS ANY SENSE WHEN THEY'RE SEVENTEEN,
DO THEY?
I...
I DON'T KNOW, HERR UNTERSTURMFÜHRER.
ARE YOU FAMILIAR WITH ARTHUR RIMBAUD?
NO. NO, HERR UNTERSTURMFÜHRER, SORRY.
DON'T BE SORRY, GROB, AN SS IS NEVER SORRY. RIMBAUD WAS A FRENCH POET, AN ADVENTURER, AND AN AESTHETE.
ALL RIGHT, RUN ALONG. YOU'RE GOING TO BE LATE, GROB.
YES, SIR, HERR UNTERSTURMFÜHRER.
WHAT DID THE LIEUTENANT WANT WITH YOU? GIVING YOU SHIT?
NO, NOT AT ALL. ON THE CONTRARY. I JUST HAD MY JACKET COLLAR TURNED UP.

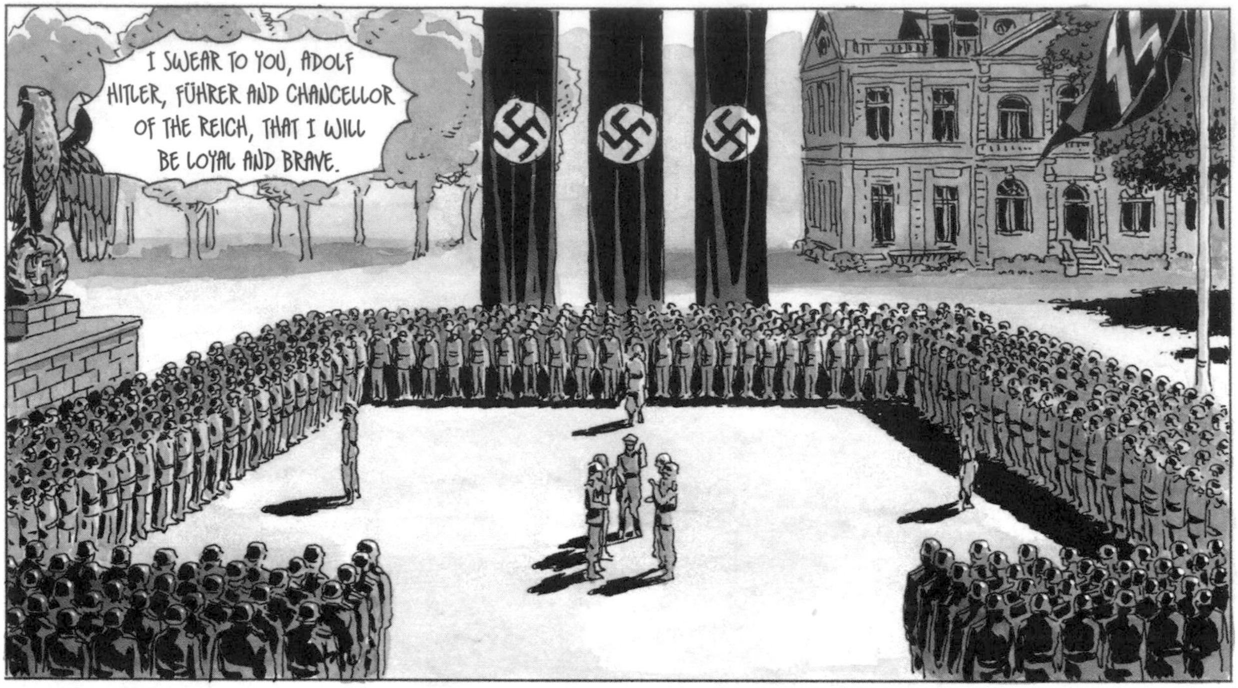
I SWEAR TO YOU, ADOLF HITLER, FÜHRER AND CHANCELLOR OF THE REICH, THAT I WILL BE LOYAL AND BRAVE.

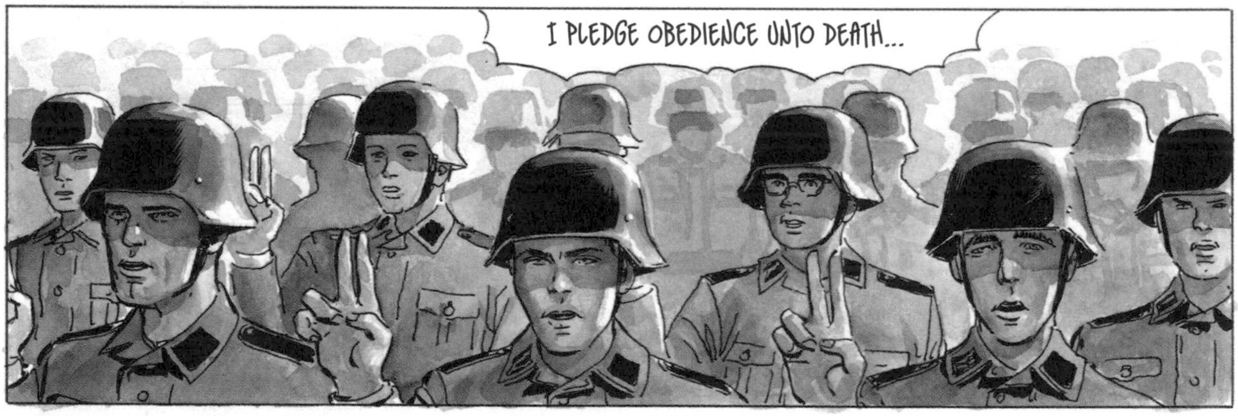
I PLEDGE OBEDIENCE UNTO DEATH...

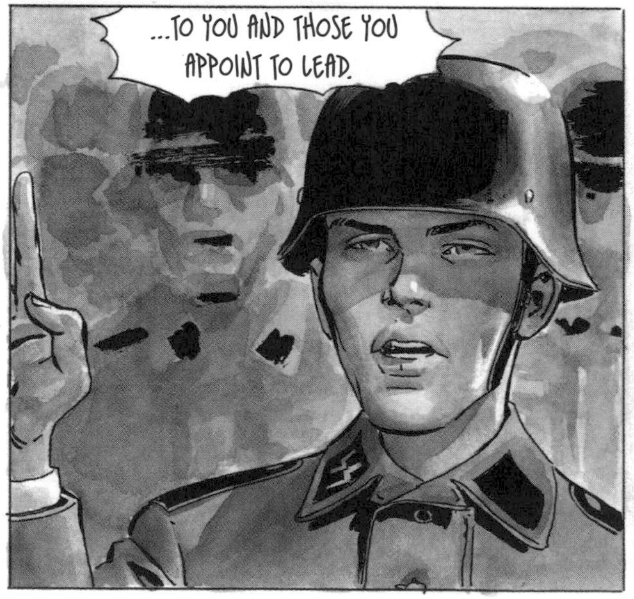
...TO YOU AND THOSE YOU APPOINT TO LEAD.

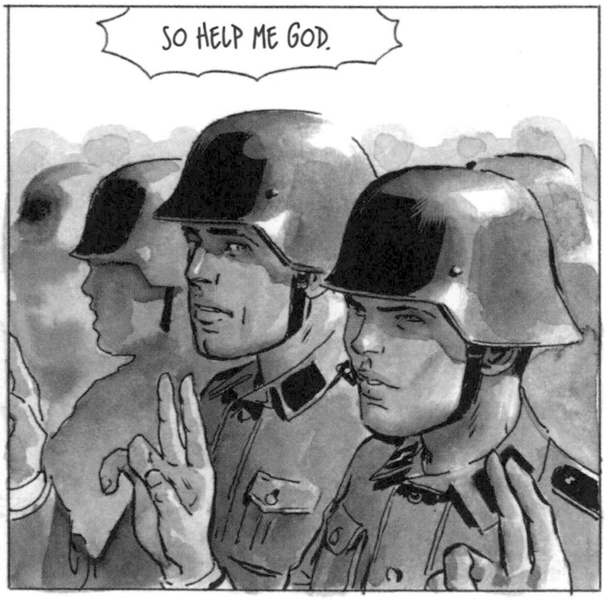
SO HELP ME GOD.

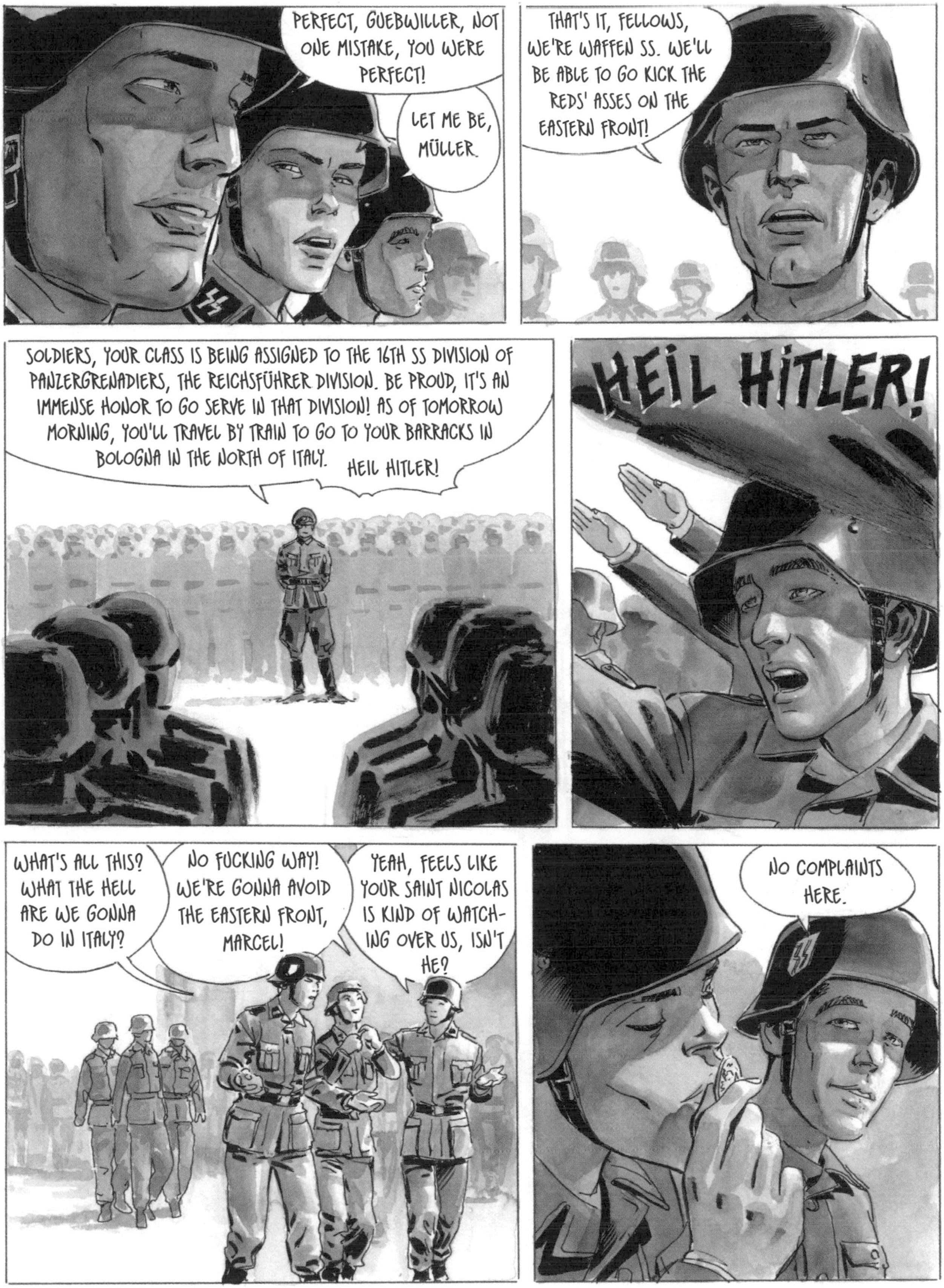
PERFECT, GUEBWILLER, NOT ONE MISTAKE, YOU WERE PERFECT!
LET ME BE, MÜLLER.
THAT'S IT, FELLOWS, WE'RE WAFFEN SS. WE'LL BE ABLE TO GO KICK THE REDS' ASSES ON THE EASTERN FRONT!
SOLDIERS, YOUR CLASS IS BEING ASSIGNED TO THE 16TH SS DIVISION OF PANZERGRENADIERS, THE REICHSFÜHRER DIVISION. BE PROUD, IT'S AN IMMENSE HONOR TO GO SERVE IN THAT DIVISION! AS OF TOMORROW MORNING, YOU'LL TRAVEL BY TRAIN TO GO TO YOUR BARRACKS IN BOLOGNA IN THE NORTH OF ITALY. HEIL HITLER!
HEIL HITLER!
WHAT'S ALL THIS? WHAT THE HELL ARE WE GONNA DO IN ITALY?
NO FUCKING WAY! WE'RE GONNA AVOID THE EASTERN FRONT, MARCEL!
YEAH, FEELS LIKE YOUR SAINT NICOLAS IS KIND OF WATCHING OVER US, ISN'T HE?
NO COMPLAINTS HERE.

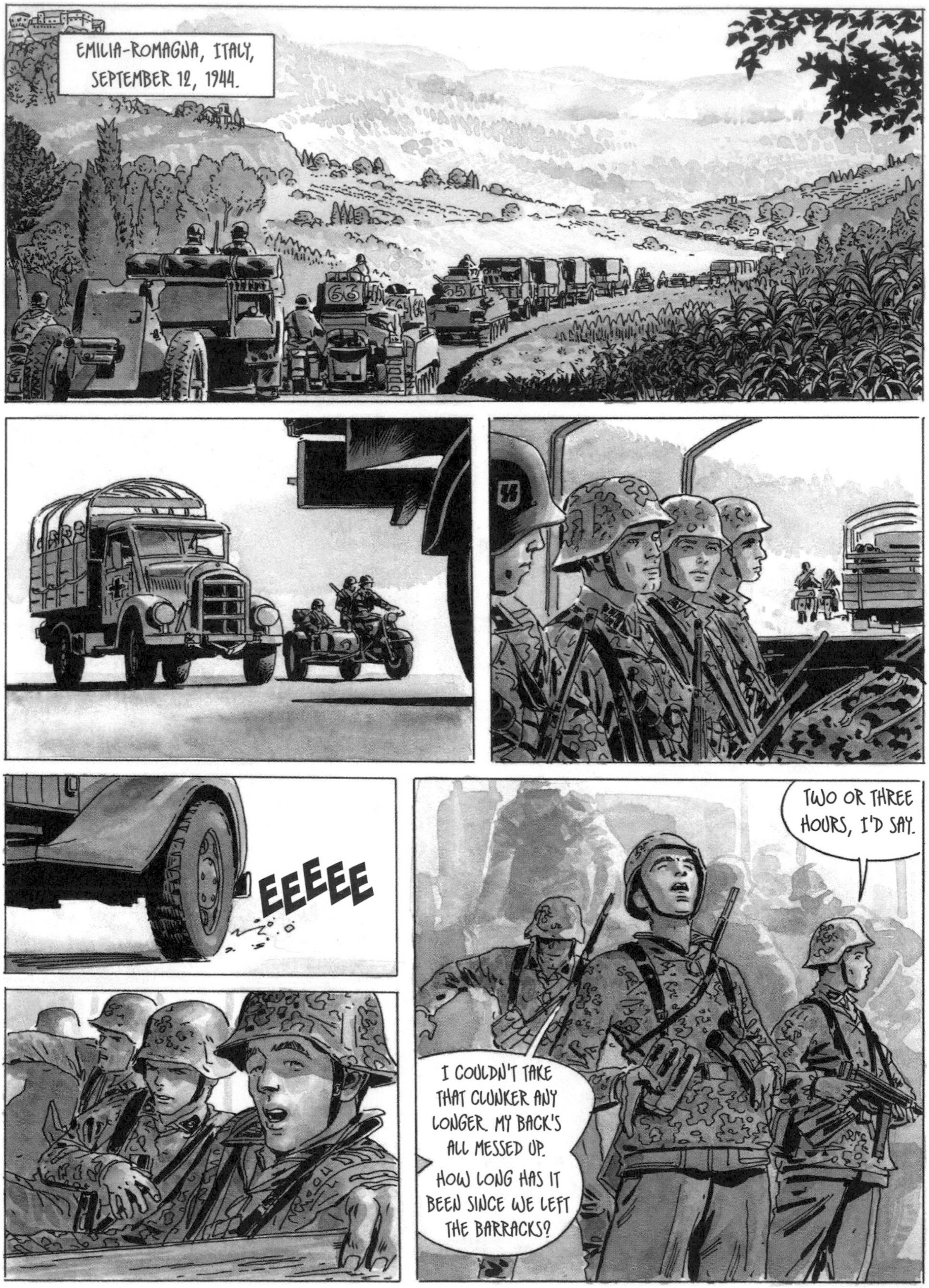
EMILIA-ROMAGNA, ITALY, SEPTEMBER 12, 1944.
EEEEE
I COULDN'T TAKE THAT CLUNKER ANY LONGER. MY BACK'S ALL MESSED UP.
HOW LONG HAS IT BEEN SINCE WE LEFT THE BARRACKS?
TWO OR THREE HOURS, I'D SAY.

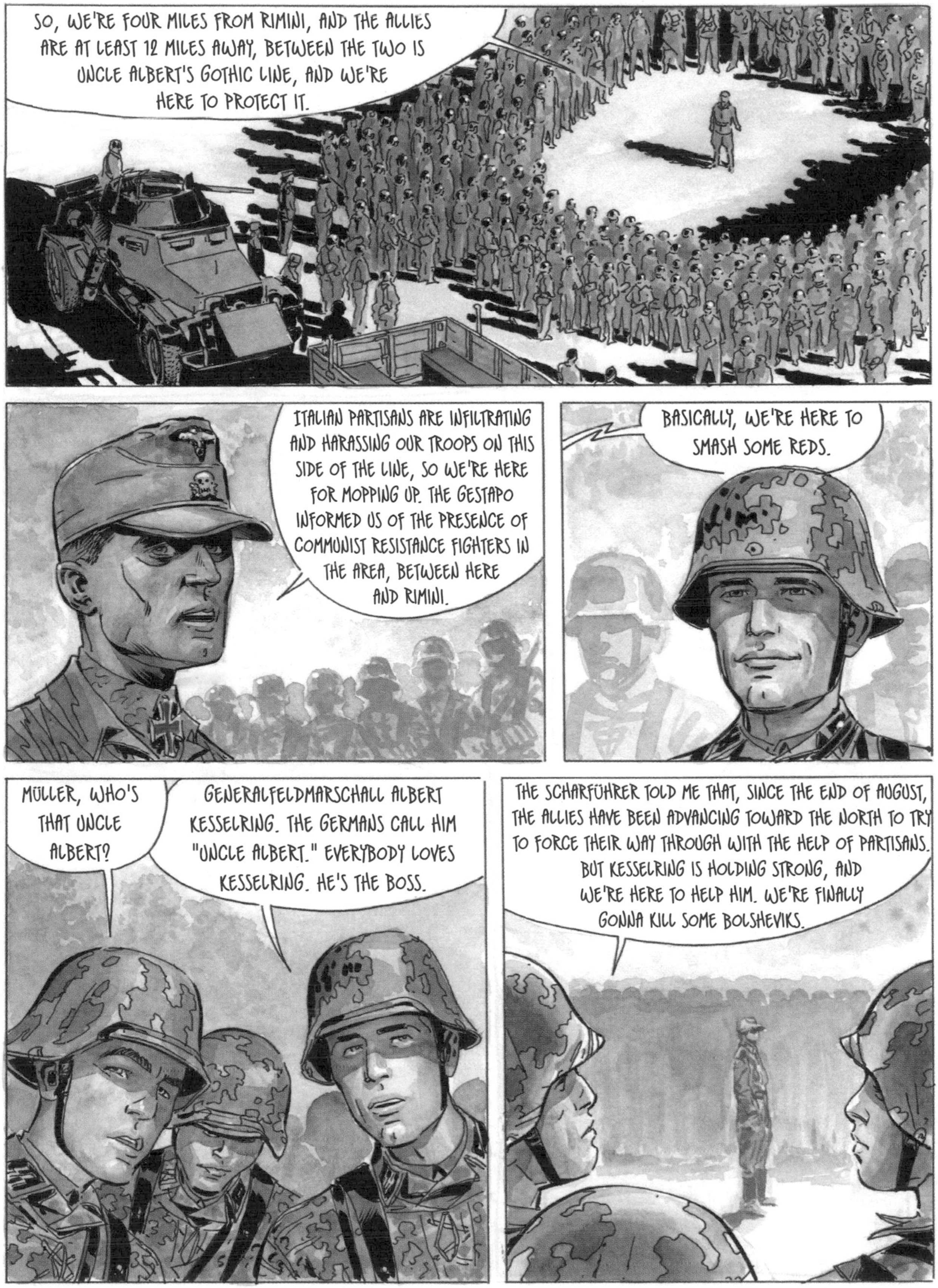
SO, WE'RE FOUR MILES FROM RIMINI, AND THE ALLIES ARE AT LEAST 12 MILES AWAY, BETWEEN THE TWO IS UNCLE ALBERT'S GOTHIC LINE, AND WE'RE HERE TO PROTECT IT.
ITALIAN PARTISANS ARE INFILTRATING AND HARASSING OUR TROOPS ON THIS SIDE OF THE LINE, SO WE'RE HERE FOR MOPPING UP. THE GESTAPO INFORMED US OF THE PRESENCE OF COMMUNIST RESISTANCE FIGHTERS IN THE AREA, BETWEEN HERE AND RIMINI.
BASICALLY, WE'RE HERE TO SMASH SOME REDS.
MÜLLER, WHO'S THAT UNCLE ALBERT?
GENERALFELDMARSCHALL ALBERT KESSELRING. THE GERMANS CALL HIM "UNCLE ALBERT." EVERYBODY LOVES KESSELRING. HE'S THE BOSS.
THE SCHARFÜHRER TOLD ME THAT, SINCE THE END OF AUGUST, THE ALLIES HAVE BEEN ADVANCING TOWARD THE NORTH TO TRY TO FORCE THEIR WAY THROUGH WITH THE HELP OF PARTISANS. BUT KESSELRING IS HOLDING STRONG, AND WE'RE HERE TO HELP HIM. WE'RE FINALLY GONNA KILL SOME BOLSHEVIKS.

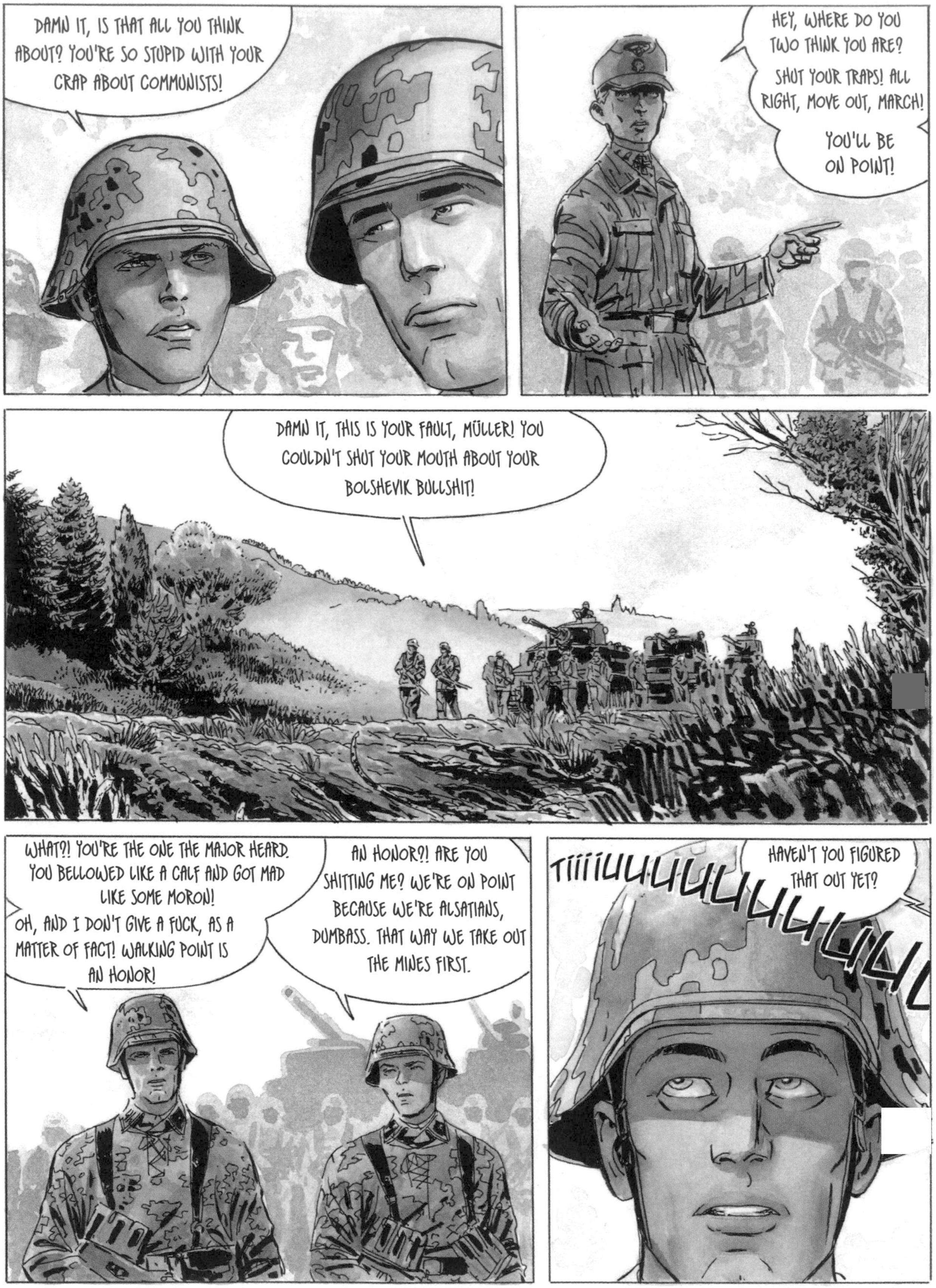
DAMN IT, IS THAT ALL YOU THINK ABOUT? YOU'RE SO STUPID WITH YOUR CRAP ABOUT COMMUNISTS!
HEY, WHERE DO YOU TWO THINK YOU ARE?
SHUT YOUR TRAPS! ALL RIGHT, MOVE OUT, MARCH!
YOU'LL BE ON POINT!
DAMN IT, THIS IS YOUR FAULT, MÜLLER! YOU COULDN'T SHUT YOUR MOUTH ABOUT YOUR BOLSHEVIK BULLSHIT!
WHAT?! YOU'RE THE ONE THE MAJOR HEARD. YOU BELLOWED LIKE A CALF AND GOT MAD LIKE SOME MORON!
OH, AND I DON'T GIVE A FUCK, AS A MATTER OF FACT! WALKING POINT IS AN HONOR!
AN HONOR?! ARE YOU SHITTING ME? WE'RE ON POINT BECAUSE WE'RE ALSATIANS, DUMBASS. THAT WAY WE TAKE OUT THE MINES FIRST.
HAVEN'T YOU FIGURED THAT OUT YET?
TIIIIUUUUUUUUUUUUU

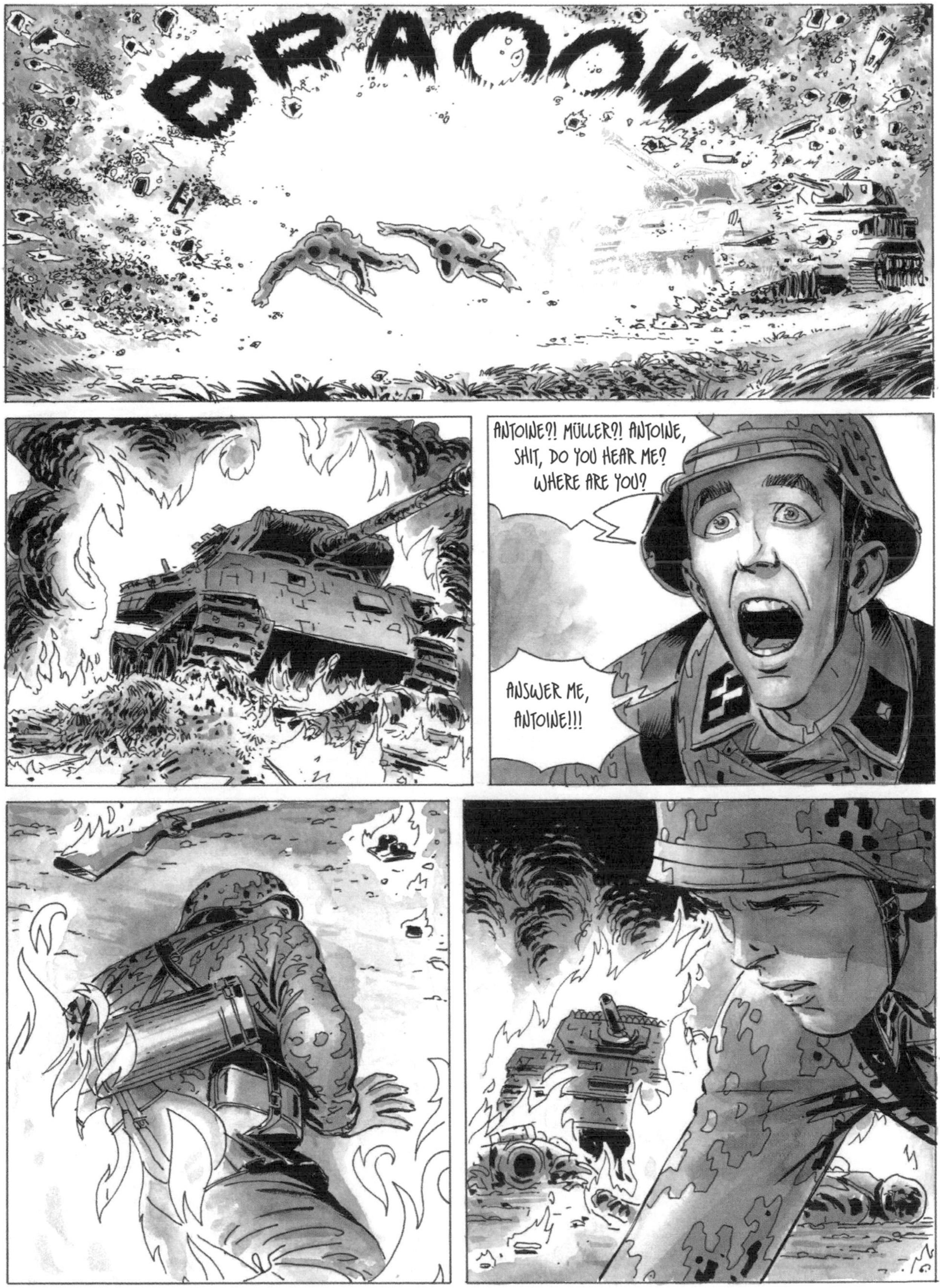
BRAOOW
ANTOINE?! MÜLLER?! ANTOINE, SHIT, DO YOU HEAR ME? WHERE ARE YOU?
ANSWER ME, ANTOINE!!!

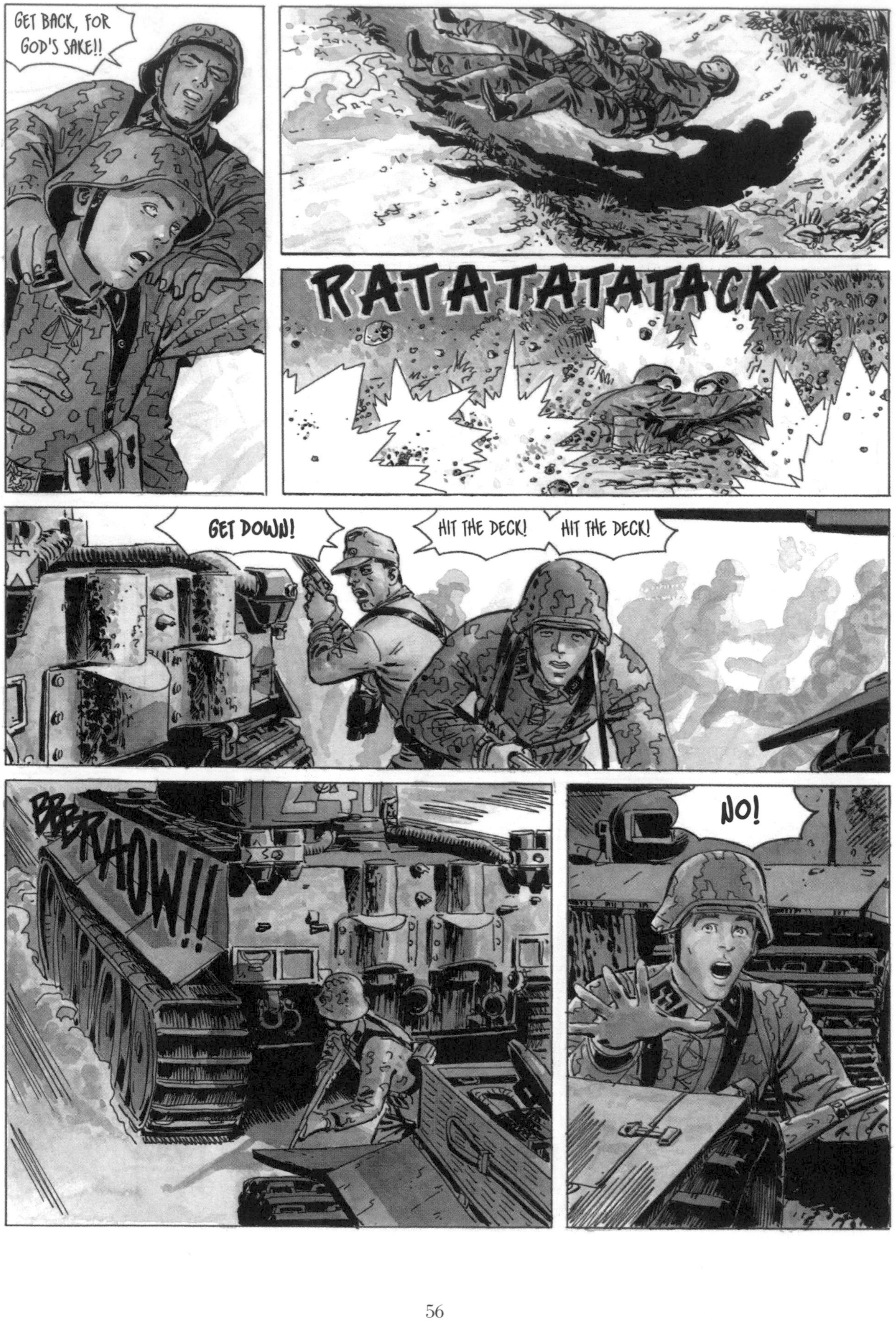
GET BACK, FOR GOD'S SAKE!!
RATATATATACK
GET DOWN!
HIT THE DECK!
HIT THE DECK!
BBBRAOW!!
NO!

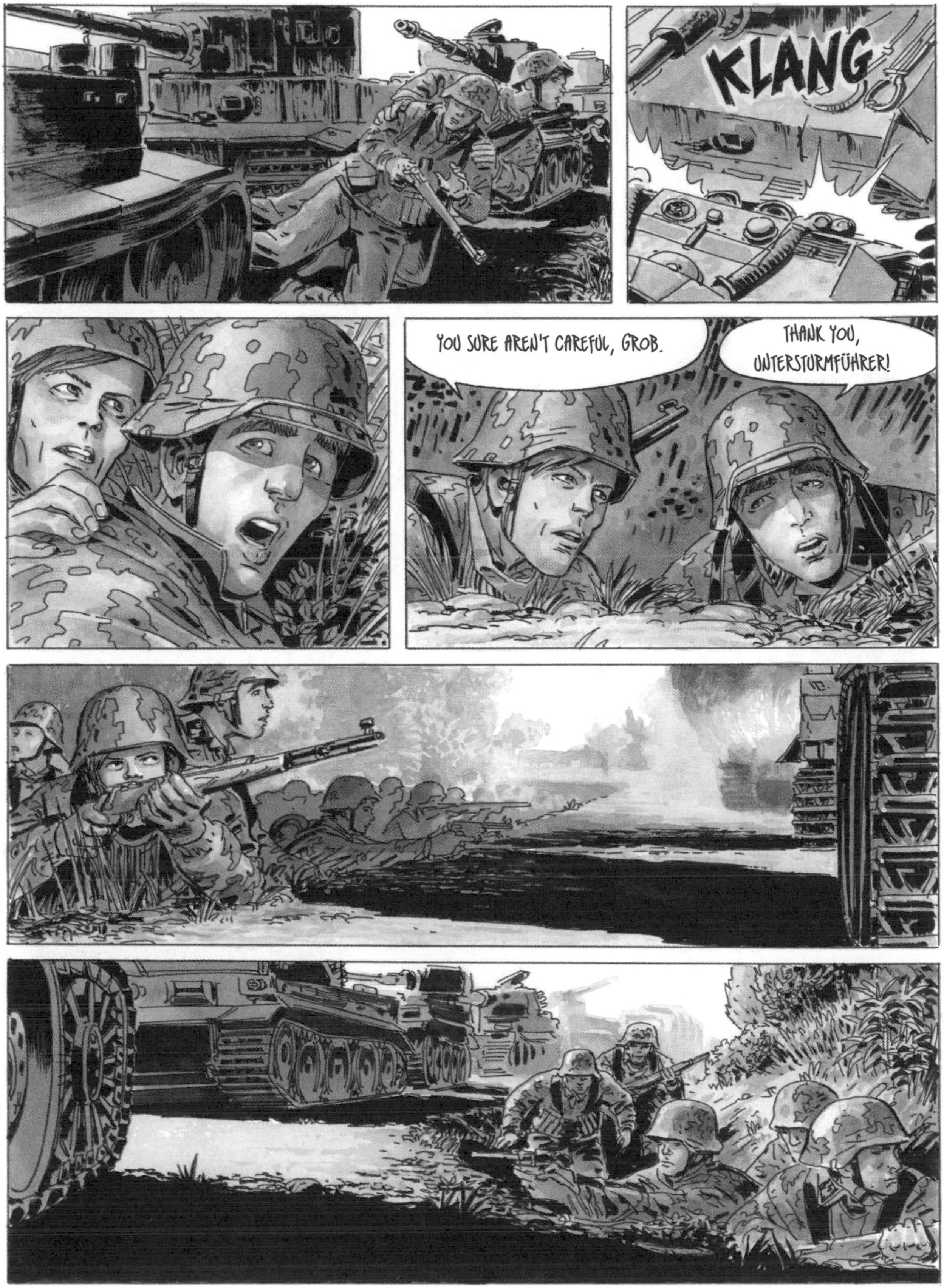
KLANG
YOU SURE AREN'T CAREFUL, GROB.
THANK YOU, UNTERSTURMFÜHRER!

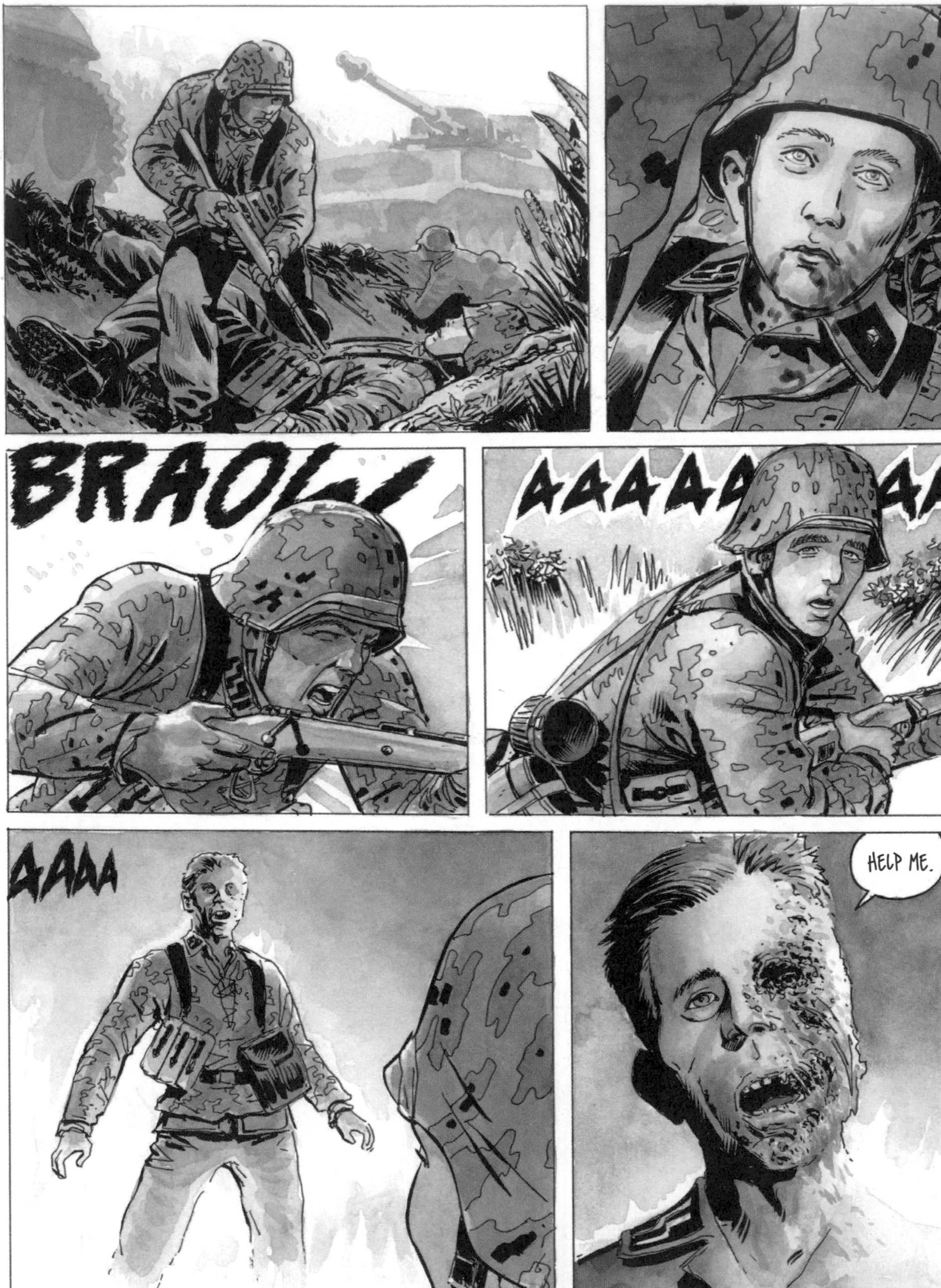
BRAOW!
AAAAAAAA
AAAA
HELP ME.

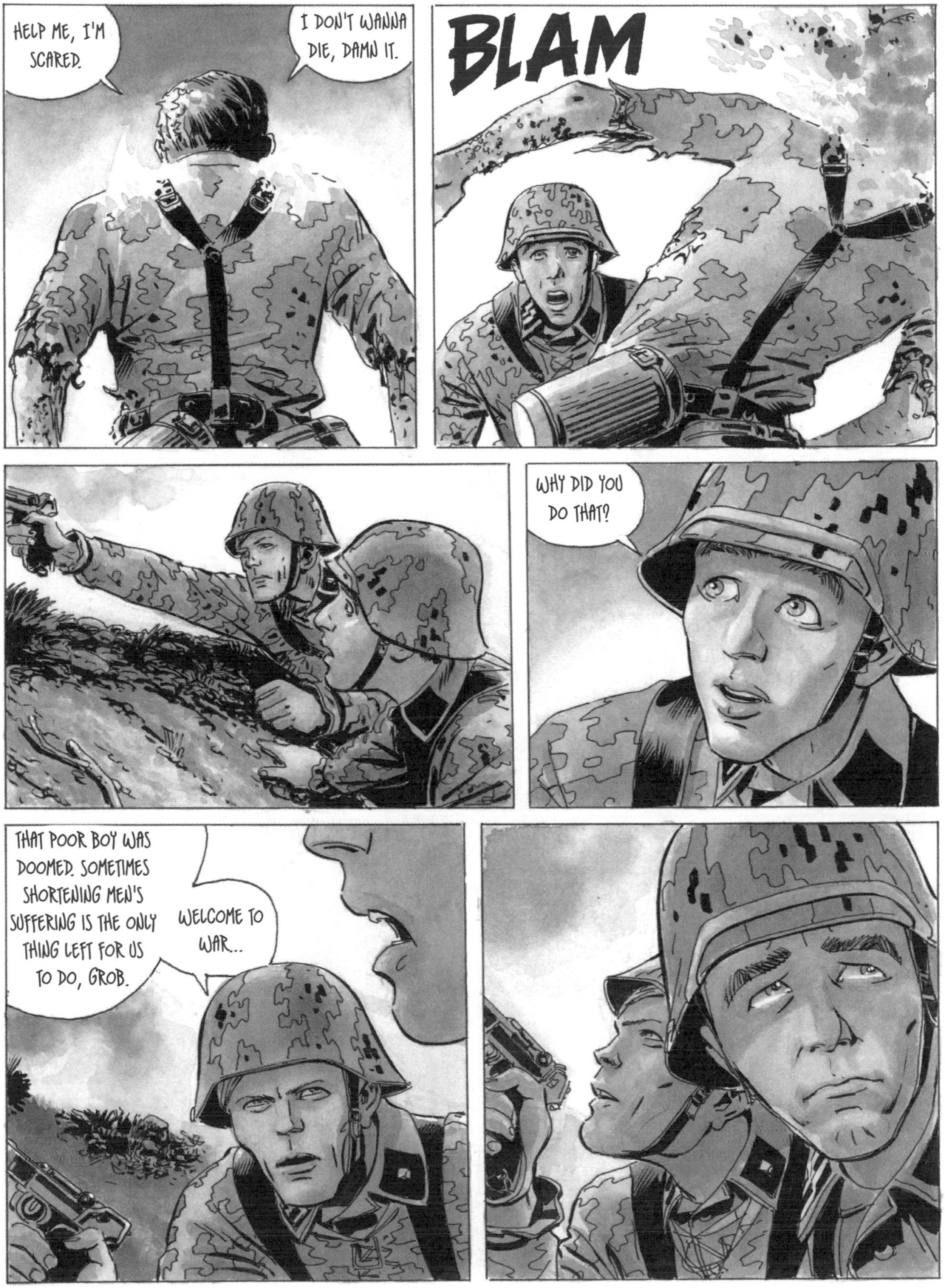
HELP ME, I'M SCARED.
I DON'T WANNA DIE, DAMN IT.
BLAM
WHY DID YOU DO THAT?
THAT POOR BOY WAS DOOMED. SOMETIMES SHORTENING MEN'S SUFFERING IS THE ONLY THING LEFT FOR US TO DO, GROB.
WELCOME TO WAR...

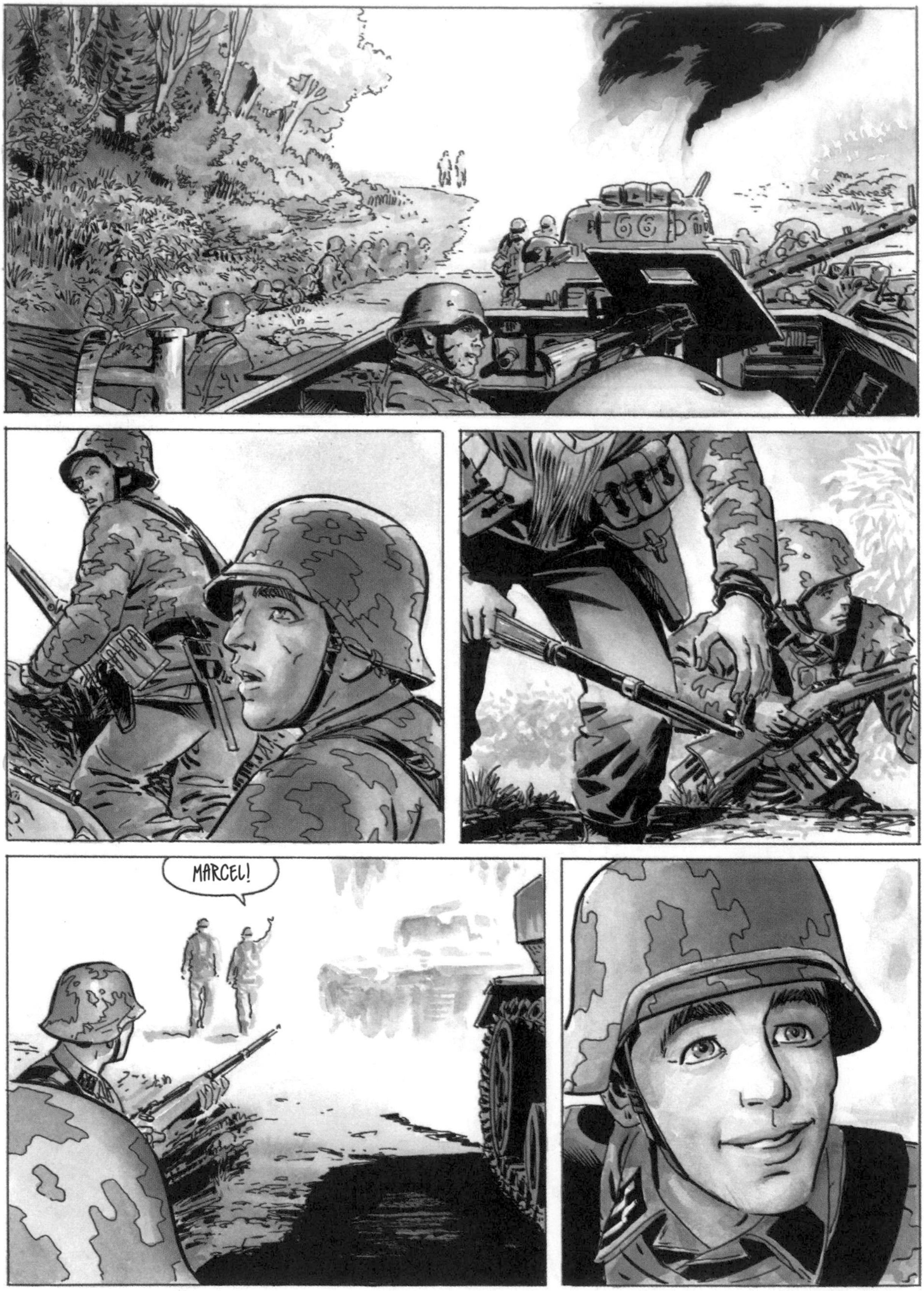
MARCEL!

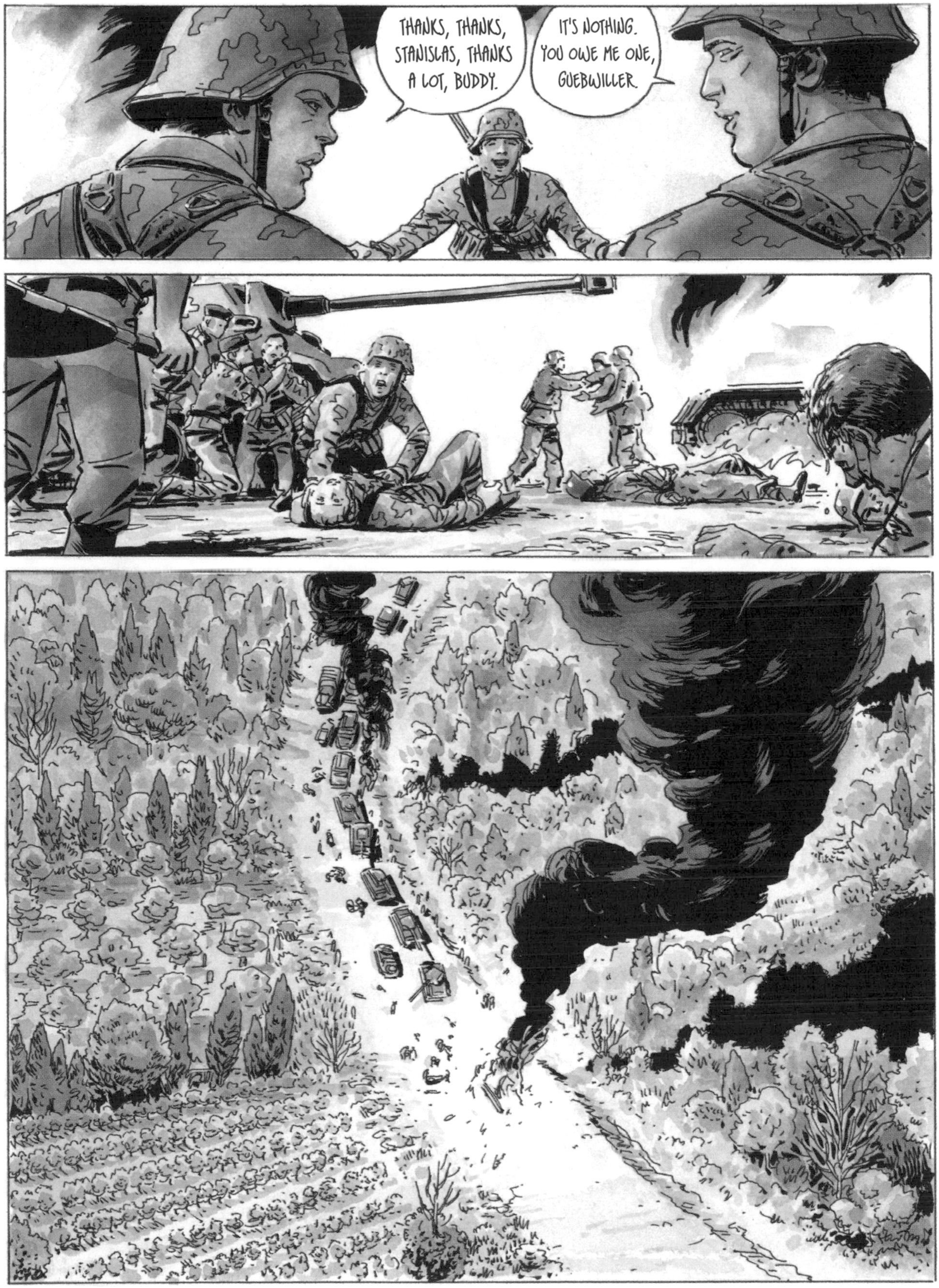
THANKS, THANKS, STANISLAS, THANKS A LOT, BUDDY.
IT'S NOTHING. YOU OWE ME ONE, GUEBWILLER.

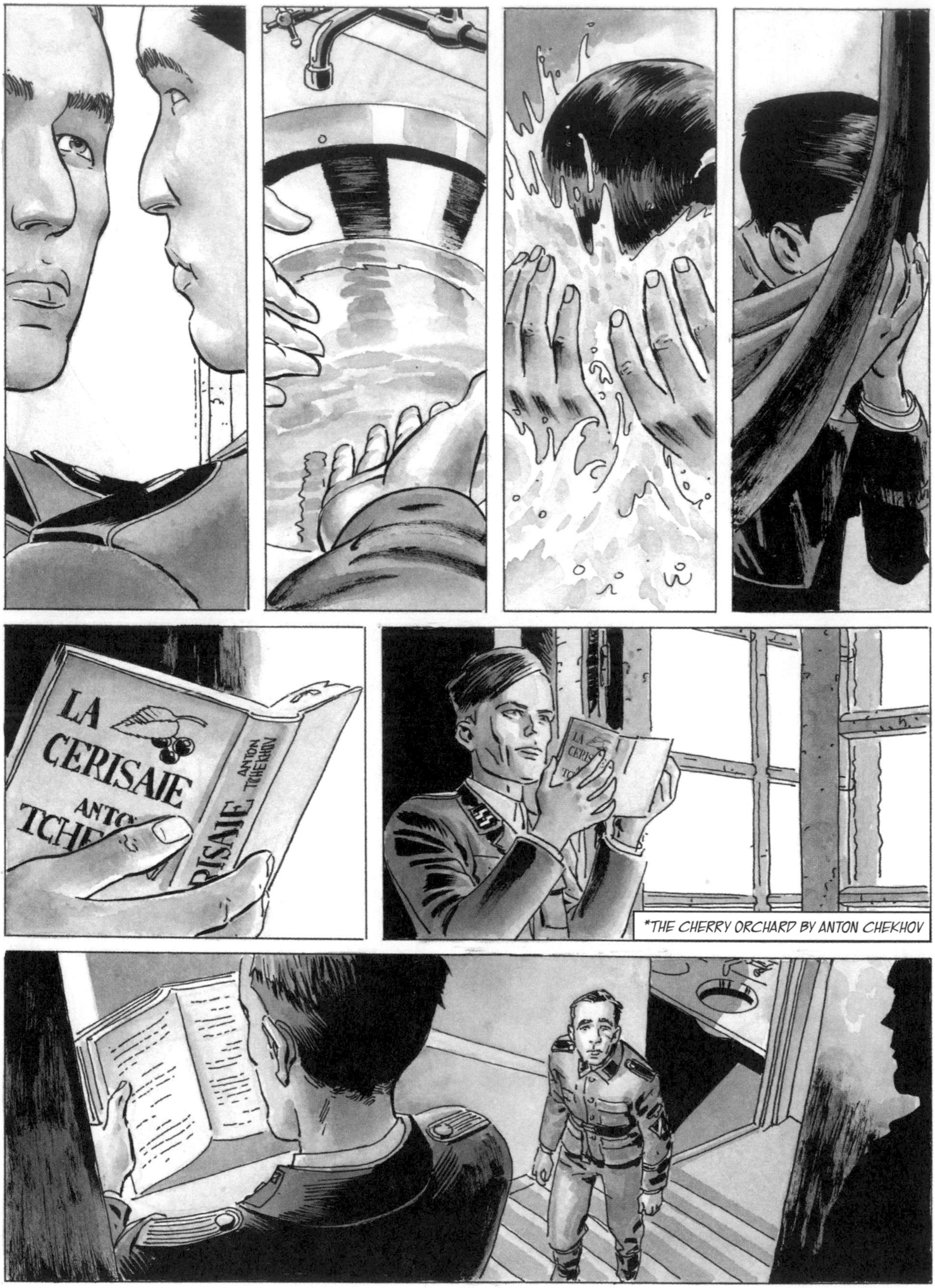
LA CERISAIE
ANTON TCHEKHOV
*THE CHERRY ORCHARD BY ANTON CHEKHOV

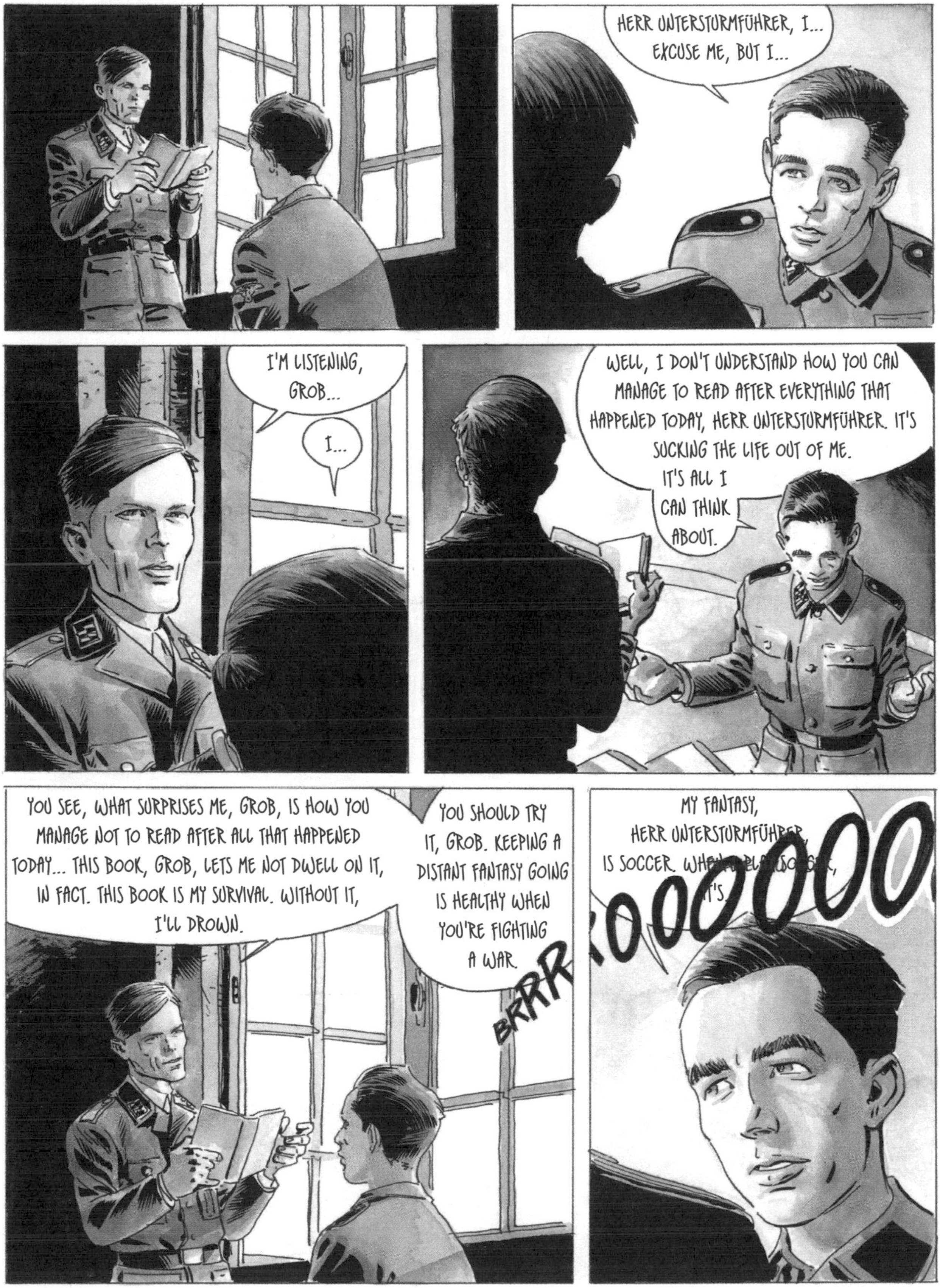
HERR UNTERSTURMFÜHRER, I... EXCUSE ME, BUT I...
I'M LISTENING, GROB...
I...
WELL, I DON'T UNDERSTAND HOW YOU CAN MANAGE TO READ AFTER EVERYTHING THAT HAPPENED TODAY, HERR UNTERSTURMFÜHRER. IT'S SUCKING THE LIFE OUT OF ME.
IT'S ALL I CAN THINK ABOUT.
YOU SEE, WHAT SURPRISES ME, GROB, IS HOW YOU MANAGE NOT TO READ AFTER ALL THAT HAPPENED TODAY... THIS BOOK, GROB, LETS ME NOT DWELL ON IT, IN FACT. THIS BOOK IS MY SURVIVAL. WITHOUT IT, I'LL DROWN.
YOU SHOULD TRY IT, GROB. KEEPING A DISTANT FANTASY GOING IS HEALTHY WHEN YOU'RE FIGHTING A WAR.
MY FANTASY, HERR UNTERSTURMFÜHRER, IS SOCCER.
BRRRROOOOOOO

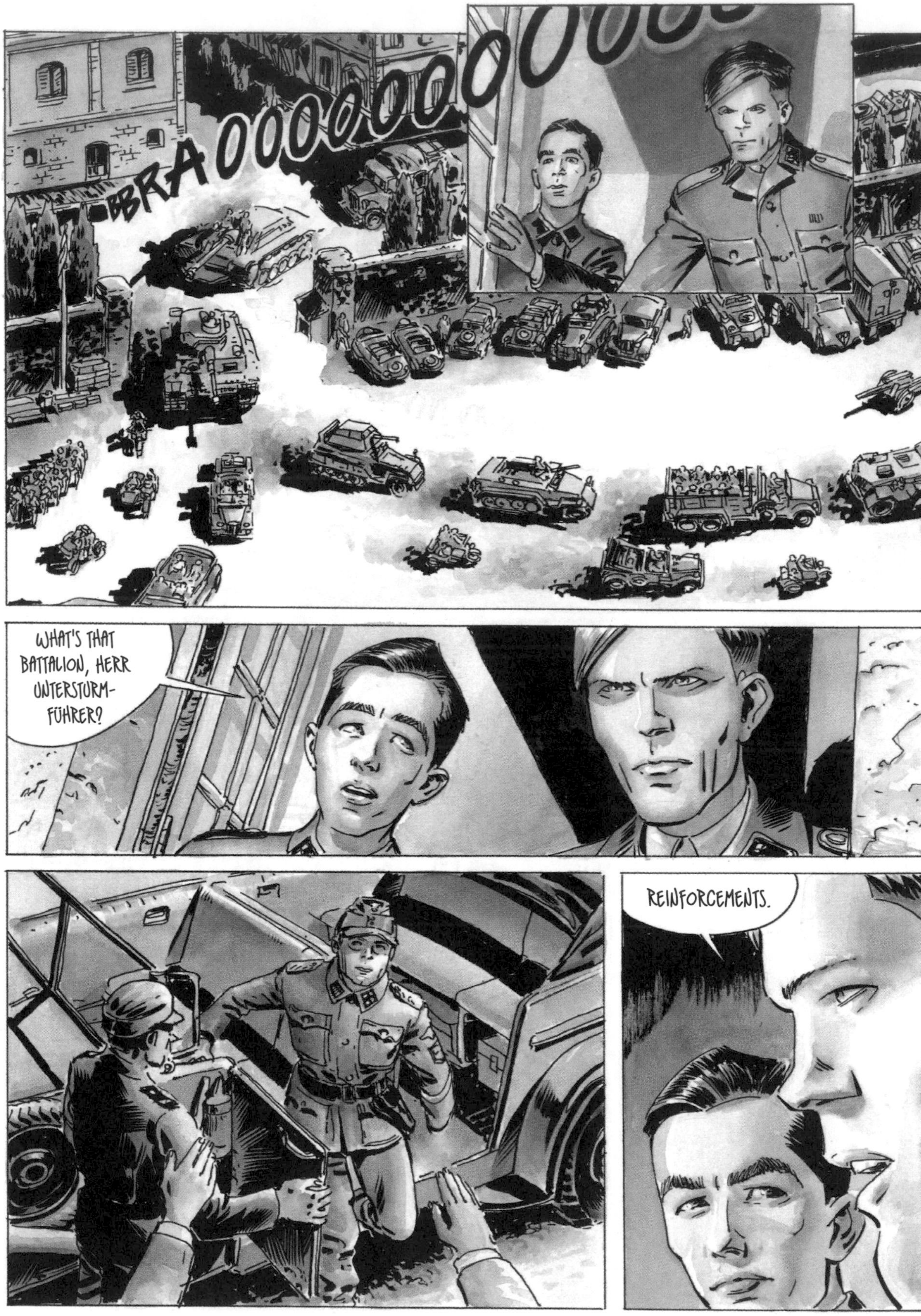
BBRAOOOOOOOOOOOO
WHAT'S THAT BATTALION, HERR UNTERSTURM-FÜHRER?
REINFORCEMENTS.

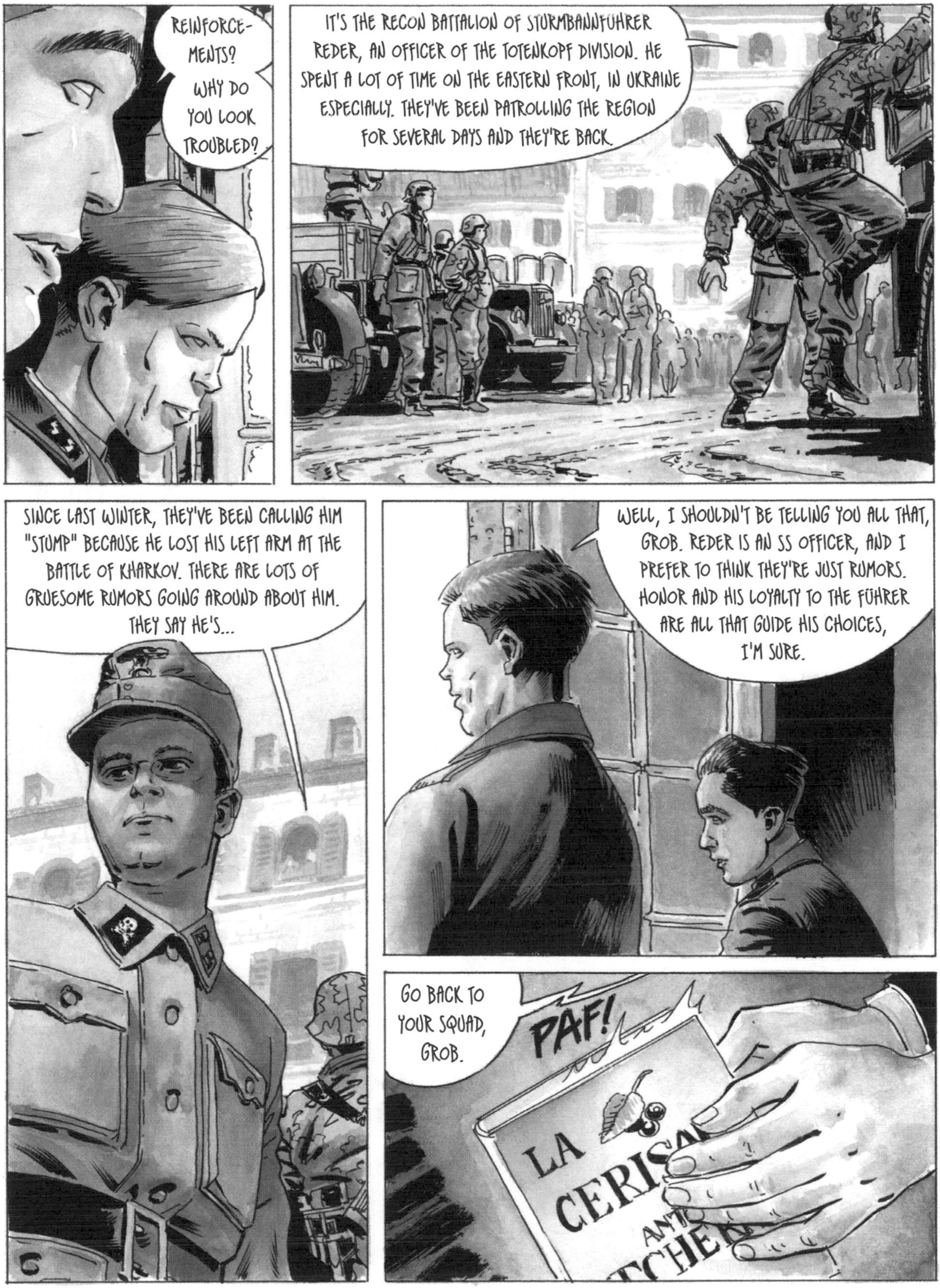
REINFORCE-MENTS?
WHY DO YOU LOOK TROUBLED?
IT'S THE RECON BATTALION OF STURMBANNFÜHRER REDER, AN OFFICER OF THE TOTENKOPF DIVISION. HE SPENT A LOT OF TIME ON THE EASTERN FRONT, IN UKRAINE ESPECIALLY. THEY'VE BEEN PATROLLING THE REGION FOR SEVERAL DAYS AND THEY'RE BACK.
SINCE LAST WINTER, THEY'VE BEEN CALLING HIM "STUMP" BECAUSE HE LOST HIS LEFT ARM AT THE BATTLE OF KHARKOV. THERE ARE LOTS OF GRUESOME RUMORS GOING AROUND ABOUT HIM. THEY SAY HE'S...
WELL, I SHOULDN'T BE TELLING YOU ALL THAT, GROB. REDER IS AN SS OFFICER, AND I PREFER TO THINK THEY'RE JUST RUMORS. HONOR AND HIS LOYALTY TO THE FÜHRER ARE ALL THAT GUIDE HIS CHOICES, I'M SURE.
GO BACK TO YOUR SQUAD, GROB.
PAF!
LA CERISA

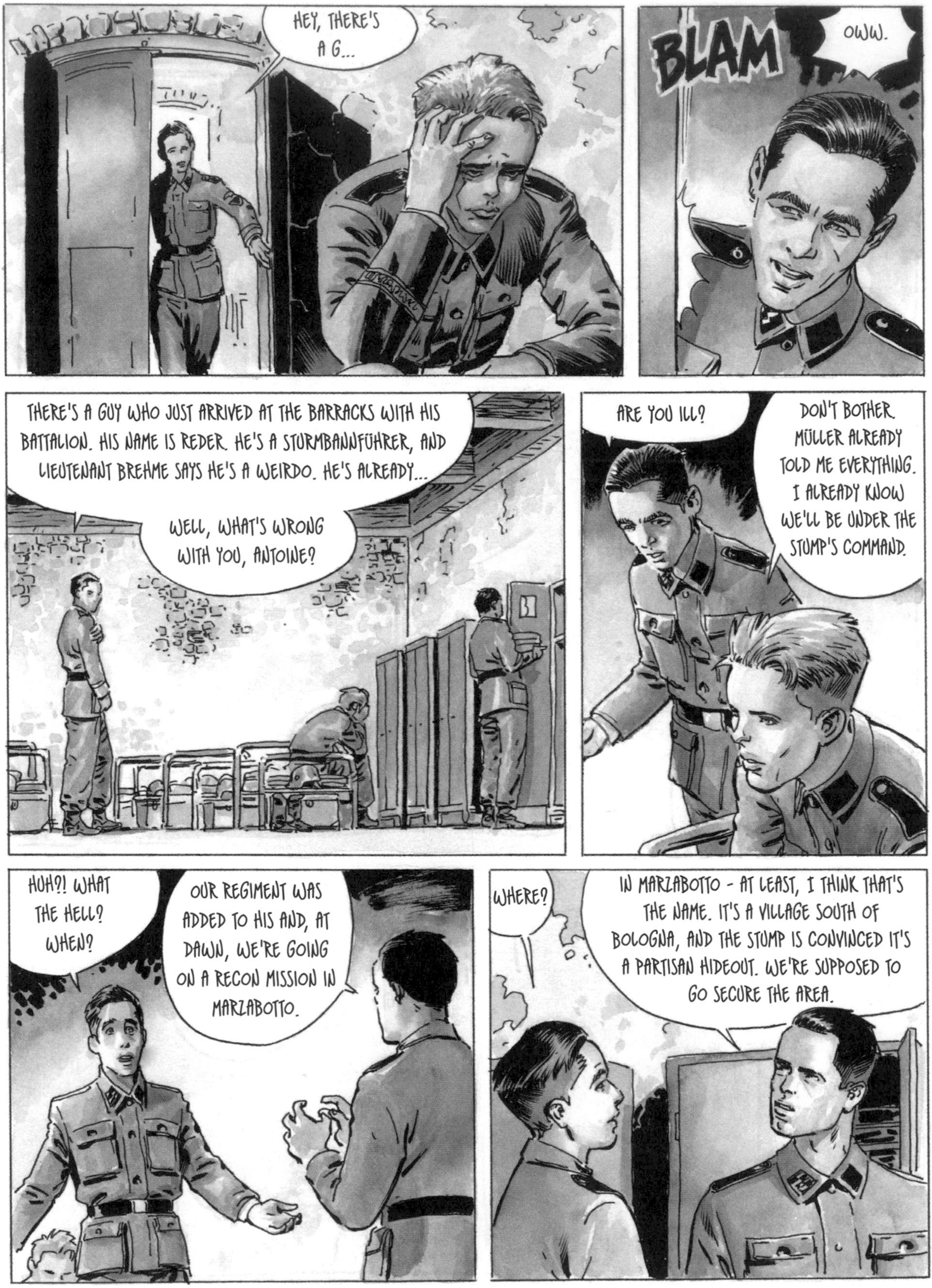

HEY, THERE'S A G...
BLAM
OWW.
THERE'S A GUY WHO JUST ARRIVED AT THE BARRACKS WITH HIS BATTALION. HIS NAME IS REDER. HE'S A STURMBANNFÜHRER, AND LIEUTENANT BREHME SAYS HE'S A WEIRDO. HE'S ALREADY...
WELL, WHAT'S WRONG WITH YOU, ANTOINE?
ARE YOU ILL?
DON'T BOTHER. MÜLLER ALREADY TOLD ME EVERYTHING. I ALREADY KNOW WE'LL BE UNDER THE STUMP'S COMMAND.
HUH?! WHAT THE HELL? WHEN?
OUR REGIMENT WAS ADDED TO HIS AND, AT DAWN, WE'RE GOING ON A RECON MISSION IN MARZABOTTO.
WHERE?
IN MARZABOTTO - AT LEAST, I THINK THAT'S THE NAME. IT'S A VILLAGE SOUTH OF BOLOGNA, AND THE STUMP IS CONVINCED IT'S A PARTISAN HIDEOUT. WE'RE SUPPOSED TO GO SECURE THE AREA.

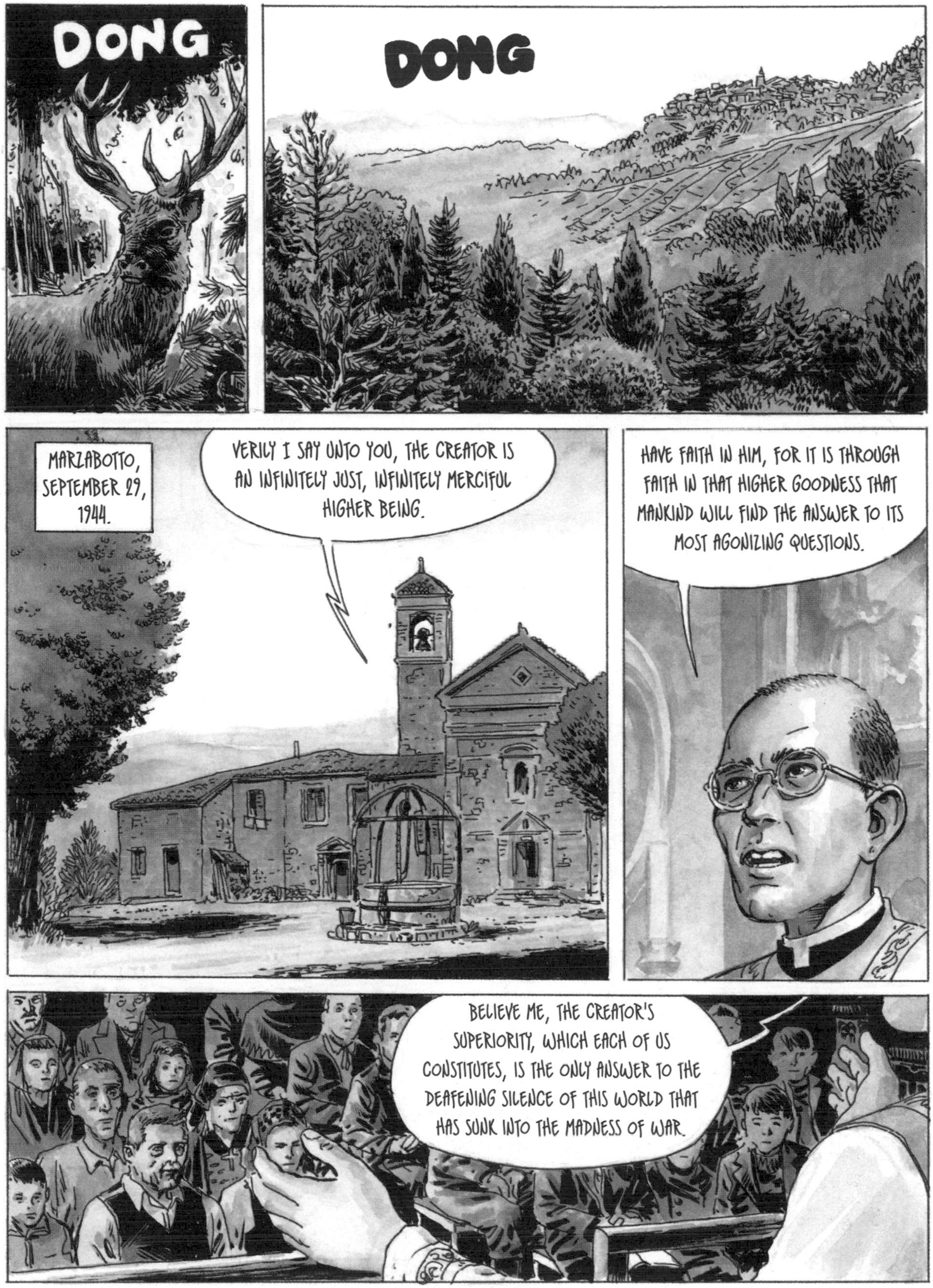
DONG
DONG
MARZABOTTO, SEPTEMBER 29, 1944.
VERILY I SAY UNTO YOU, THE CREATOR IS AN INFINITELY JUST, INFINITELY MERCIFUL HIGHER BEING.
HAVE FAITH IN HIM, FOR IT IS THROUGH FAITH IN THAT HIGHER GOODNESS THAT MANKIND WILL FIND THE ANSWER TO ITS MOST AGONIZING QUESTIONS.
BELIEVE ME, THE CREATOR'S SUPERIORITY, WHICH EACH OF US CONSTITUTES, IS THE ONLY ANSWER TO THE DEAFENING SILENCE OF THIS WORLD THAT HAS SUNK INTO THE MADNESS OF WAR.

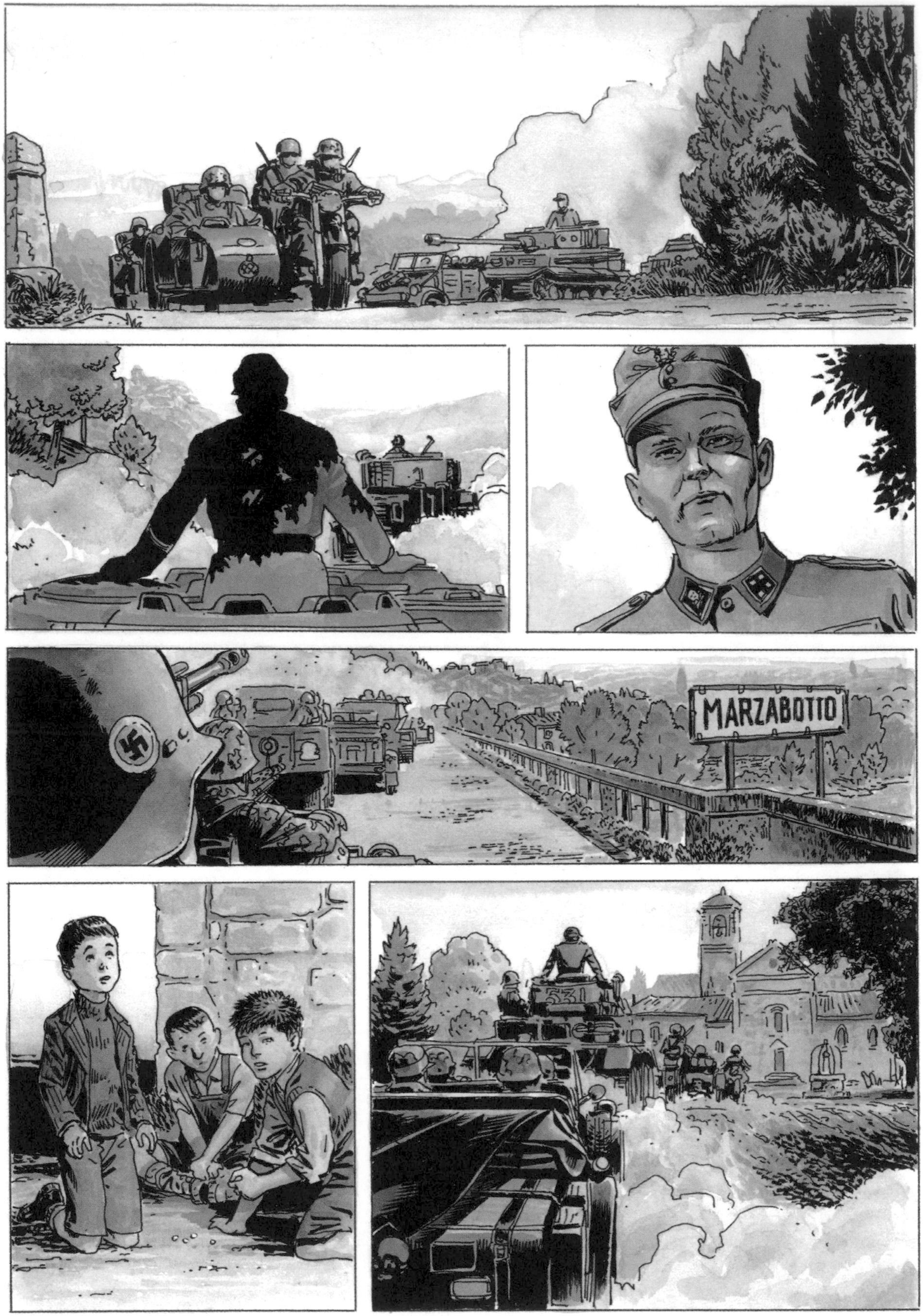
MARZABOTTO

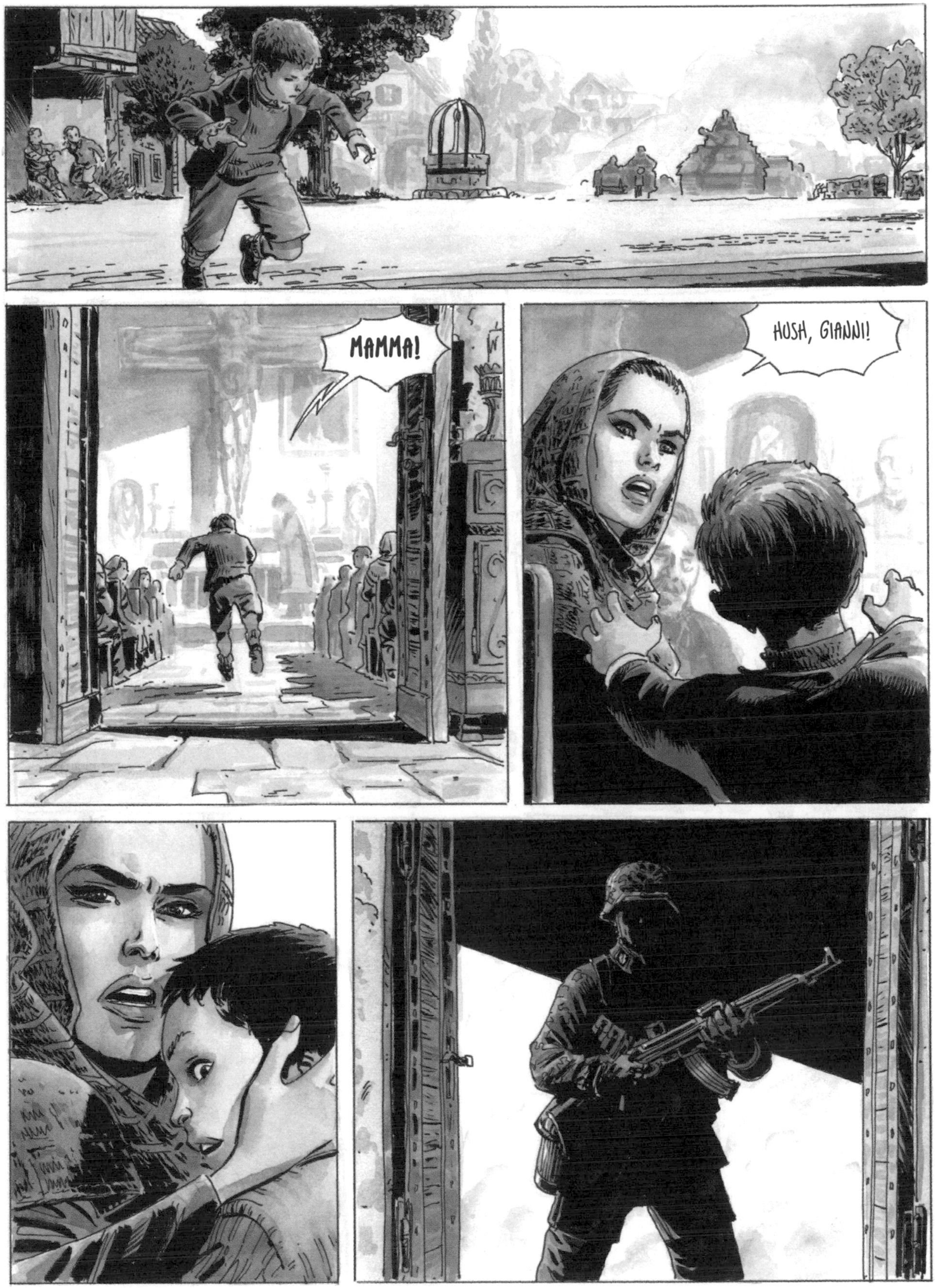
MAMMA!
HUSH, GIANNI!

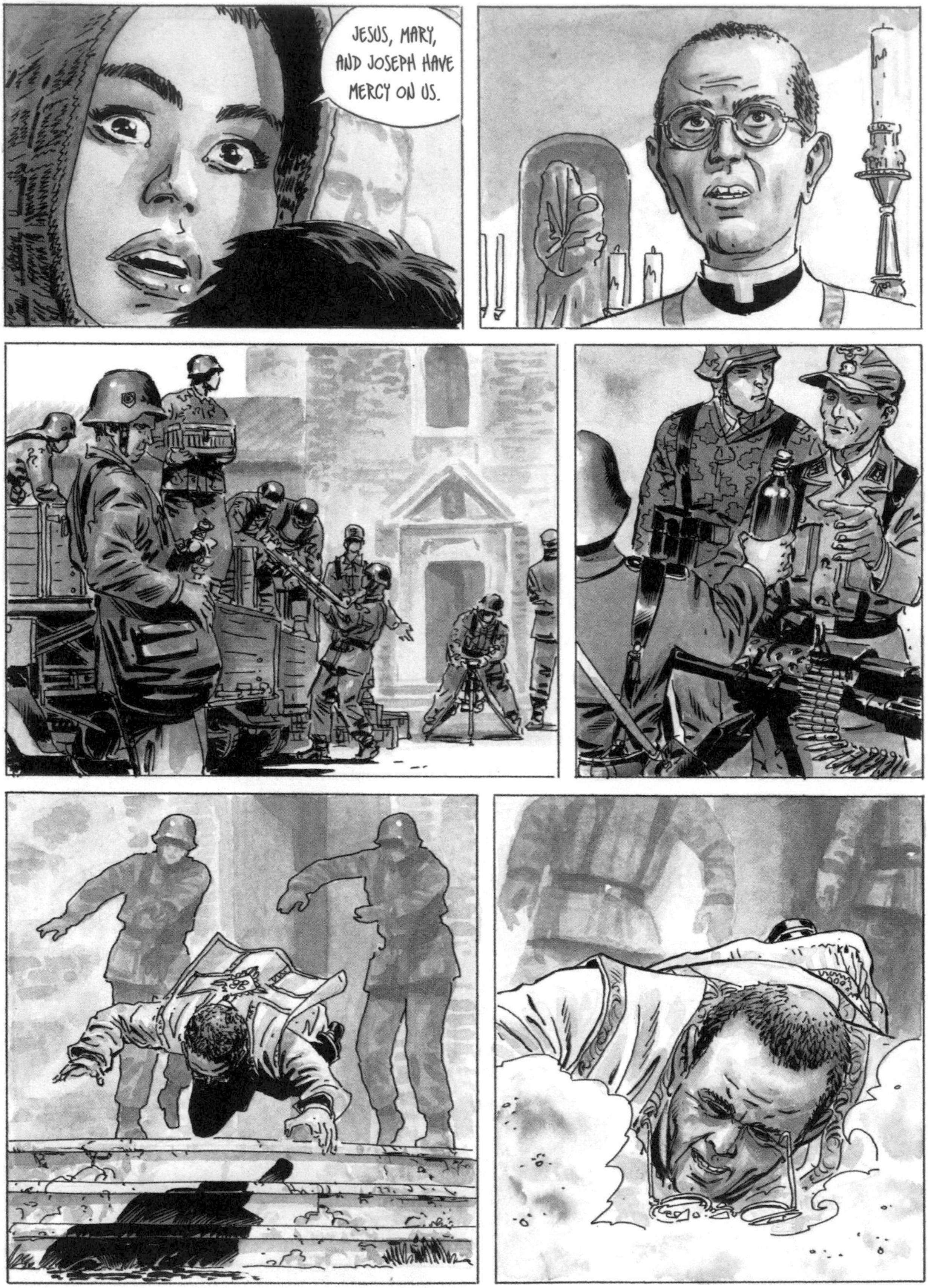
JESUS, MARY, AND JOSEPH HAVE MERCY ON US.

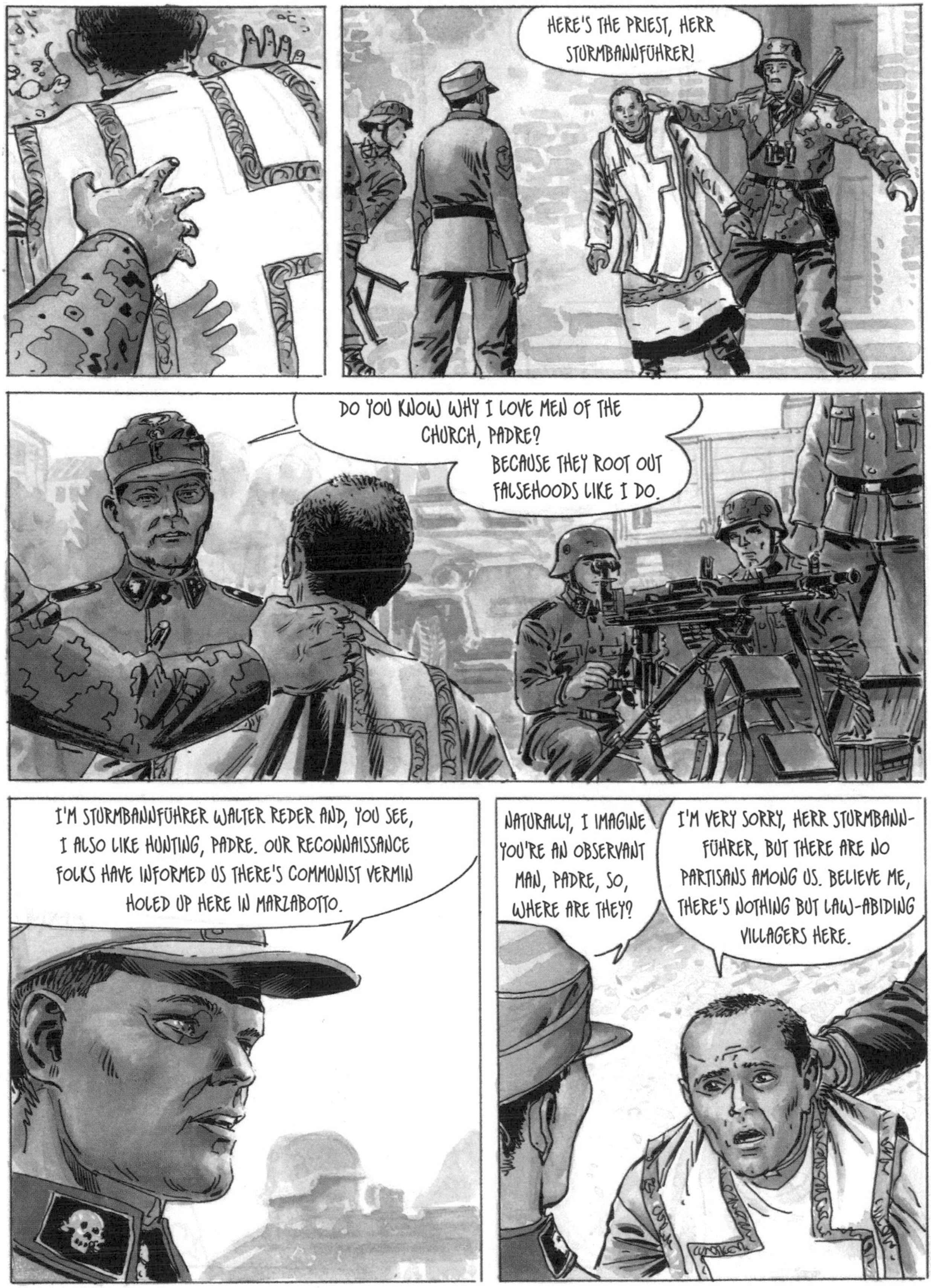
HERE'S THE PRIEST, HERR STURMBANNFÜHRER!
DO YOU KNOW WHY I LOVE MEN OF THE CHURCH, PADRE?
BECAUSE THEY ROOT OUT FALSEHOODS LIKE I DO.
I'M STURMBANNFÜHRER WALTER REDER AND, YOU SEE, I ALSO LIKE HUNTING, PADRE. OUR RECONNAISSANCE FOLKS HAVE INFORMED US THERE'S COMMUNIST VERMIN HOLED UP HERE IN MARZABOTTO.
NATURALLY, I IMAGINE YOU'RE AN OBSERVANT MAN, PADRE, SO, WHERE ARE THEY?
I'M VERY SORRY, HERR STURMBANN-FÜHRER, BUT THERE ARE NO PARTISANS AMONG US. BELIEVE ME, THERE'S NOTHING BUT LAW-ABIDING VILLAGERS HERE.

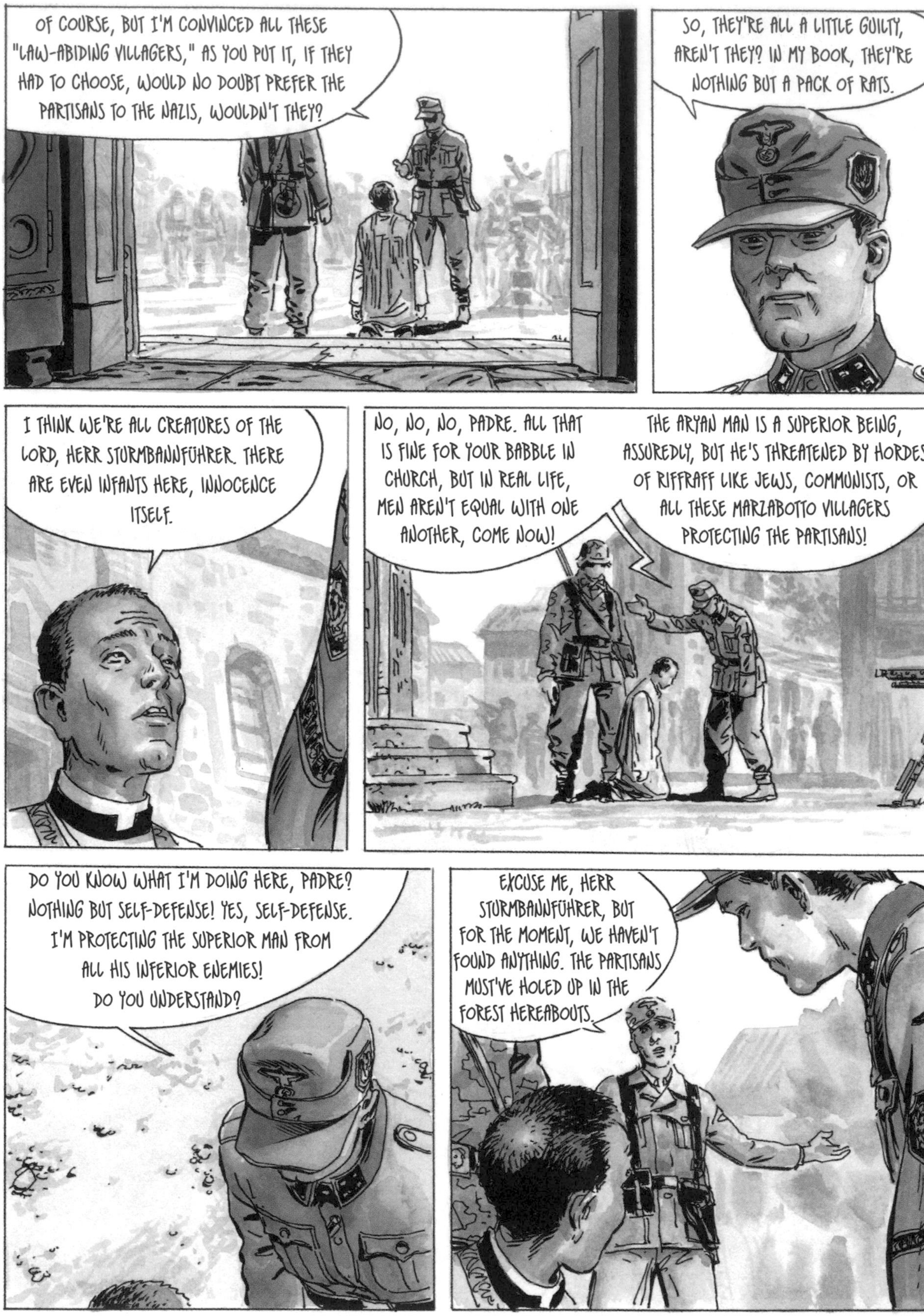

OF COURSE, BUT I'M CONVINCED ALL THESE "LAW-ABIDING VILLAGERS," AS YOU PUT IT, IF THEY HAD TO CHOOSE, WOULD NO DOUBT PREFER THE PARTISANS TO THE NAZIS, WOULDN'T THEY?
SO, THEY'RE ALL A LITTLE GUILTY, AREN'T THEY? IN MY BOOK, THEY'RE NOTHING BUT A PACK OF RATS.
I THINK WE'RE ALL CREATURES OF THE LORD, HERR STURMBANNFÜHRER. THERE ARE EVEN INFANTS HERE, INNOCENCE ITSELF.
NO, NO, NO, PADRE. ALL THAT IS FINE FOR YOUR BABBLE IN CHURCH, BUT IN REAL LIFE, MEN AREN'T EQUAL WITH ONE ANOTHER, COME NOW!
THE ARYAN MAN IS A SUPERIOR BEING, ASSUREDLY, BUT HE'S THREATENED BY HORDES OF RIFFRAFF LIKE JEWS, COMMUNISTS, OR ALL THESE MARZABOTTO VILLAGERS PROTECTING THE PARTISANS!
DO YOU KNOW WHAT I'M DOING HERE, PADRE? NOTHING BUT SELF-DEFENSE! YES, SELF-DEFENSE. I'M PROTECTING THE SUPERIOR MAN FROM ALL HIS INFERIOR ENEMIES! DO YOU UNDERSTAND?
EXCUSE ME, HERR STURMBANNFÜHRER, BUT FOR THE MOMENT, WE HAVEN'T FOUND ANYTHING. THE PARTISANS MUST'VE HOLED UP IN THE FOREST HEREABOUTS.

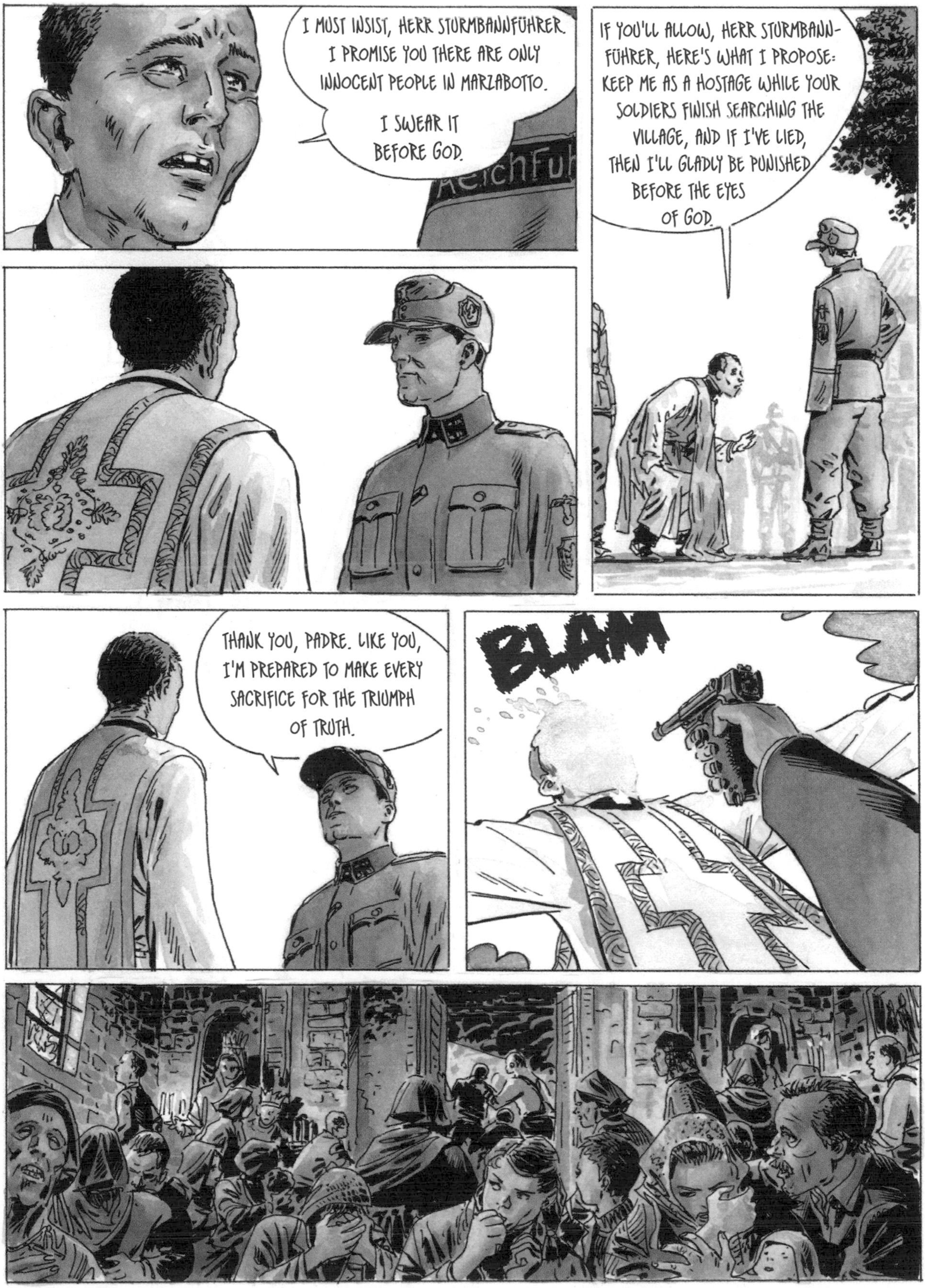
I MUST INSIST, HERR STURMBANNFÜHRER. I PROMISE YOU THERE ARE ONLY INNOCENT PEOPLE IN MARZABOTTO.
I SWEAR IT BEFORE GOD.
REICHFUH
IF YOU'LL ALLOW, HERR STURMBANN-FÜHRER, HERE'S WHAT I PROPOSE: KEEP ME AS A HOSTAGE WHILE YOUR SOLDIERS FINISH SEARCHING THE VILLAGE, AND IF I'VE LIED, THEN I'LL GLADLY BE PUNISHED BEFORE THE EYES OF GOD.
THANK YOU, PADRE. LIKE YOU, I'M PREPARED TO MAKE EVERY SACRIFICE FOR THE TRIUMPH OF TRUTH.
BLAM

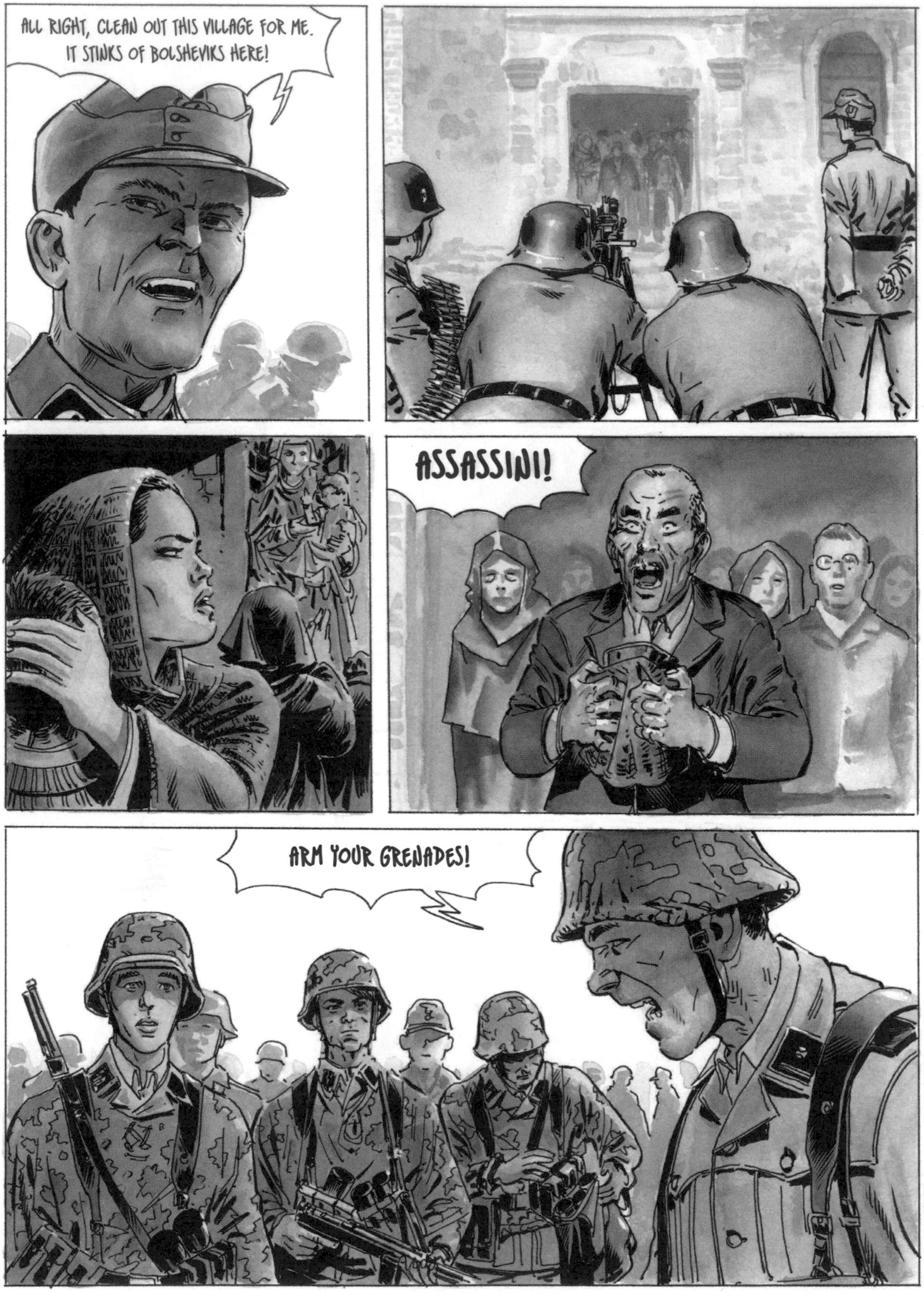
ALL RIGHT, CLEAN OUT THIS VILLAGE FOR ME. IT STINKS OF BOLSHEVIKS HERE!
ASSASSINI!
ARM YOUR GRENADES!

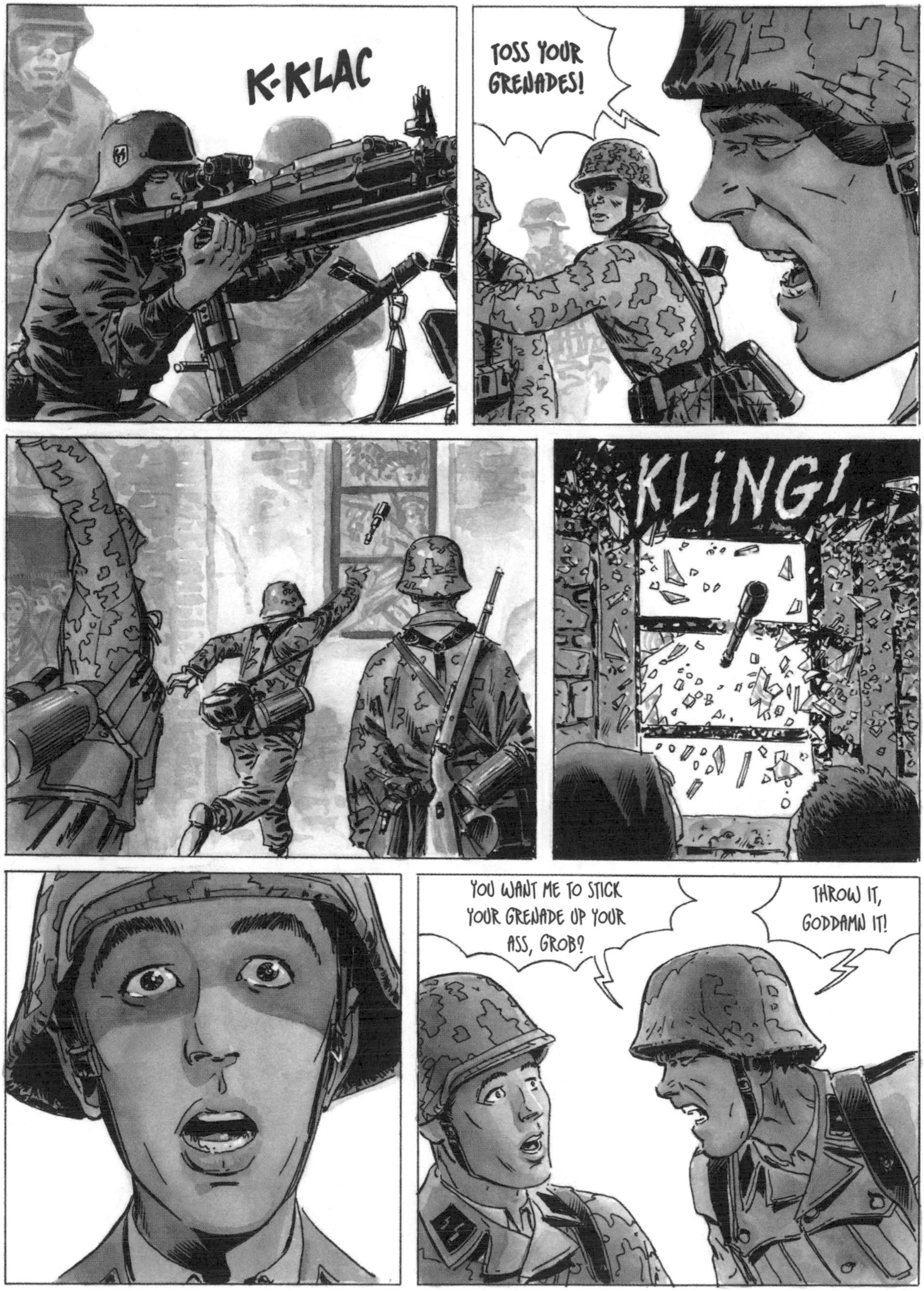
K-KLAC
TOSS YOUR GRENADES!
KLING!
YOU WANT ME TO STICK YOUR GRENADE UP YOUR ASS, GROB?
THROW IT, GODDAMN IT!

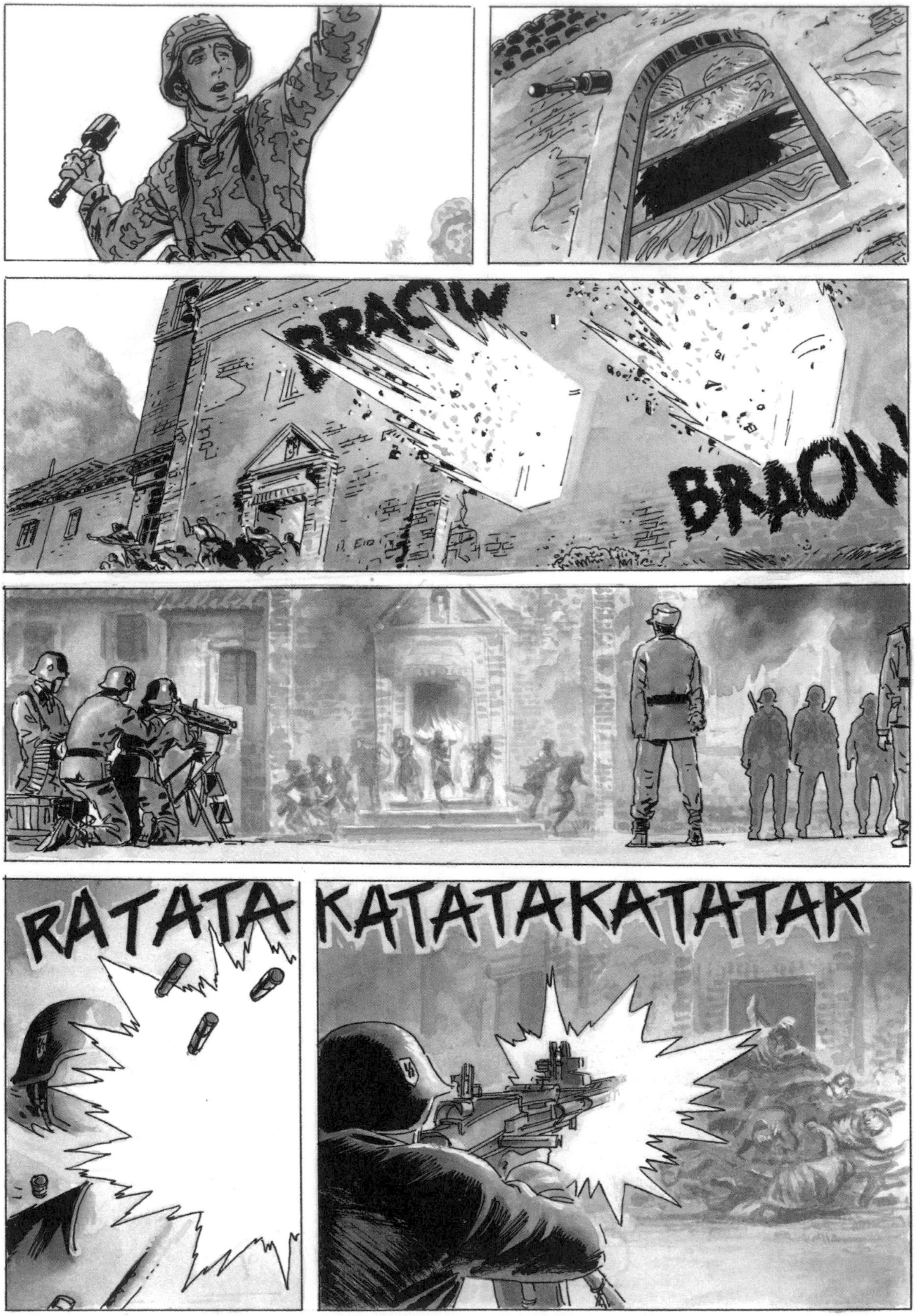
BRAOW
BRAOW
RATATA
KATATAKATATAK

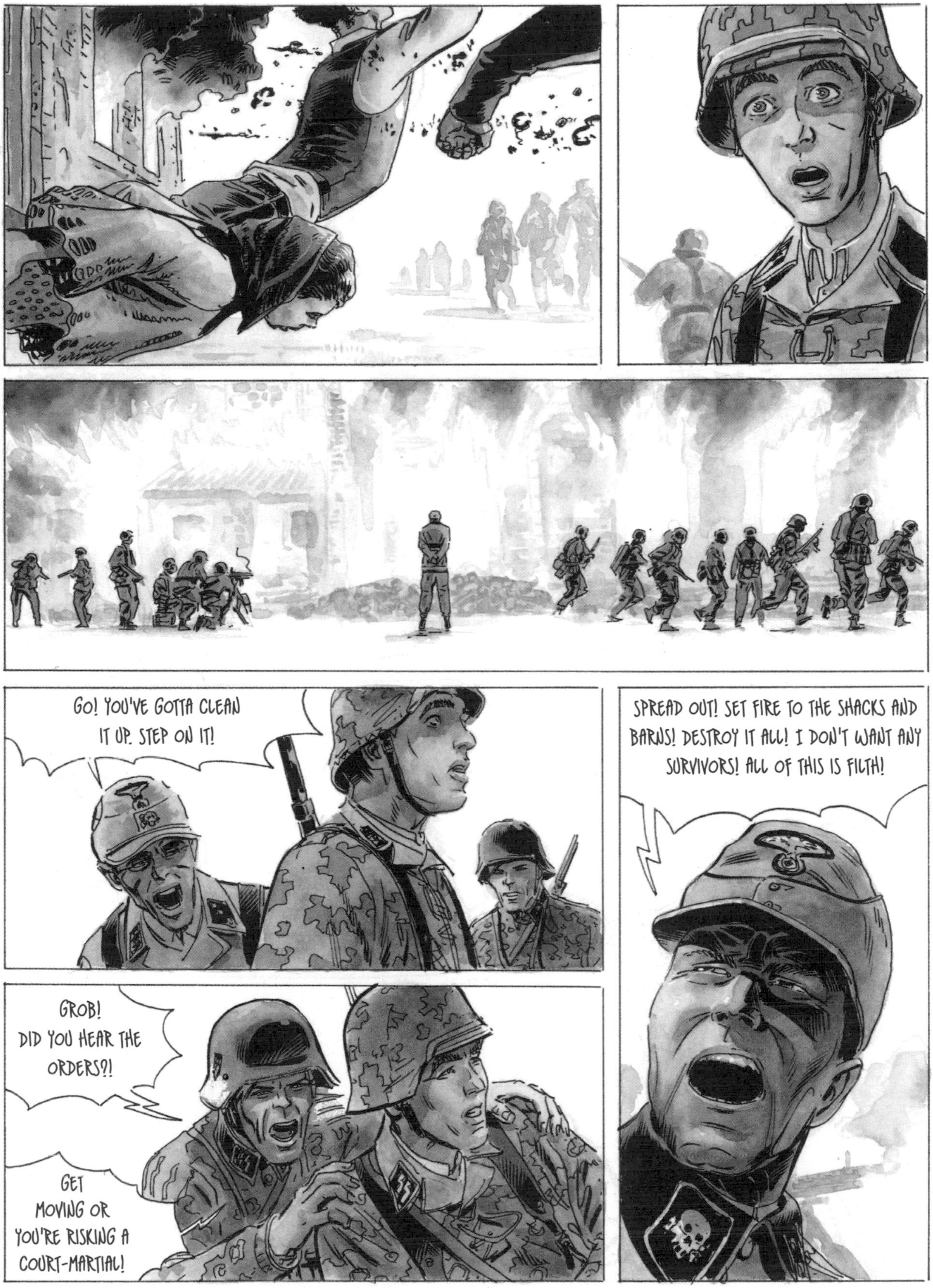

GO! YOU'VE GOTTA CLEAN IT UP. STEP ON IT!
SPREAD OUT! SET FIRE TO THE SHACKS AND BARNS! DESTROY IT ALL! I DON'T WANT ANY SURVIVORS! ALL OF THIS IS FILTH!
GROB! DID YOU HEAR THE ORDERS?!
GET MOVING OR YOU'RE RISKING A COURT-MARTIAL!

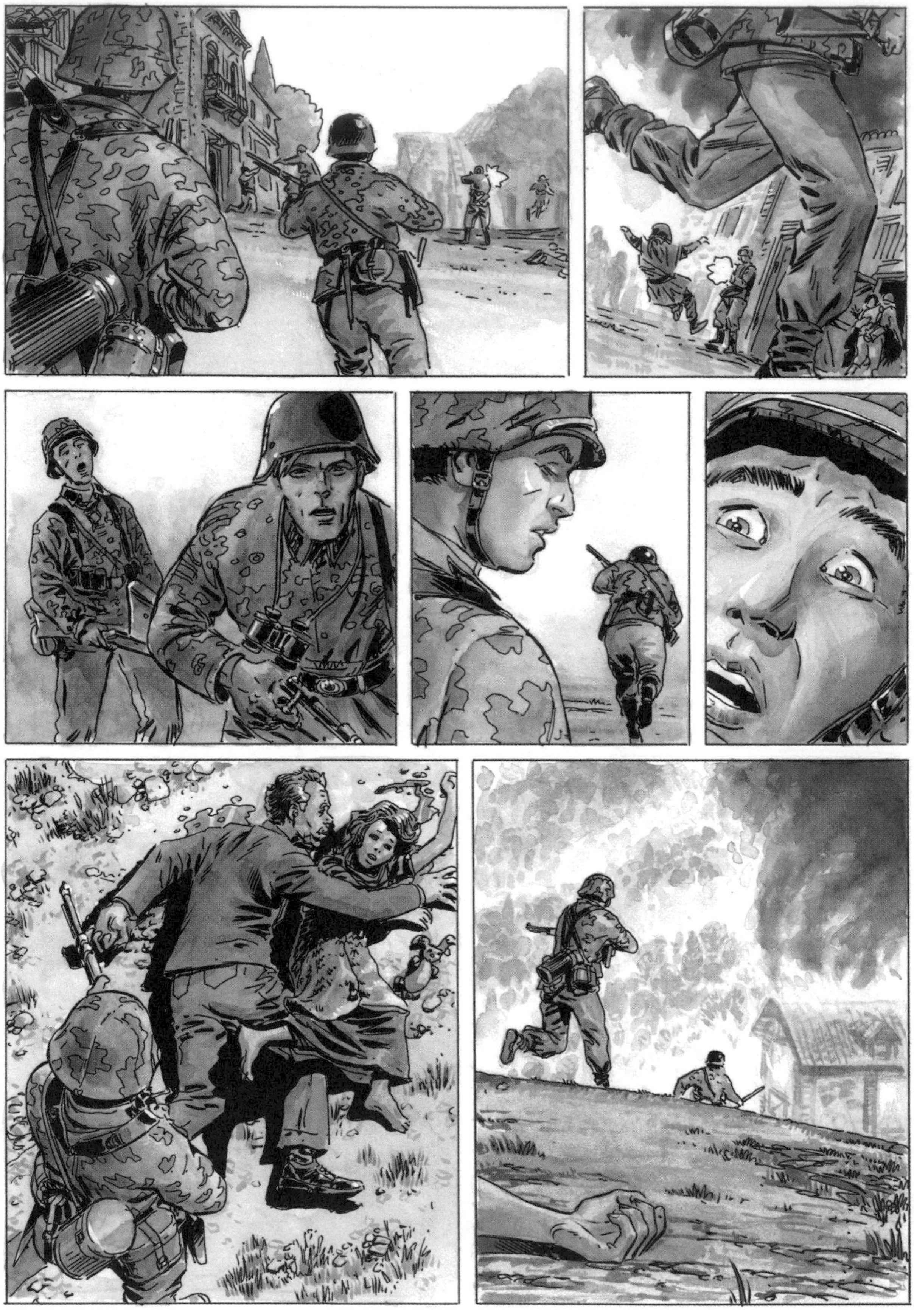

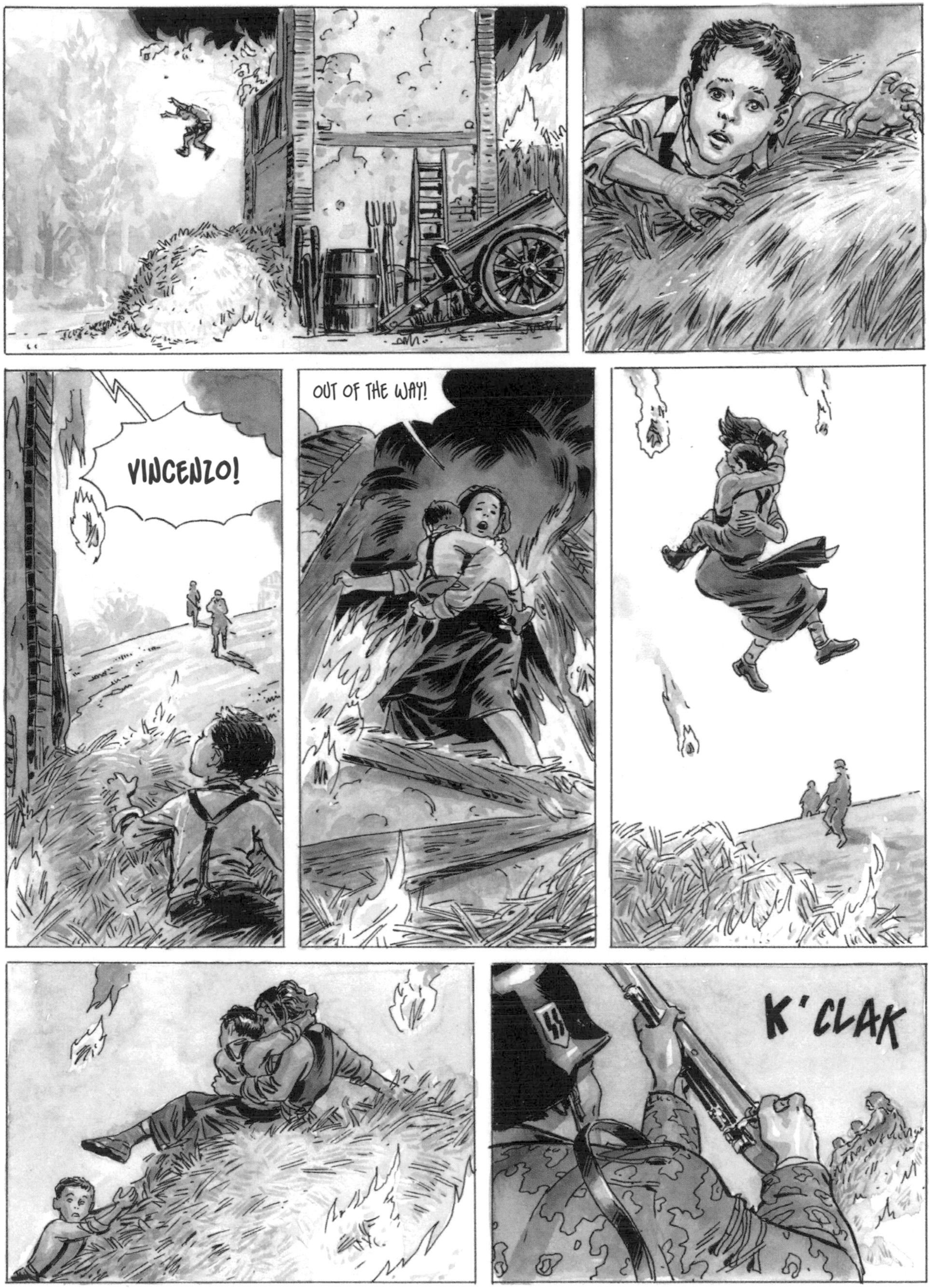
VINCENZO!
OUT OF THE WAY!
K'CLAK

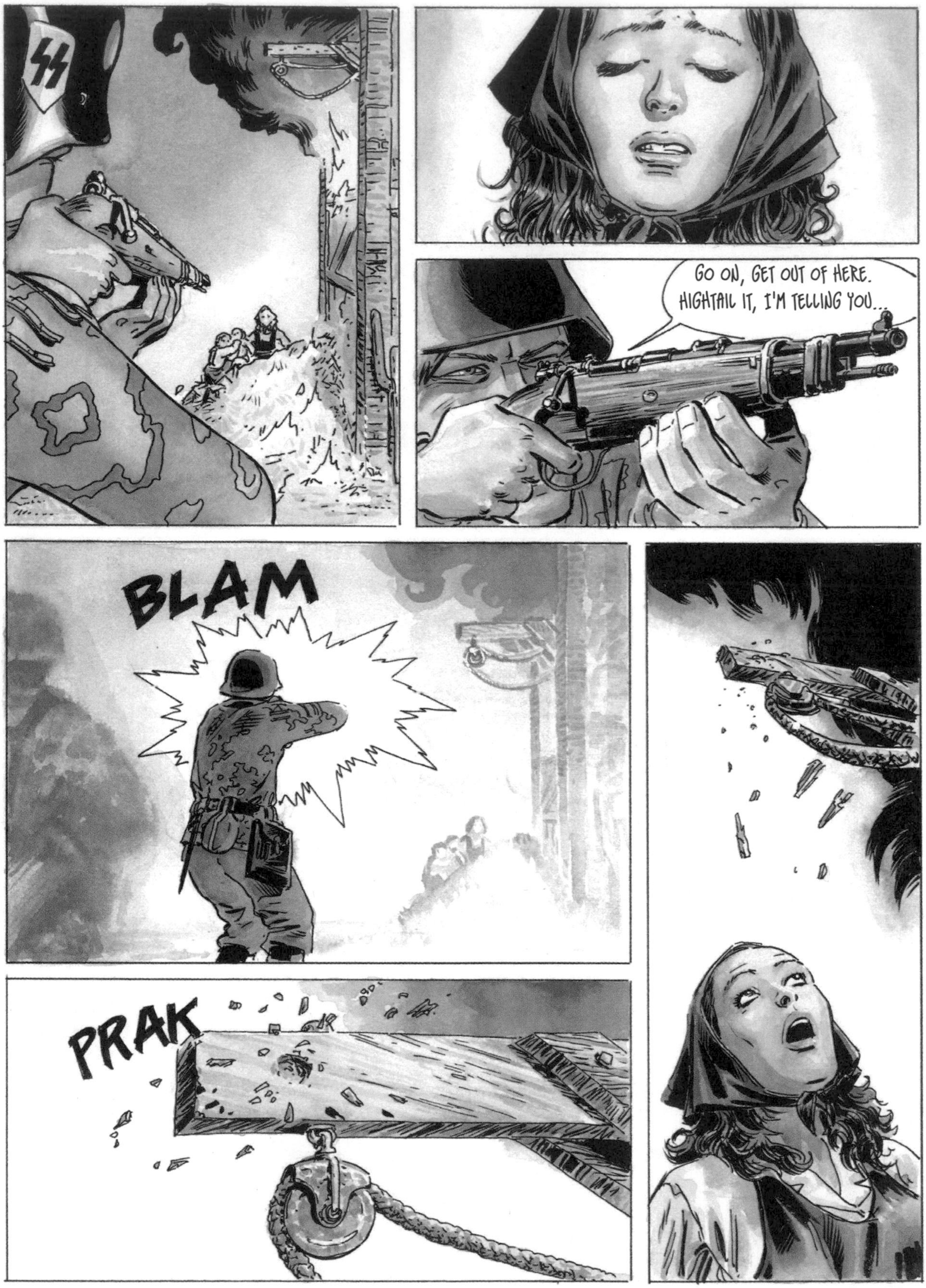
GO ON, GET OUT OF HERE. HIGHTAIL IT, I'M TELLING YOU...
BLAM
PRAK

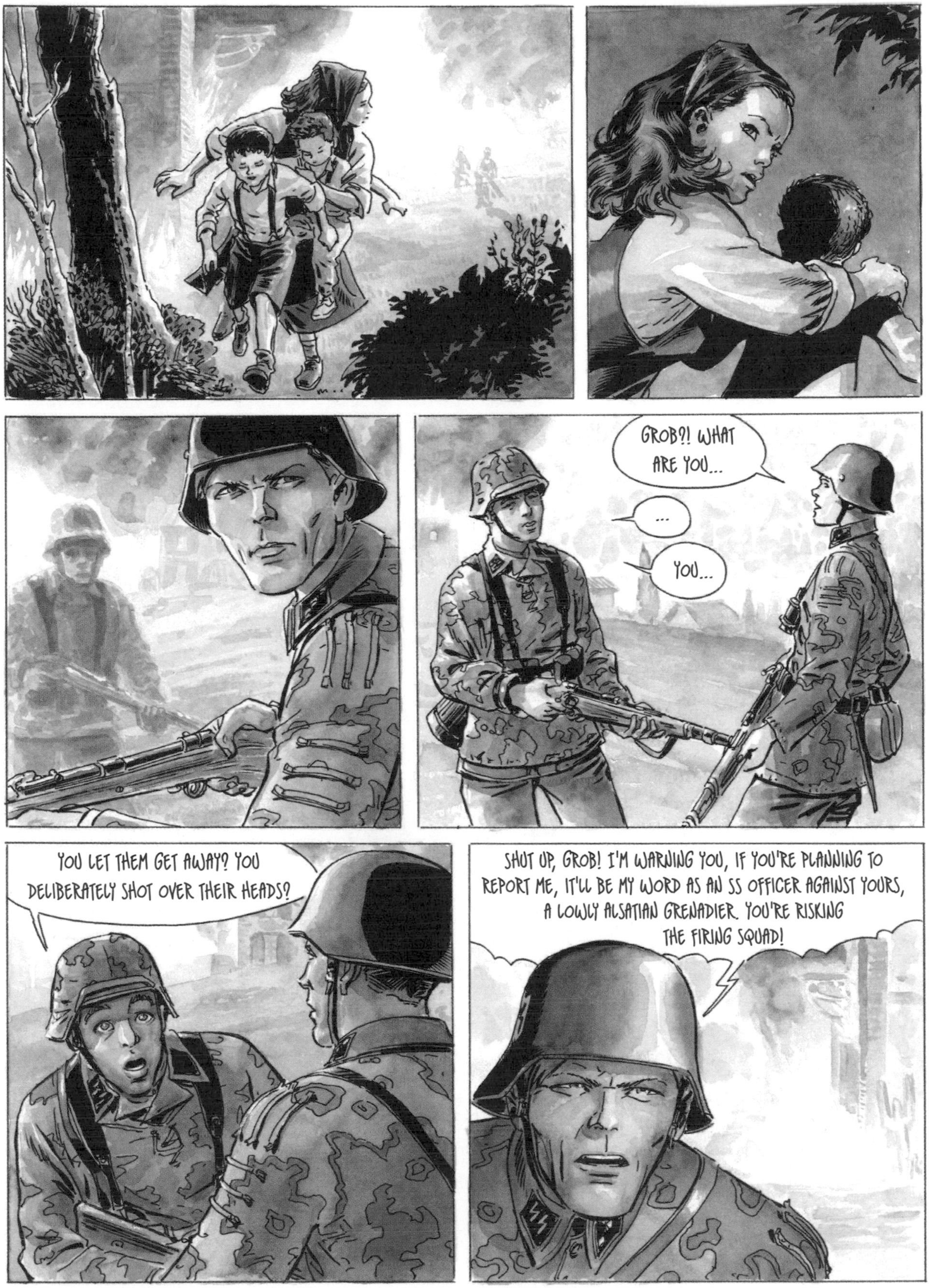
GROB?! WHAT ARE YOU...
...
YOU...
YOU LET THEM GET AWAY? YOU DELIBERATELY SHOT OVER THEIR HEADS?
SHUT UP, GROB! I'M WARNING YOU, IF YOU'RE PLANNING TO REPORT ME, IT'LL BE MY WORD AS AN SS OFFICER AGAINST YOURS, A LOWLY ALSATIAN GRENADIER. YOU'RE RISKING THE FIRING SQUAD!

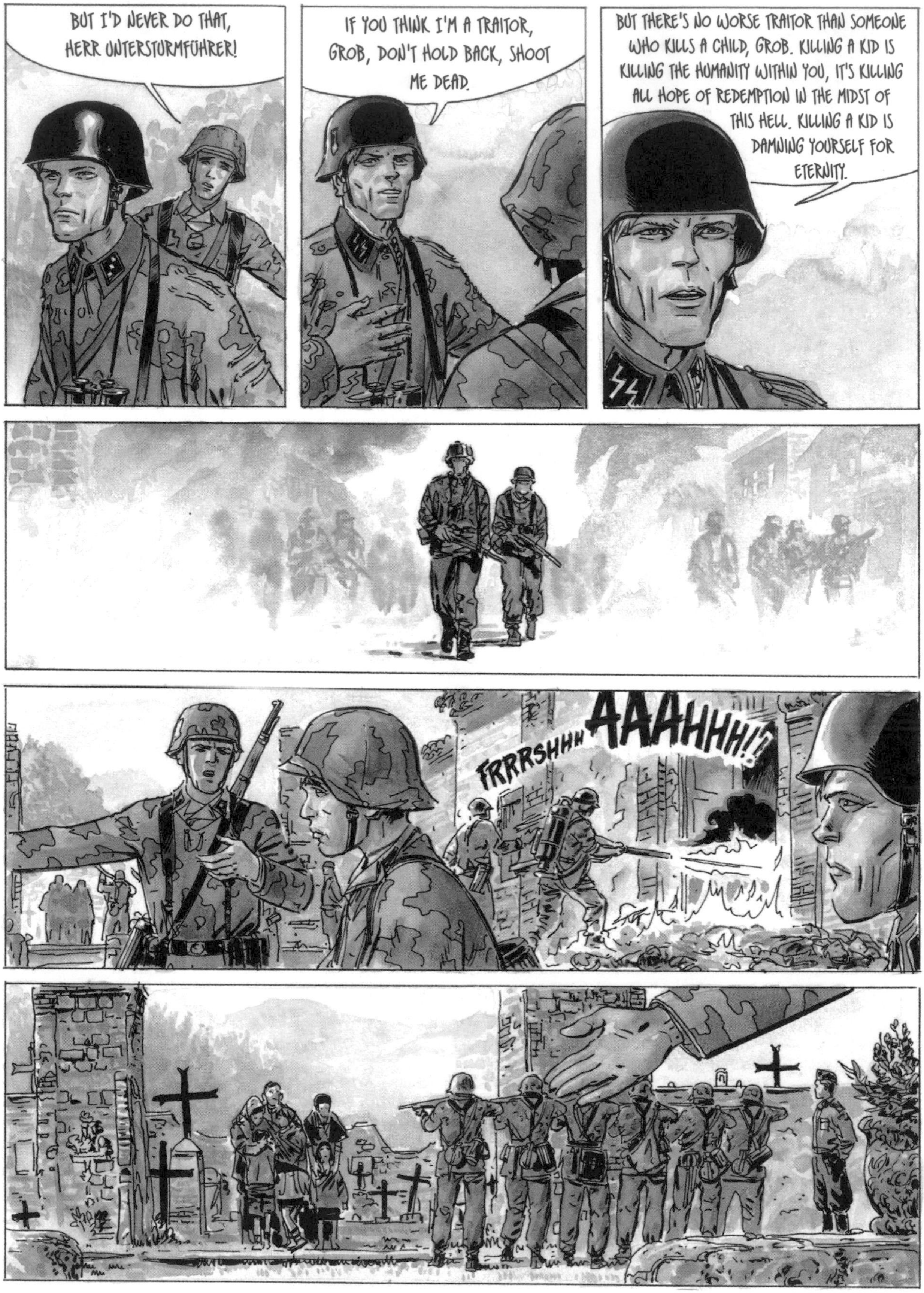
BUT I'D NEVER DO THAT, HERR UNTERSTURMFÜHRER!
IF YOU THINK I'M A TRAITOR, GROB, DON'T HOLD BACK, SHOOT ME DEAD.
BUT THERE'S NO WORSE TRAITOR THAN SOMEONE WHO KILLS A CHILD, GROB. KILLING A KID IS KILLING THE HUMANITY WITHIN YOU, IT'S KILLING ALL HOPE OF REDEMPTION IN THE MIDST OF THIS HELL. KILLING A KID IS DAMNING YOURSELF FOR ETERNITY.
FRRRSHHH
AAAHHH!!

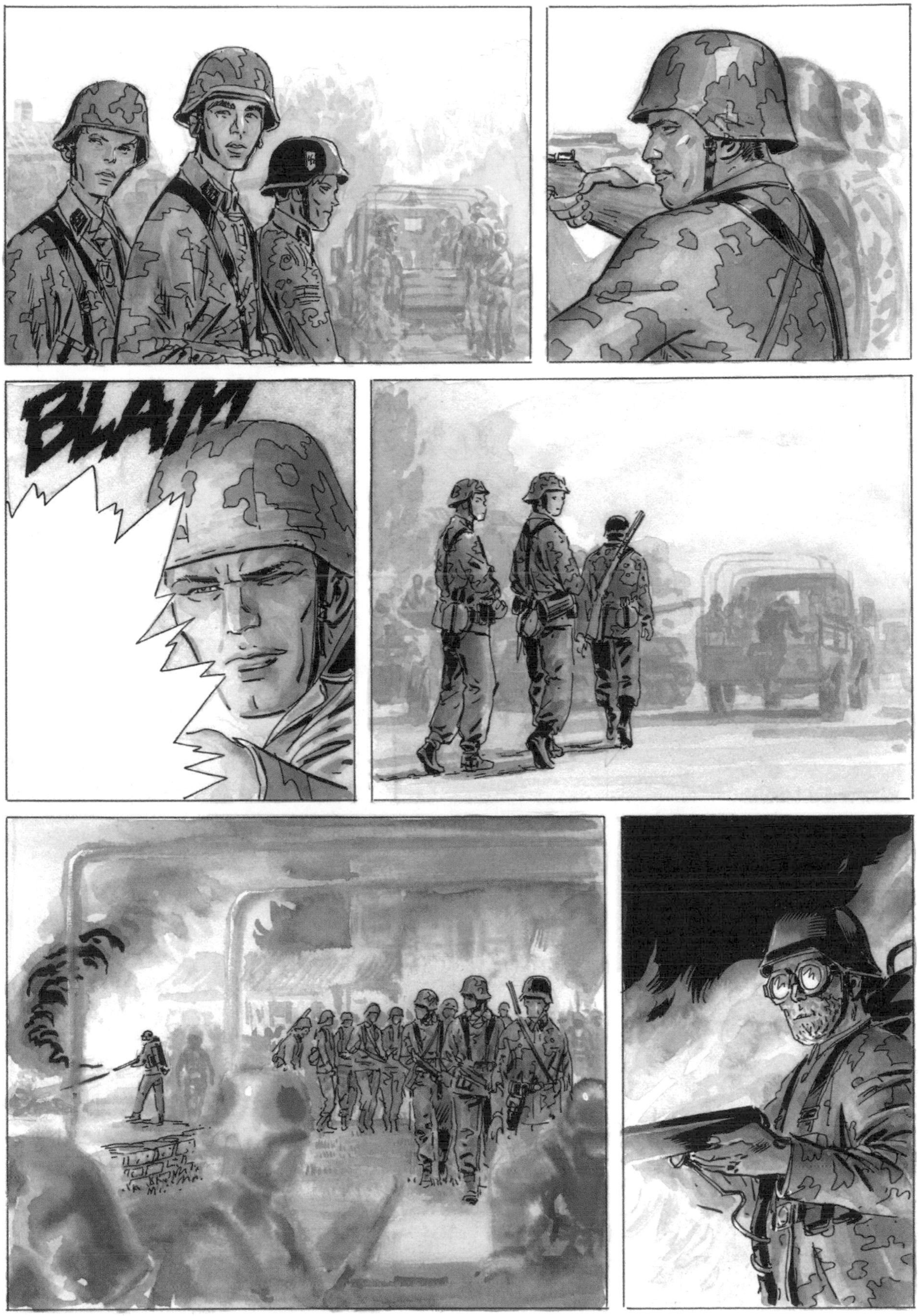
BLAM

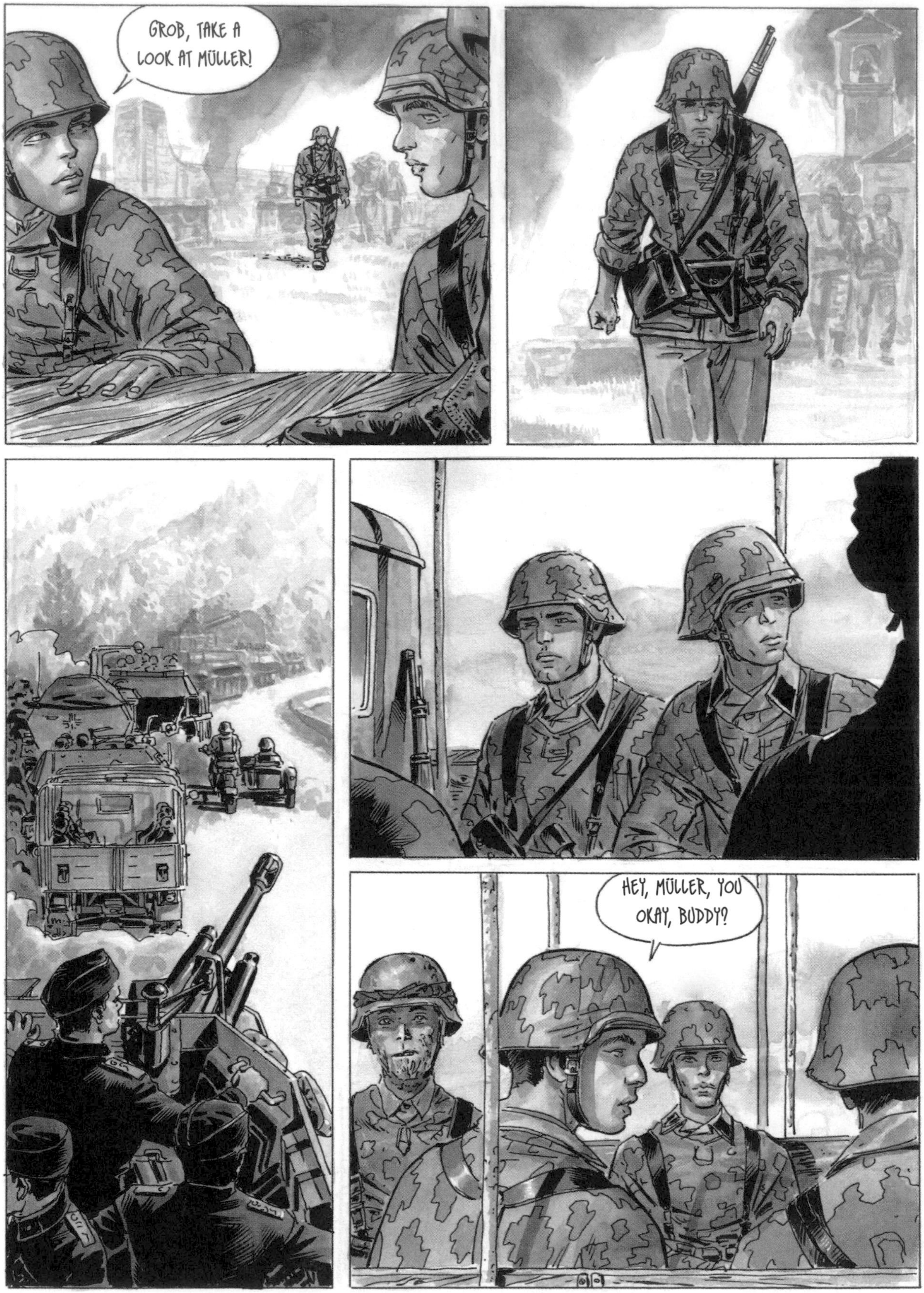
GROB, TAKE A LOOK AT MÜLLER!
HEY, MÜLLER, YOU OKAY, BUDDY?

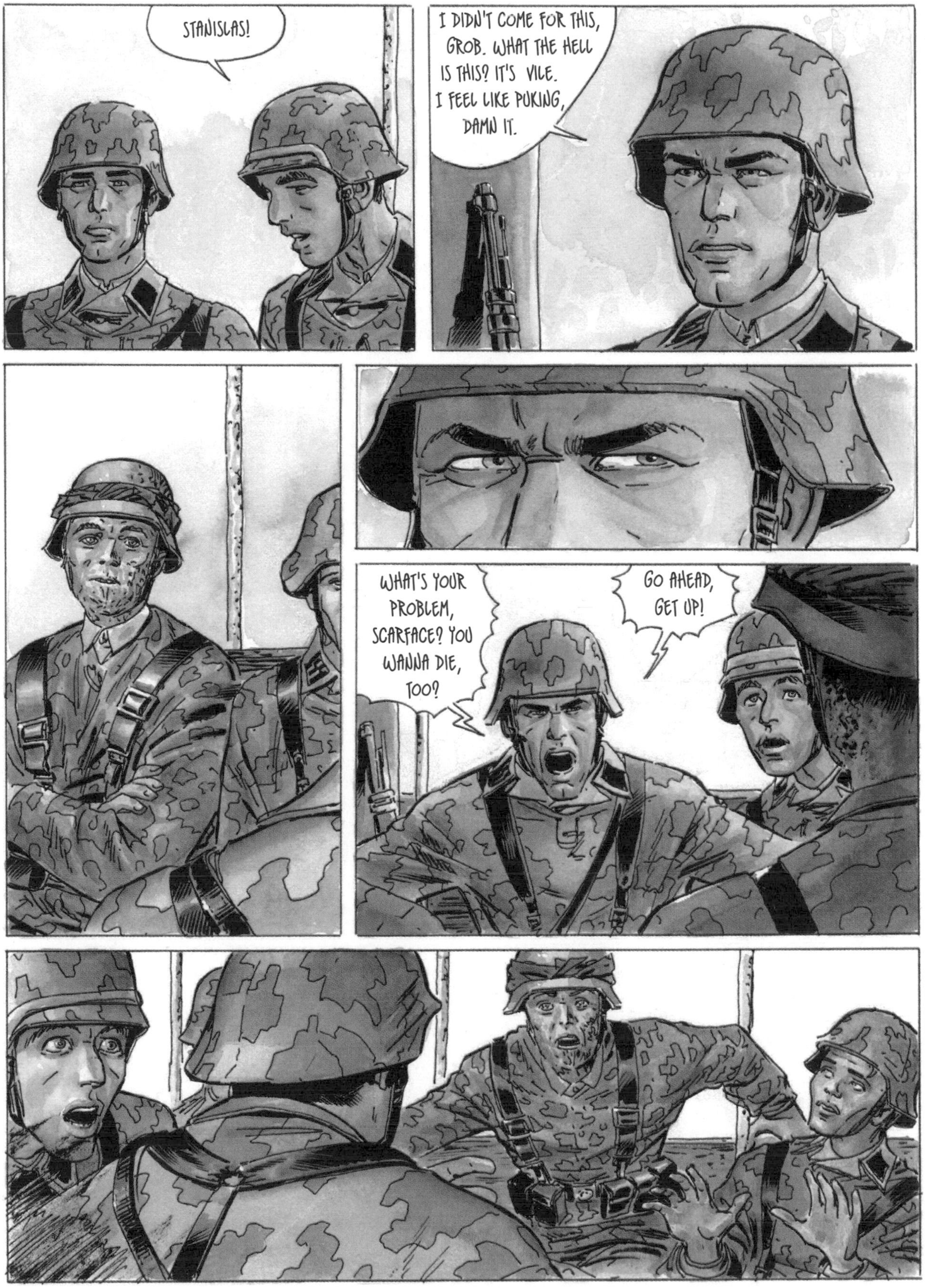
STANISLAS!
I DIDN'T COME FOR THIS, GROB. WHAT THE HELL IS THIS? IT'S VILE. I FEEL LIKE PUKING, DAMN IT.
WHAT'S YOUR PROBLEM, SCARFACE? YOU WANNA DIE, TOO?
GO AHEAD, GET UP!

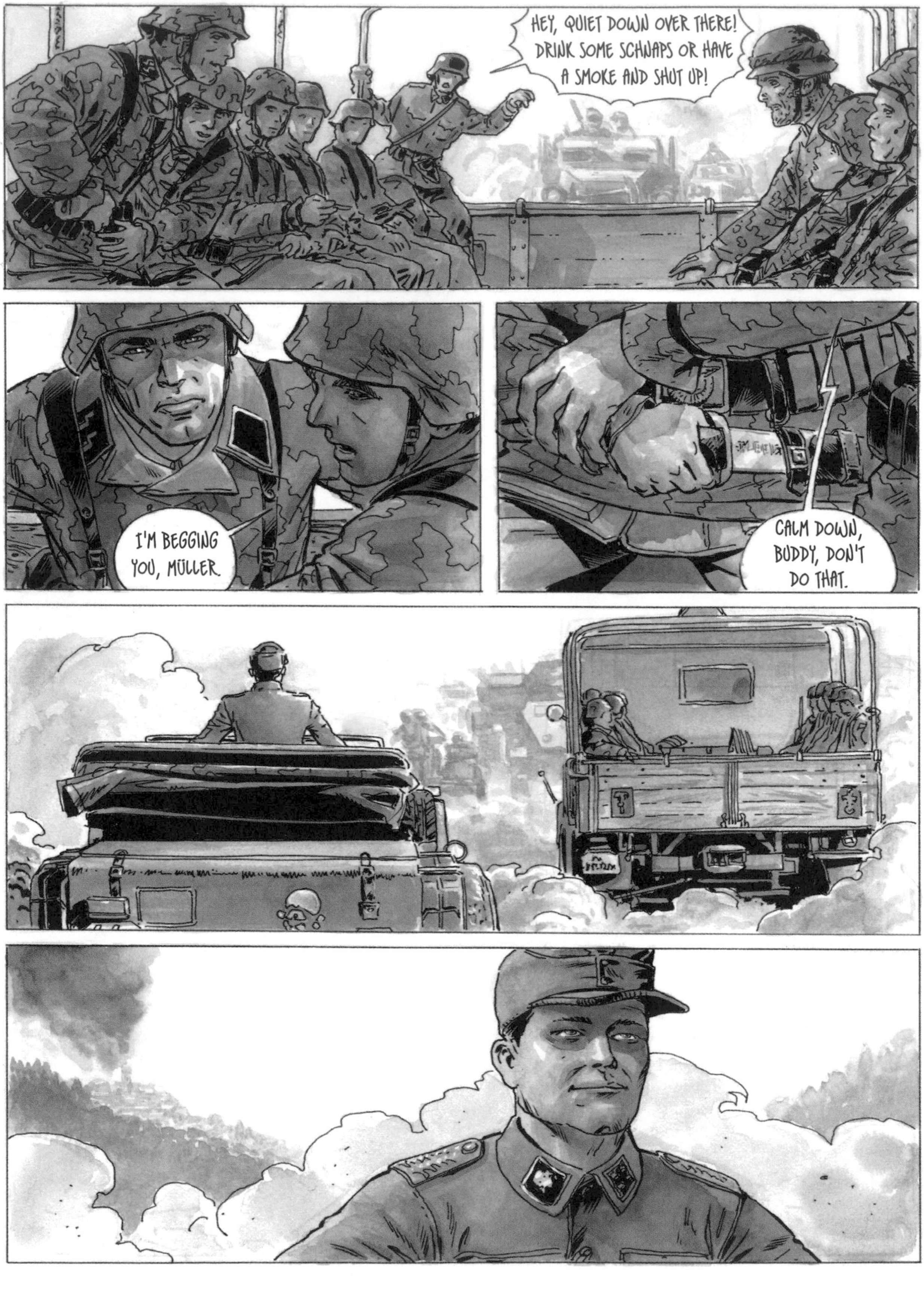
HEY, QUIET DOWN OVER THERE! DRINK SOME SCHNAPS OR HAVE A SMOKE AND SHUT UP!
I'M BEGGING YOU, MÜLLER.
CALM DOWN, BUDDY, DON'T DO THAT.

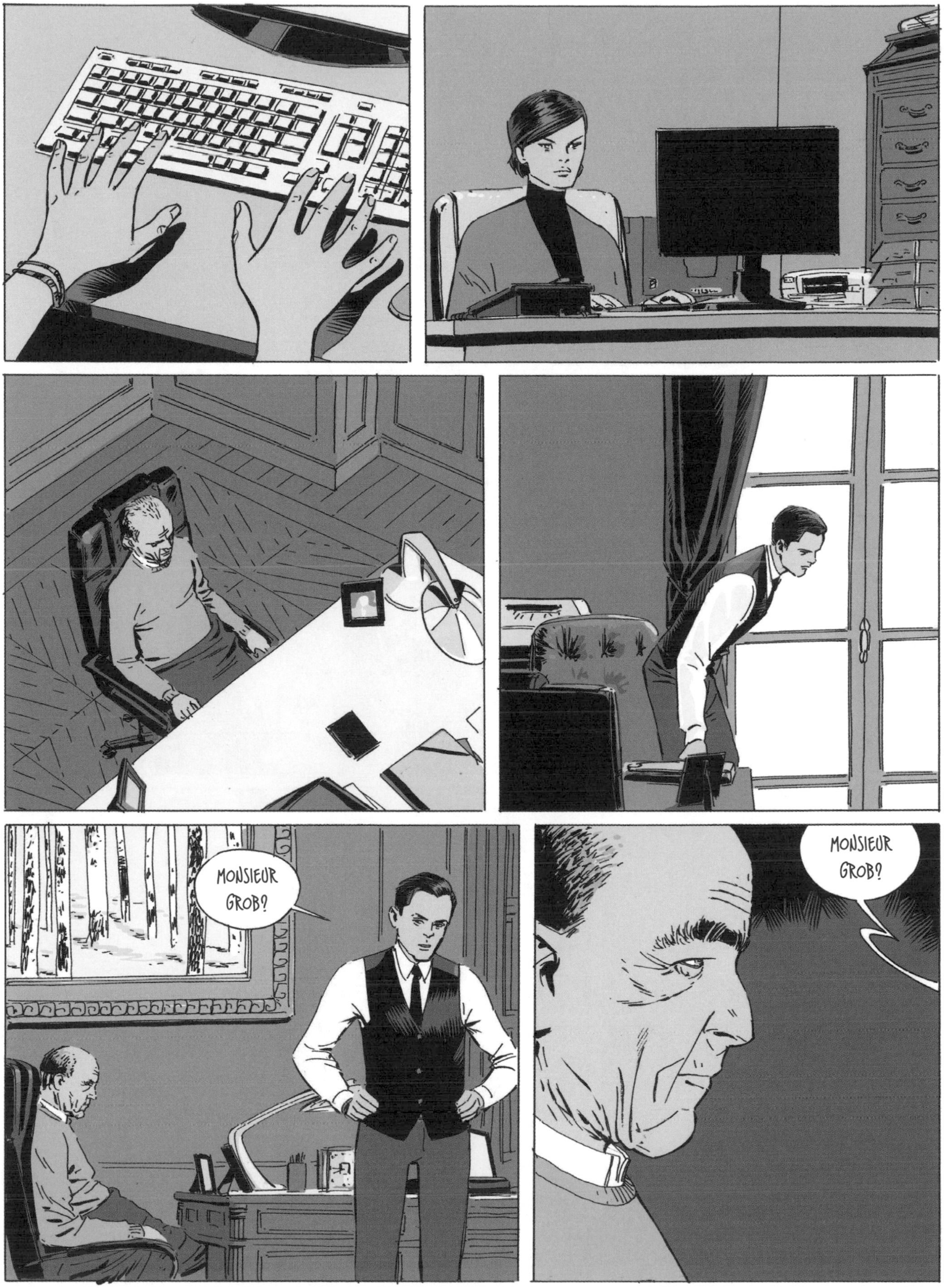
MONSIEUR GROB?
MONSIEUR GROB?

YES...

CAN WE CONTINUE?

YES.

DO YOU KNOW THE EXACT COUNT OF THE MASSACRE OF MARZABOTTO, MONSIEUR GROB?

NO, NO, NOT EXACTLY.

SEVEN HUNDRED AND SEVENTY DEAD, MONSIEUR GROB! A HUNDRED OF THE VICTIMS WERE UNDER 10 YEARS OLD. THREE HUNDRED WOMEN EXECUTED, ELEVEN CEMETERIES DESECRATED. IT WAS THE DEADLIEST MASSACRE OF CIVILIANS PERPETRATED BY THE NAZIS IN WESTERN EUROPE.

HOW DOES SOMEONE GET OVER THAT, MONSIEUR GROB, HUH?!

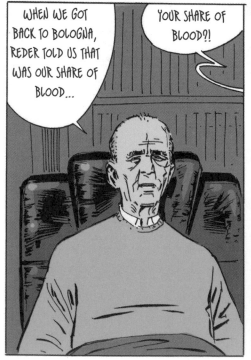

WHEN WE GOT BACK TO BOLOGNA, REDER TOLD US THAT WAS OUR SHARE OF BLOOD...

YOUR SHARE OF BLOOD?!

YES, HE TOLD US THAT WOULD BIND US TO THE CORPS OF THE SS AND THAT IT WAS PERMANENT. HE WAS RIGHT, YOU DON'T GET OVER IT.

YOU NEVER GET OVER IT.

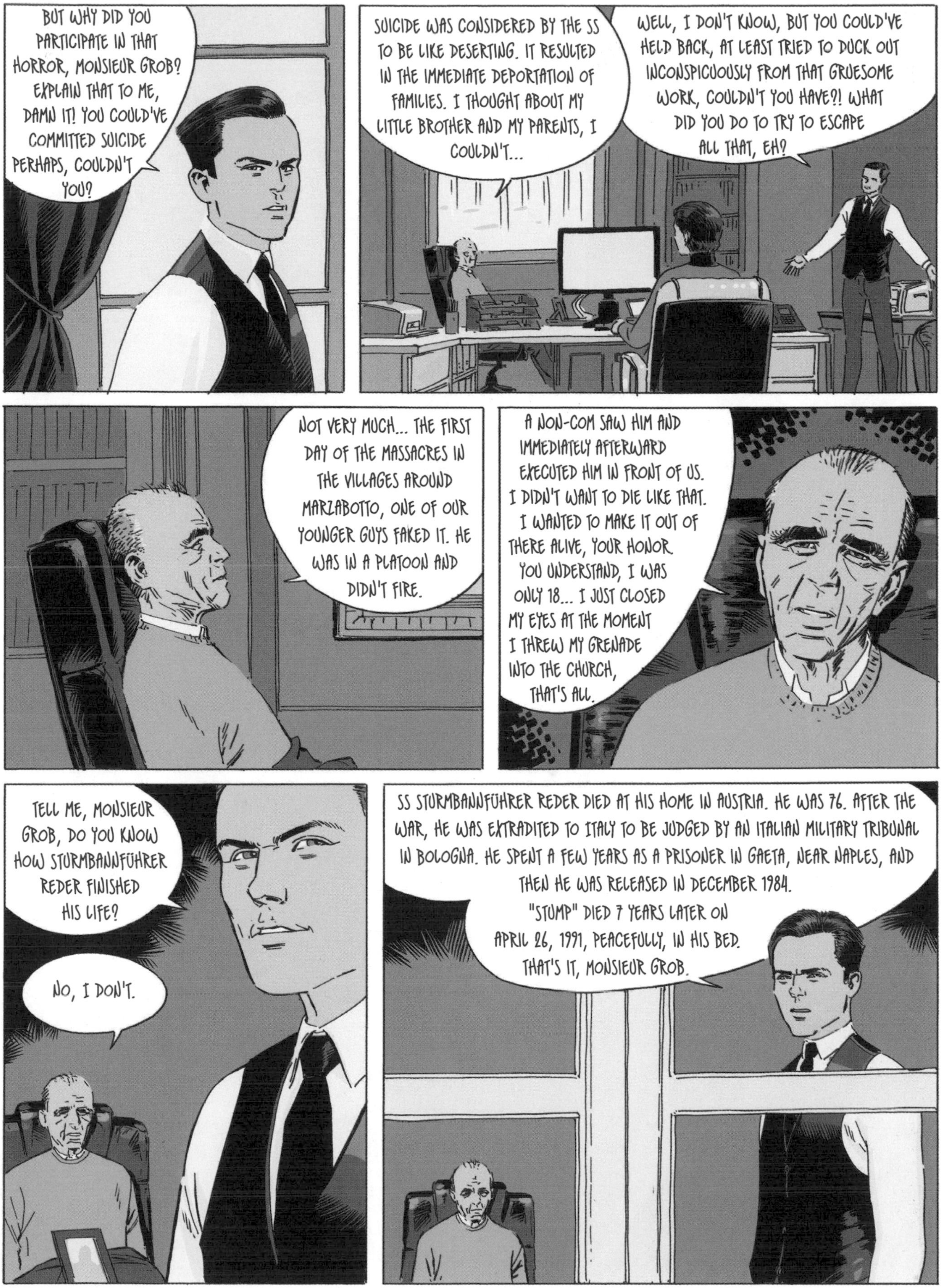
BUT WHY DID YOU PARTICIPATE IN THAT HORROR, MONSIEUR GROB? EXPLAIN THAT TO ME, DAMN IT! YOU COULD'VE COMMITTED SUICIDE PERHAPS, COULDN'T YOU?
SUICIDE WAS CONSIDERED BY THE SS TO BE LIKE DESERTING. IT RESULTED IN THE IMMEDIATE DEPORTATION OF FAMILIES. I THOUGHT ABOUT MY LITTLE BROTHER AND MY PARENTS, I COULDN'T...
WELL, I DON'T KNOW, BUT YOU COULD'VE HELD BACK, AT LEAST TRIED TO DUCK OUT INCONSPICUOUSLY FROM THAT GRUESOME WORK, COULDN'T YOU HAVE?! WHAT DID YOU DO TO TRY TO ESCAPE ALL THAT, EH?
NOT VERY MUCH... THE FIRST DAY OF THE MASSACRES IN THE VILLAGES AROUND MARZABOTTO, ONE OF OUR YOUNGER GUYS FAKED IT. HE WAS IN A PLATOON AND DIDN'T FIRE.
A NON-COM SAW HIM AND IMMEDIATELY AFTERWARD EXECUTED HIM IN FRONT OF US. I DIDN'T WANT TO DIE LIKE THAT. I WANTED TO MAKE IT OUT OF THERE ALIVE, YOUR HONOR. YOU UNDERSTAND, I WAS ONLY 18... I JUST CLOSED MY EYES AT THE MOMENT I THREW MY GRENADE INTO THE CHURCH, THAT'S ALL.
TELL ME, MONSIEUR GROB, DO YOU KNOW HOW STURMBANNFÜHRER REDER FINISHED HIS LIFE?
NO, I DON'T.
SS STURMBANNFÜHRER REDER DIED AT HIS HOME IN AUSTRIA. HE WAS 76. AFTER THE WAR, HE WAS EXTRADITED TO ITALY TO BE JUDGED BY AN ITALIAN MILITARY TRIBUNAL IN BOLOGNA. HE SPENT A FEW YEARS AS A PRISONER IN GAETA, NEAR NAPLES, AND THEN HE WAS RELEASED IN DECEMBER 1984. "STUMP" DIED 7 YEARS LATER ON APRIL 26, 1991, PEACEFULLY, IN HIS BED. THAT'S IT, MONSIEUR GROB.

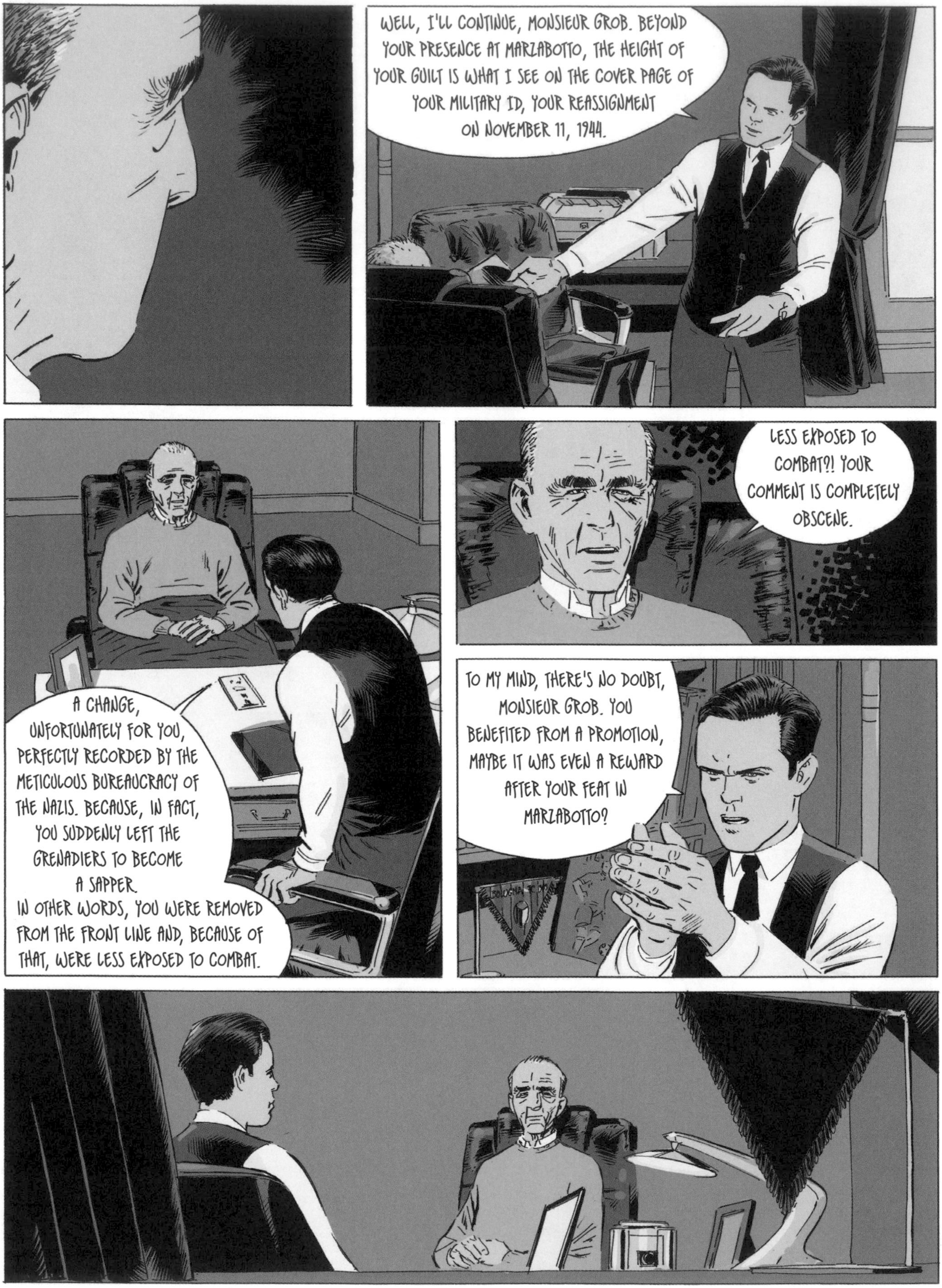
WELL, I'LL CONTINUE, MONSIEUR GROB. BEYOND YOUR PRESENCE AT MARZABOTTO, THE HEIGHT OF YOUR GUILT IS WHAT I SEE ON THE COVER PAGE OF YOUR MILITARY ID, YOUR REASSIGNMENT ON NOVEMBER 11, 1944.
A CHANGE, UNFORTUNATELY FOR YOU, PERFECTLY RECORDED BY THE METICULOUS BUREAUCRACY OF THE NAZIS. BECAUSE, IN FACT, YOU SUDDENLY LEFT THE GRENADIERS TO BECOME A SAPPER.
IN OTHER WORDS, YOU WERE REMOVED FROM THE FRONT LINE AND, BECAUSE OF THAT, WERE LESS EXPOSED TO COMBAT.
LESS EXPOSED TO COMBAT?! YOUR COMMENT IS COMPLETELY OBSCENE.
TO MY MIND, THERE'S NO DOUBT, MONSIEUR GROB. YOU BENEFITED FROM A PROMOTION, MAYBE IT WAS EVEN A REWARD AFTER YOUR FEAT IN MARZABOTTO?

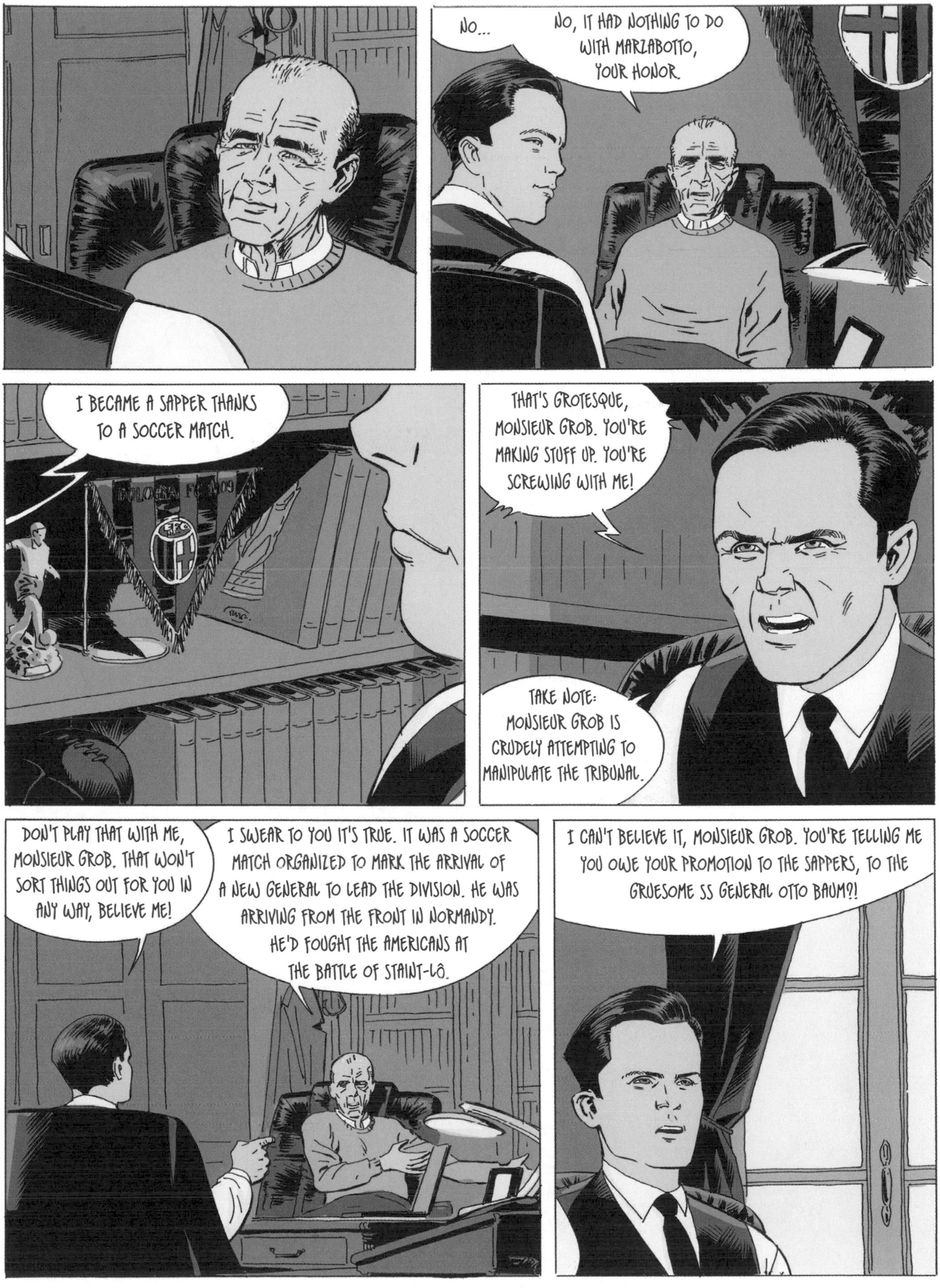
NO...
NO, IT HAD NOTHING TO DO WITH MARZABOTTO, YOUR HONOR.
I BECAME A SAPPER THANKS TO A SOCCER MATCH.
THAT'S GROTESQUE, MONSIEUR GROB. YOU'RE MAKING STUFF UP. YOU'RE SCREWING WITH ME!
TAKE NOTE: MONSIEUR GROB IS CRUDELY ATTEMPTING TO MANIPULATE THE TRIBUNAL.
DON'T PLAY THAT WITH ME, MONSIEUR GROB. THAT WON'T SORT THINGS OUT FOR YOU IN ANY WAY, BELIEVE ME!
I SWEAR TO YOU IT'S TRUE. IT WAS A SOCCER MATCH ORGANIZED TO MARK THE ARRIVAL OF A NEW GENERAL TO LEAD THE DIVISION. HE WAS ARRIVING FROM THE FRONT IN NORMANDY. HE'D FOUGHT THE AMERICANS AT THE BATTLE OF STAINT-LÔ.
I CAN'T BELIEVE IT, MONSIEUR GROB. YOU'RE TELLING ME YOU OWE YOUR PROMOTION TO THE SAPPERS, TO THE GRUESOME SS GENERAL OTTO BAUM?!

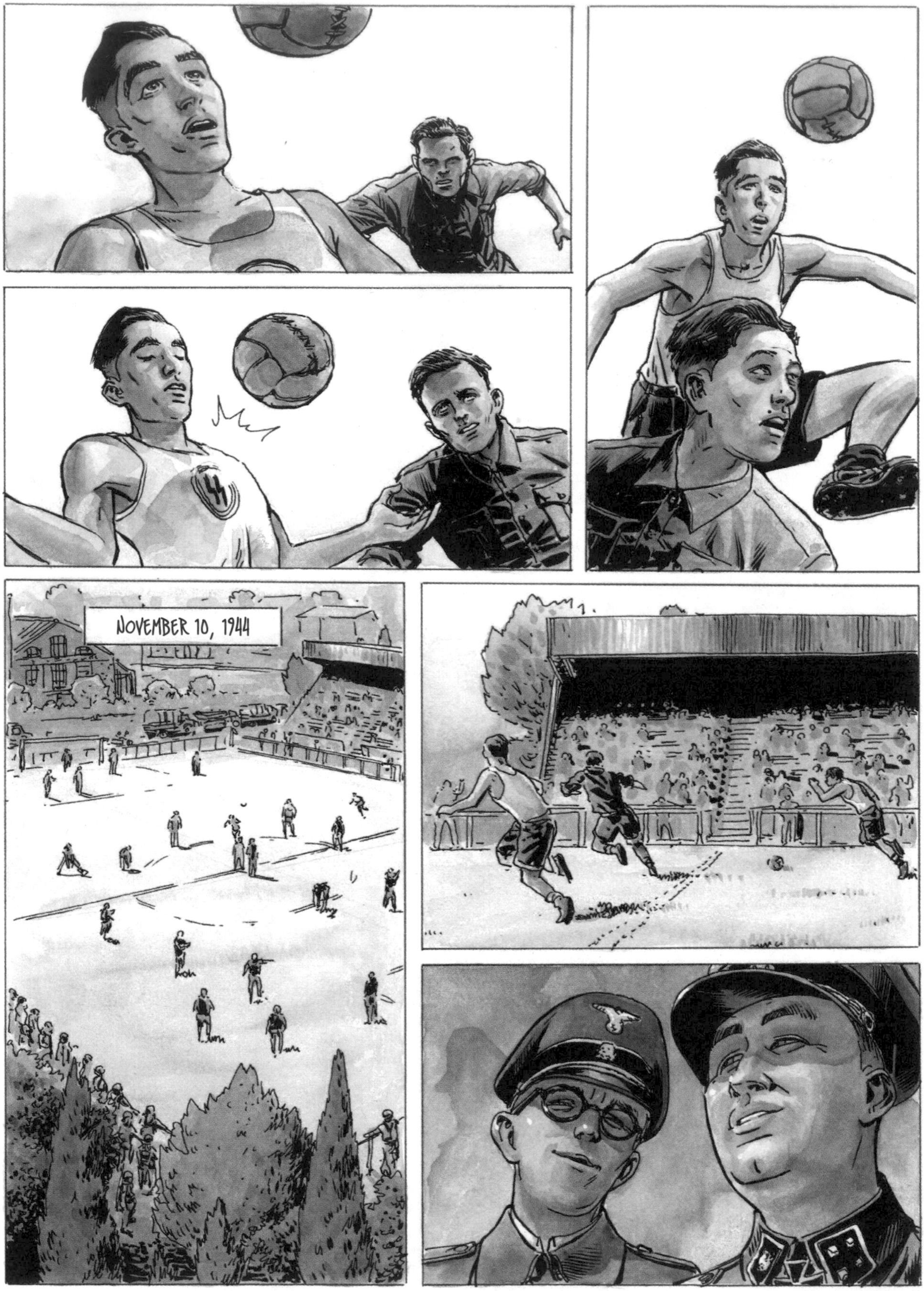
November 10, 1944

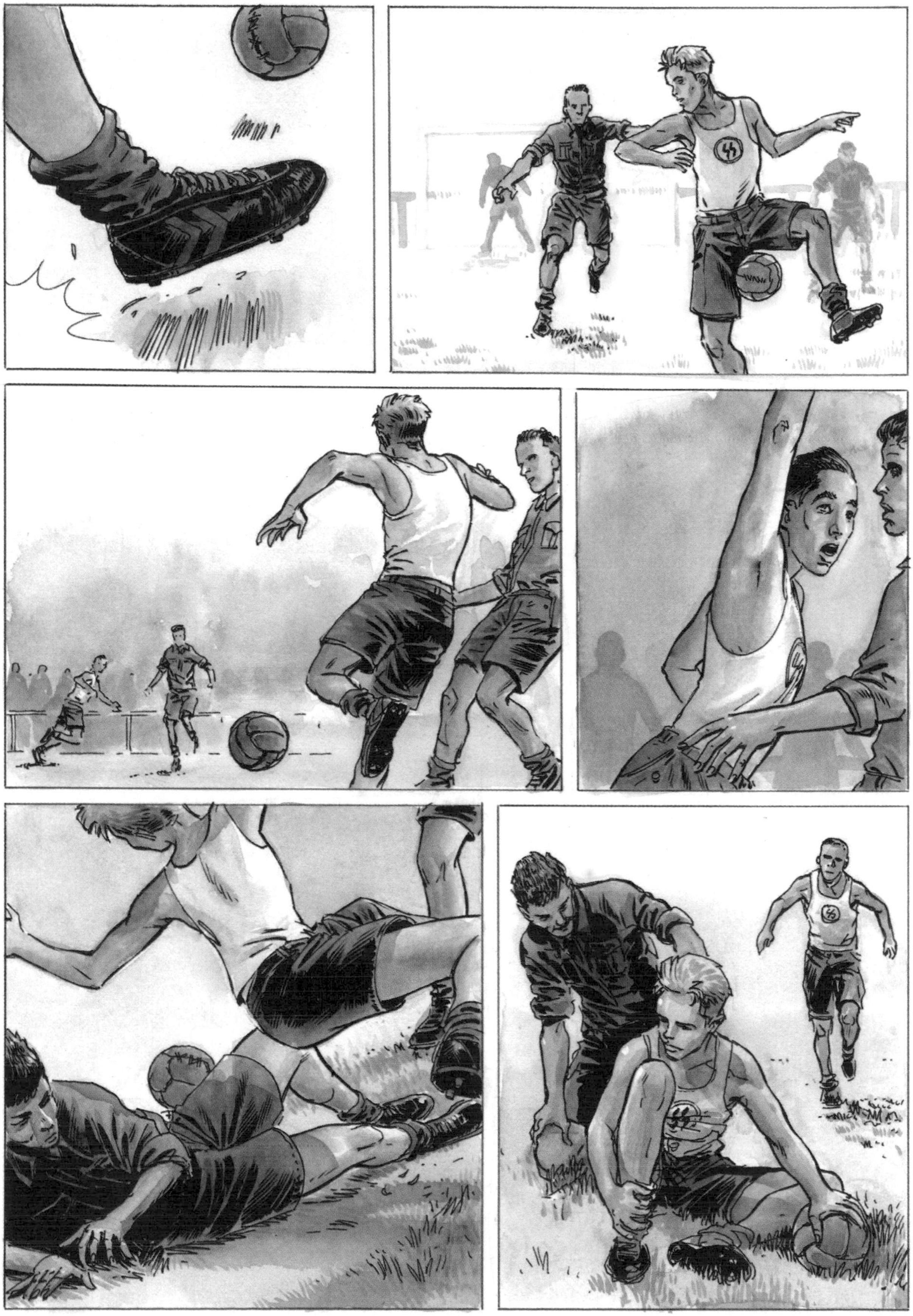

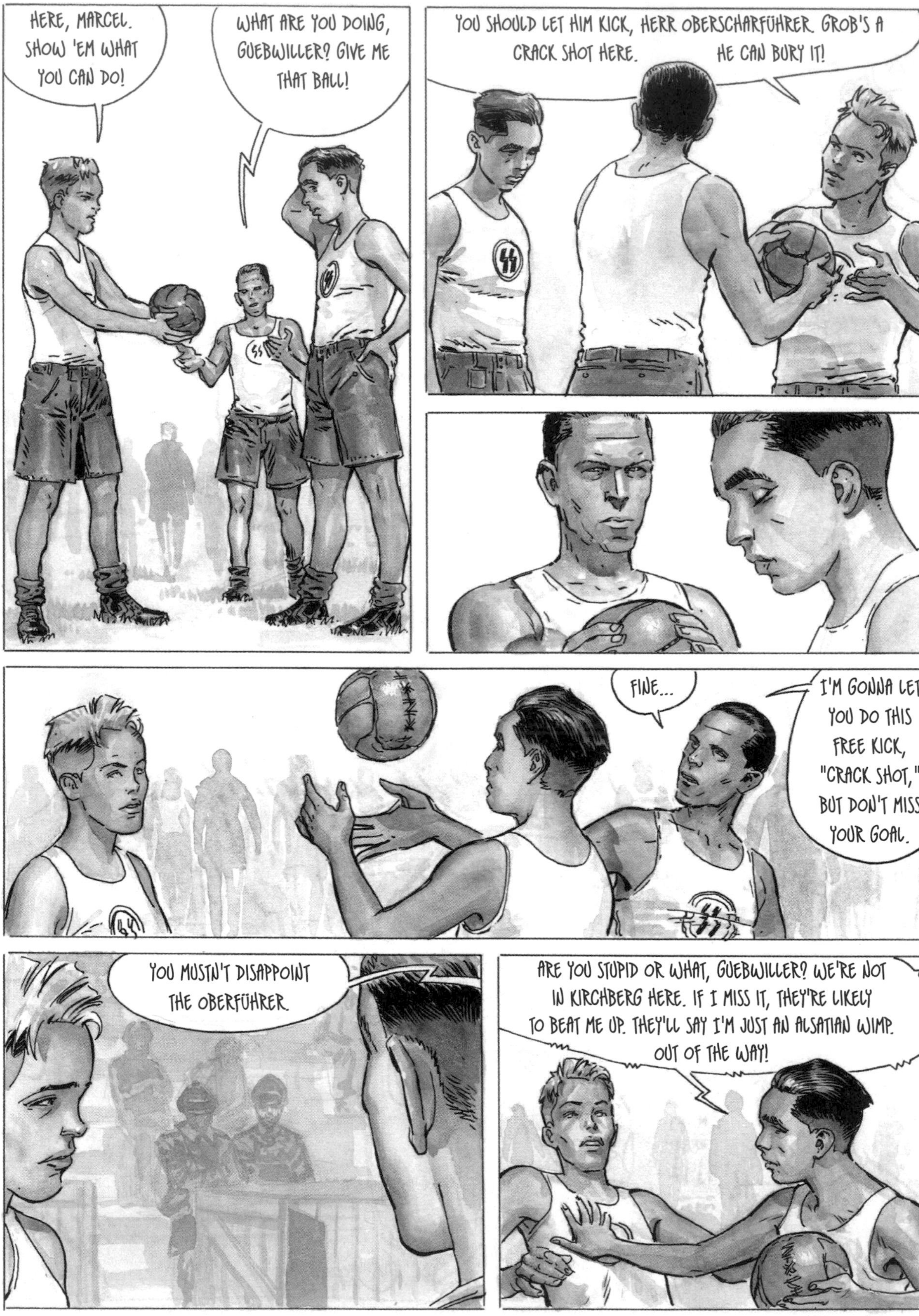
HERE, MARCEL. SHOW 'EM WHAT YOU CAN DO!
WHAT ARE YOU DOING, GUEBWILLER? GIVE ME THAT BALL!
YOU SHOULD LET HIM KICK, HERR OBERSCHARFÜHRER. GROB'S A CRACK SHOT HERE. HE CAN BURY IT!
FINE...
I'M GONNA LET YOU DO THIS FREE KICK, "CRACK SHOT," BUT DON'T MISS YOUR GOAL.
YOU MUSTN'T DISAPPOINT THE OBERFÜHRER.
ARE YOU STUPID OR WHAT, GUEBWILLER? WE'RE NOT IN KIRCHBERG HERE. IF I MISS IT, THEY'RE LIKELY TO BEAT ME UP. THEY'LL SAY I'M JUST AN ALSATIAN WIMP. OUT OF THE WAY!

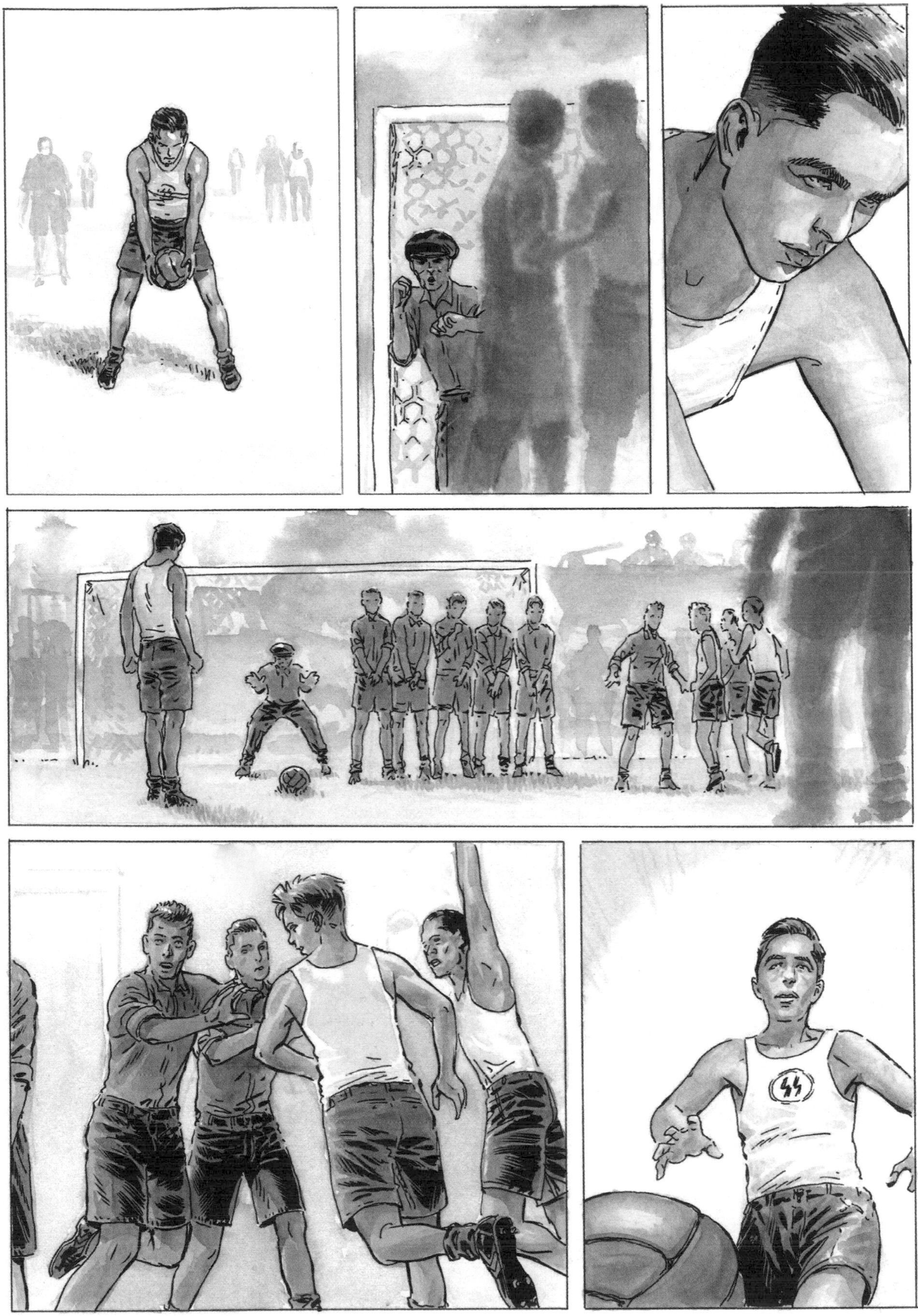

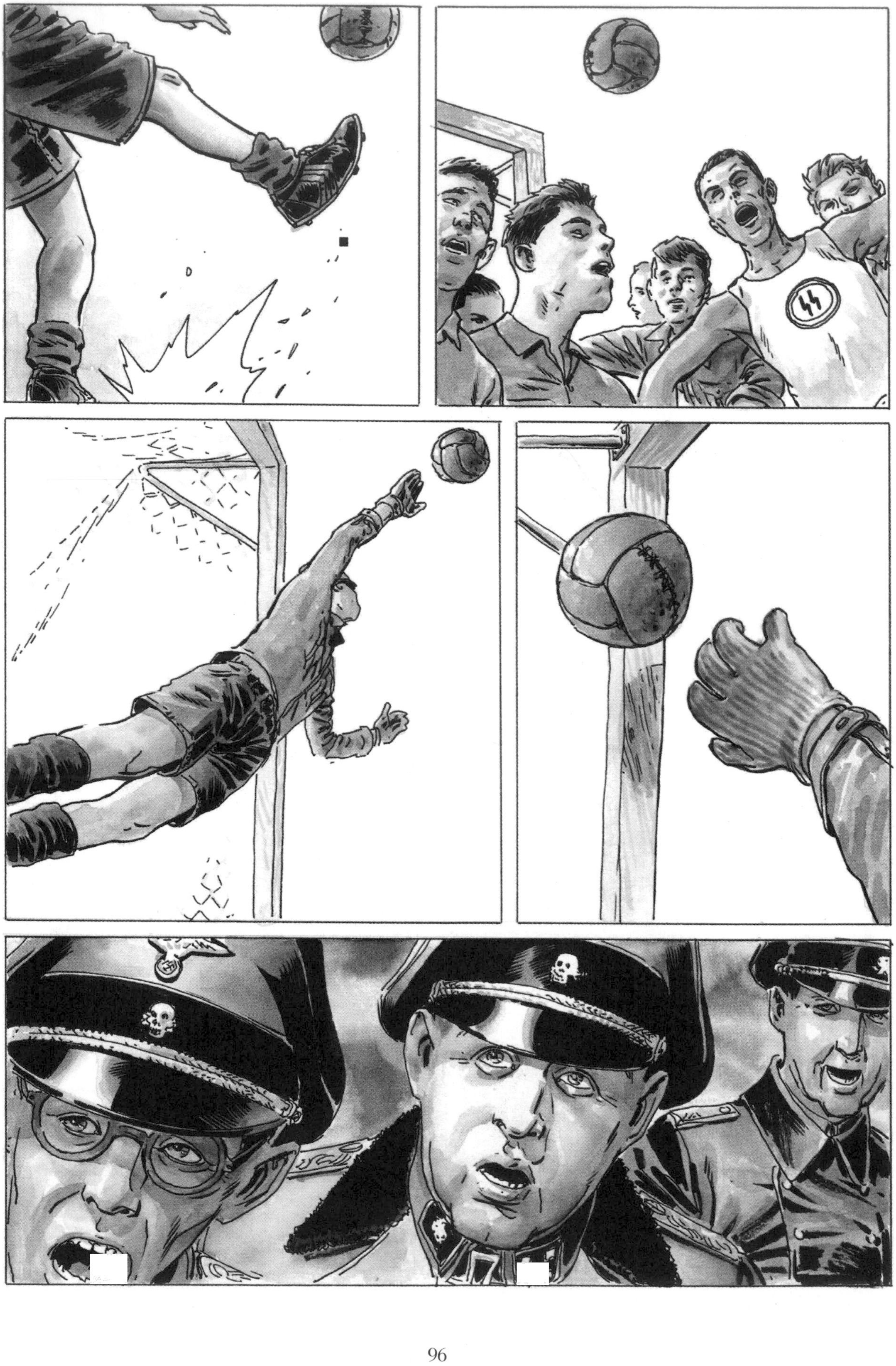

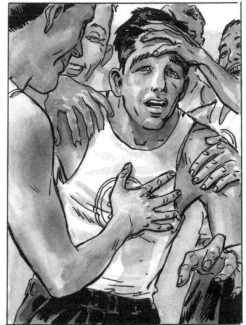

CLAP
CLAP

CLAP

CLAP
CLAP

CLAP

GROB! THE OBERFÜHRER WANTS TO CHAT WITH YOU.

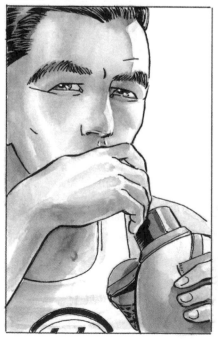

YES, SCHARFÜHRER!

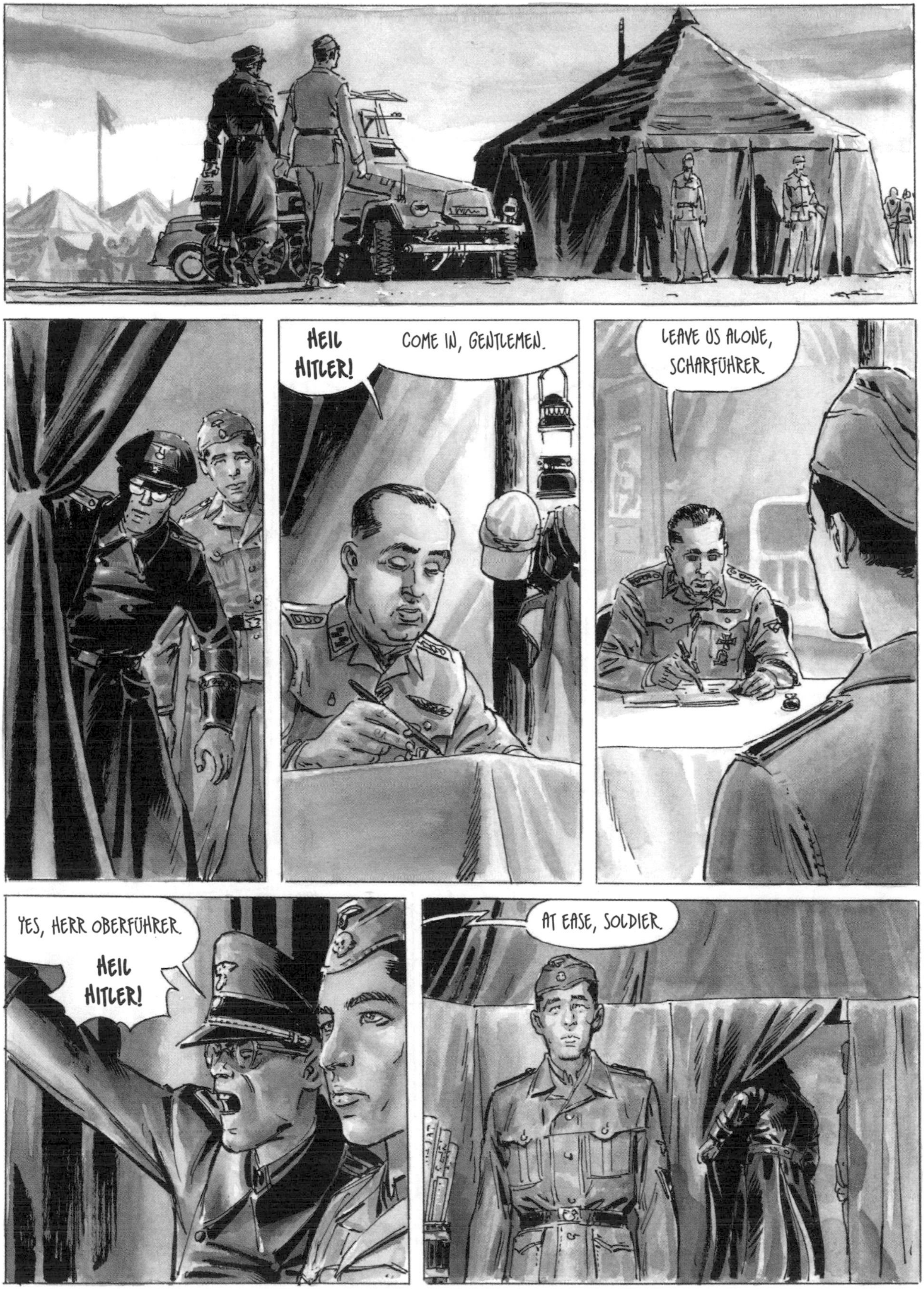
HEIL HITLER!
COME IN, GENTLEMEN.
LEAVE US ALONE, SCHARFÜHRER.
YES, HERR OBERFÜHRER.
HEIL HITLER!
AT EASE, SOLDIER.

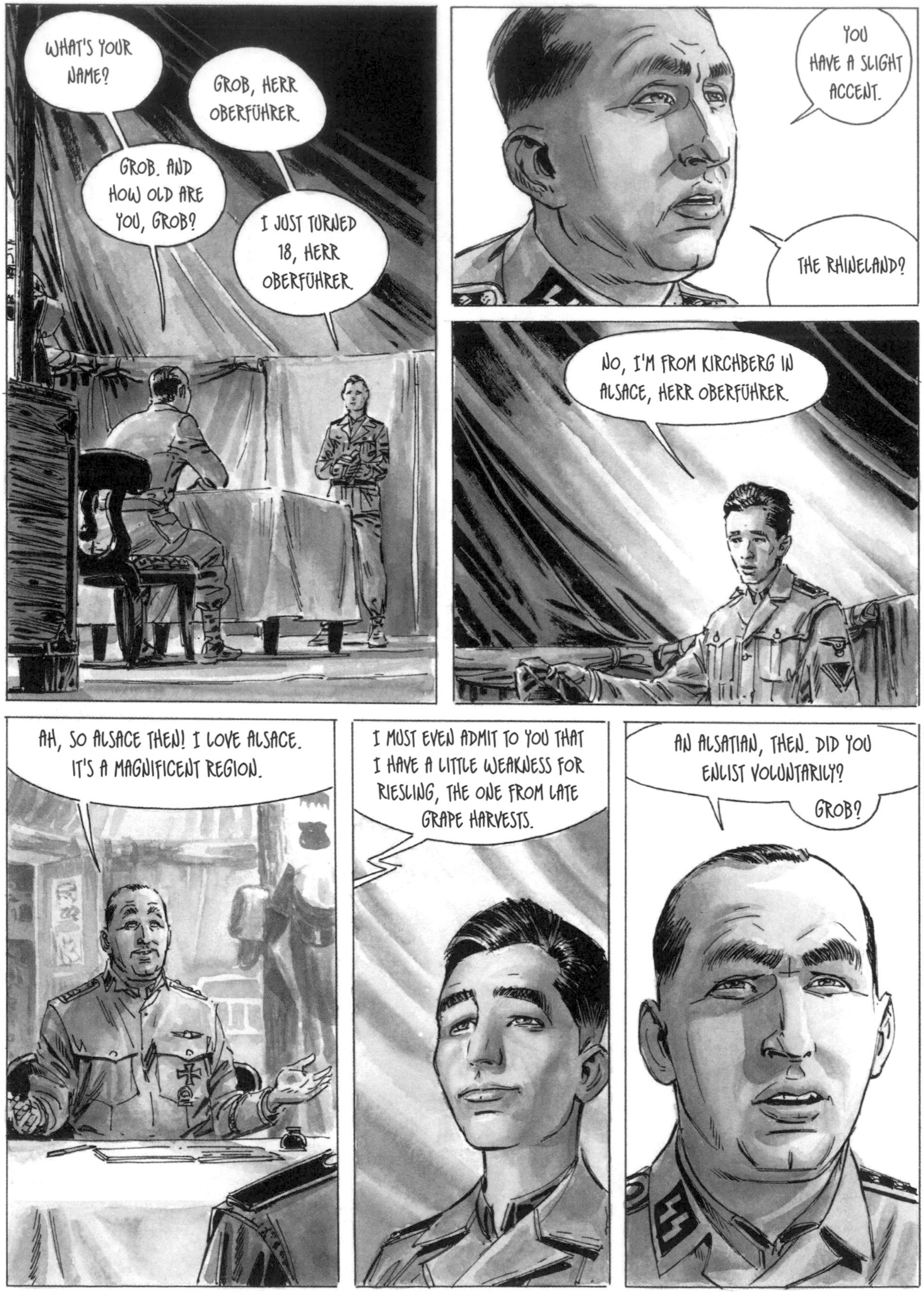
WHAT'S YOUR NAME?
GROB, HERR OBERFÜHRER.
GROB. AND HOW OLD ARE YOU, GROB?
I JUST TURNED 18, HERR OBERFÜHRER.
YOU HAVE A SLIGHT ACCENT.
THE RHINELAND?
NO, I'M FROM KIRCHBERG IN ALSACE, HERR OBERFÜHRER.
AH, SO ALSACE THEN! I LOVE ALSACE. IT'S A MAGNIFICENT REGION.
I MUST EVEN ADMIT TO YOU THAT I HAVE A LITTLE WEAKNESS FOR RIESLING, THE ONE FROM LATE GRAPE HARVESTS.
AN ALSATIAN, THEN. DID YOU ENLIST VOLUNTARILY?
GROB?

NO. NO, HERR OBERFÜHRER.

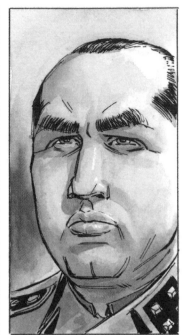

WHAT DID YOU DO IN ALSACE, GROB? WERE YOU A SOCCER PLAYER?

NO, I WORKED IN A FACTORY.

OH COME NOW, YOU DON'T LEARN TO PLAY SOCCER LIKE YOU DO IN A FACTORY.

YES, YES, HERR OBERFÜHRER. I LEARNED TO PLAY WITH MY BUDDIES AT THE FACTORY.

AND DID YOU PULL FOR A TEAM? I MEAN A REAL SOCCER TEAM?

ABSOLUTELY. I PULL FOR RACING CLUB OF STRASBOURG.

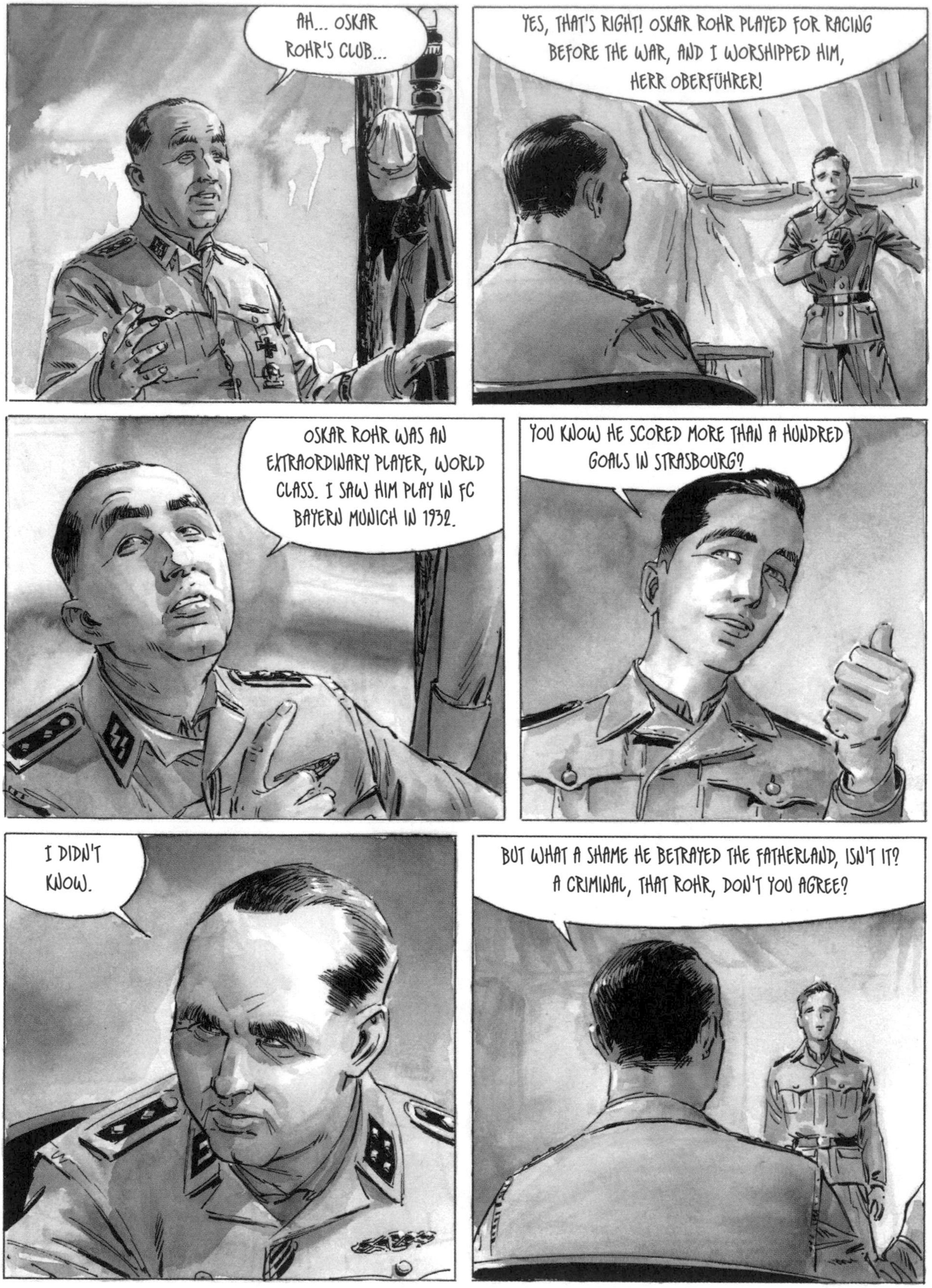
AH... OSKAR ROHR'S CLUB...
YES, THAT'S RIGHT! OSKAR ROHR PLAYED FOR RACING BEFORE THE WAR, AND I WORSHIPPED HIM, HERR OBERFÜHRER!
OSKAR ROHR WAS AN EXTRAORDINARY PLAYER, WORLD CLASS. I SAW HIM PLAY IN FC BAYERN MUNICH IN 1932.
YOU KNOW HE SCORED MORE THAN A HUNDRED GOALS IN STRASBOURG?
I DIDN'T KNOW.
BUT WHAT A SHAME HE BETRAYED THE FATHERLAND, ISN'T IT? A CRIMINAL, THAT ROHR, DON'T YOU AGREE?

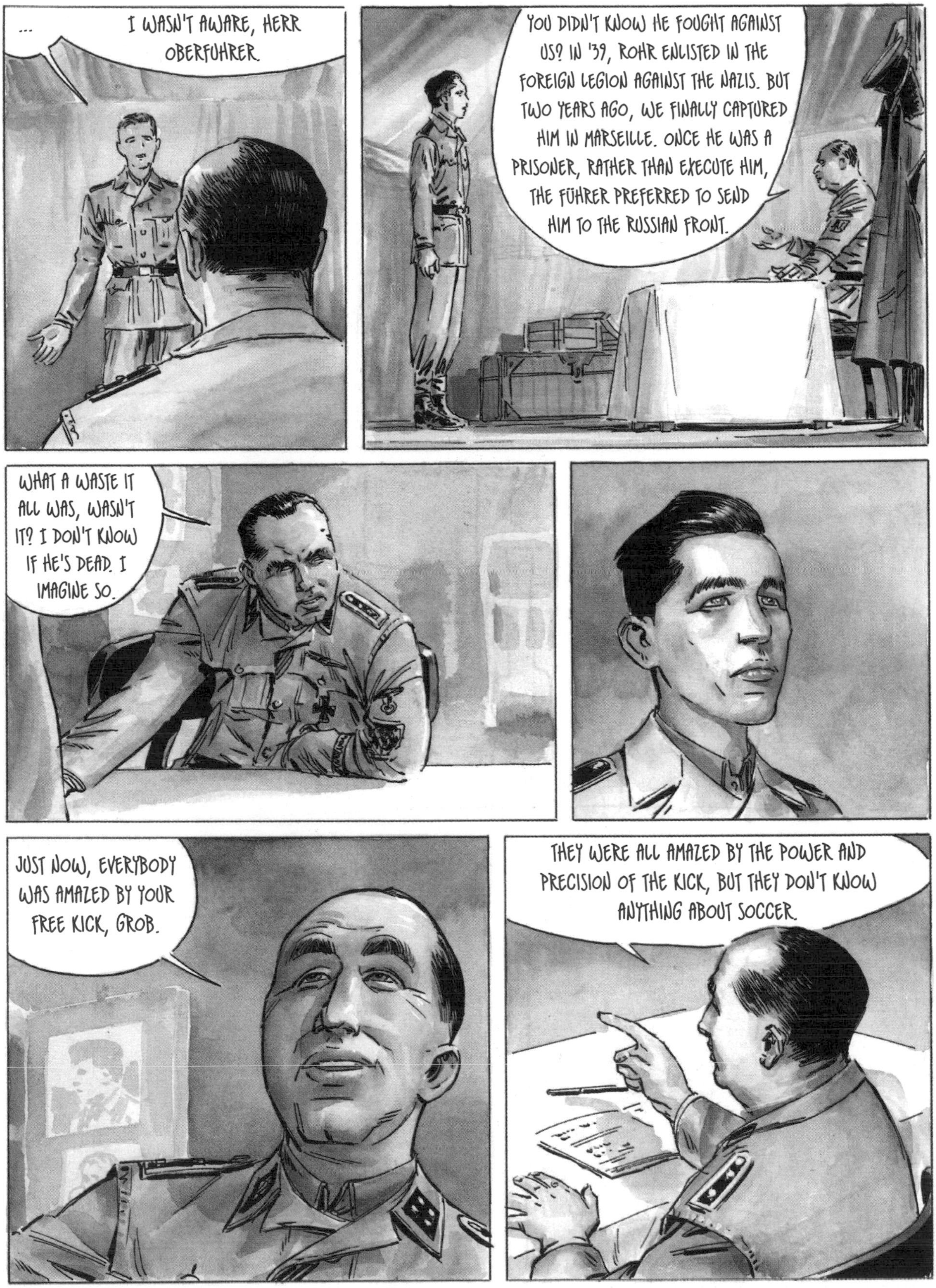
... I WASN'T AWARE, HERR OBERFUHRER.
YOU DIDN'T KNOW HE FOUGHT AGAINST US? IN '39, ROHR ENLISTED IN THE FOREIGN LEGION AGAINST THE NAZIS. BUT TWO YEARS AGO, WE FINALLY CAPTURED HIM IN MARSEILLE. ONCE HE WAS A PRISONER, RATHER THAN EXECUTE HIM, THE FÜHRER PREFERRED TO SEND HIM TO THE RUSSIAN FRONT.
WHAT A WASTE IT ALL WAS, WASN'T IT? I DON'T KNOW IF HE'S DEAD. I IMAGINE SO.
JUST NOW, EVERYBODY WAS AMAZED BY YOUR FREE KICK, GROB.
THEY WERE ALL AMAZED BY THE POWER AND PRECISION OF THE KICK, BUT THEY DON'T KNOW ANYTHING ABOUT SOCCER.

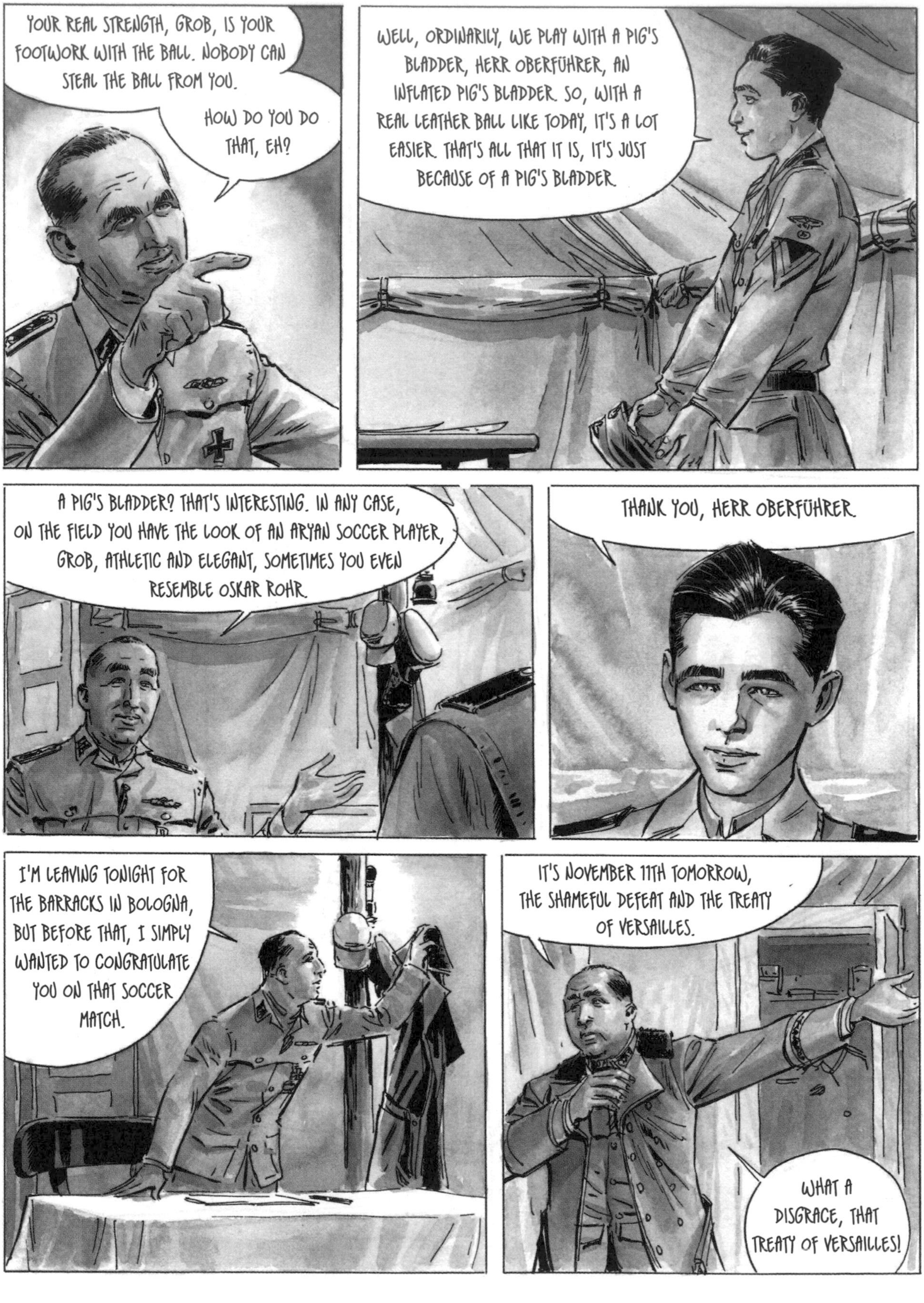
YOUR REAL STRENGTH, GROB, IS YOUR FOOTWORK WITH THE BALL. NOBODY CAN STEAL THE BALL FROM YOU.
HOW DO YOU DO THAT, EH?
WELL, ORDINARILY, WE PLAY WITH A PIG'S BLADDER, HERR OBERFÜHRER, AN INFLATED PIG'S BLADDER. SO, WITH A REAL LEATHER BALL LIKE TODAY, IT'S A LOT EASIER. THAT'S ALL THAT IT IS, IT'S JUST BECAUSE OF A PIG'S BLADDER.
A PIG'S BLADDER? THAT'S INTERESTING. IN ANY CASE, ON THE FIELD YOU HAVE THE LOOK OF AN ARYAN SOCCER PLAYER, GROB, ATHLETIC AND ELEGANT, SOMETIMES YOU EVEN RESEMBLE OSKAR ROHR.
THANK YOU, HERR OBERFÜHRER.
I'M LEAVING TONIGHT FOR THE BARRACKS IN BOLOGNA, BUT BEFORE THAT, I SIMPLY WANTED TO CONGRATULATE YOU ON THAT SOCCER MATCH.
IT'S NOVEMBER 11TH TOMORROW, THE SHAMEFUL DEFEAT AND THE TREATY OF VERSAILLES.
WHAT A DISGRACE, THAT TREATY OF VERSAILLES!

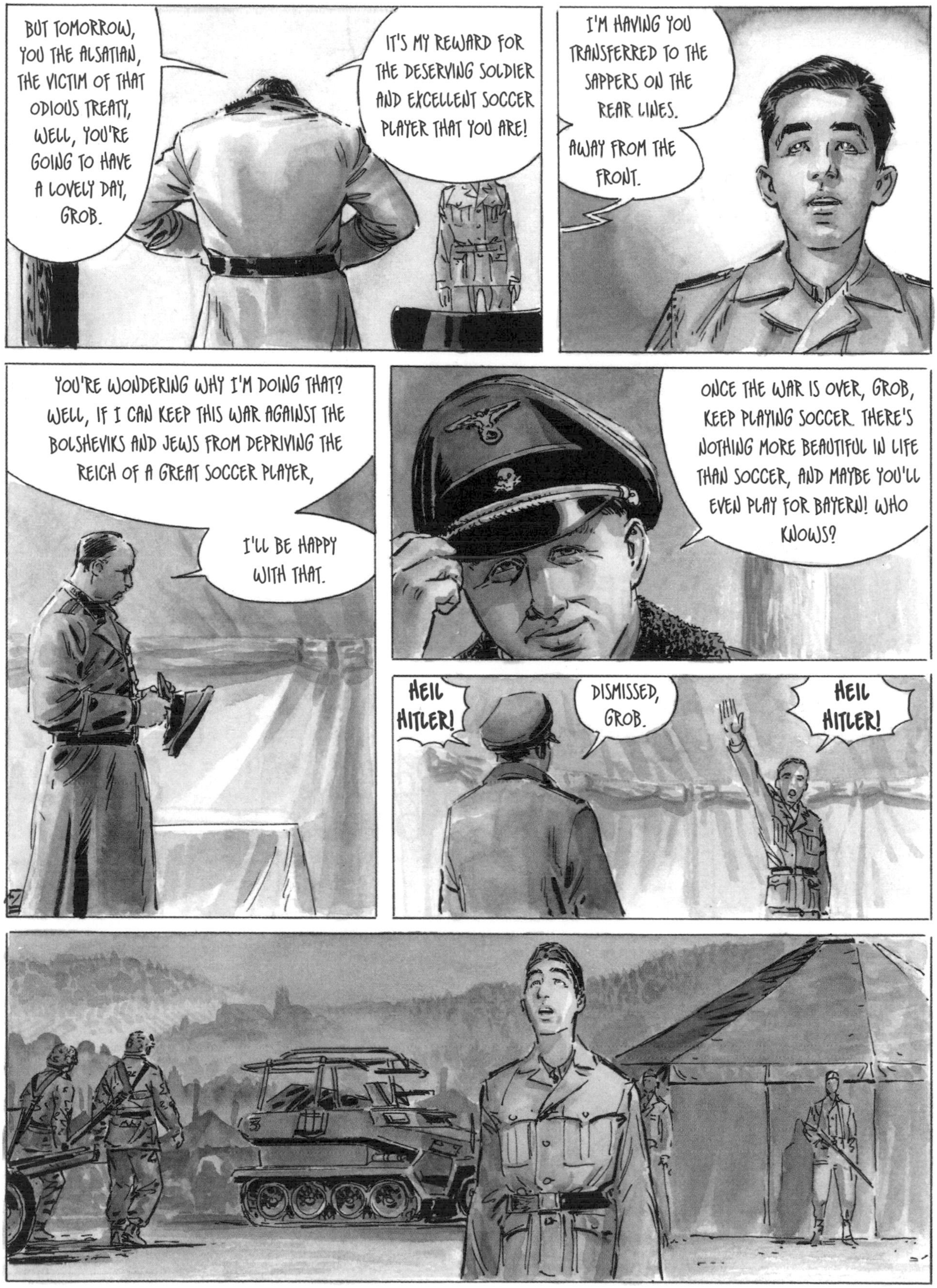
BUT TOMORROW, YOU THE ALSATIAN, THE VICTIM OF THAT ODIOUS TREATY, WELL, YOU'RE GOING TO HAVE A LOVELY DAY, GROB.
IT'S MY REWARD FOR THE DESERVING SOLDIER AND EXCELLENT SOCCER PLAYER THAT YOU ARE!
I'M HAVING YOU TRANSFERRED TO THE SAPPERS ON THE REAR LINES.
AWAY FROM THE FRONT.
YOU'RE WONDERING WHY I'M DOING THAT? WELL, IF I CAN KEEP THIS WAR AGAINST THE BOLSHEVIKS AND JEWS FROM DEPRIVING THE REICH OF A GREAT SOCCER PLAYER,
I'LL BE HAPPY WITH THAT.
ONCE THE WAR IS OVER, GROB, KEEP PLAYING SOCCER. THERE'S NOTHING MORE BEAUTIFUL IN LIFE THAN SOCCER, AND MAYBE YOU'LL EVEN PLAY FOR BAYERN! WHO KNOWS?
HEIL HITLER!
DISMISSED, GROB.
HEIL HITLER!

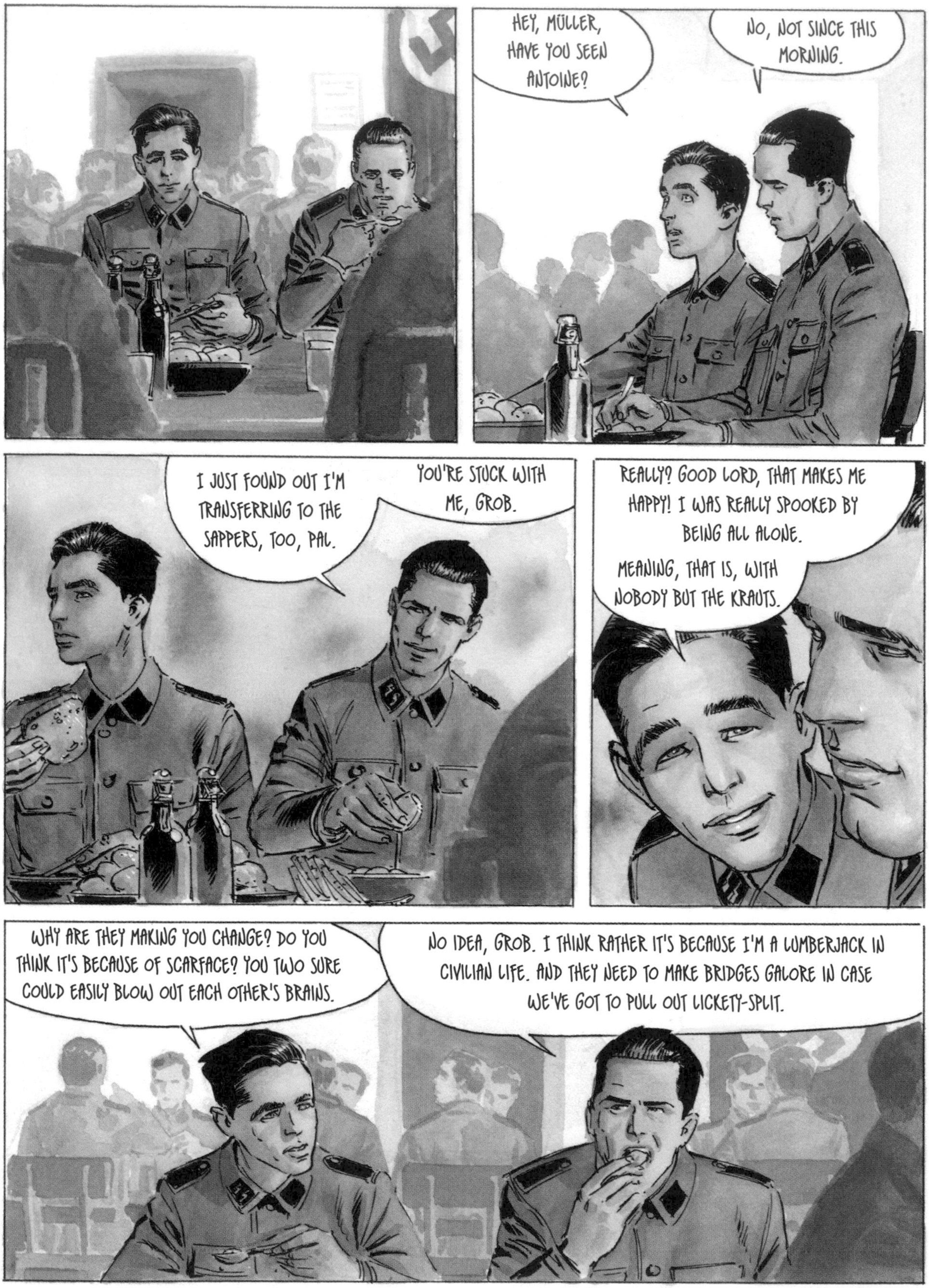
HEY, MÜLLER, HAVE YOU SEEN ANTOINE?
NO, NOT SINCE THIS MORNING.
I JUST FOUND OUT I'M TRANSFERRING TO THE SAPPERS, TOO, PAL.
YOU'RE STUCK WITH ME, GROB.
REALLY? GOOD LORD, THAT MAKES ME HAPPY! I WAS REALLY SPOOKED BY BEING ALL ALONE.
MEANING, THAT IS, WITH NOBODY BUT THE KRAUTS.
WHY ARE THEY MAKING YOU CHANGE? DO YOU THINK IT'S BECAUSE OF SCARFACE? YOU TWO SURE COULD EASILY BLOW OUT EACH OTHER'S BRAINS.
NO IDEA, GROB. I THINK RATHER IT'S BECAUSE I'M A LUMBERJACK IN CIVILIAN LIFE. AND THEY NEED TO MAKE BRIDGES GALORE IN CASE WE'VE GOT TO PULL OUT LICKETY-SPLIT.

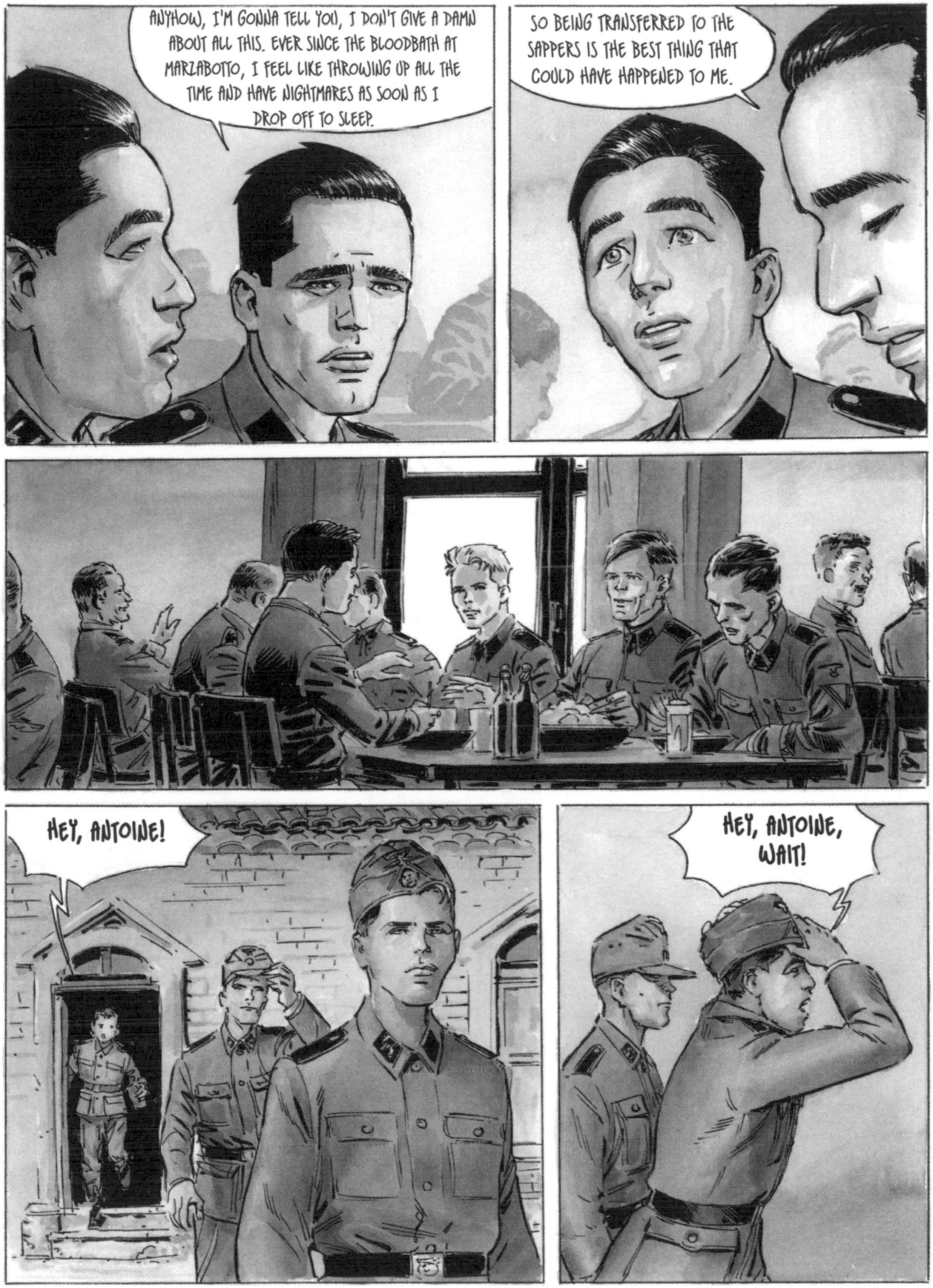
ANYHOW, I'M GONNA TELL YOU, I DON'T GIVE A DAMN ABOUT ALL THIS. EVER SINCE THE BLOODBATH AT MARZABOTTO, I FEEL LIKE THROWING UP ALL THE TIME AND HAVE NIGHTMARES AS SOON AS I DROP OFF TO SLEEP.
SO BEING TRANSFERRED TO THE SAPPERS IS THE BEST THING THAT COULD HAVE HAPPENED TO ME.
HEY, ANTOINE!
HEY, ANTOINE, WAIT!

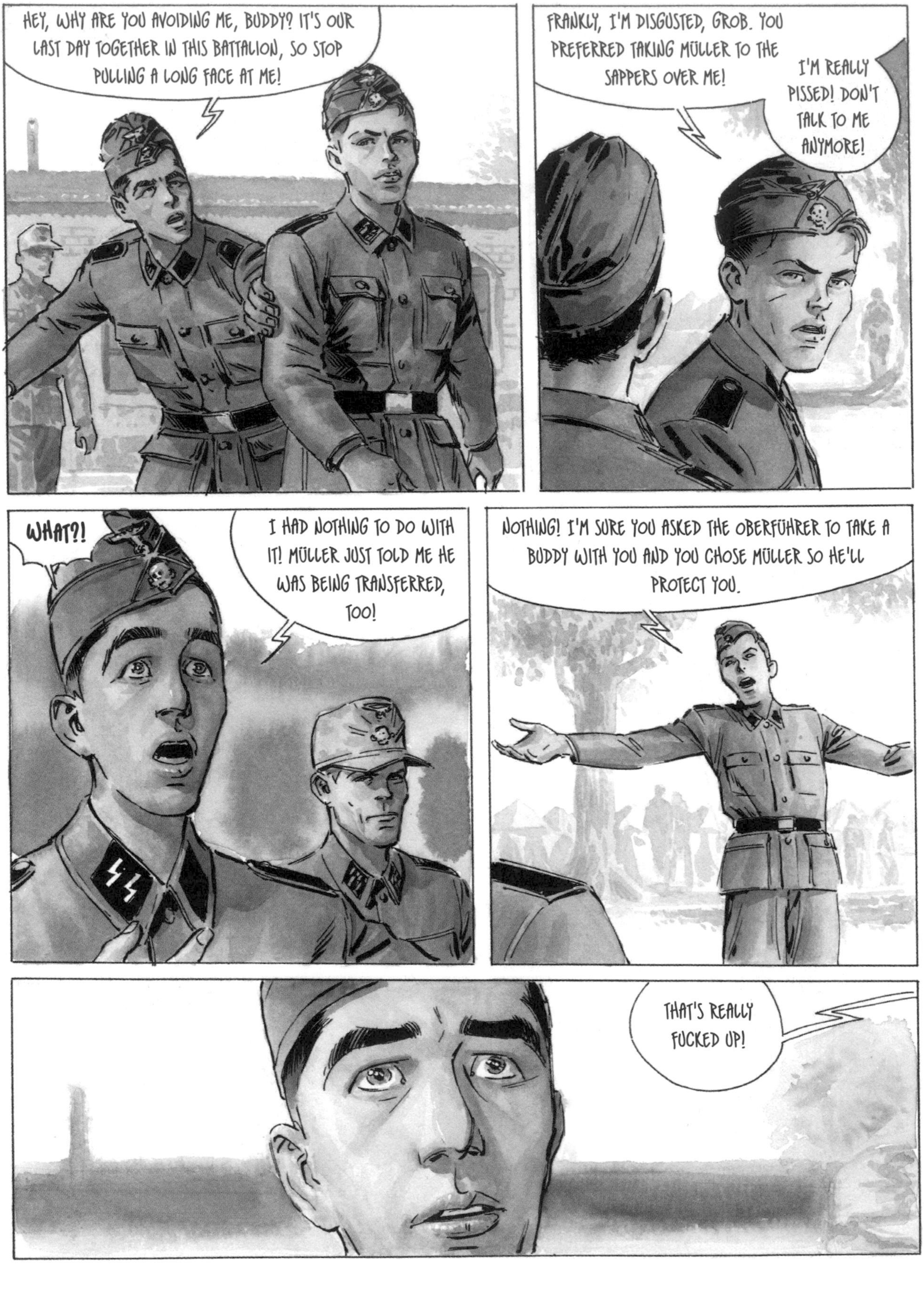
HEY, WHY ARE YOU AVOIDING ME, BUDDY? IT'S OUR LAST DAY TOGETHER IN THIS BATTALION, SO STOP PULLING A LONG FACE AT ME!
FRANKLY, I'M DISGUSTED, GROB. YOU PREFERRED TAKING MÜLLER TO THE SAPPERS OVER ME!
I'M REALLY PISSED! DON'T TALK TO ME ANYMORE!
WHAT?!
I HAD NOTHING TO DO WITH IT! MÜLLER JUST TOLD ME HE WAS BEING TRANSFERRED, TOO!
NOTHING! I'M SURE YOU ASKED THE OBERFÜHRER TO TAKE A BUDDY WITH YOU AND YOU CHOSE MÜLLER SO HE'LL PROTECT YOU.
THAT'S REALLY FUCKED UP!

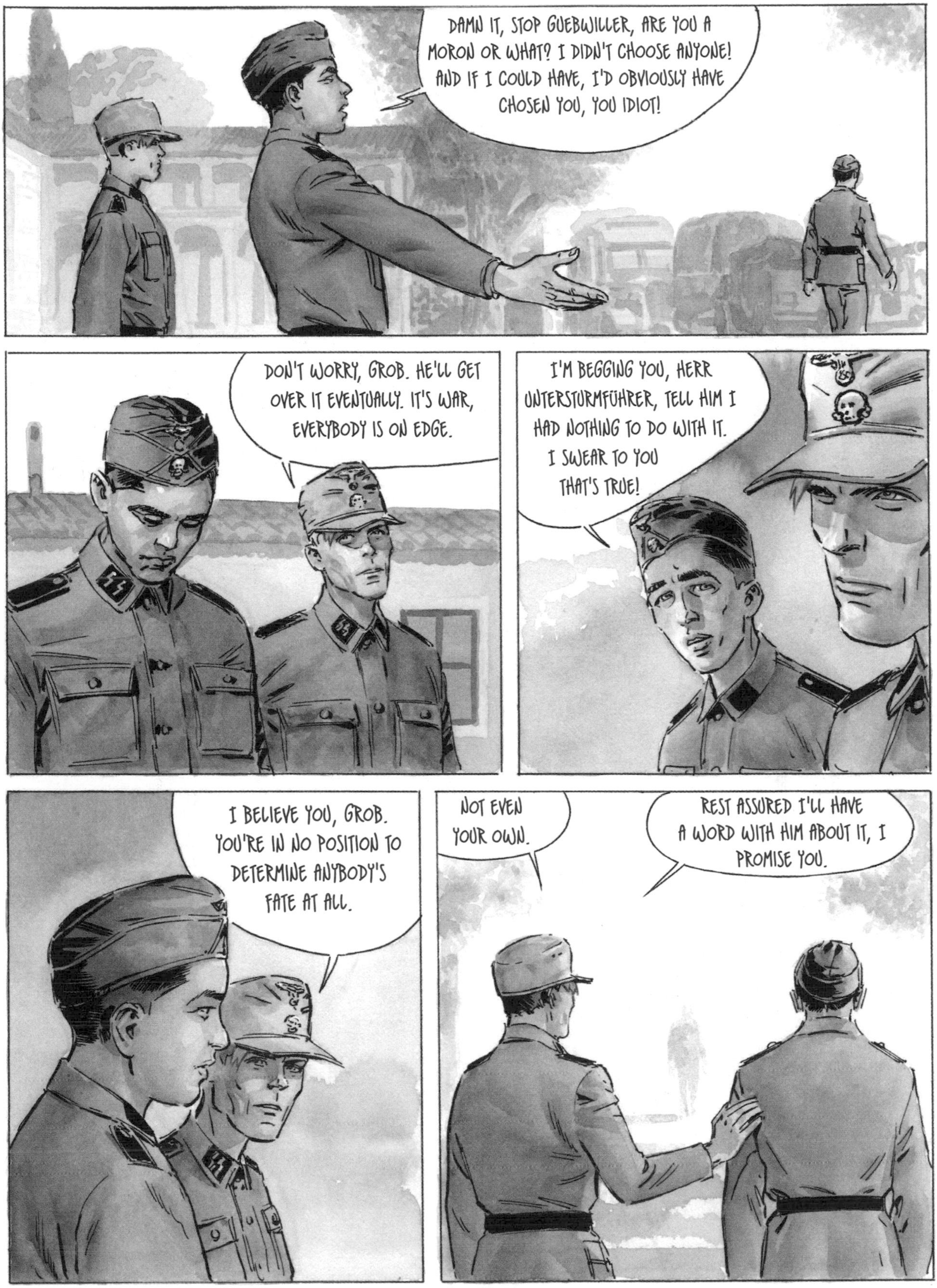
DAMN IT, STOP GUEBWILLER, ARE YOU A MORON OR WHAT? I DIDN'T CHOOSE ANYONE! AND IF I COULD HAVE, I'D OBVIOUSLY HAVE CHOSEN YOU, YOU IDIOT!
DON'T WORRY, GROB. HE'LL GET OVER IT EVENTUALLY. IT'S WAR, EVERYBODY IS ON EDGE.
I'M BEGGING YOU, HERR UNTERSTURMFÜHRER, TELL HIM I HAD NOTHING TO DO WITH IT. I SWEAR TO YOU THAT'S TRUE!
I BELIEVE YOU, GROB. YOU'RE IN NO POSITION TO DETERMINE ANYBODY'S FATE AT ALL.
NOT EVEN YOUR OWN.
REST ASSURED I'LL HAVE A WORD WITH HIM ABOUT IT, I PROMISE YOU.

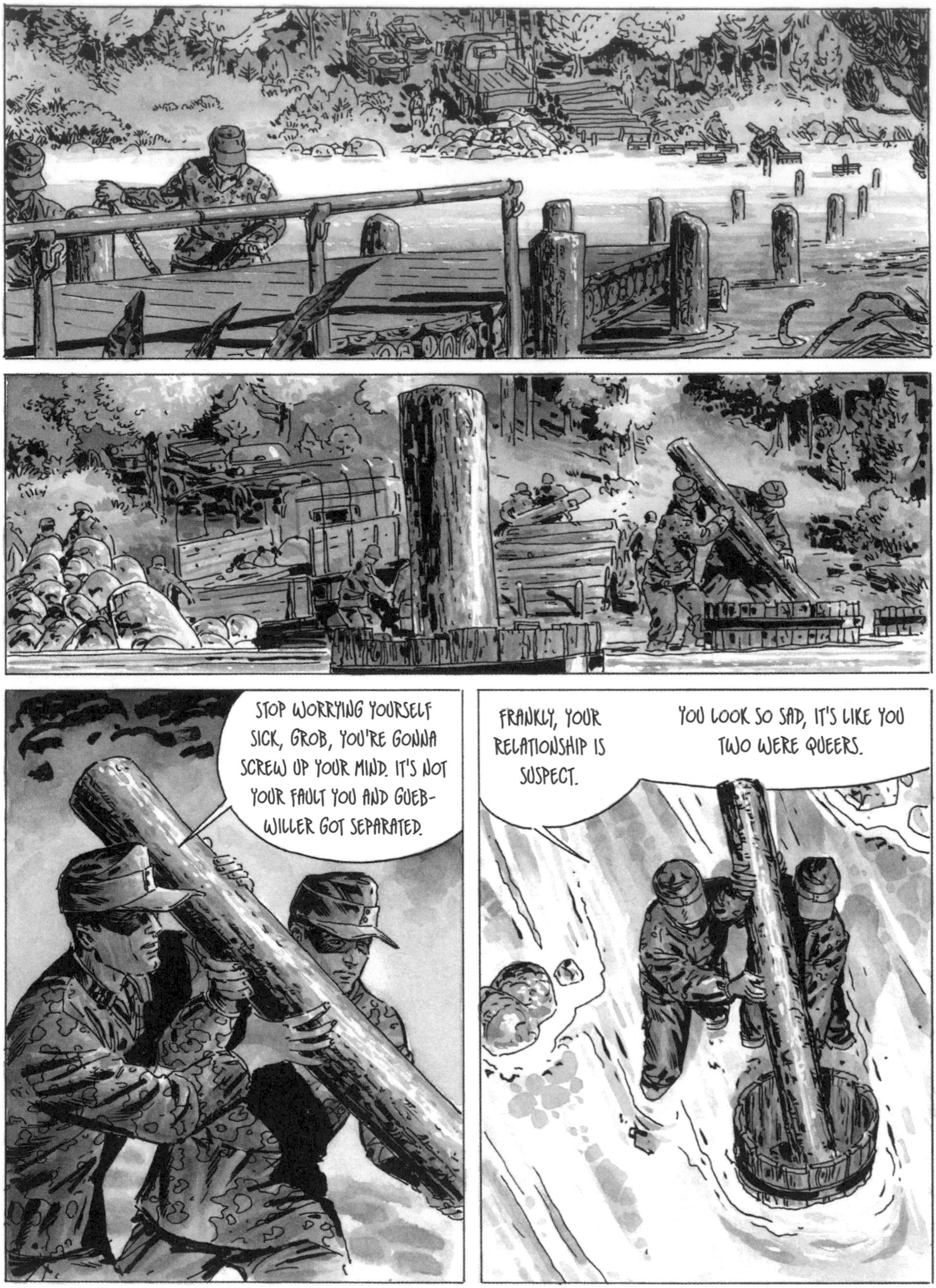
STOP WORRYING YOURSELF SICK, GROB, YOU'RE GONNA SCREW UP YOUR MIND. IT'S NOT YOUR FAULT YOU AND GUEB-WILLER GOT SEPARATED.
FRANKLY, YOUR RELATIONSHIP IS SUSPECT.
YOU LOOK SO SAD, IT'S LIKE YOU TWO WERE QUEERS.

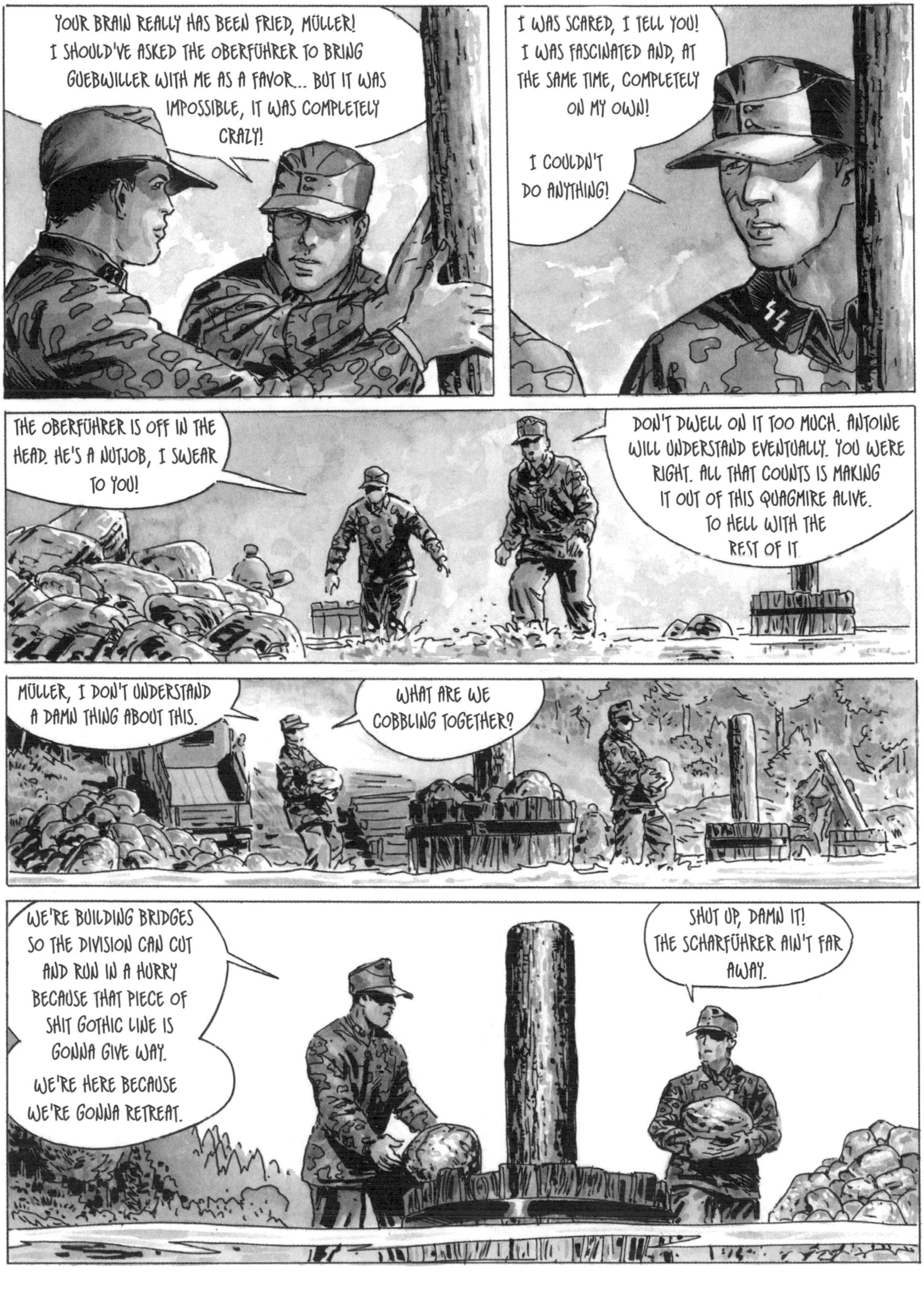
YOUR BRAIN REALLY HAS BEEN FRIED, MÜLLER! I SHOULD'VE ASKED THE OBERFÜHRER TO BRING GUEBWILLER WITH ME AS A FAVOR... BUT IT WAS IMPOSSIBLE, IT WAS COMPLETELY CRAZY!
I WAS SCARED, I TELL YOU! I WAS FASCINATED AND, AT THE SAME TIME, COMPLETELY ON MY OWN!
I COULDN'T DO ANYTHING!
THE OBERFÜHRER IS OFF IN THE HEAD. HE'S A NUTJOB, I SWEAR TO YOU!
DON'T DWELL ON IT TOO MUCH. ANTOINE WILL UNDERSTAND EVENTUALLY. YOU WERE RIGHT. ALL THAT COUNTS IS MAKING IT OUT OF THIS QUAGMIRE ALIVE. TO HELL WITH THE REST OF IT.
MÜLLER, I DON'T UNDERSTAND A DAMN THING ABOUT THIS.
WHAT ARE WE COBBLING TOGETHER?
WE'RE BUILDING BRIDGES SO THE DIVISION CAN CUT AND RUN IN A HURRY BECAUSE THAT PIECE OF SHIT GOTHIC LINE IS GONNA GIVE WAY.
WE'RE HERE BECAUSE WE'RE GONNA RETREAT.
SHUT UP, DAMN IT! THE SCHARFÜHRER AIN'T FAR AWAY.

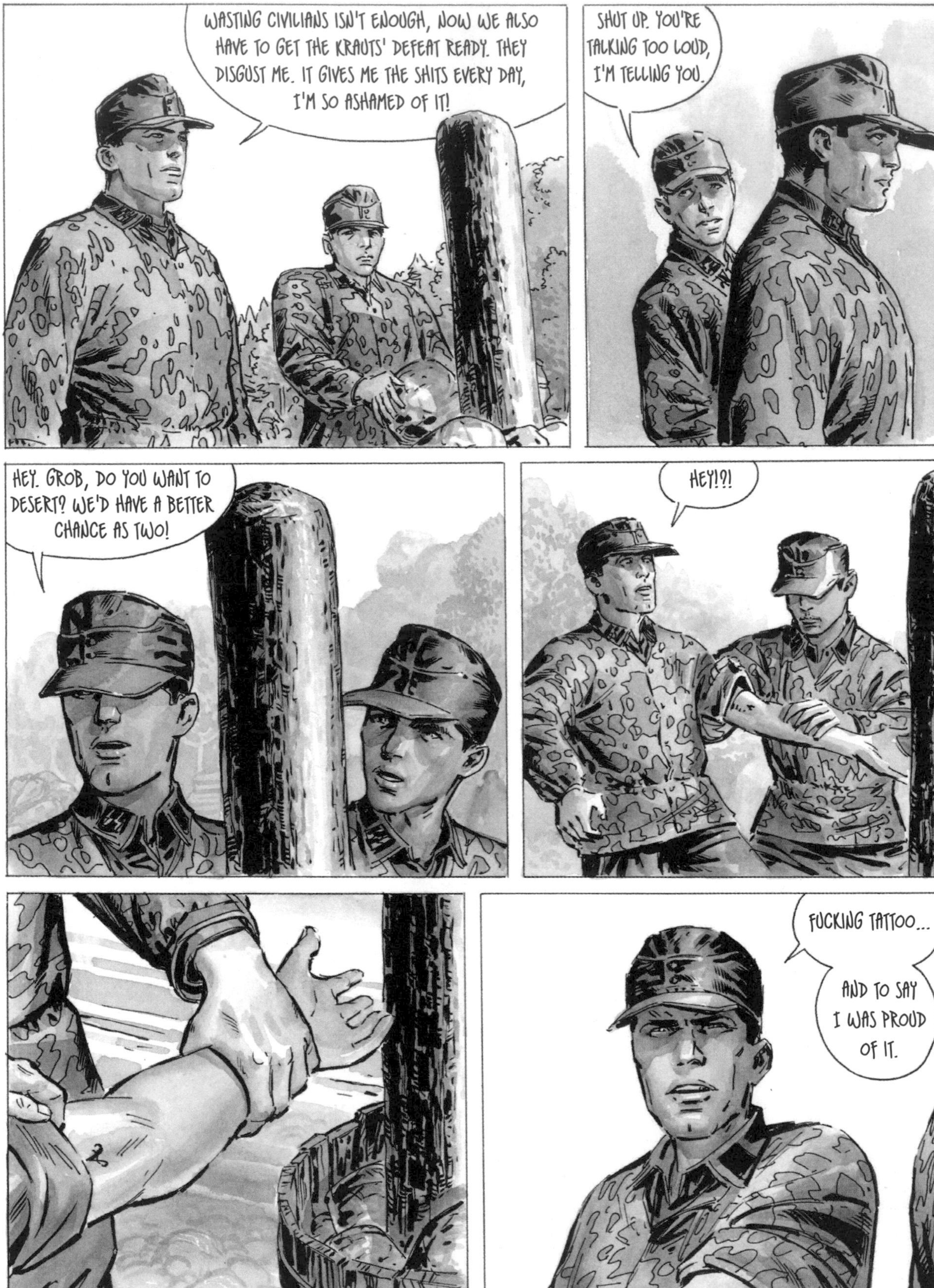
WASTING CIVILIANS ISN'T ENOUGH, NOW WE ALSO HAVE TO GET THE KRAUTS' DEFEAT READY. THEY DISGUST ME. IT GIVES ME THE SHITS EVERY DAY, I'M SO ASHAMED OF IT!
SHUT UP. YOU'RE TALKING TOO LOUD, I'M TELLING YOU.
HEY. GROB, DO YOU WANT TO DESERT? WE'D HAVE A BETTER CHANCE AS TWO!
HEY!?!
FUCKING TATTOO...
AND TO SAY I WAS PROUD OF IT.

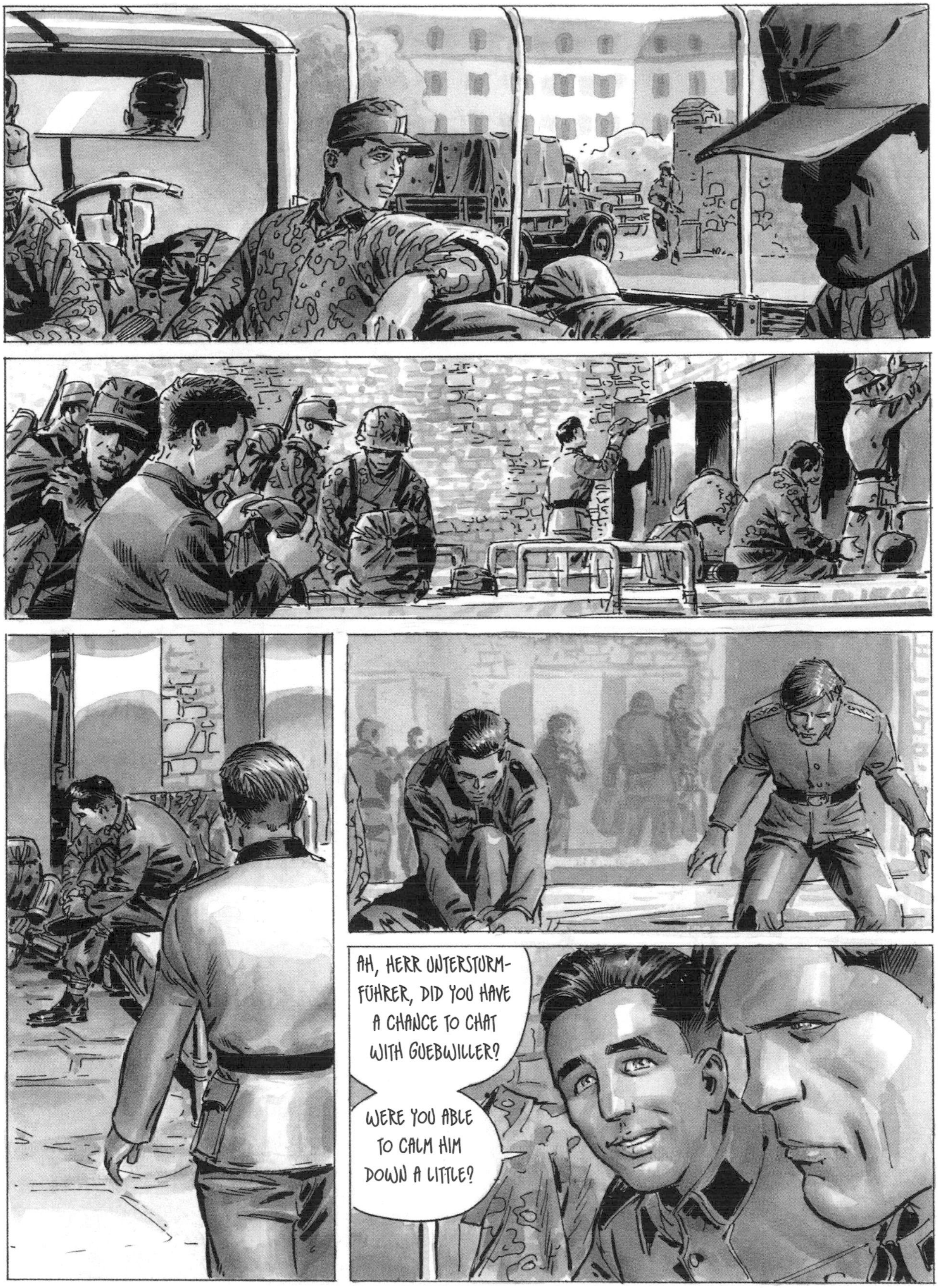
AH, HERR UNTERSTURM-FÜHRER, DID YOU HAVE A CHANCE TO CHAT WITH GUEBWILLER?
WERE YOU ABLE TO CALM HIM DOWN A LITTLE?

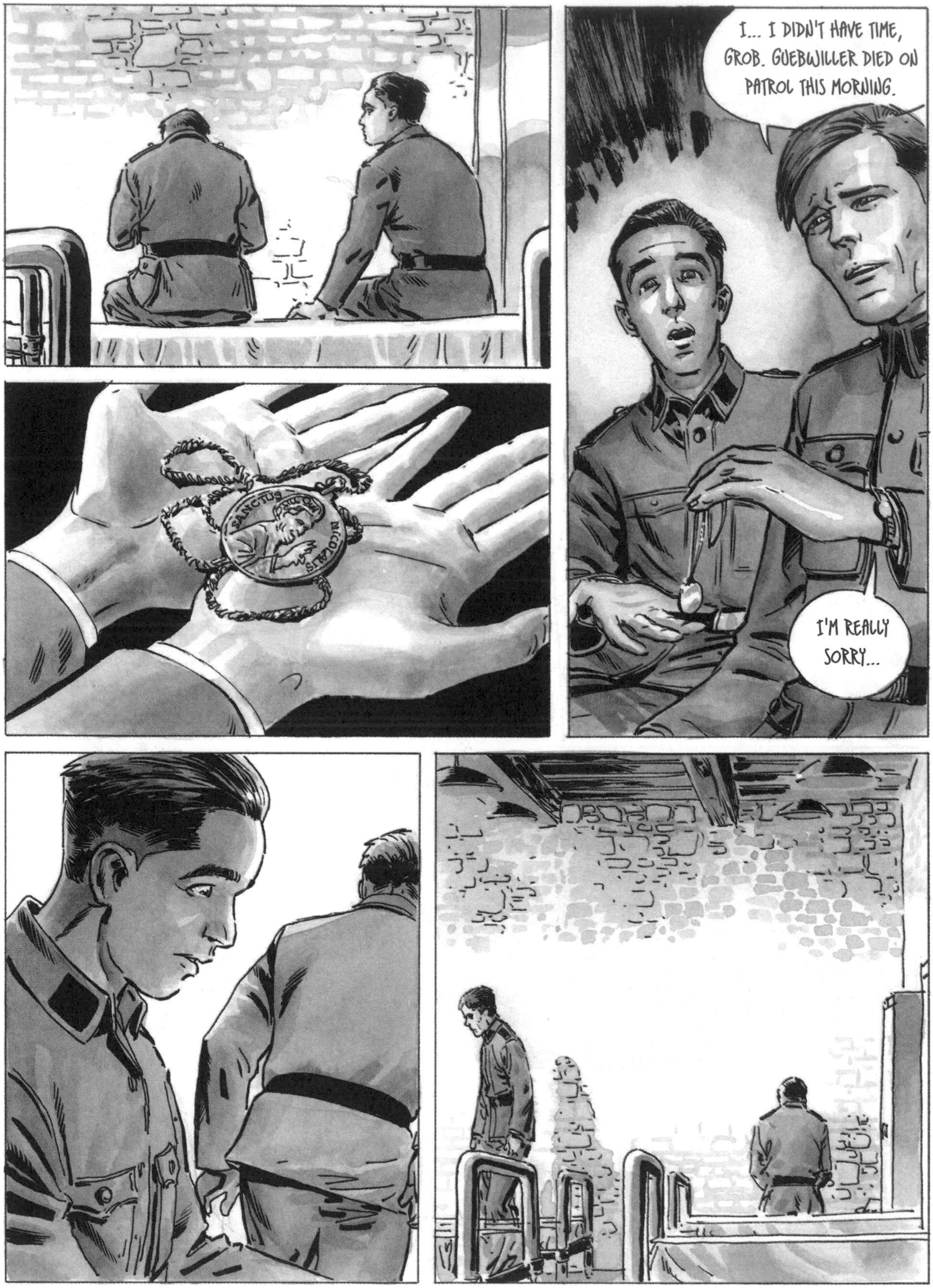
I... I DIDN'T HAVE TIME, GROB. GUEBWILLER DIED ON PATROL THIS MORNING.
SANCTUS NICOLAUS
I'M REALLY SORRY...

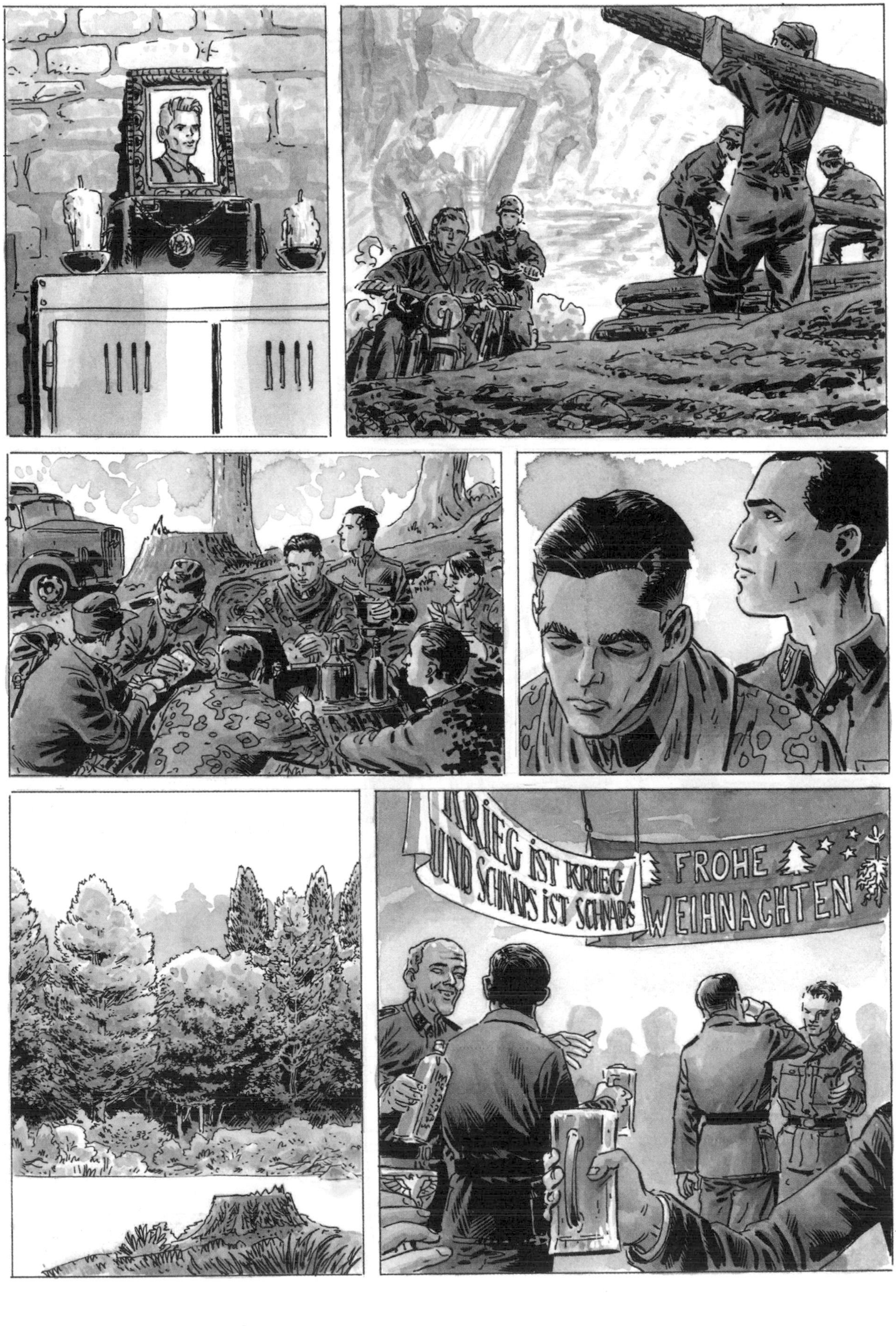
RIEG IST KRIEG
UND SCHNAPS IST SCHNAPS
FROHE WEIHNACHTEN

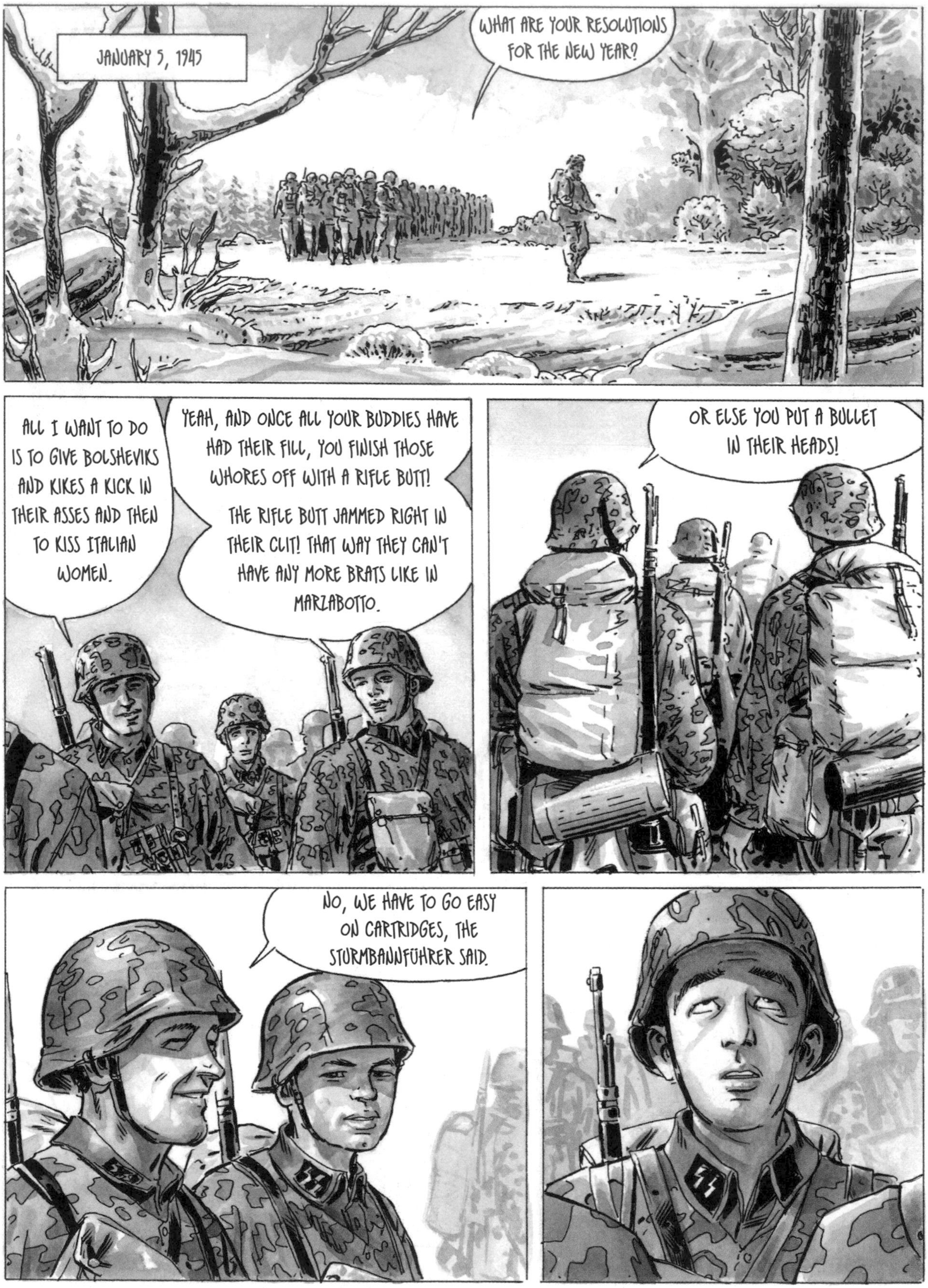
JANUARY 5, 1945
WHAT ARE YOUR RESOLUTIONS FOR THE NEW YEAR?
ALL I WANT TO DO IS TO GIVE BOLSHEVIKS AND KIKES A KICK IN THEIR ASSES AND THEN TO KISS ITALIAN WOMEN.
YEAH, AND ONCE ALL YOUR BUDDIES HAVE HAD THEIR FILL, YOU FINISH THOSE WHORES OFF WITH A RIFLE BUTT!
THE RIFLE BUTT JAMMED RIGHT IN THEIR CLIT! THAT WAY THEY CAN'T HAVE ANY MORE BRATS LIKE IN MARZABOTTO.
OR ELSE YOU PUT A BULLET IN THEIR HEADS!
NO, WE HAVE TO GO EASY ON CARTRIDGES, THE STURMBANNFÜHRER SAID.

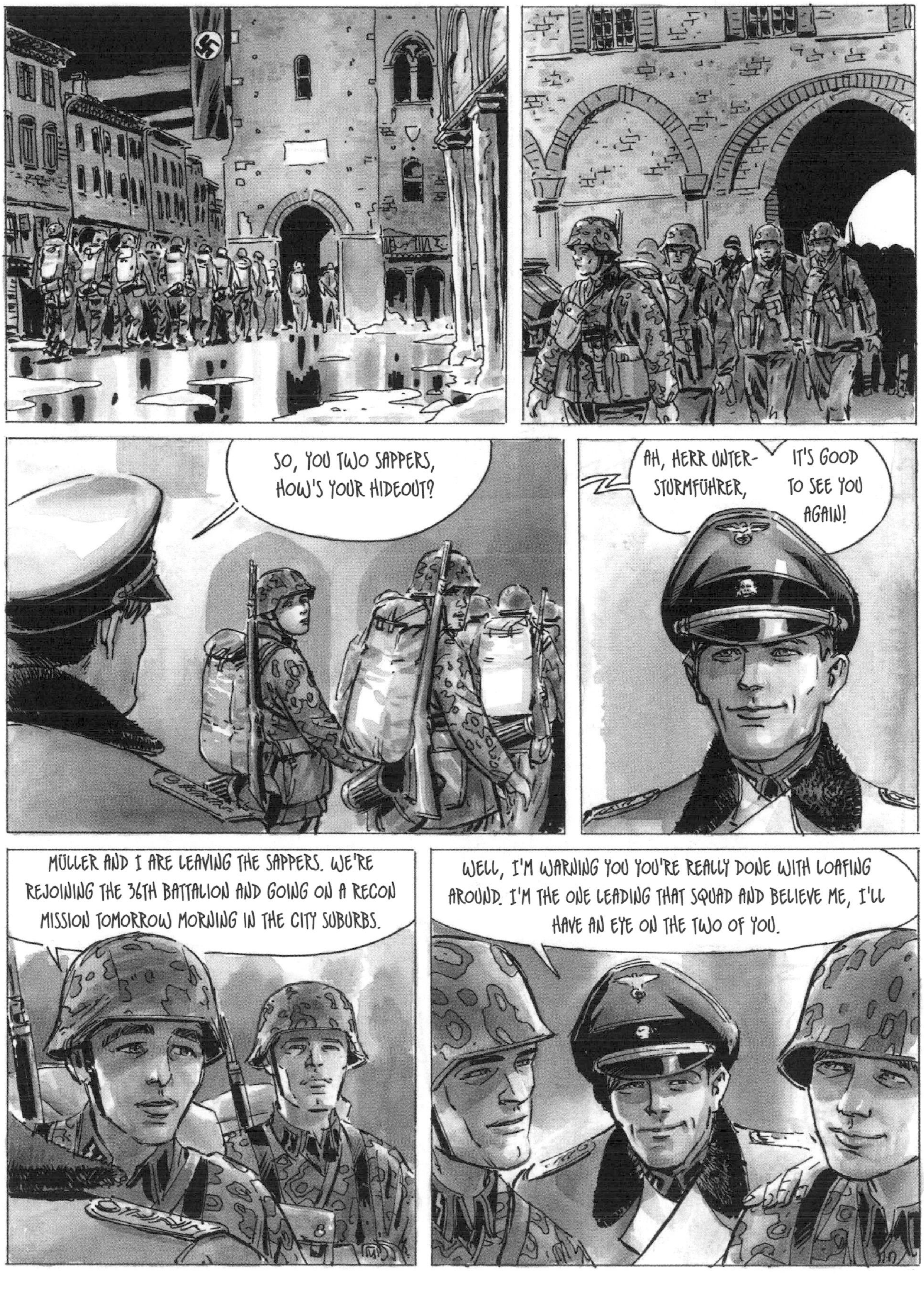

SO, YOU TWO SAPPERS, HOW'S YOUR HIDEOUT?
AH, HERR UNTER-STURMFÜHRER,
IT'S GOOD TO SEE YOU AGAIN!
MÜLLER AND I ARE LEAVING THE SAPPERS. WE'RE REJOINING THE 36TH BATTALION AND GOING ON A RECON MISSION TOMORROW MORNING IN THE CITY SUBURBS.
WELL, I'M WARNING YOU YOU'RE REALLY DONE WITH LOAFING AROUND. I'M THE ONE LEADING THAT SQUAD AND BELIEVE ME, I'LL HAVE AN EYE ON THE TWO OF YOU.

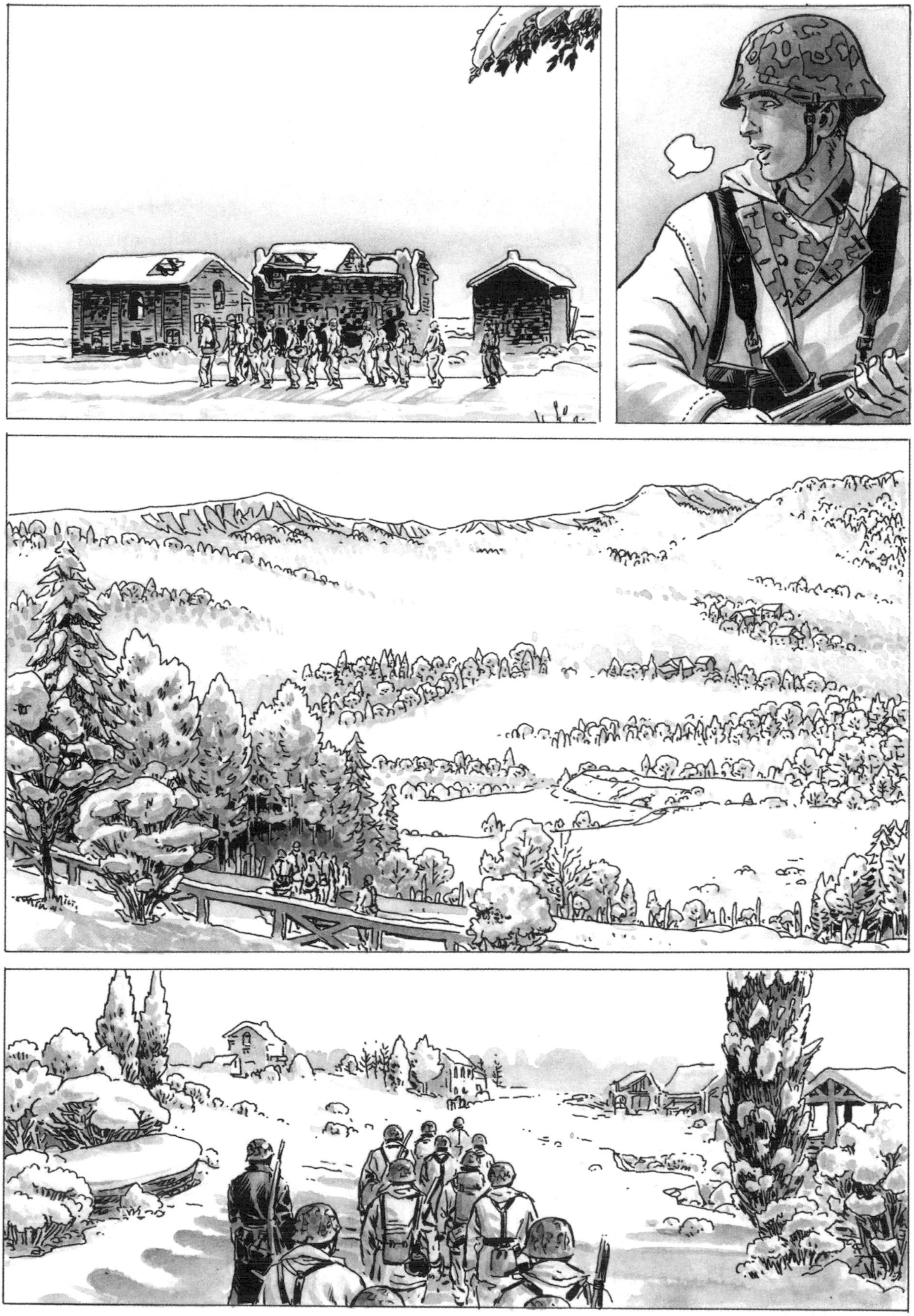

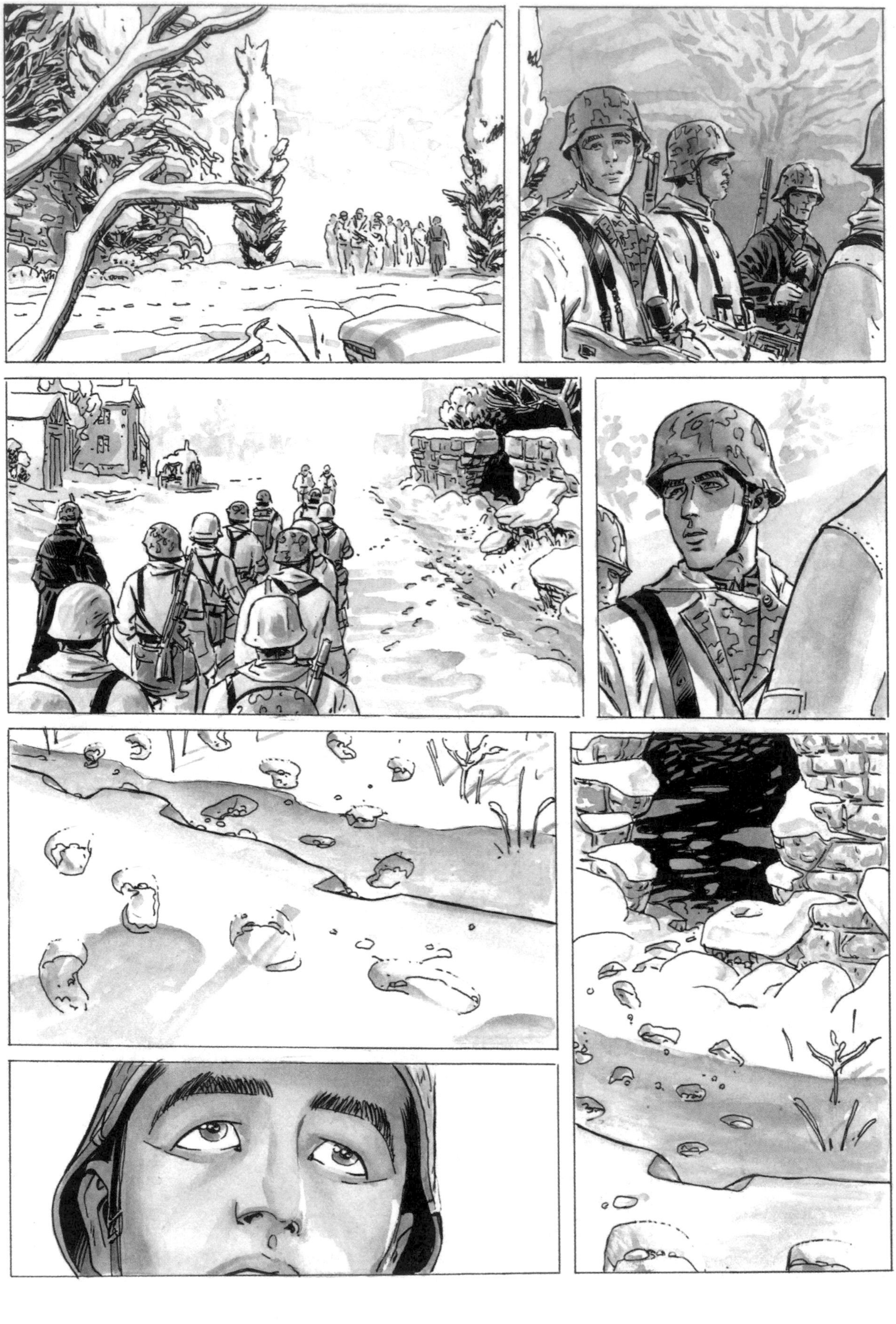

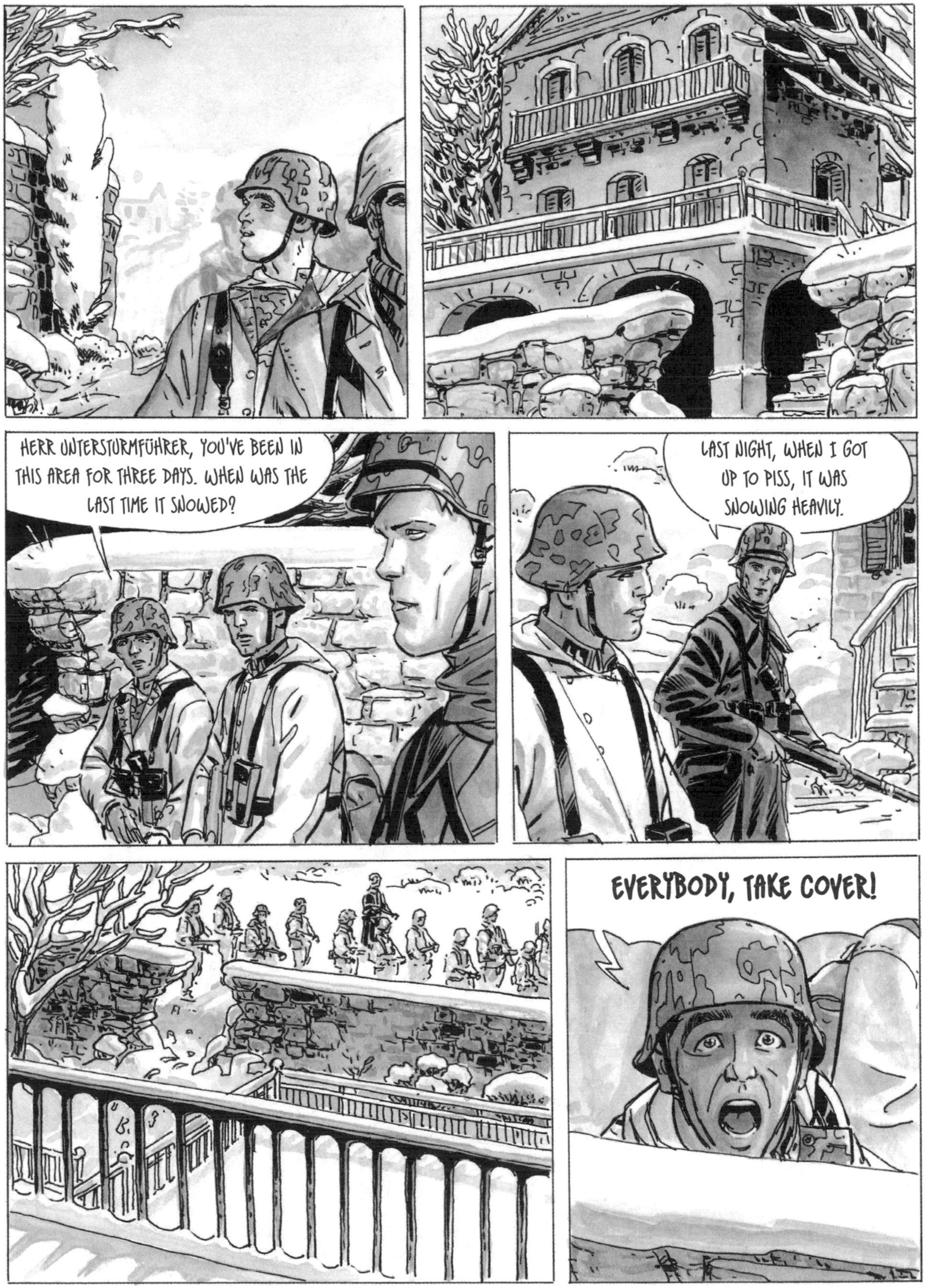
HERR UNTERSTURMFÜHRER, YOU'VE BEEN IN THIS AREA FOR THREE DAYS. WHEN WAS THE LAST TIME IT SNOWED?
LAST NIGHT, WHEN I GOT UP TO PISS, IT WAS SNOWING HEAVILY.
EVERYBODY, TAKE COVER!

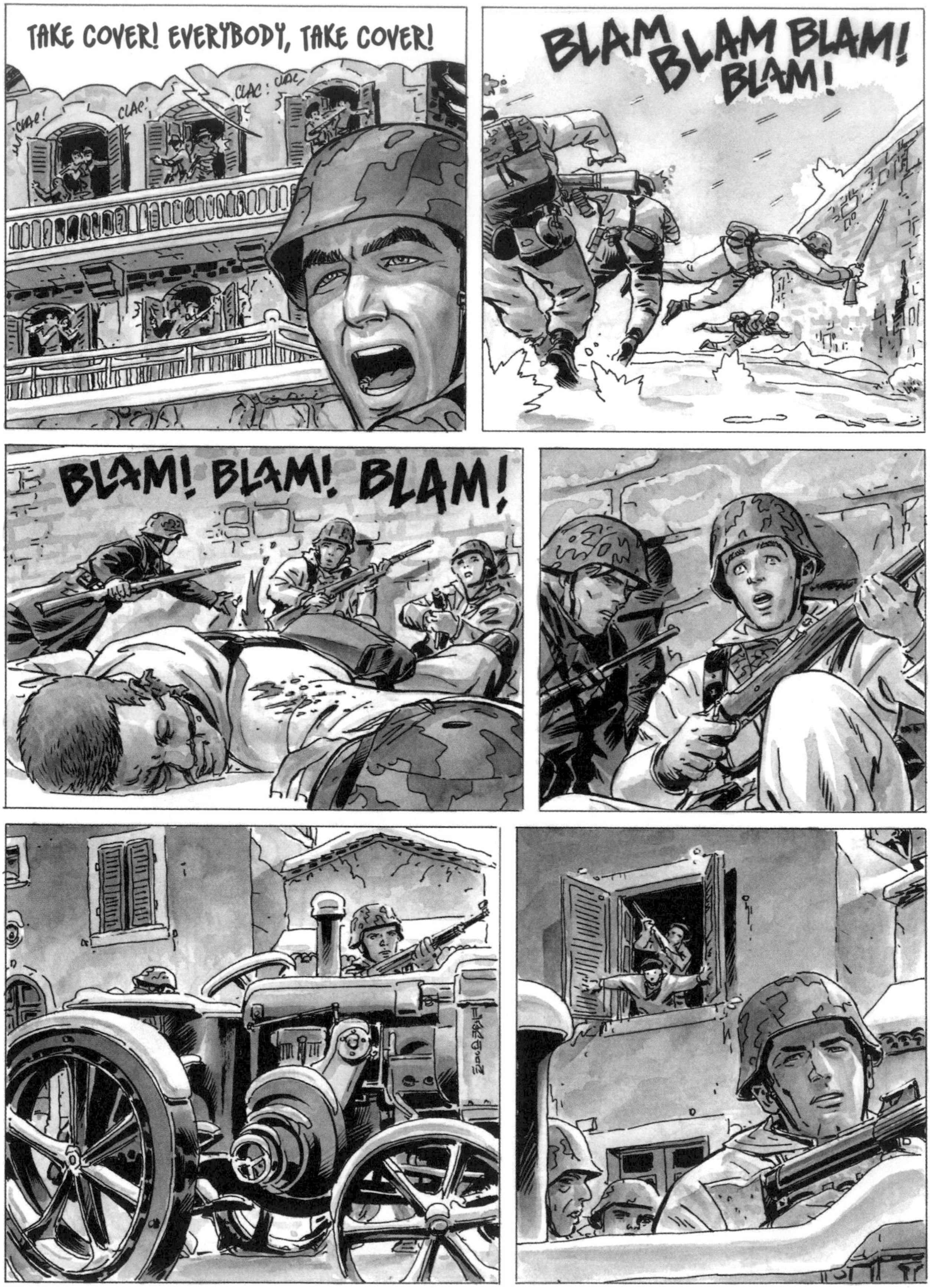
TAKE COVER! EVERYBODY, TAKE COVER!
CLAC!
CLAC!
CLAC!
CLAC!
BLAM BLAM BLAM!
BLAM!
BLAM! BLAM! BLAM!

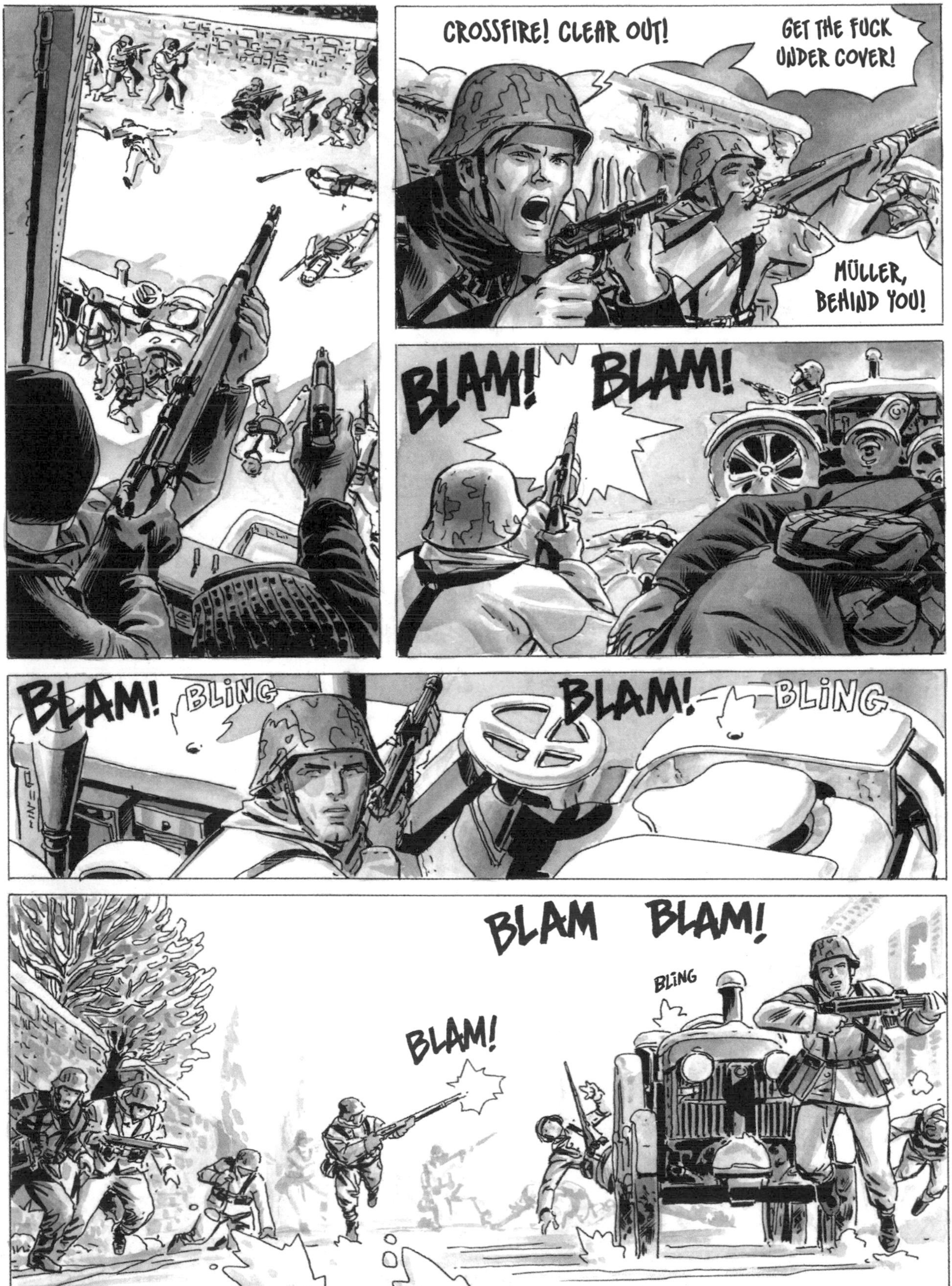
CROSSFIRE! CLEAR OUT!
GET THE FUCK UNDER COVER!
MÜLLER, BEHIND YOU!
BLAM! BLAM!
BLAM! BLING
BLAM! BLING
BLAM BLAM!
BLING
BLAM!

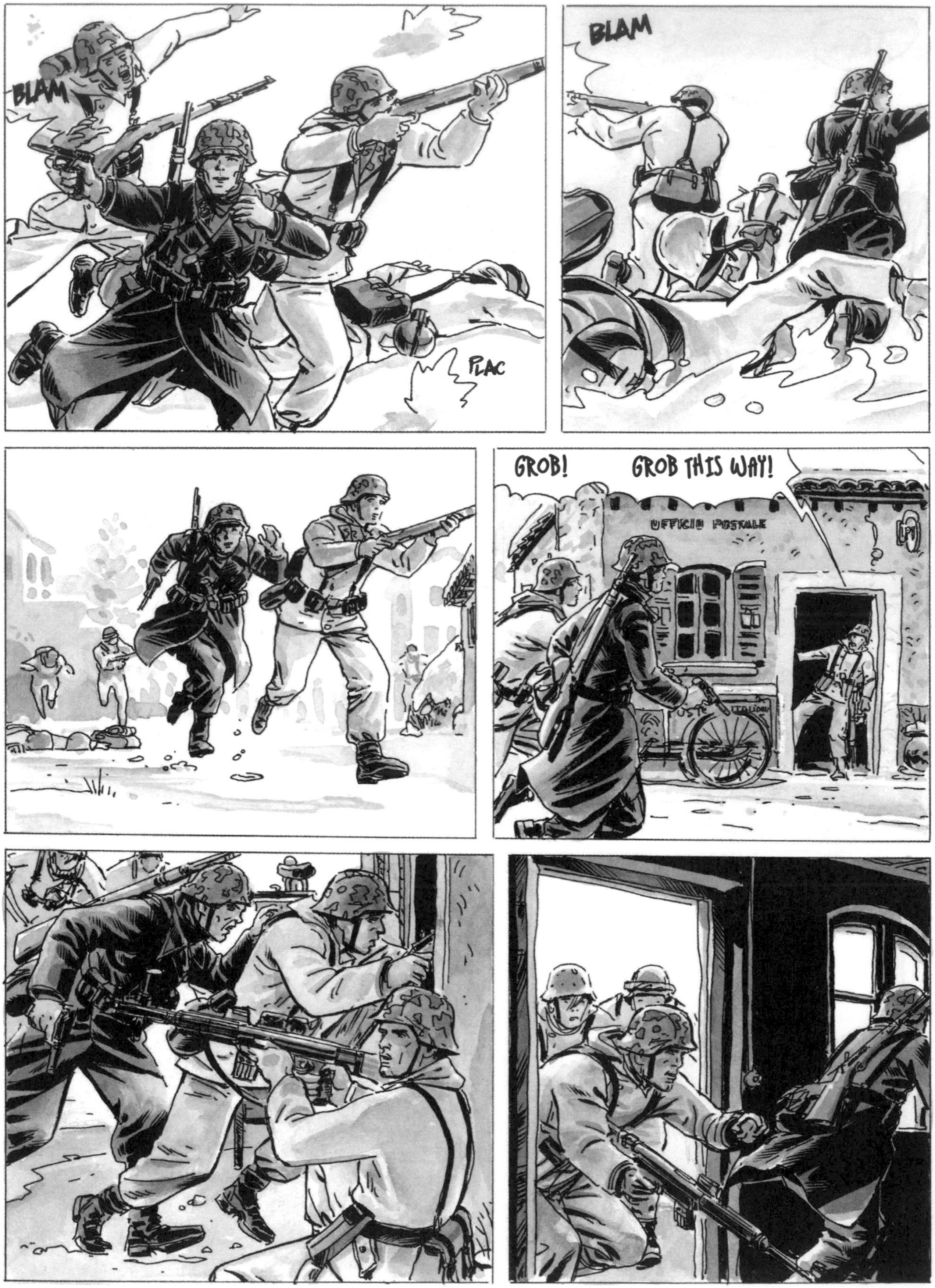
BLAM
PLAC
BLAM
GROB!
GROB THIS WAY!
UFFICIO POSTALE

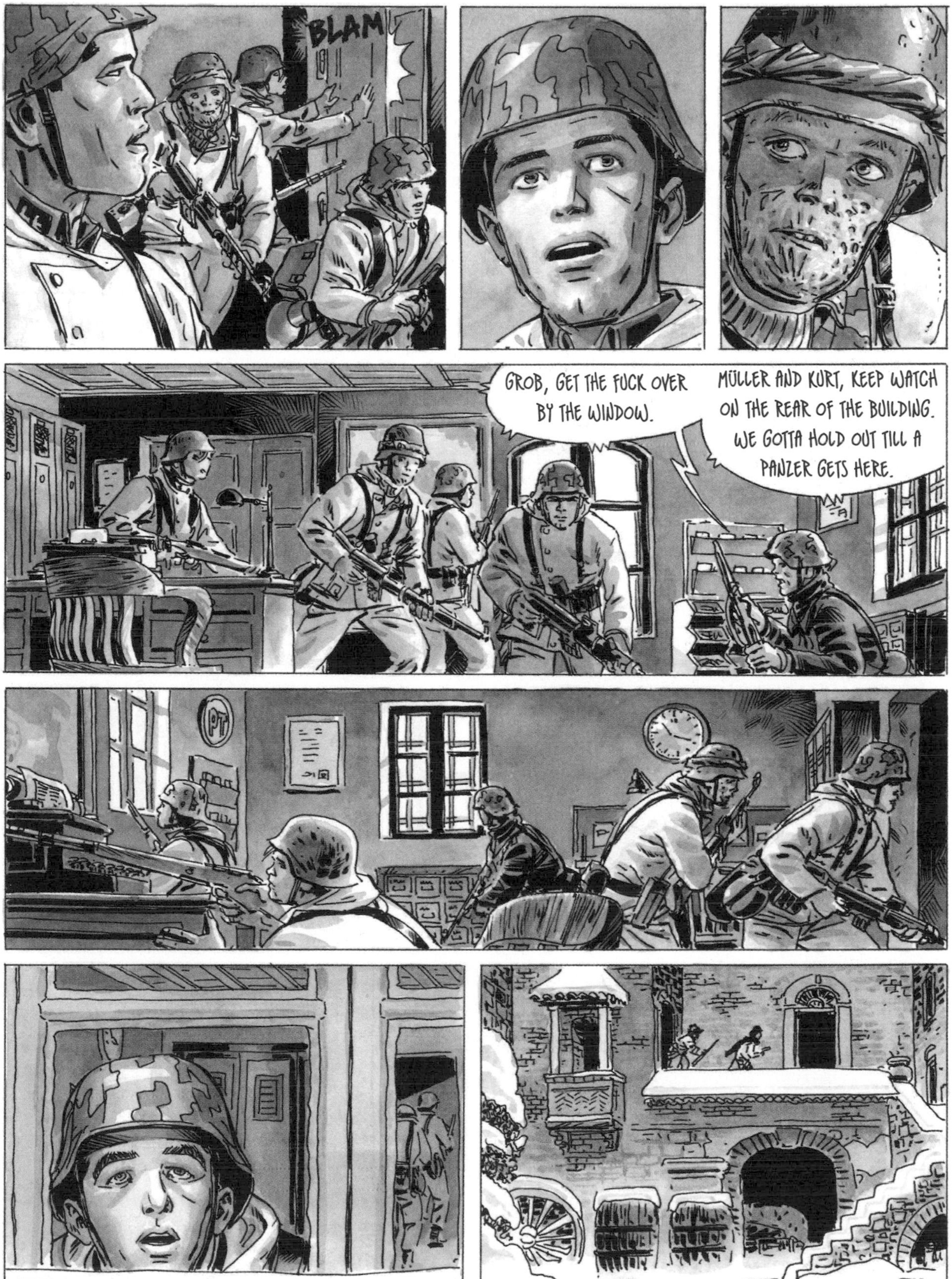
BLAM
GROB, GET THE FUCK OVER BY THE WINDOW.
MÜLLER AND KURT, KEEP WATCH ON THE REAR OF THE BUILDING. WE GOTTA HOLD OUT TILL A PANZER GETS HERE.
PT

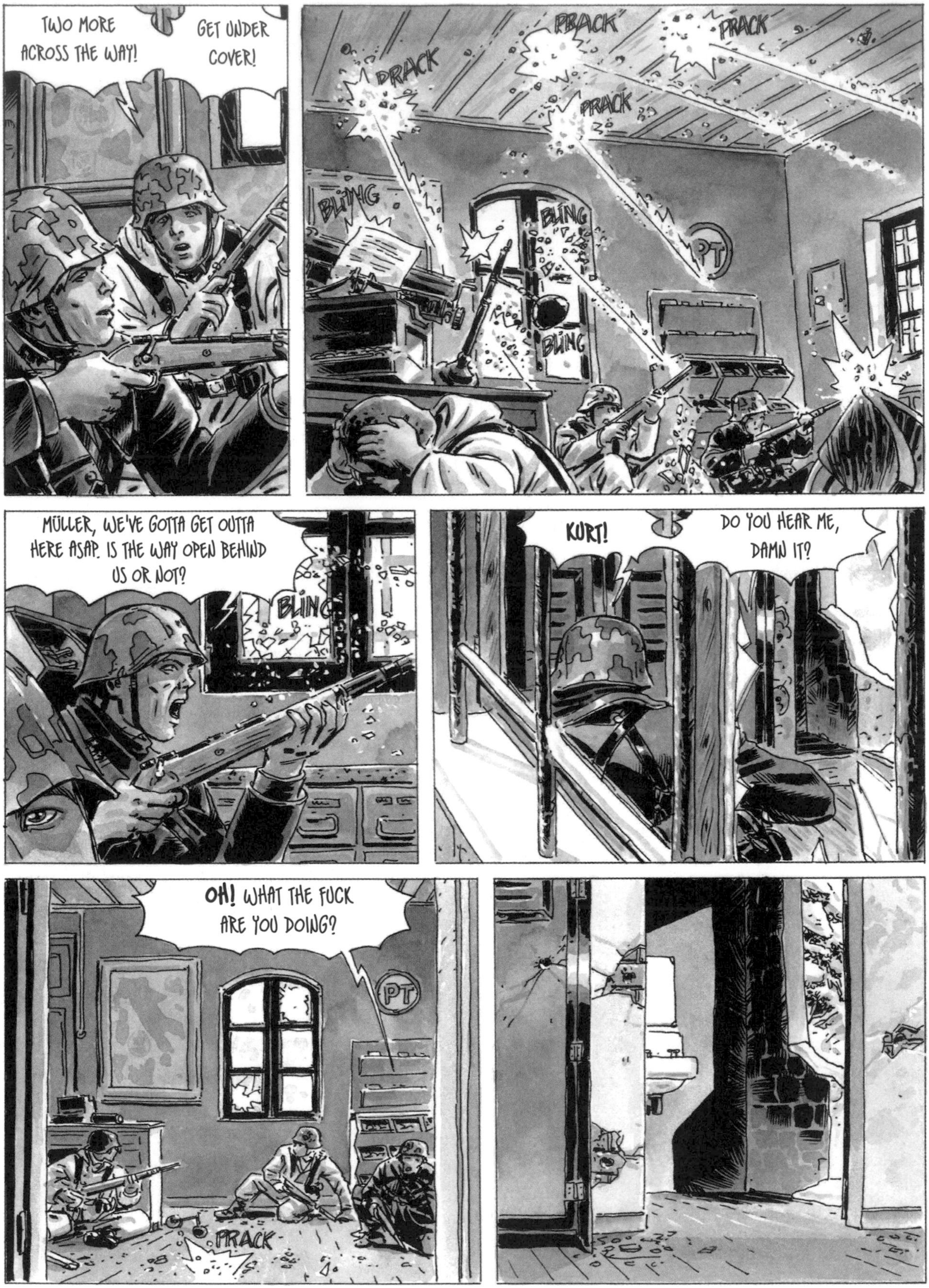
TWO MORE ACROSS THE WAY!
GET UNDER COVER!
PRACK
PRACK
PRACK
PRACK
BLING
BLING
BLING
MÜLLER, WE'VE GOTTA GET OUTTA HERE ASAP. IS THE WAY OPEN BEHIND US OR NOT?
BLING
KURT!
DO YOU HEAR ME, DAMN IT?
OH! WHAT THE FUCK ARE YOU DOING?
PRACK

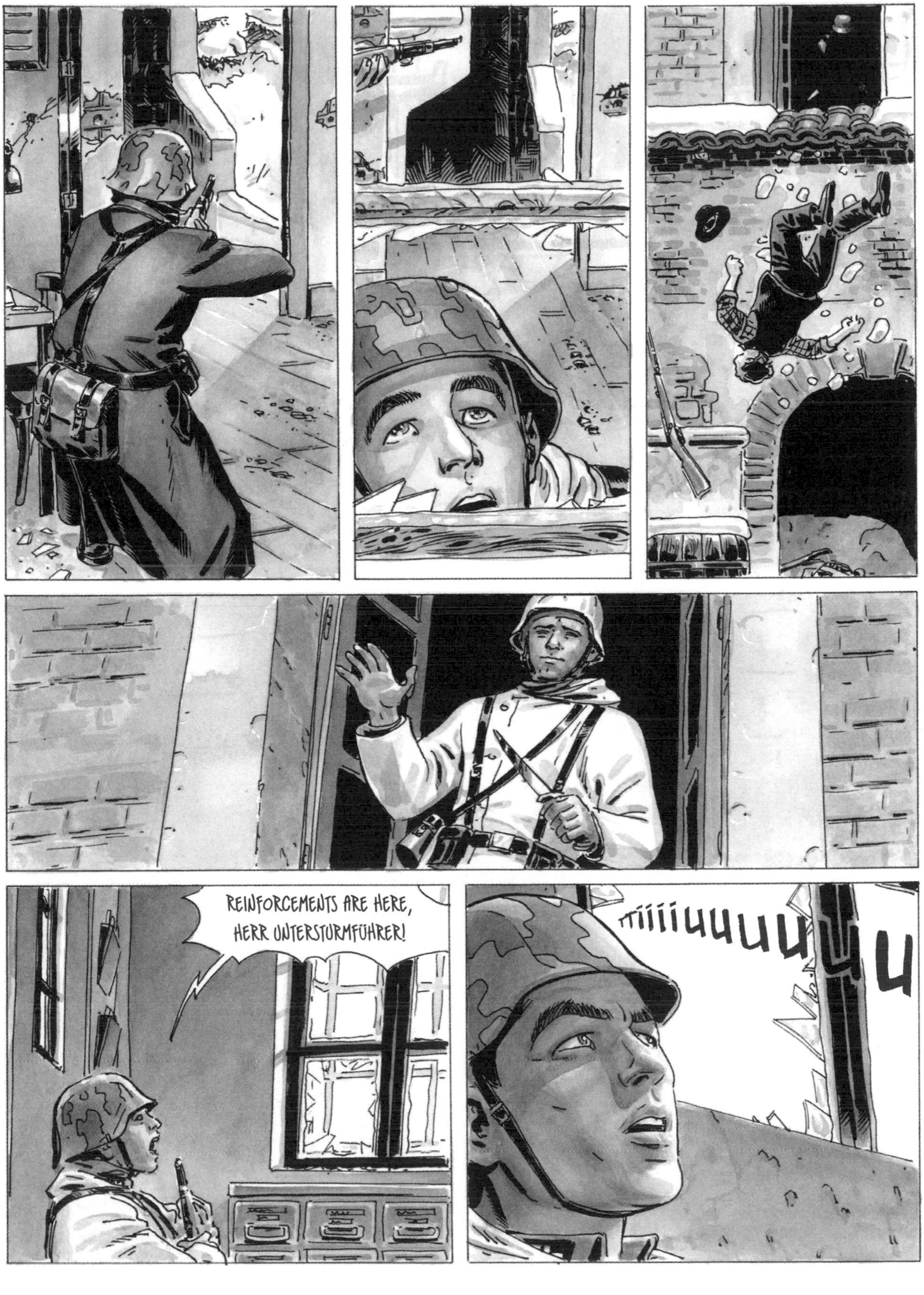
REINFORCEMENTS ARE HERE, HERR UNTERSTURMFÜHRER!
IIIIIUUUUUUUU

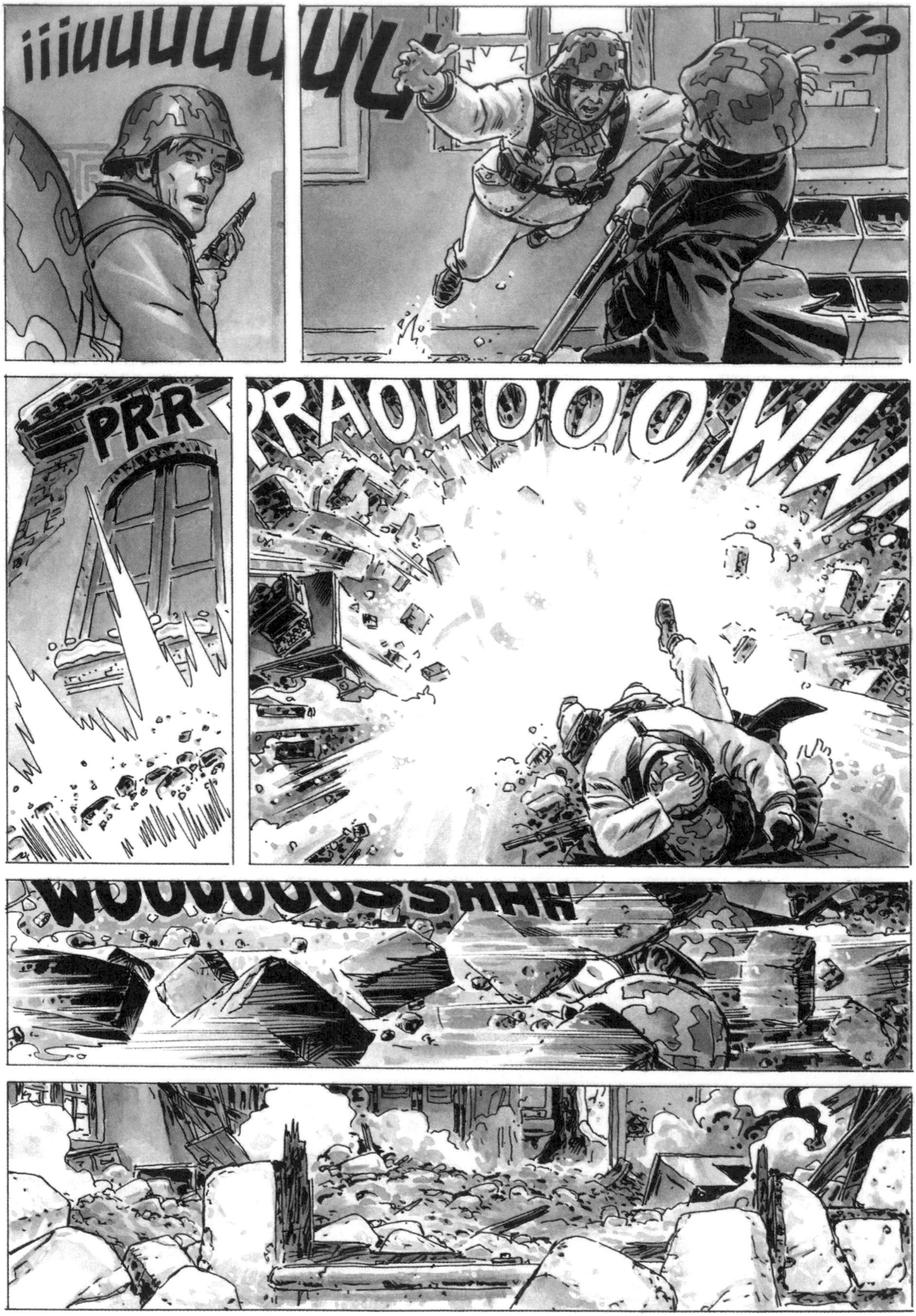
iiiuuuuuUL
!?
PRR
PRAOUOOOWW
WOOOOOOSSHHH

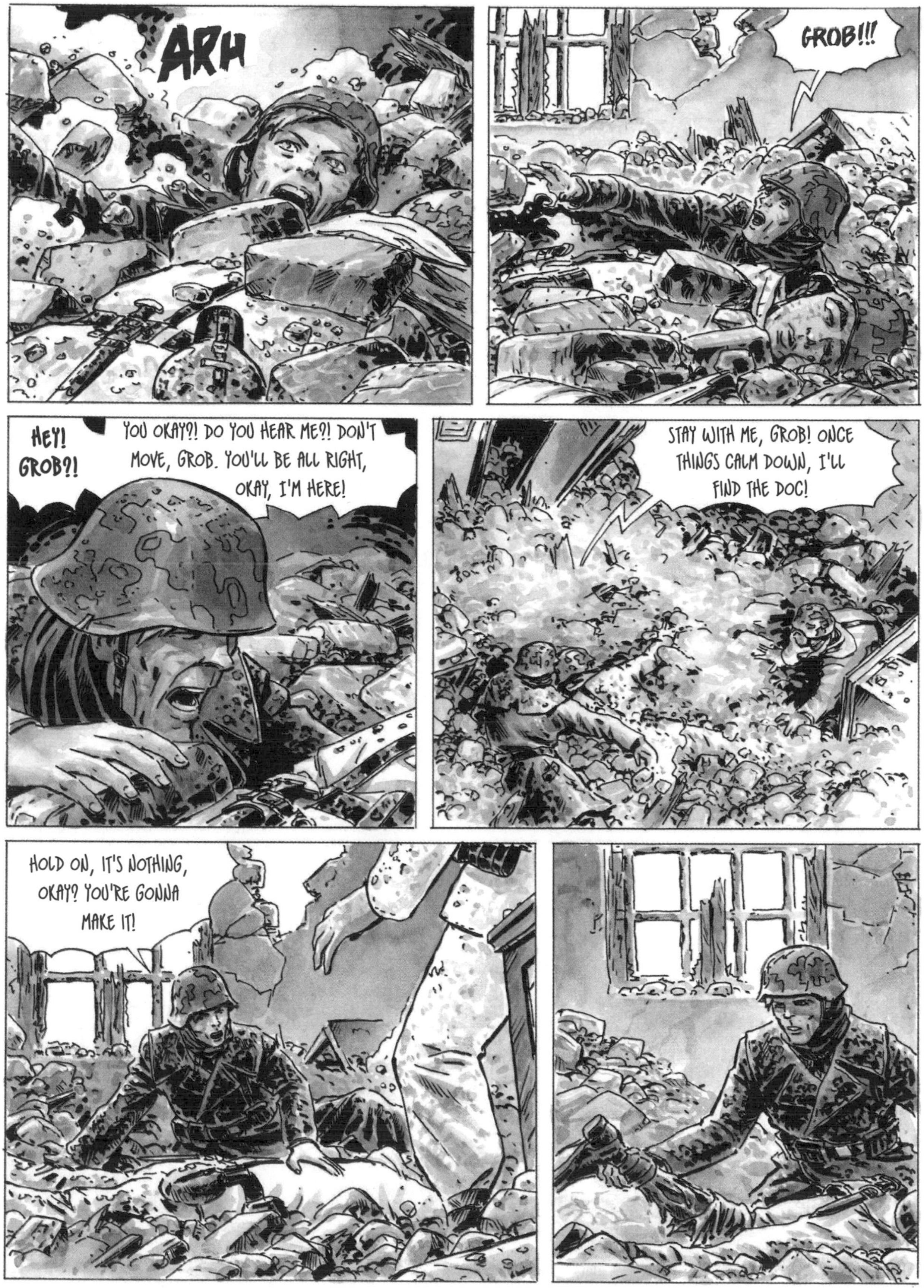
ARH
GROB!!!
HEY! GROB?!
YOU OKAY?! DO YOU HEAR ME?! DON'T MOVE, GROB. YOU'LL BE ALL RIGHT, OKAY, I'M HERE!
STAY WITH ME, GROB! ONCE THINGS CALM DOWN, I'LL FIND THE DOC!
HOLD ON, IT'S NOTHING, OKAY? YOU'RE GONNA MAKE IT!

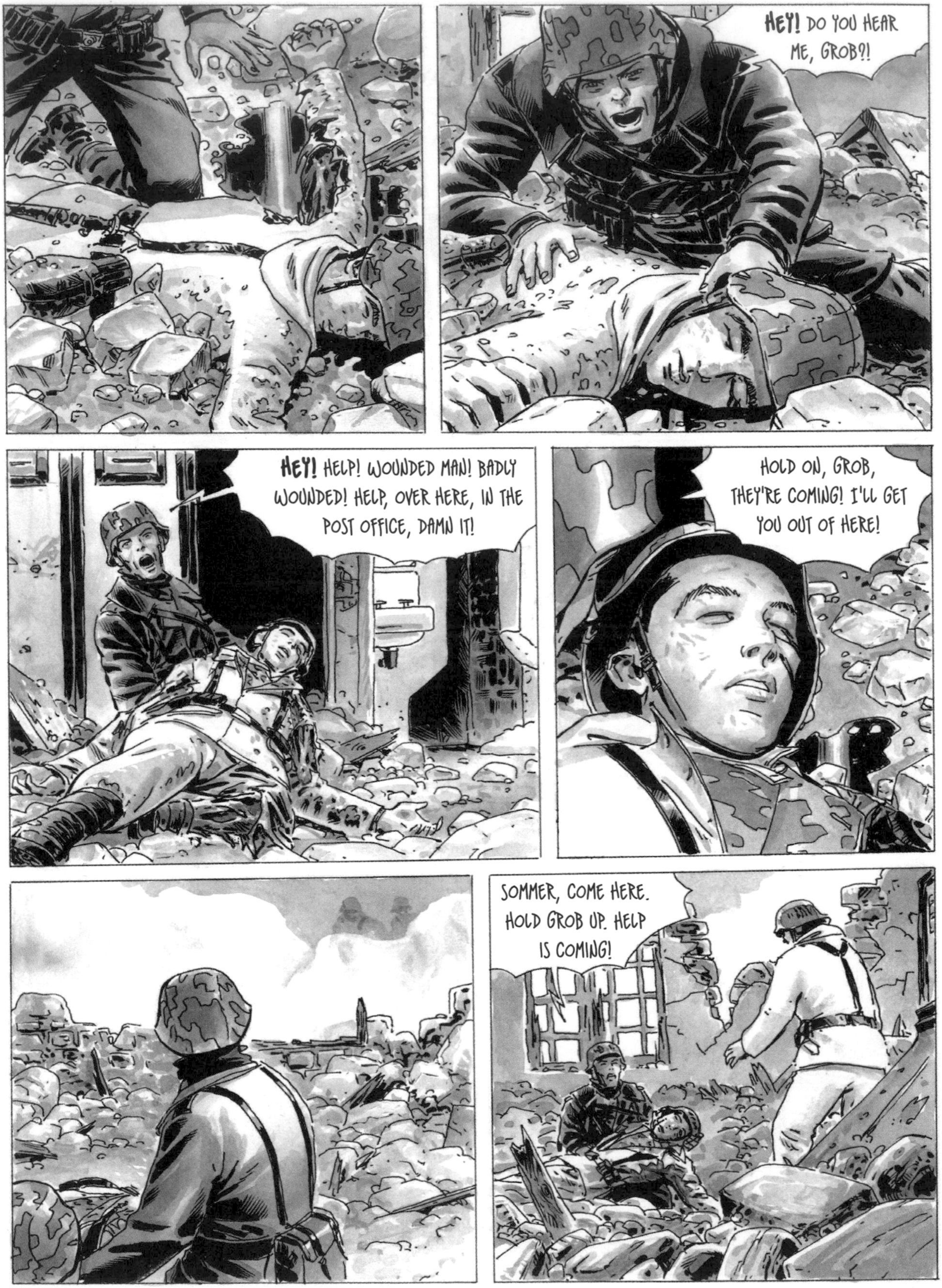
HEY! DO YOU HEAR ME, GROB?!
HEY! HELP! WOUNDED MAN! BADLY WOUNDED! HELP, OVER HERE, IN THE POST OFFICE, DAMN IT!
HOLD ON, GROB, THEY'RE COMING! I'LL GET YOU OUT OF HERE!
SOMMER, COME HERE. HOLD GROB UP. HELP IS COMING!

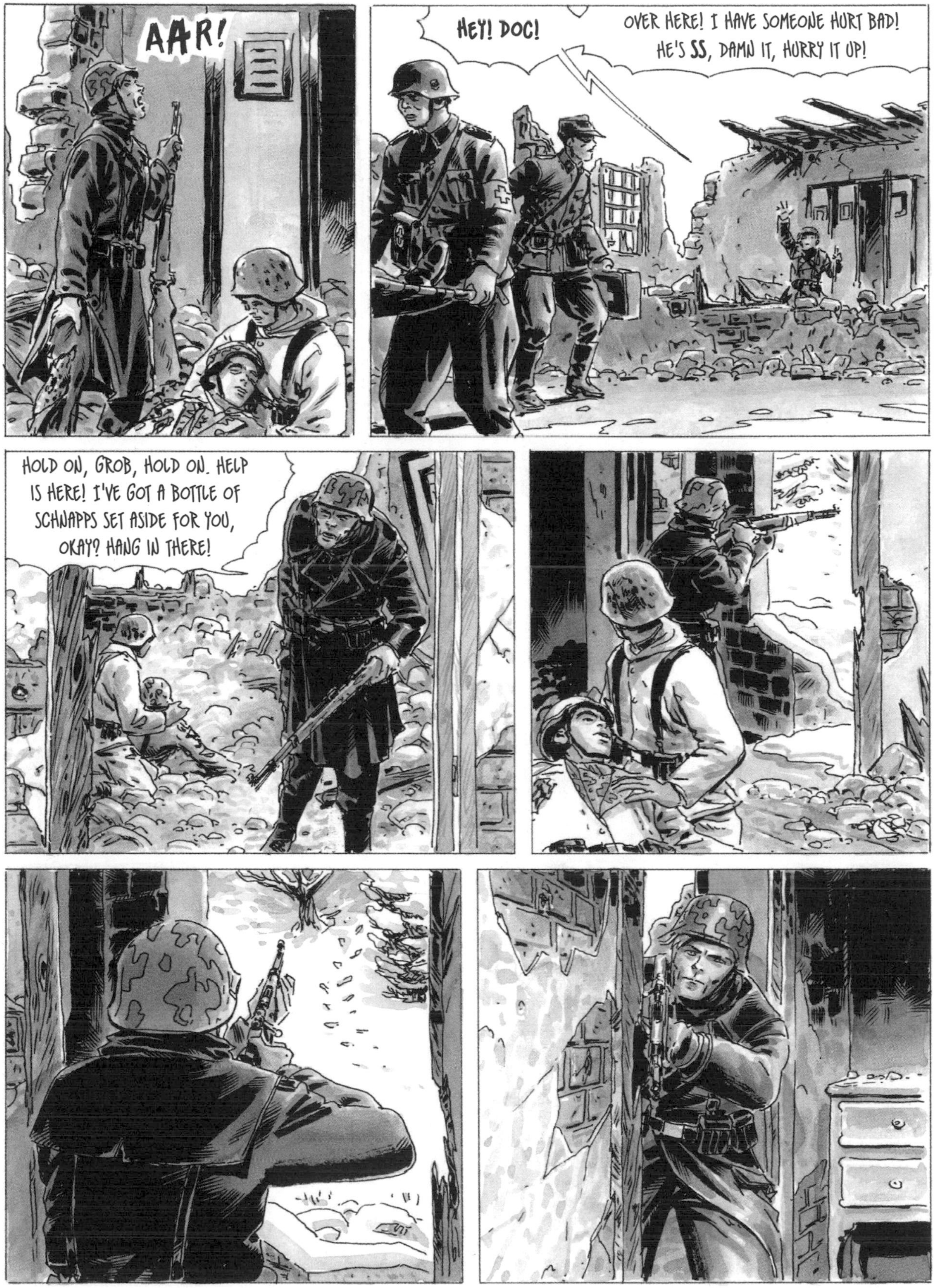
AAR!
HEY! DOC!
OVER HERE! I HAVE SOMEONE HURT BAD! HE'S SS, DAMN IT, HURRY IT UP!
HOLD ON, GROB, HOLD ON. HELP IS HERE! I'VE GOT A BOTTLE OF SCHNAPPS SET ASIDE FOR YOU, OKAY? HANG IN THERE!

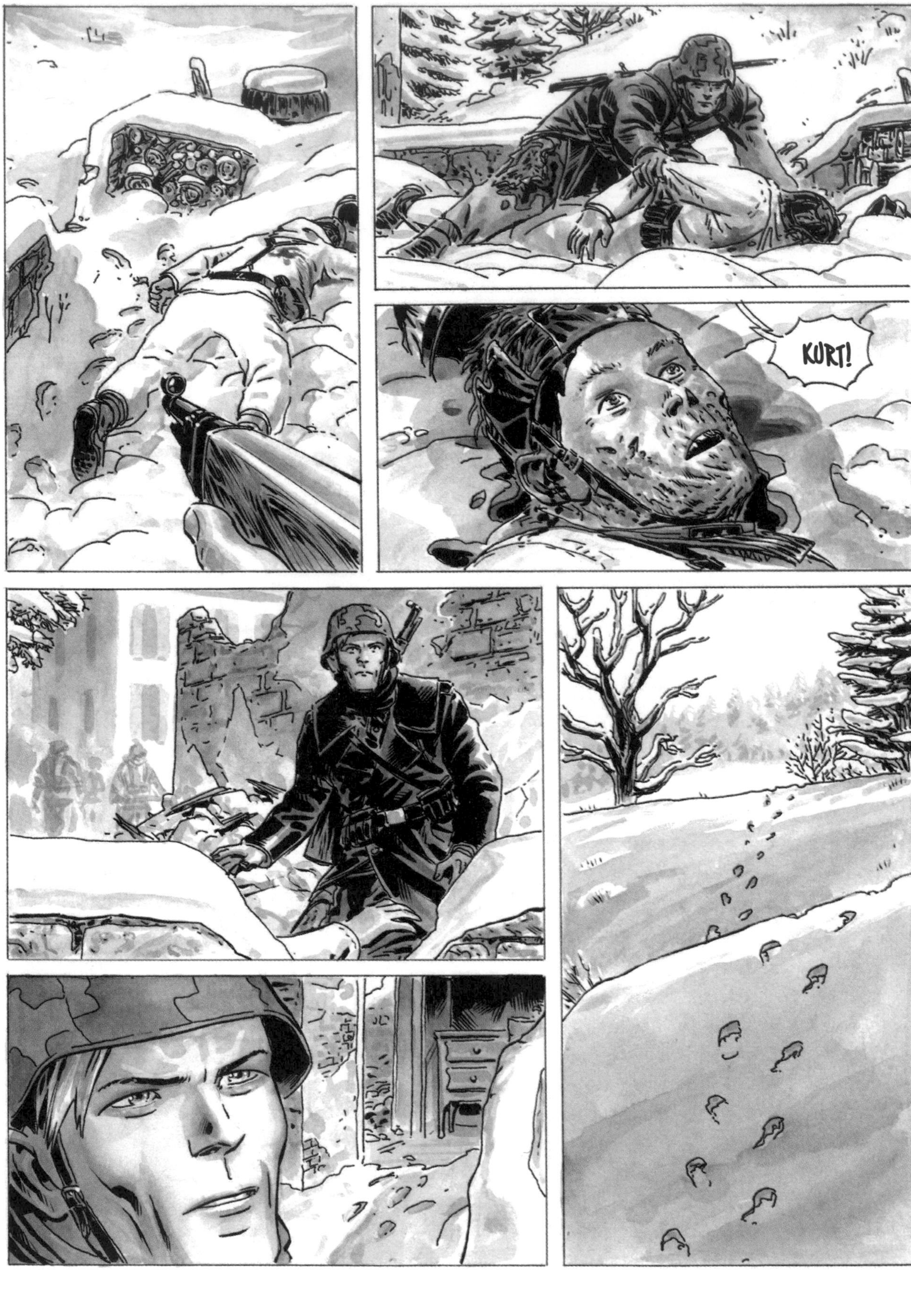
KURT!

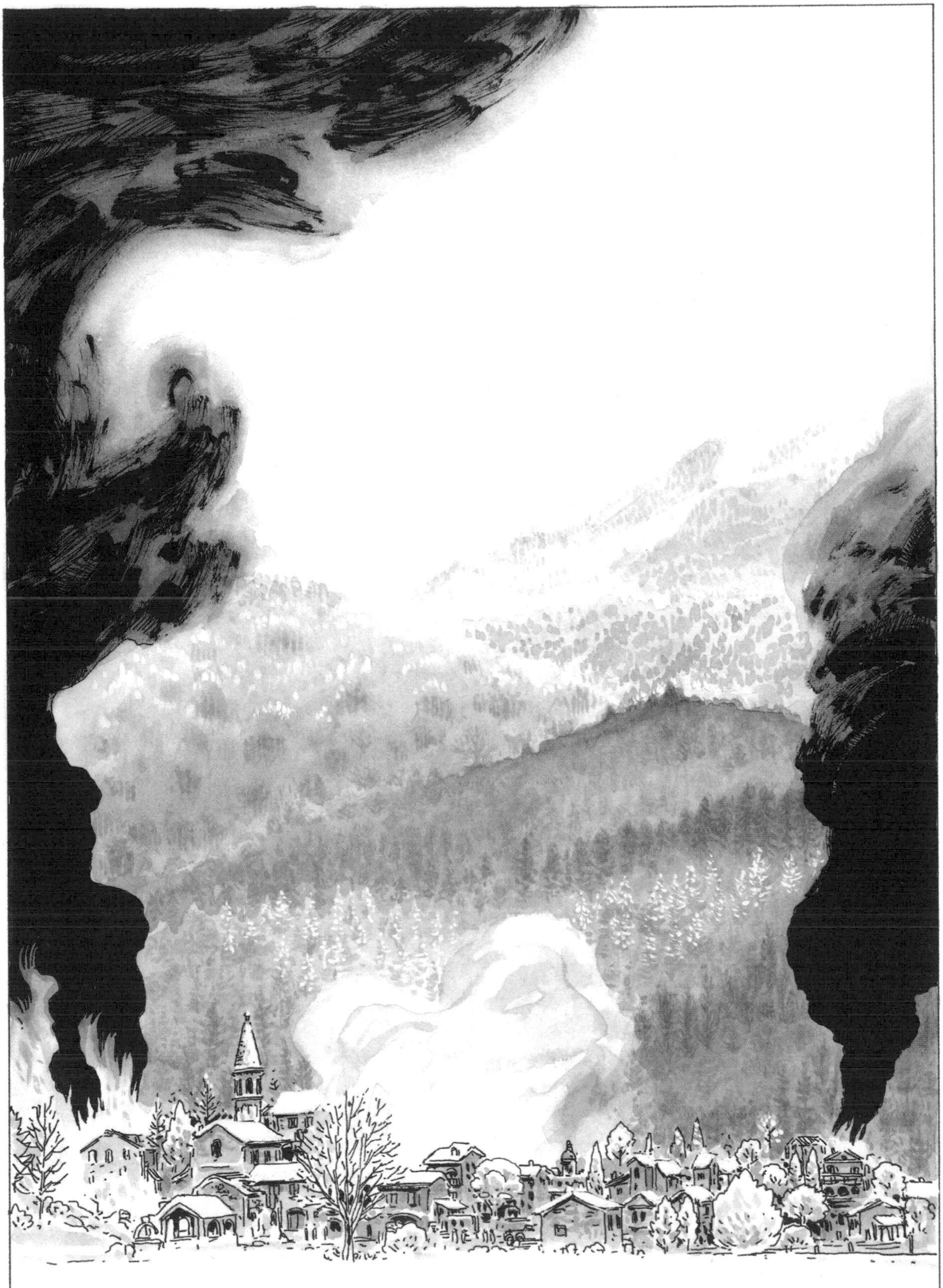

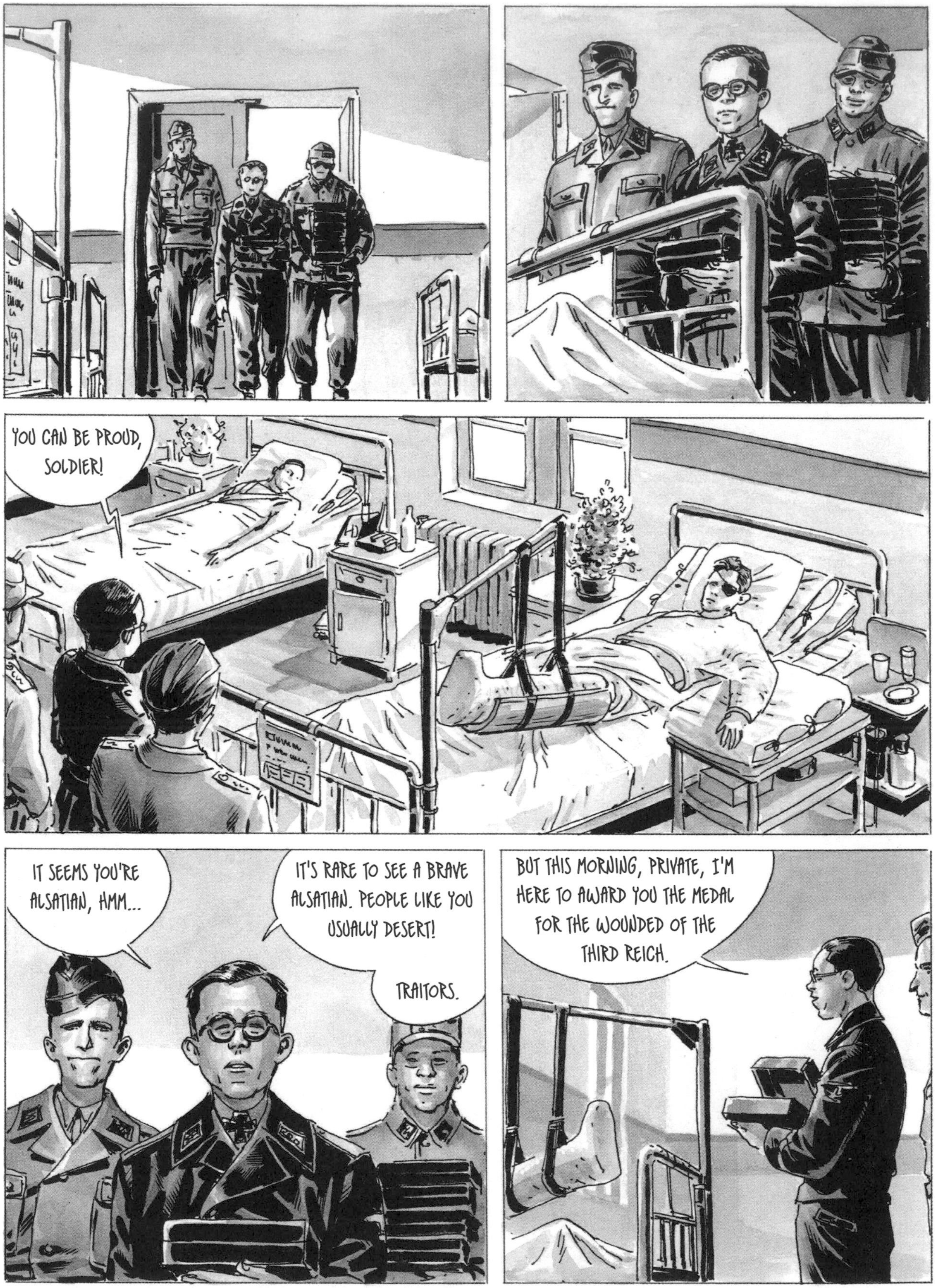
YOU CAN BE PROUD, SOLDIER!
IT SEEMS YOU'RE ALSATIAN, HMM...
IT'S RARE TO SEE A BRAVE ALSATIAN. PEOPLE LIKE YOU USUALLY DESERT!
TRAITORS.
BUT THIS MORNING, PRIVATE, I'M HERE TO AWARD YOU THE MEDAL FOR THE WOUNDED OF THE THIRD REICH.

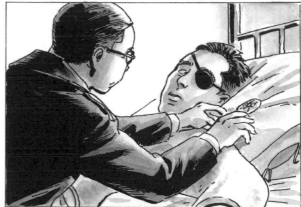

I HOPE THIS MEDAL WILL GIVE YOU STRENGTH AND COURAGE ONCE YOU COME BACK TO KICK THE REDS' ASSES!

FINAL VICTORY IS NEAR!

WHERE'S THE NEXT ONE, HERR DOKTOR?

JUST A BIT FARTHER ALONG, HERR HAUPT-STURMFÜHRER

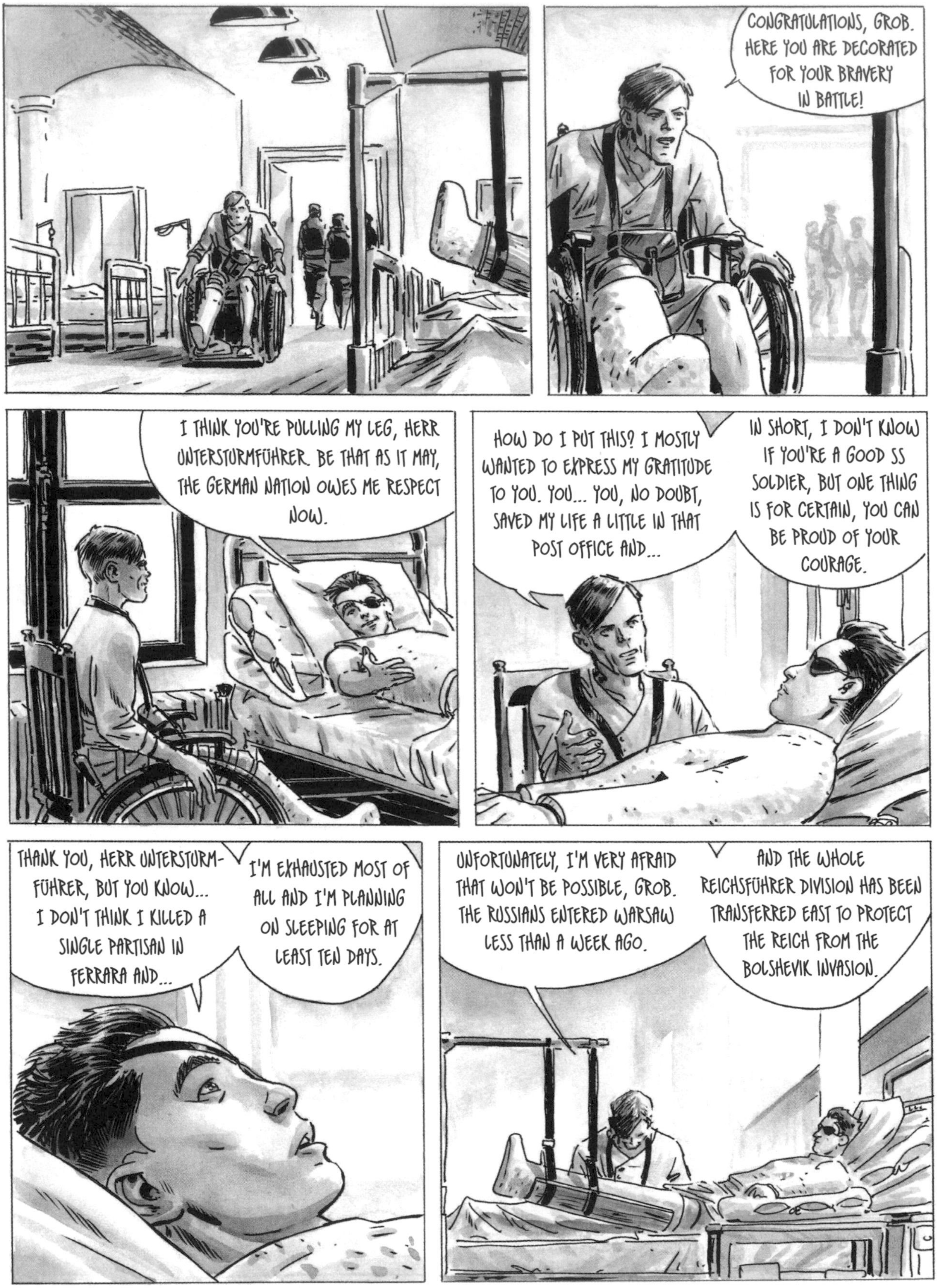
CONGRATULATIONS, GROB. HERE YOU ARE DECORATED FOR YOUR BRAVERY IN BATTLE!
I THINK YOU'RE PULLING MY LEG, HERR UNTERSTURMFÜHRER. BE THAT AS IT MAY, THE GERMAN NATION OWES ME RESPECT NOW.
HOW DO I PUT THIS? I MOSTLY WANTED TO EXPRESS MY GRATITUDE TO YOU. YOU... YOU, NO DOUBT, SAVED MY LIFE A LITTLE IN THAT POST OFFICE AND...
IN SHORT, I DON'T KNOW IF YOU'RE A GOOD SS SOLDIER, BUT ONE THING IS FOR CERTAIN, YOU CAN BE PROUD OF YOUR COURAGE.
THANK YOU, HERR UNTERSTURM-FÜHRER, BUT YOU KNOW... I DON'T THINK I KILLED A SINGLE PARTISAN IN FERRARA AND...
I'M EXHAUSTED MOST OF ALL AND I'M PLANNING ON SLEEPING FOR AT LEAST TEN DAYS.
UNFORTUNATELY, I'M VERY AFRAID THAT WON'T BE POSSIBLE, GROB. THE RUSSIANS ENTERED WARSAW LESS THAN A WEEK AGO.
AND THE WHOLE REICHSFÜHRER DIVISION HAS BEEN TRANSFERRED EAST TO PROTECT THE REICH FROM THE BOLSHEVIK INVASION.

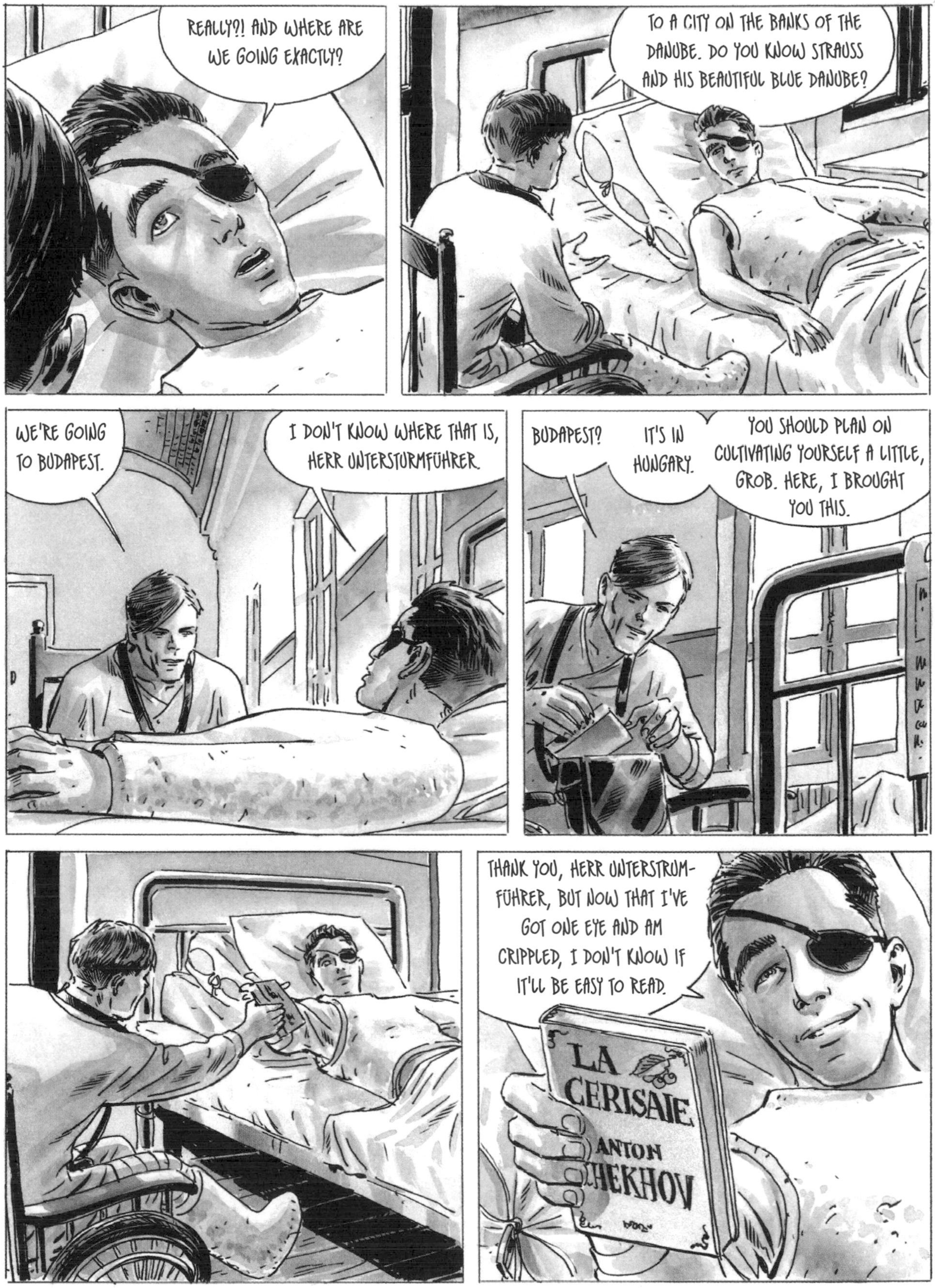
REALLY?! AND WHERE ARE WE GOING EXACTLY?
TO A CITY ON THE BANKS OF THE DANUBE. DO YOU KNOW STRAUSS AND HIS BEAUTIFUL BLUE DANUBE?
WE'RE GOING TO BUDAPEST.
I DON'T KNOW WHERE THAT IS, HERR UNTERSTURMFÜHRER.
BUDAPEST?
IT'S IN HUNGARY.
YOU SHOULD PLAN ON CULTIVATING YOURSELF A LITTLE, GROB. HERE, I BROUGHT YOU THIS.
THANK YOU, HERR UNTERSTRUMFÜHRER, BUT NOW THAT I'VE GOT ONE EYE AND AM CRIPPLED, I DON'T KNOW IF IT'LL BE EASY TO READ.
LA CERISAIE
ANTON CHEKHOV

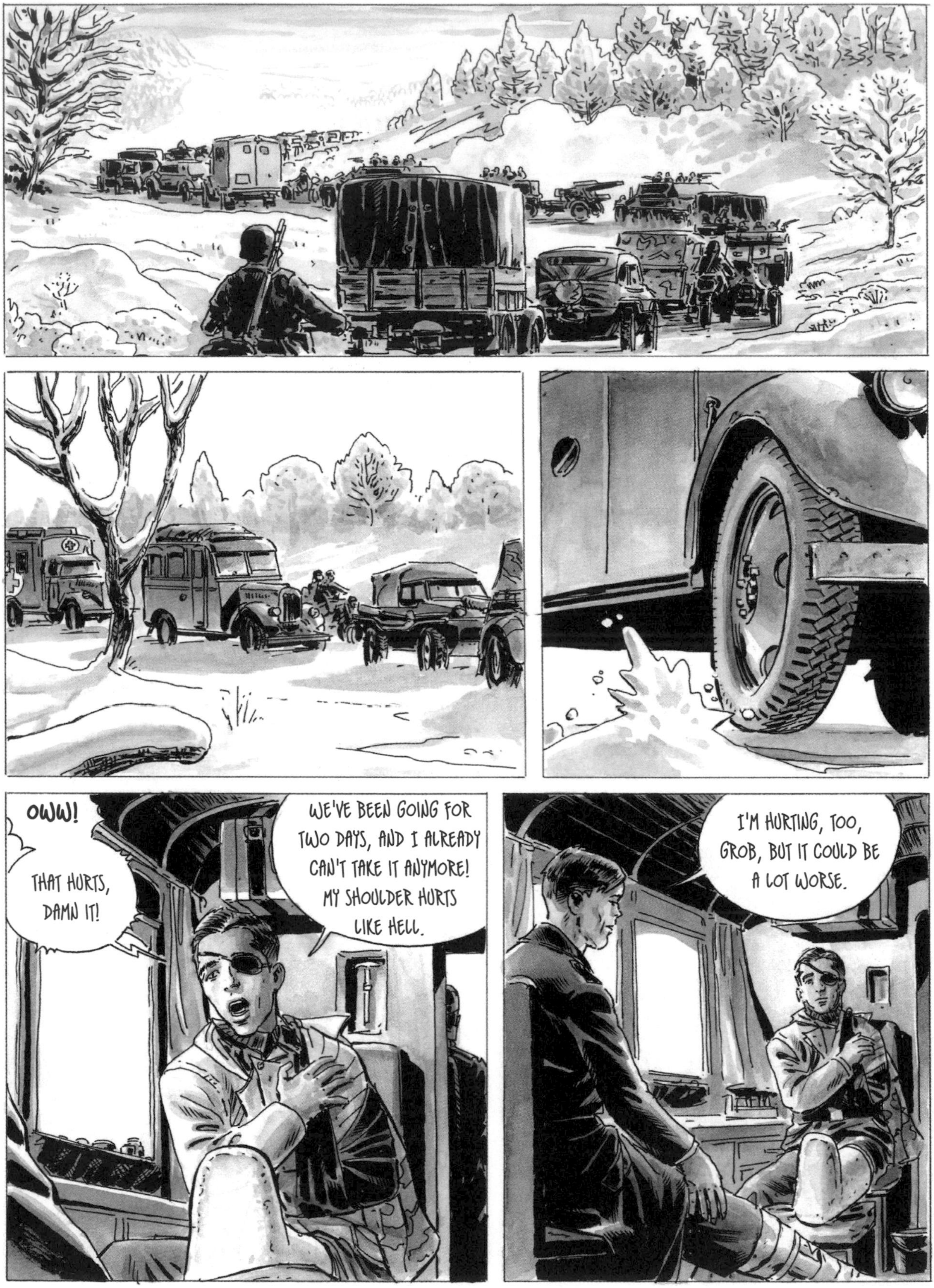
OWW!
THAT HURTS, DAMN IT!
WE'VE BEEN GOING FOR TWO DAYS, AND I ALREADY CAN'T TAKE IT ANYMORE! MY SHOULDER HURTS LIKE HELL.
I'M HURTING, TOO, GROB, BUT IT COULD BE A LOT WORSE.

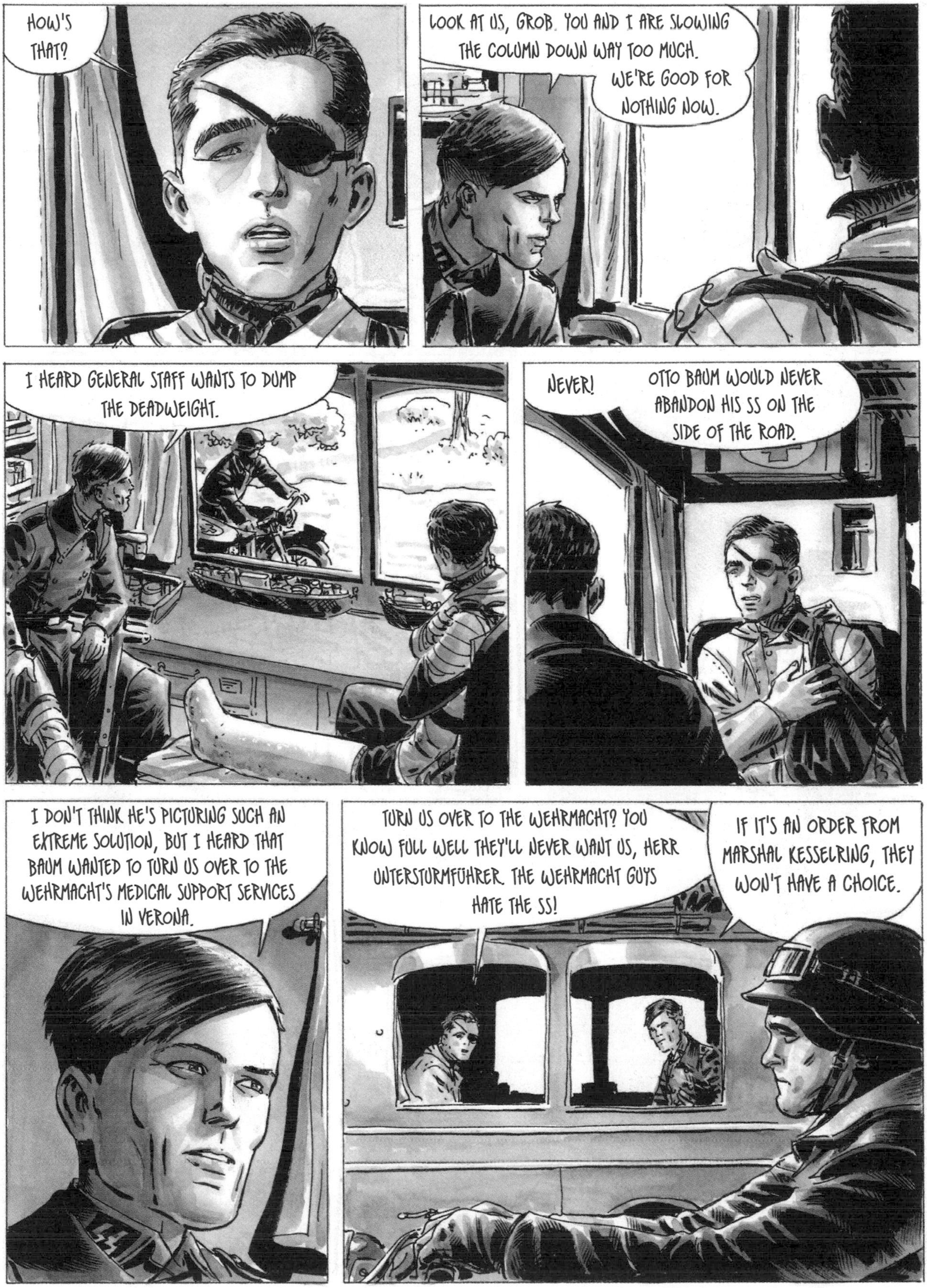
HOW'S THAT?
LOOK AT US, GROB. YOU AND I ARE SLOWING THE COLUMN DOWN WAY TOO MUCH.
WE'RE GOOD FOR NOTHING NOW.
I HEARD GENERAL STAFF WANTS TO DUMP THE DEADWEIGHT.
NEVER!
OTTO BAUM WOULD NEVER ABANDON HIS SS ON THE SIDE OF THE ROAD.
I DON'T THINK HE'S PICTURING SUCH AN EXTREME SOLUTION, BUT I HEARD THAT BAUM WANTED TO TURN US OVER TO THE WEHRMACHT'S MEDICAL SUPPORT SERVICES IN VERONA.
TURN US OVER TO THE WEHRMACHT? YOU KNOW FULL WELL THEY'LL NEVER WANT US, HERR UNTERSTURMFÜHRER. THE WEHRMACHT GUYS HATE THE SS!
IF IT'S AN ORDER FROM MARSHAL KESSELRING, THEY WON'T HAVE A CHOICE.

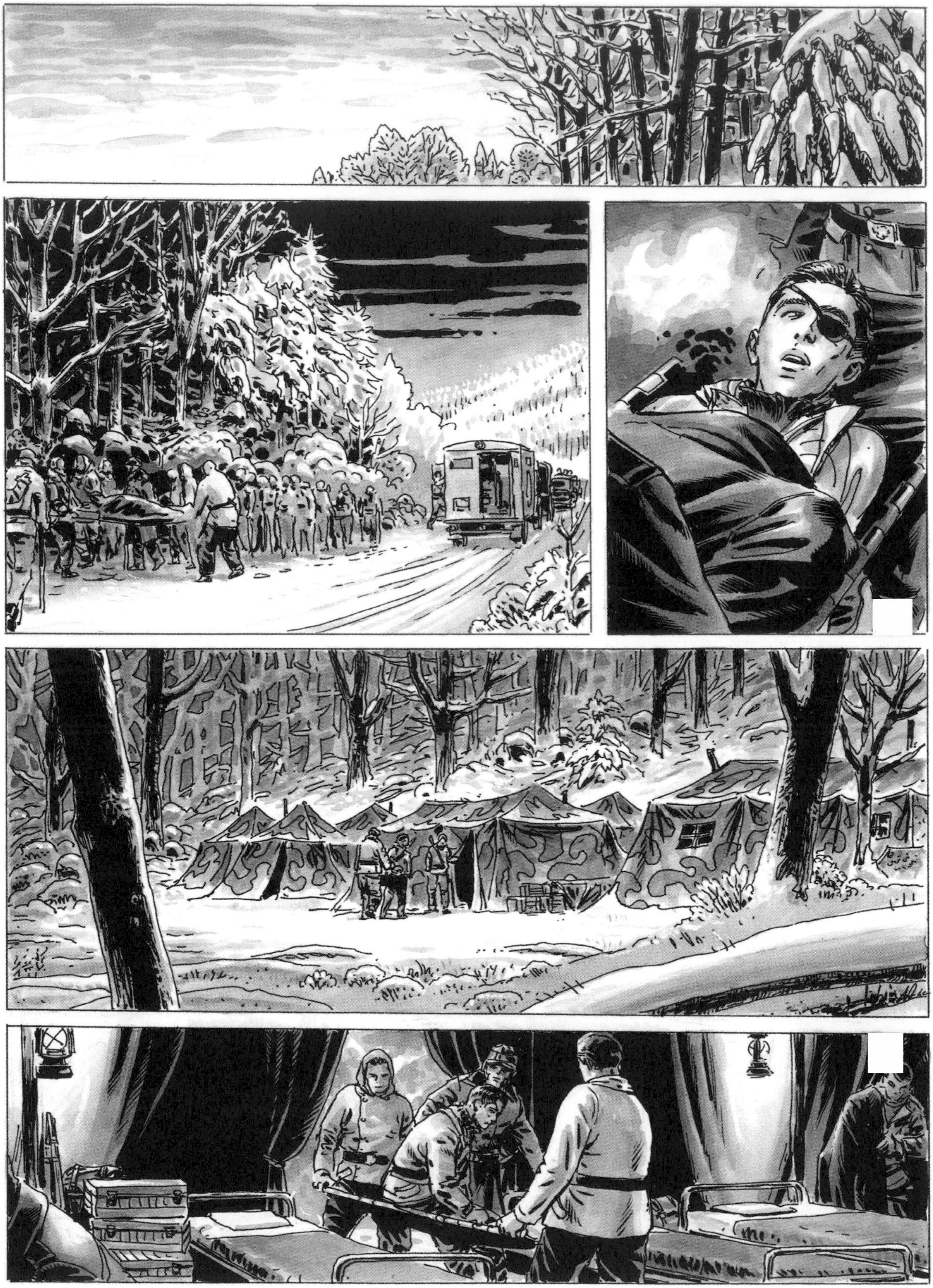

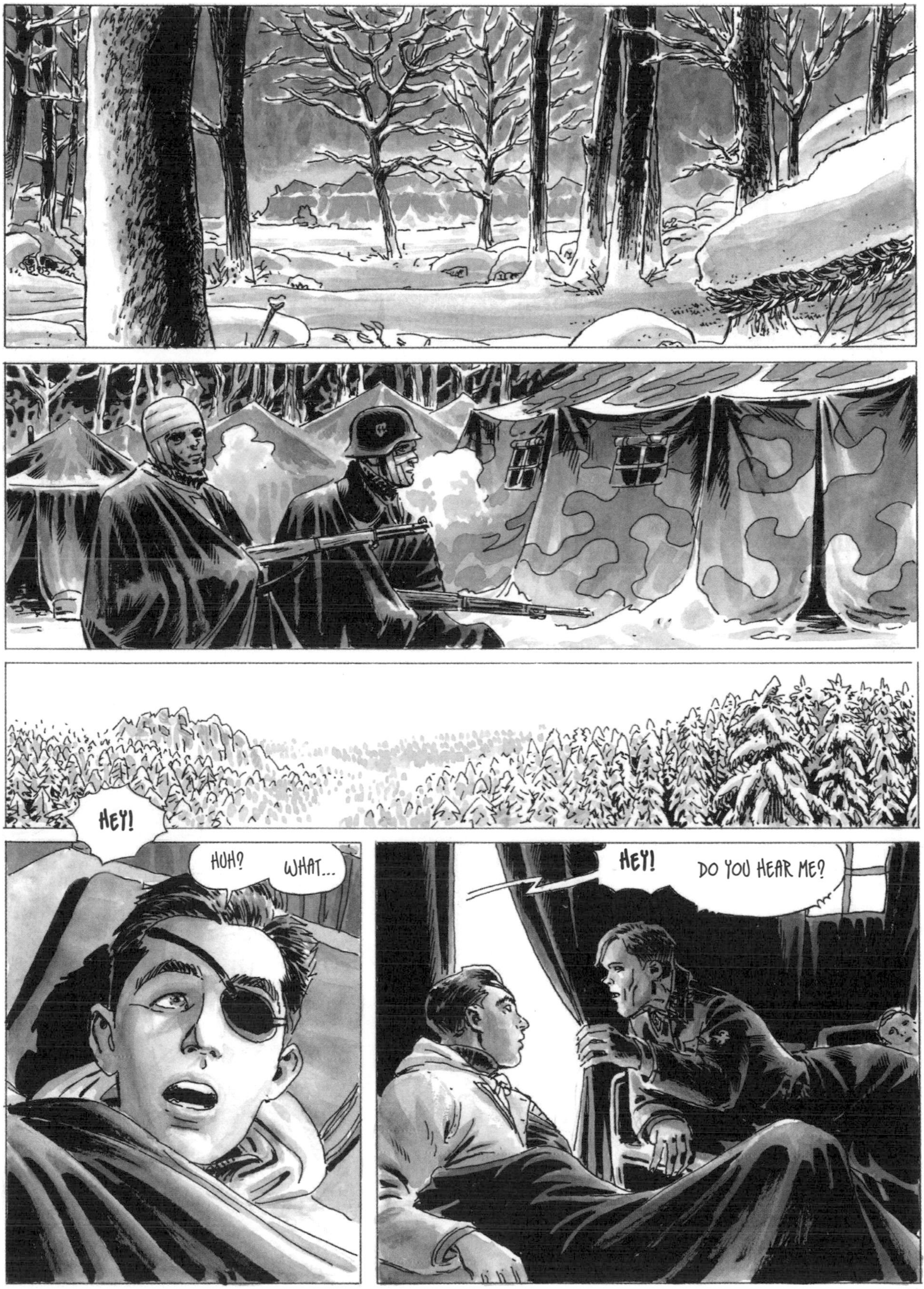
HEY!
HUH?
WHAT...
HEY!
DO YOU HEAR ME?

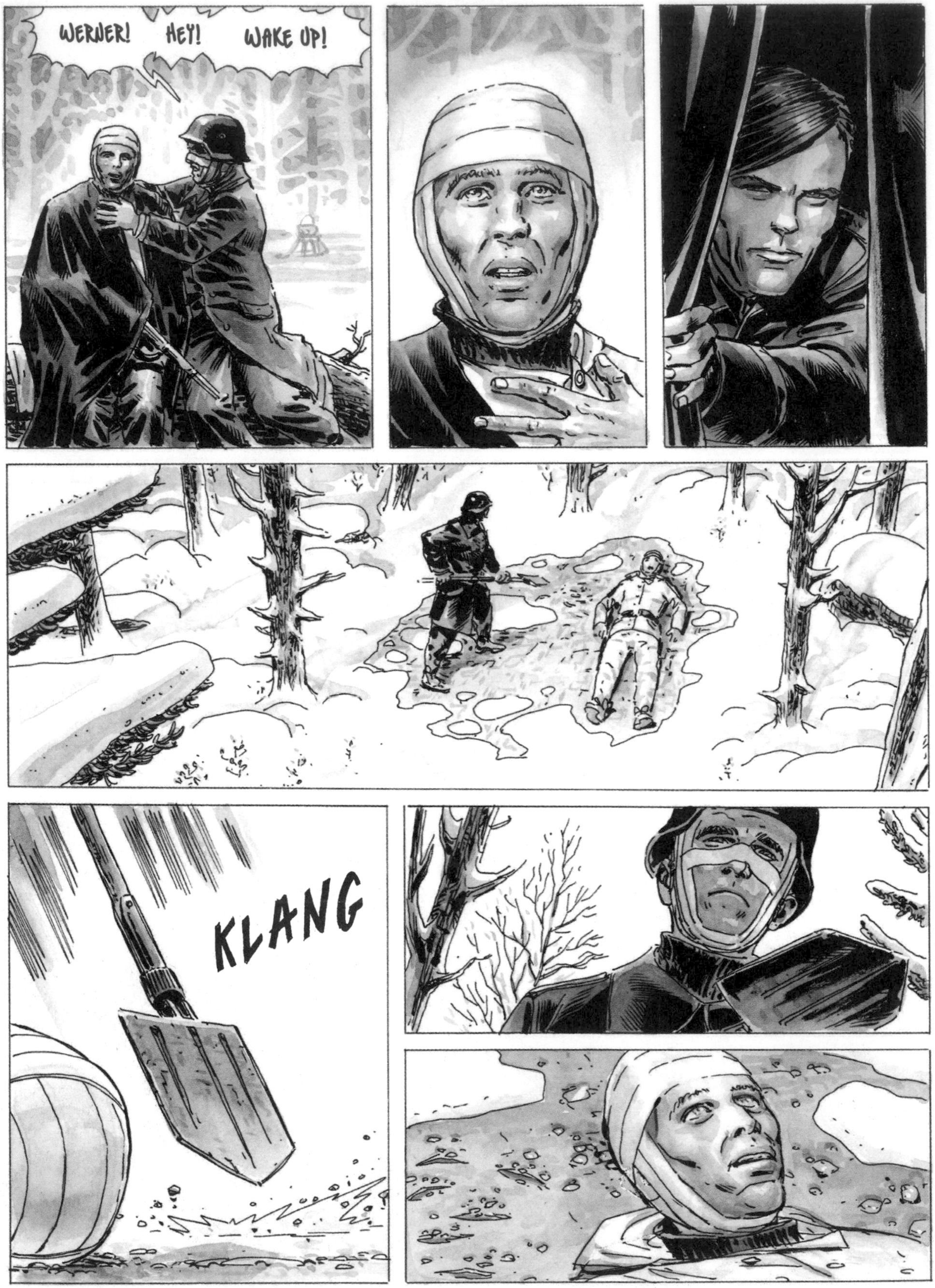
WERNER! HEY! WAKE UP!
KLANG

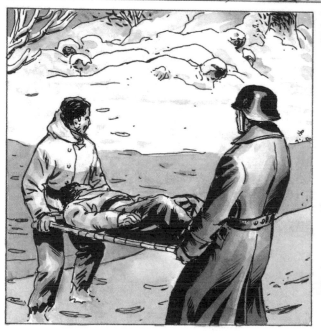

POF

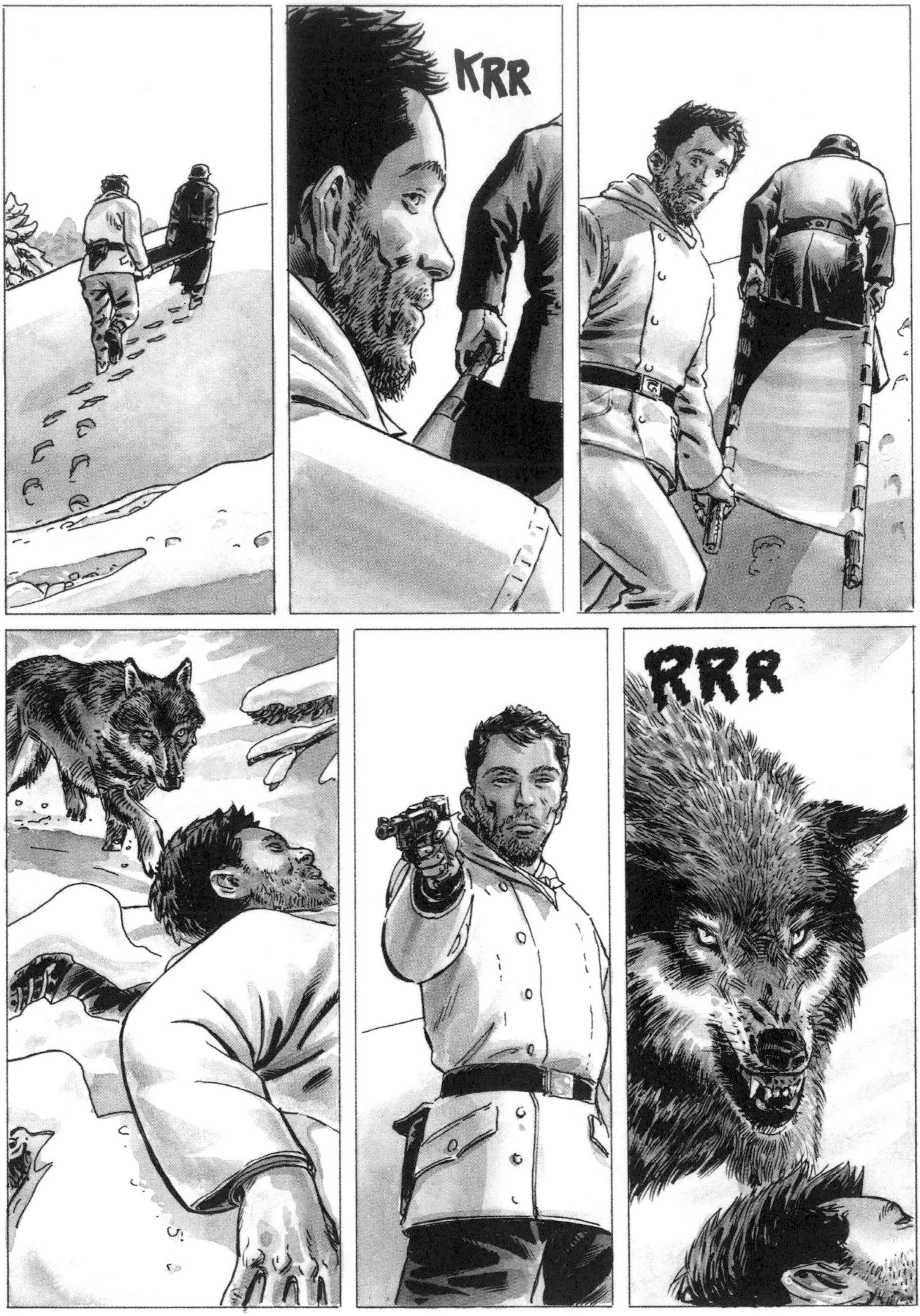
KRR
RRR

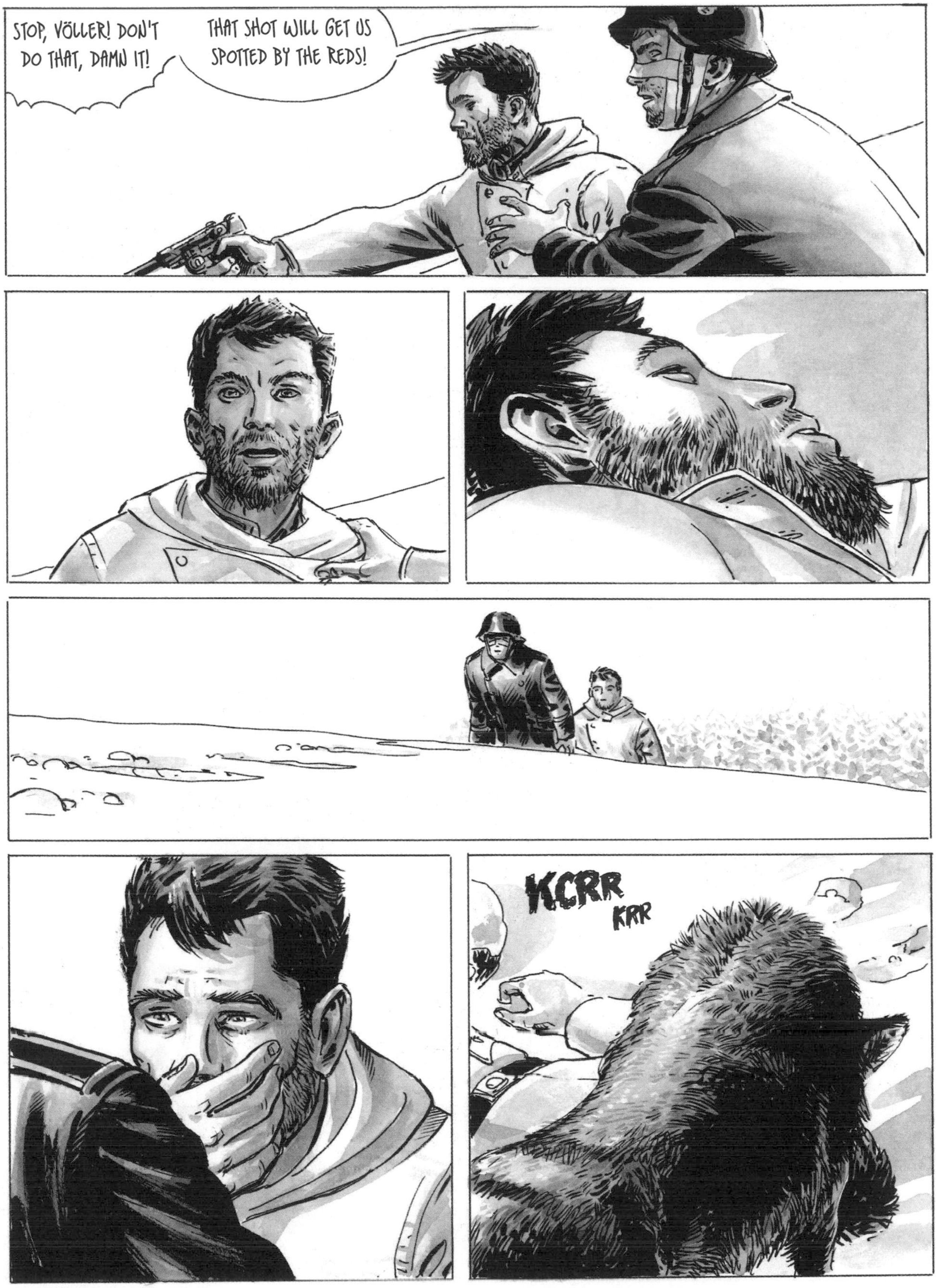

STOP, VÖLLER! DON'T DO THAT, DAMN IT!
THAT SHOT WILL GET US SPOTTED BY THE REDS!
KCRR
KRR

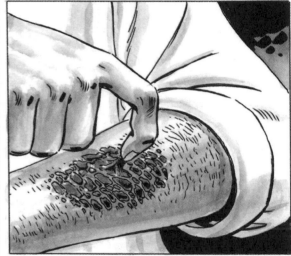

AHOUUWWOO

THEY'RE GOING TO LET US DIE HERE IN THIS UNDERBRUSH, DEVOURED BY WOLVES.

SHUT THOSE FUCKING WOLVES UP! WE'VE BEEN HERE THREE DAYS WITH NOTHING AND THAT FUCKING WERHMACHT STILL HASN'T COME!

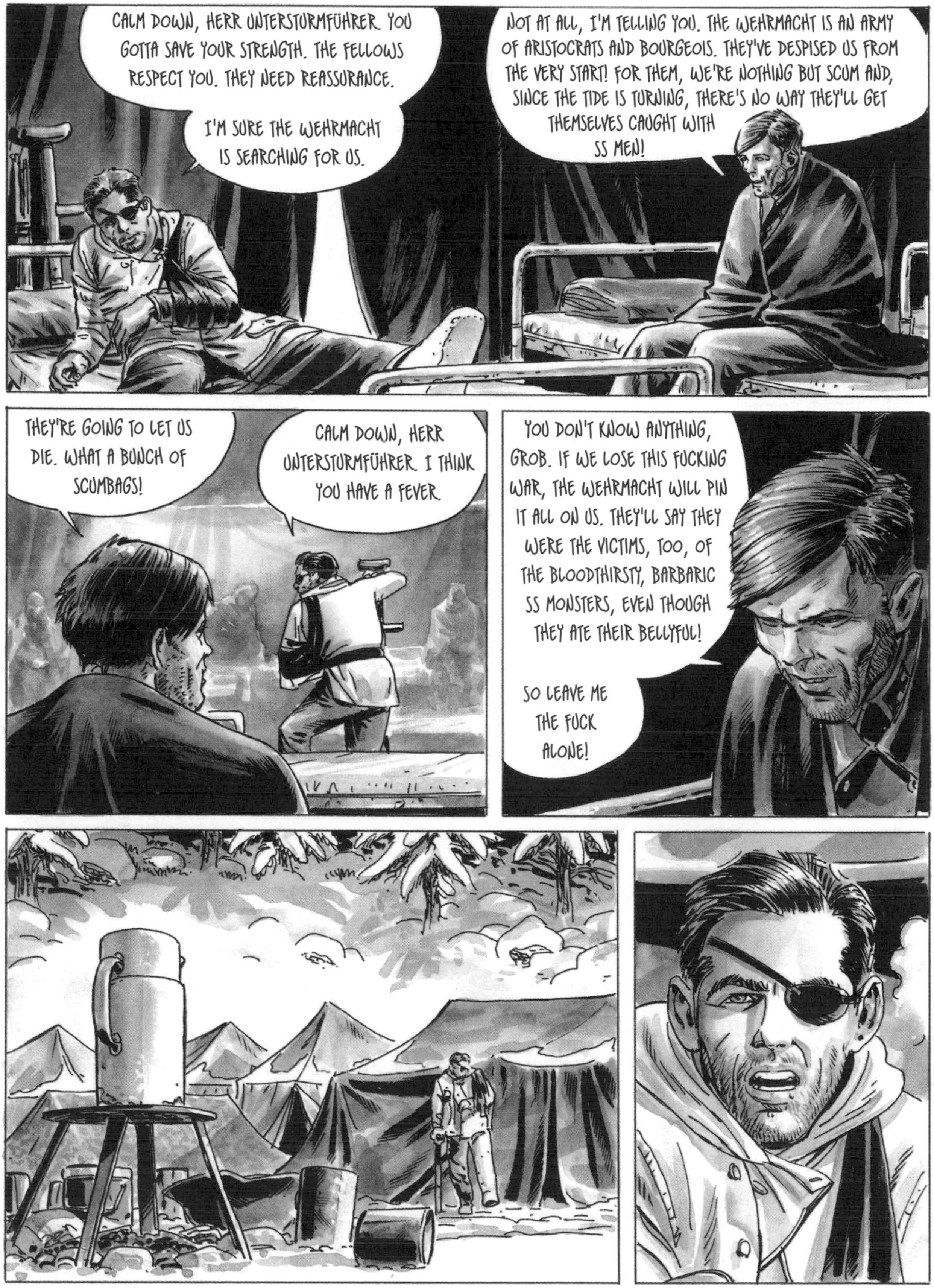
CALM DOWN, HERR UNTERSTURMFÜHRER. YOU GOTTA SAVE YOUR STRENGTH. THE FELLOWS RESPECT YOU. THEY NEED REASSURANCE.
I'M SURE THE WEHRMACHT IS SEARCHING FOR US.
NOT AT ALL, I'M TELLING YOU. THE WEHRMACHT IS AN ARMY OF ARISTOCRATS AND BOURGEOIS. THEY'VE DESPISED US FROM THE VERY START! FOR THEM, WE'RE NOTHING BUT SCUM AND, SINCE THE TIDE IS TURNING, THERE'S NO WAY THEY'LL GET THEMSELVES CAUGHT WITH SS MEN!
THEY'RE GOING TO LET US DIE. WHAT A BUNCH OF SCUMBAGS!
CALM DOWN, HERR UNTERSTURMFÜHRER. I THINK YOU HAVE A FEVER.
YOU DON'T KNOW ANYTHING, GROB. IF WE LOSE THIS FUCKING WAR, THE WEHRMACHT WILL PIN IT ALL ON US. THEY'LL SAY THEY WERE THE VICTIMS, TOO, OF THE BLOODTHIRSTY, BARBARIC SS MONSTERS, EVEN THOUGH THEY ATE THEIR BELLYFUL!
SO LEAVE ME THE FUCK ALONE!

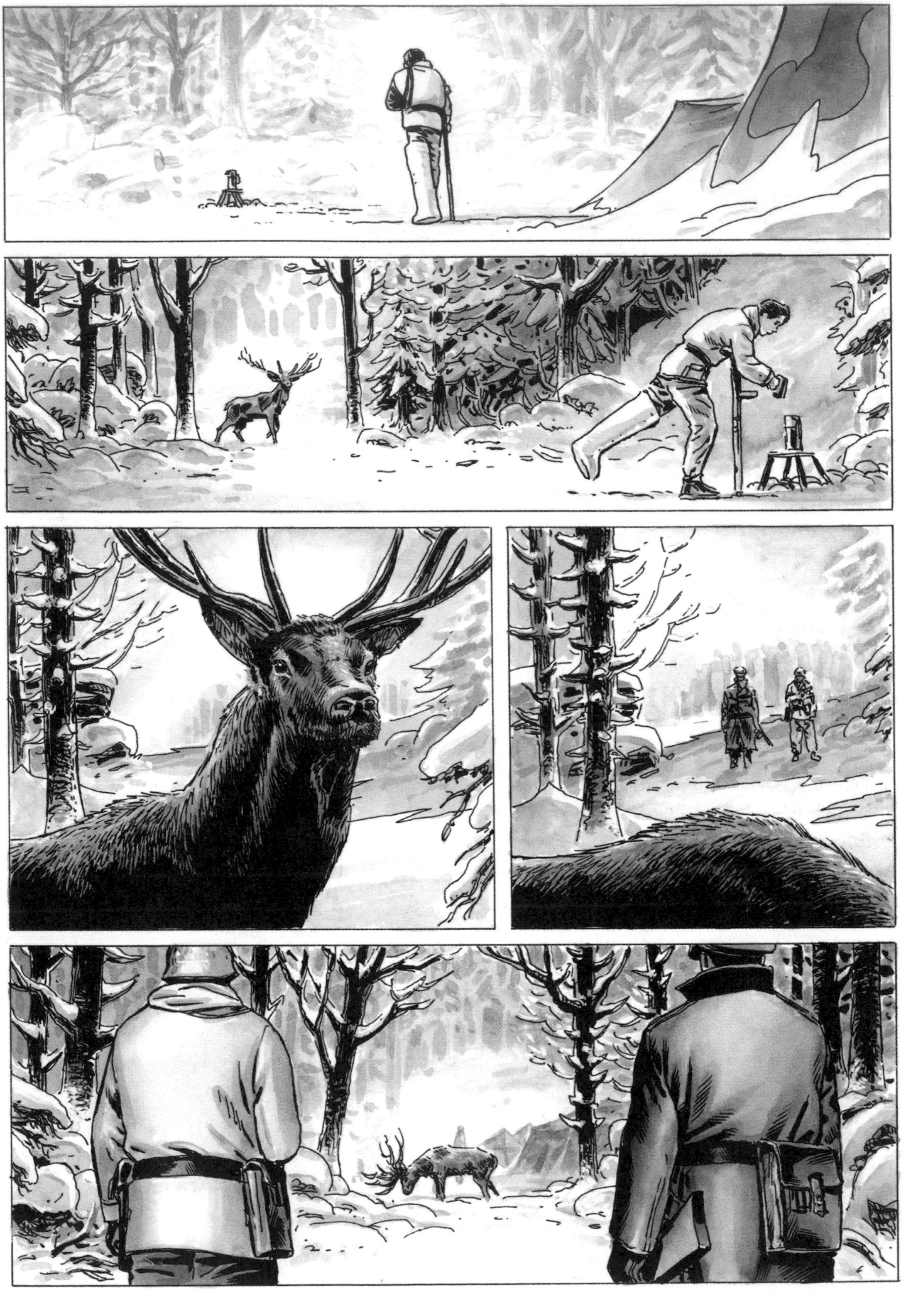

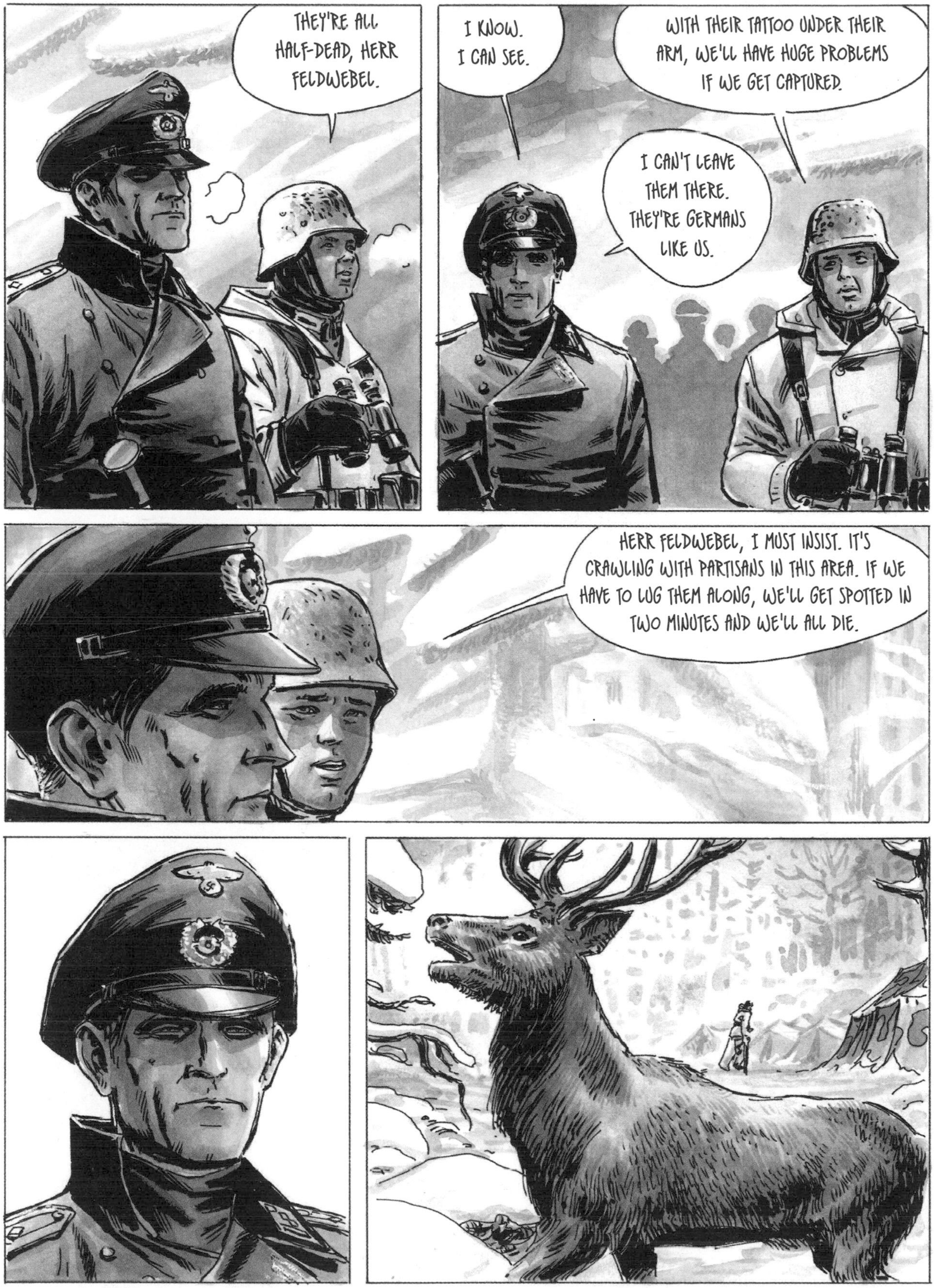
THEY'RE ALL HALF-DEAD, HERR FELDWEBEL.
I KNOW. I CAN SEE.
WITH THEIR TATTOO UNDER THEIR ARM, WE'LL HAVE HUGE PROBLEMS IF WE GET CAPTURED.
I CAN'T LEAVE THEM THERE. THEY'RE GERMANS LIKE US.
HERR FELDWEBEL, I MUST INSIST. IT'S CRAWLING WITH PARTISANS IN THIS AREA. IF WE HAVE TO LUG THEM ALONG, WE'LL GET SPOTTED IN TWO MINUTES AND WE'LL ALL DIE.

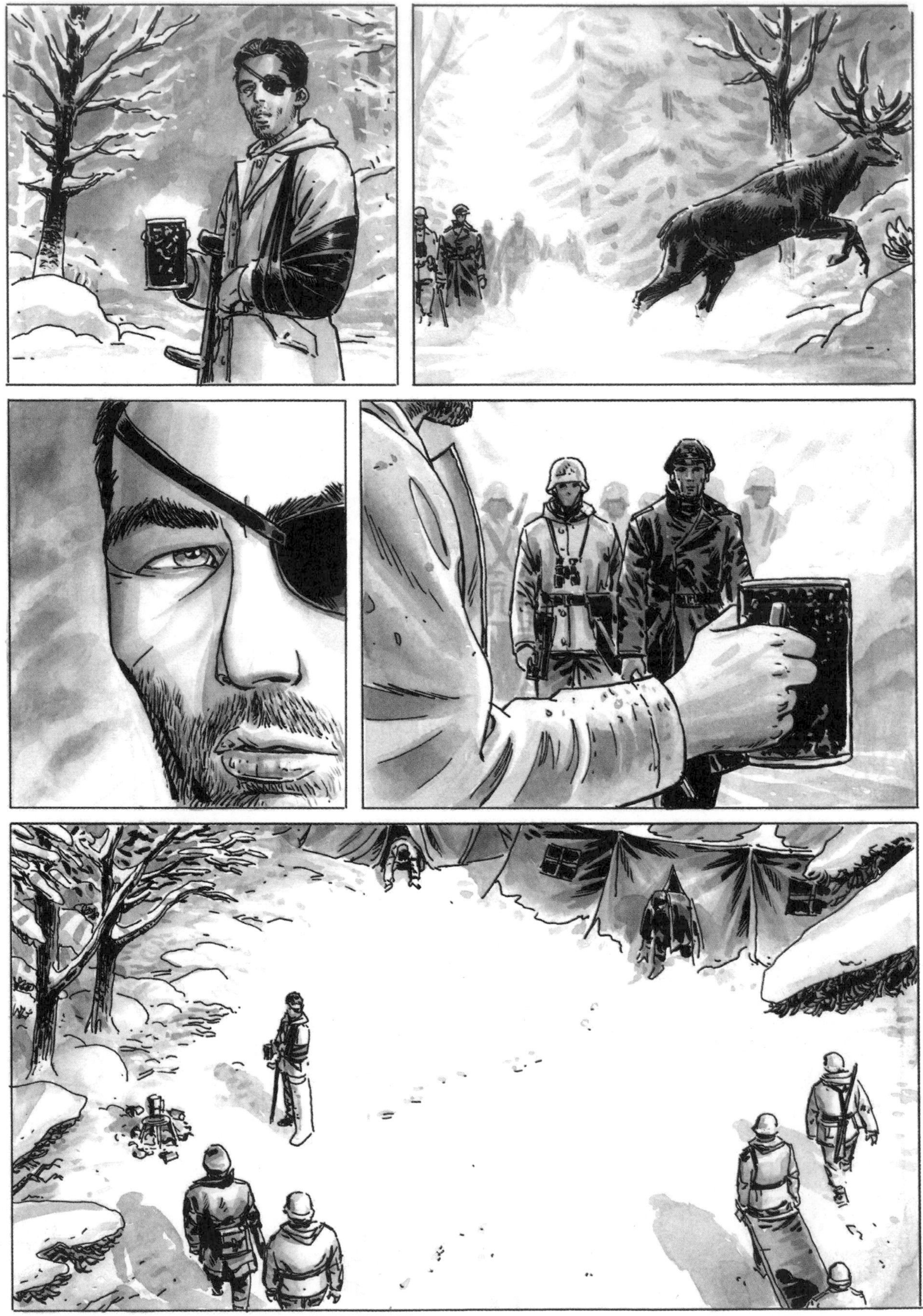

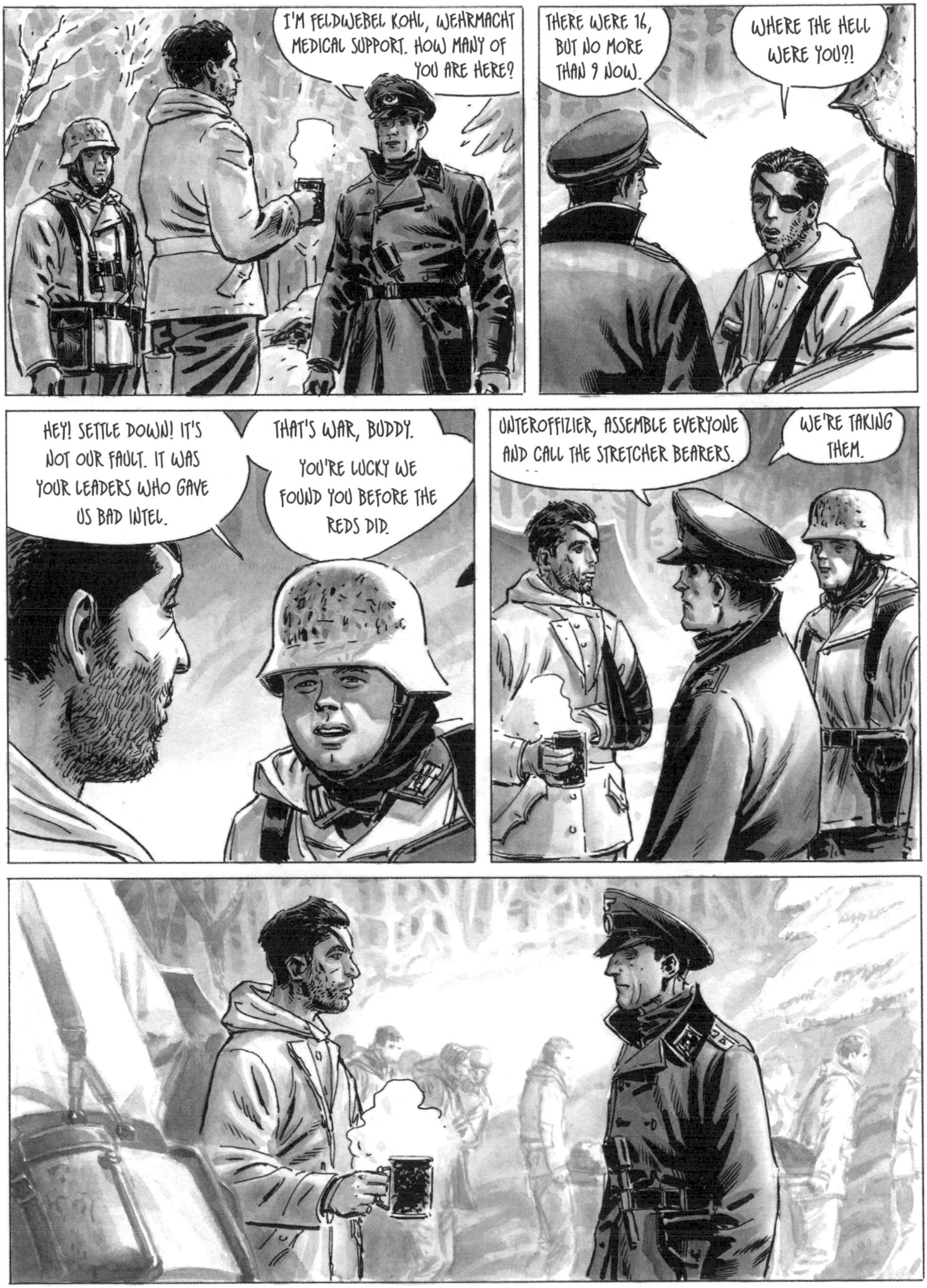
I'M FELDWEBEL KOHL, WEHRMACHT MEDICAL SUPPORT. HOW MANY OF YOU ARE HERE?
THERE WERE 16, BUT NO MORE THAN 9 NOW.
WHERE THE HELL WERE YOU?!
HEY! SETTLE DOWN! IT'S NOT OUR FAULT. IT WAS YOUR LEADERS WHO GAVE US BAD INTEL.
THAT'S WAR, BUDDY.
YOU'RE LUCKY WE FOUND YOU BEFORE THE REDS DID.
UNTEROFFIZIER, ASSEMBLE EVERYONE AND CALL THE STRETCHER BEARERS.
WE'RE TAKING THEM.

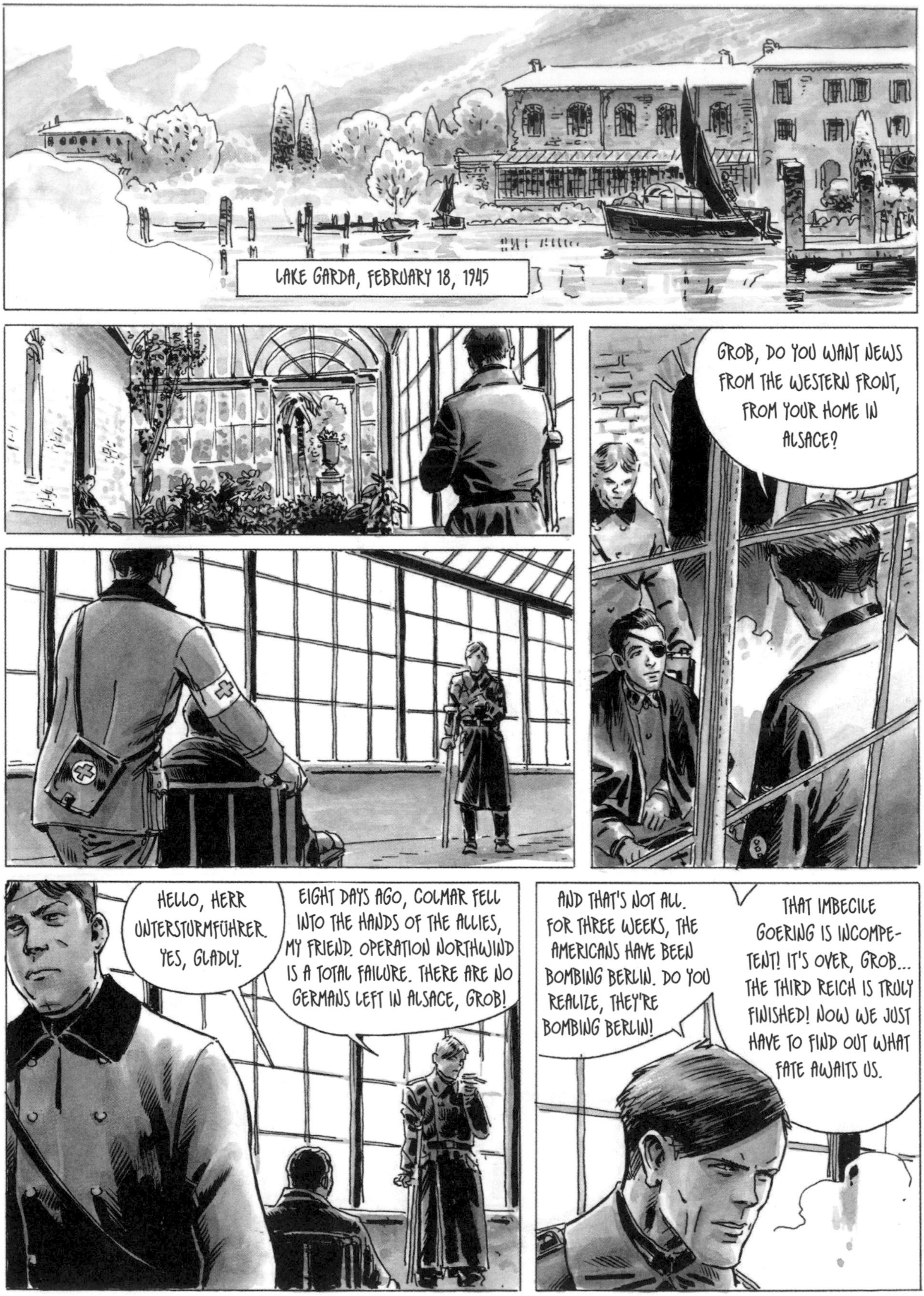
LAKE GARDA, FEBRUARY 18, 1945
GROB, DO YOU WANT NEWS FROM THE WESTERN FRONT, FROM YOUR HOME IN ALSACE?
HELLO, HERR UNTERSTURMFÜHRER. YES, GLADLY.
EIGHT DAYS AGO, COLMAR FELL INTO THE HANDS OF THE ALLIES, MY FRIEND. OPERATION NORTHWIND IS A TOTAL FAILURE. THERE ARE NO GERMANS LEFT IN ALSACE, GROB!
AND THAT'S NOT ALL. FOR THREE WEEKS, THE AMERICANS HAVE BEEN BOMBING BERLIN. DO YOU REALIZE, THEY'RE BOMBING BERLIN!
THAT IMBECILE GOERING IS INCOMPE-TENT! IT'S OVER, GROB... THE THIRD REICH IS TRULY FINISHED! NOW WE JUST HAVE TO FIND OUT WHAT FATE AWAITS US.

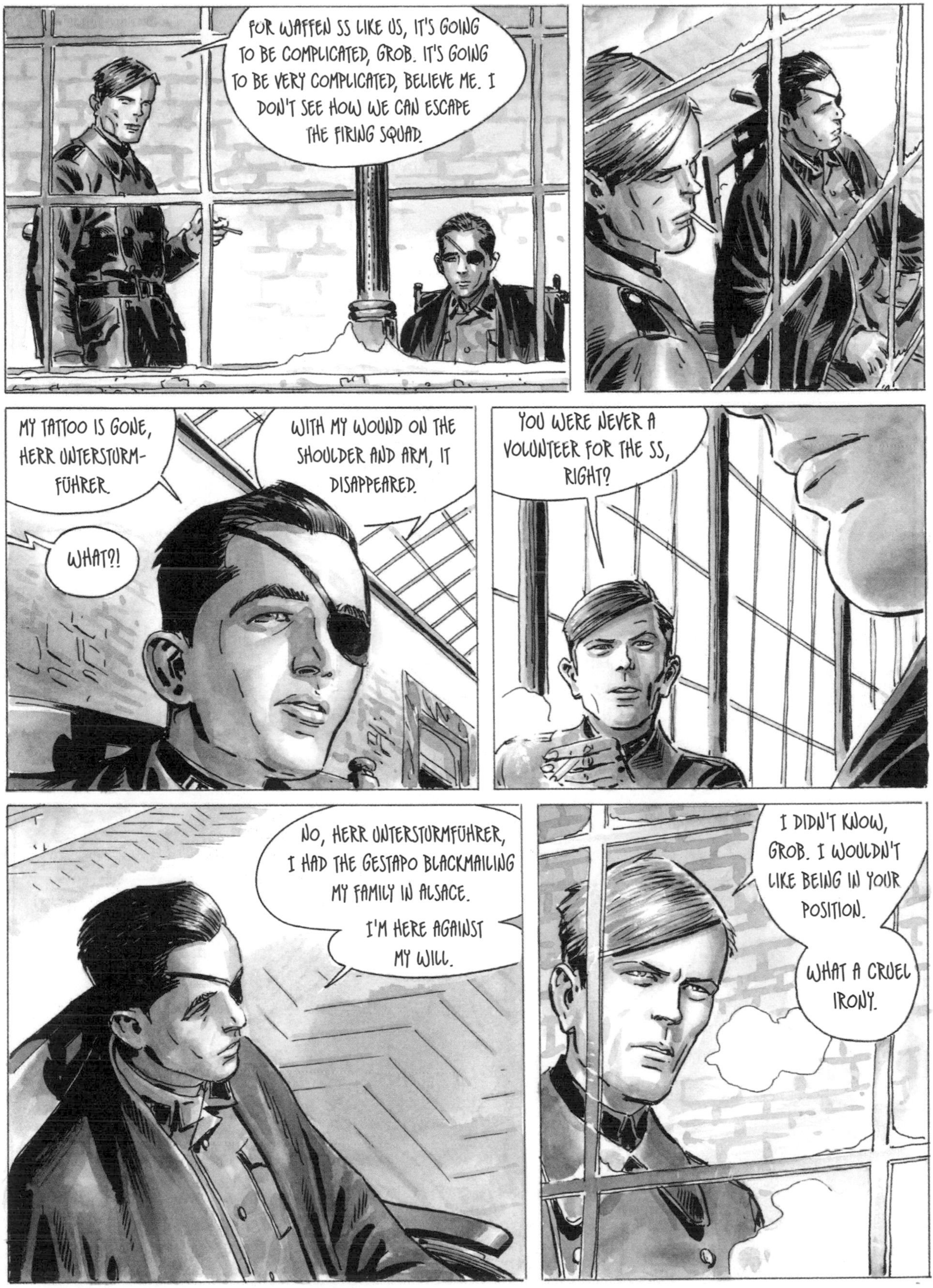
FOR WAFFEN SS LIKE US, IT'S GOING TO BE COMPLICATED, GROB. IT'S GOING TO BE VERY COMPLICATED, BELIEVE ME. I DON'T SEE HOW WE CAN ESCAPE THE FIRING SQUAD.
MY TATTOO IS GONE, HERR UNTERSTURMFÜHRER.
WITH MY WOUND ON THE SHOULDER AND ARM, IT DISAPPEARED.
WHAT?!
YOU WERE NEVER A VOLUNTEER FOR THE SS, RIGHT?
NO, HERR UNTERSTURMFÜHRER, I HAD THE GESTAPO BLACKMAILING MY FAMILY IN ALSACE.
I'M HERE AGAINST MY WILL.
I DIDN'T KNOW, GROB. I WOULDN'T LIKE BEING IN YOUR POSITION.
WHAT A CRUEL IRONY.

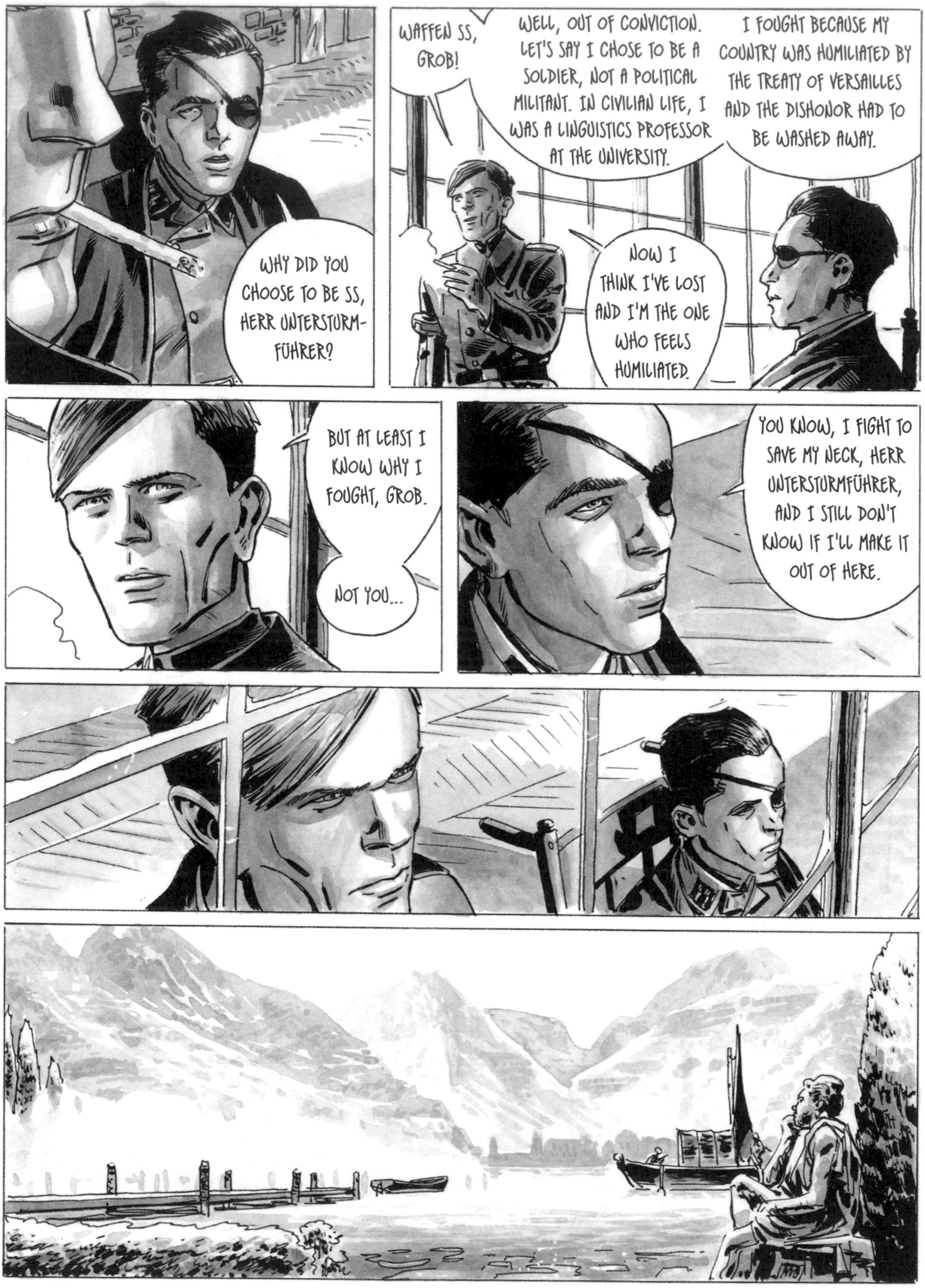
WHY DID YOU CHOOSE TO BE SS, HERR UNTERSTURMFÜHRER?
WAFFEN SS, GROB!
WELL, OUT OF CONVICTION. LET'S SAY I CHOSE TO BE A SOLDIER, NOT A POLITICAL MILITANT. IN CIVILIAN LIFE, I WAS A LINGUISTICS PROFESSOR AT THE UNIVERSITY.
I FOUGHT BECAUSE MY COUNTRY WAS HUMILIATED BY THE TREATY OF VERSAILLES AND THE DISHONOR HAD TO BE WASHED AWAY.
NOW I THINK I'VE LOST AND I'M THE ONE WHO FEELS HUMILIATED.
BUT AT LEAST I KNOW WHY I FOUGHT, GROB.
NOT YOU...
YOU KNOW, I FIGHT TO SAVE MY NECK, HERR UNTERSTURMFÜHRER, AND I STILL DON'T KNOW IF I'LL MAKE IT OUT OF HERE.

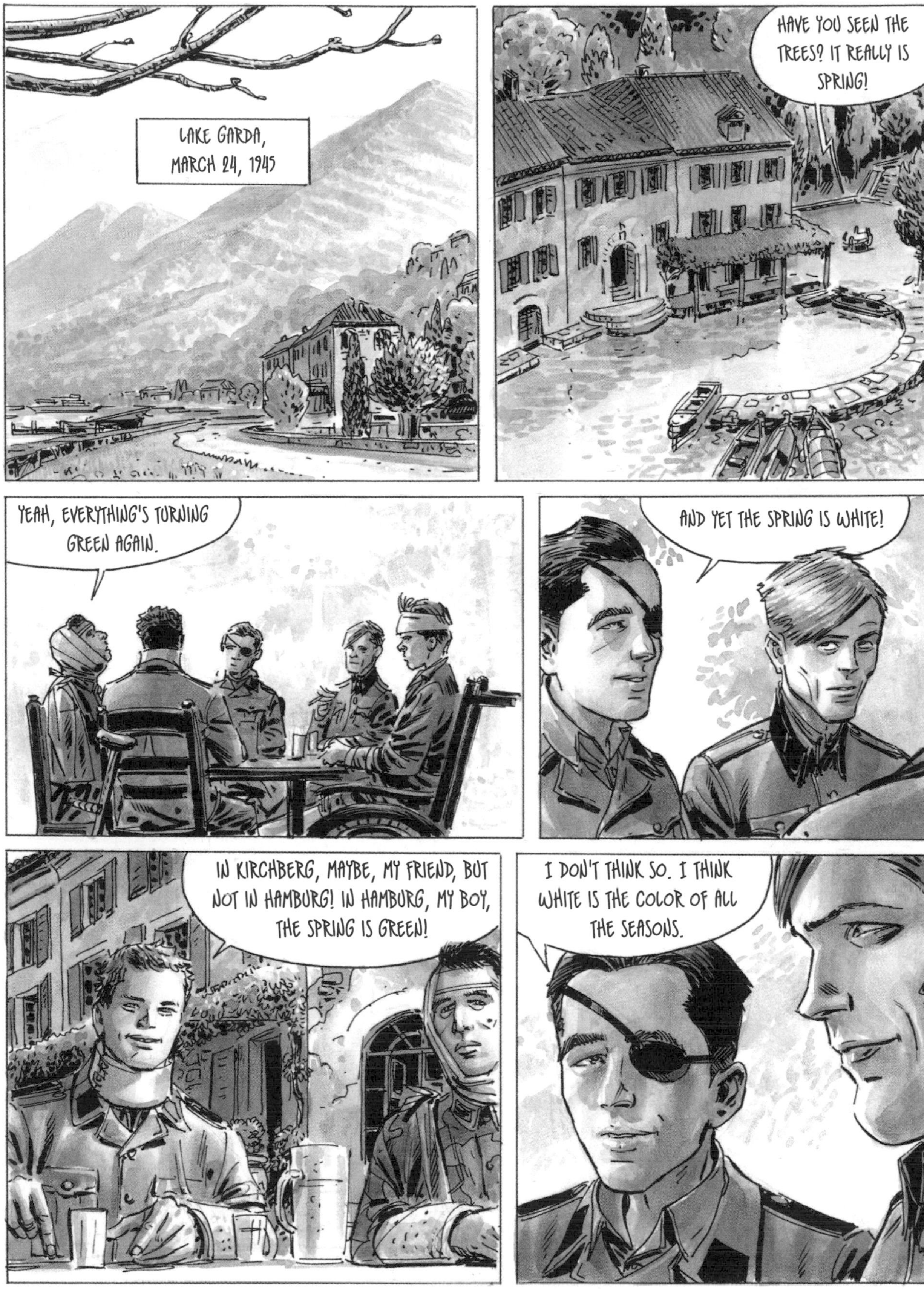

LAKE GARDA,
MARCH 24, 1945
HAVE YOU SEEN THE TREES? IT REALLY IS SPRING!
YEAH, EVERYTHING'S TURNING GREEN AGAIN.
AND YET THE SPRING IS WHITE!
IN KIRCHBERG, MAYBE, MY FRIEND, BUT NOT IN HAMBURG! IN HAMBURG, MY BOY, THE SPRING IS GREEN!
I DON'T THINK SO. I THINK WHITE IS THE COLOR OF ALL THE SEASONS.

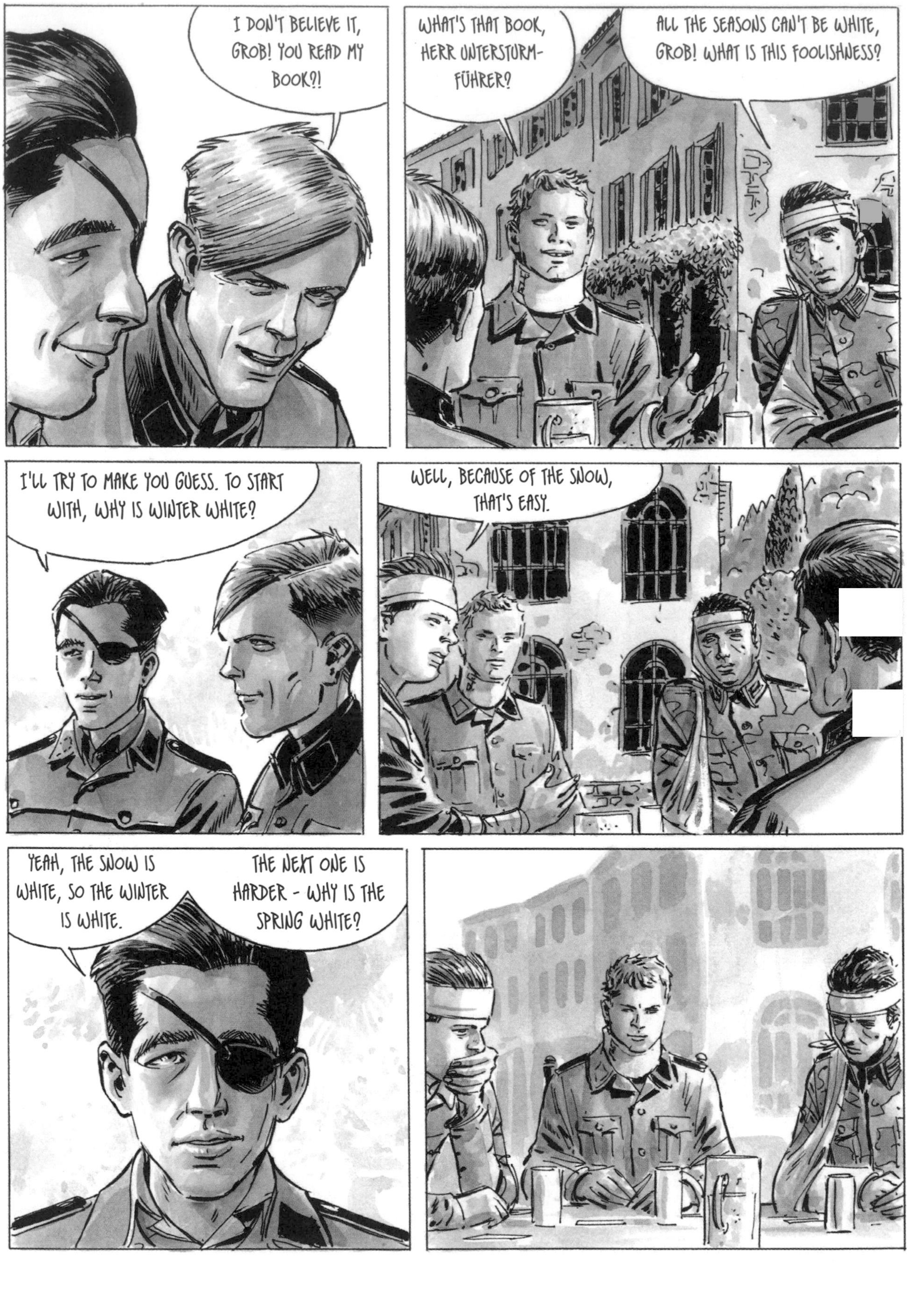
I DON'T BELIEVE IT, GROB! YOU READ MY BOOK?!
WHAT'S THAT BOOK, HERR UNTERSTURM-FÜHRER?
ALL THE SEASONS CAN'T BE WHITE, GROB! WHAT IS THIS FOOLISHNESS?
I'LL TRY TO MAKE YOU GUESS. TO START WITH, WHY IS WINTER WHITE?
WELL, BECAUSE OF THE SNOW, THAT'S EASY.
YEAH, THE SNOW IS WHITE, SO THE WINTER IS WHITE.
THE NEXT ONE IS HARDER - WHY IS THE SPRING WHITE?

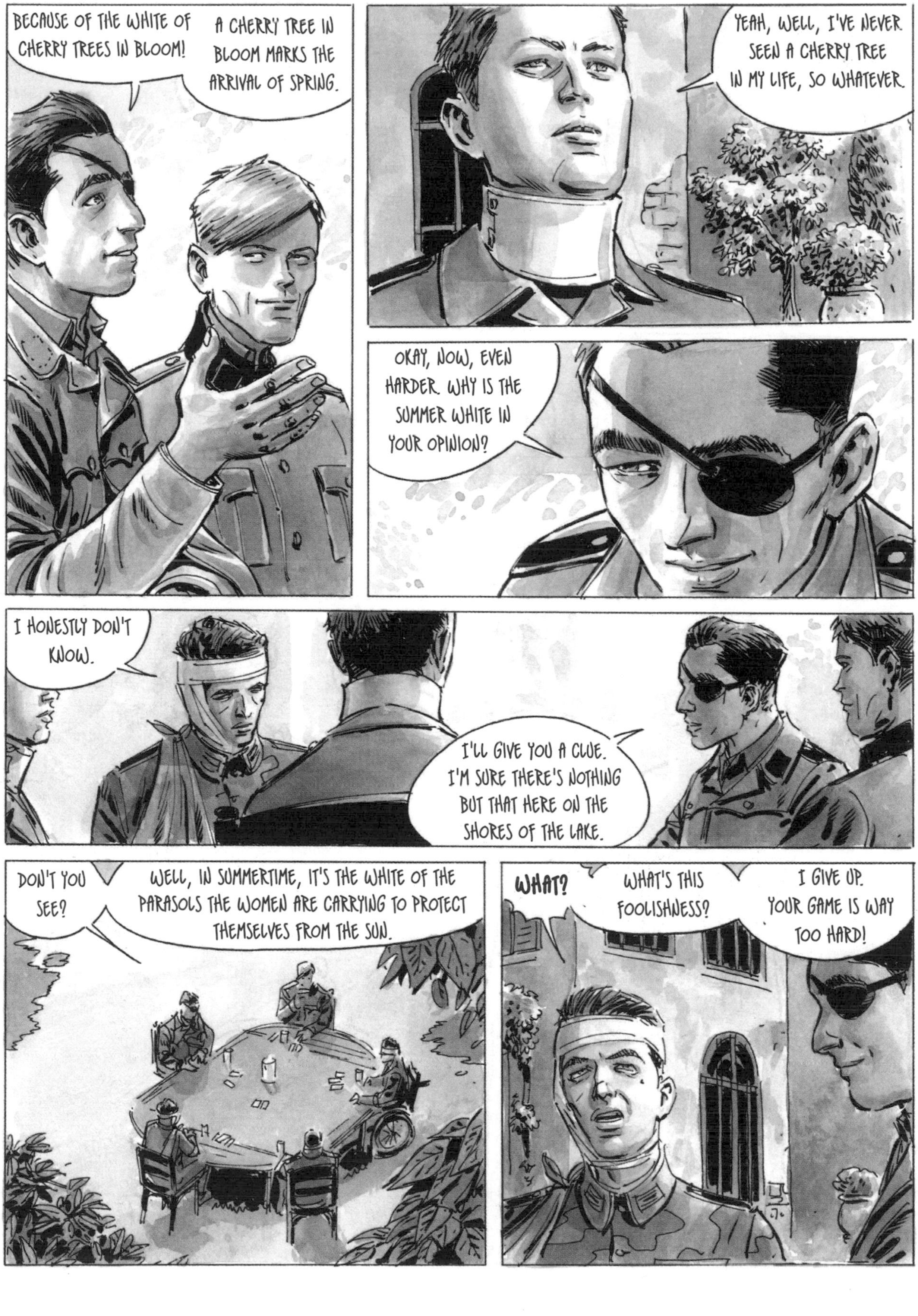
BECAUSE OF THE WHITE OF CHERRY TREES IN BLOOM!
A CHERRY TREE IN BLOOM MARKS THE ARRIVAL OF SPRING.
YEAH, WELL, I'VE NEVER SEEN A CHERRY TREE IN MY LIFE, SO WHATEVER.
OKAY, NOW, EVEN HARDER. WHY IS THE SUMMER WHITE IN YOUR OPINION?
I HONESTLY DON'T KNOW.
I'LL GIVE YOU A CLUE. I'M SURE THERE'S NOTHING BUT THAT HERE ON THE SHORES OF THE LAKE.
DON'T YOU SEE?
WELL, IN SUMMERTIME, IT'S THE WHITE OF THE PARASOLS THE WOMEN ARE CARRYING TO PROTECT THEMSELVES FROM THE SUN.
WHAT?
WHAT'S THIS FOOLISHNESS?
I GIVE UP. YOUR GAME IS WAY TOO HARD!

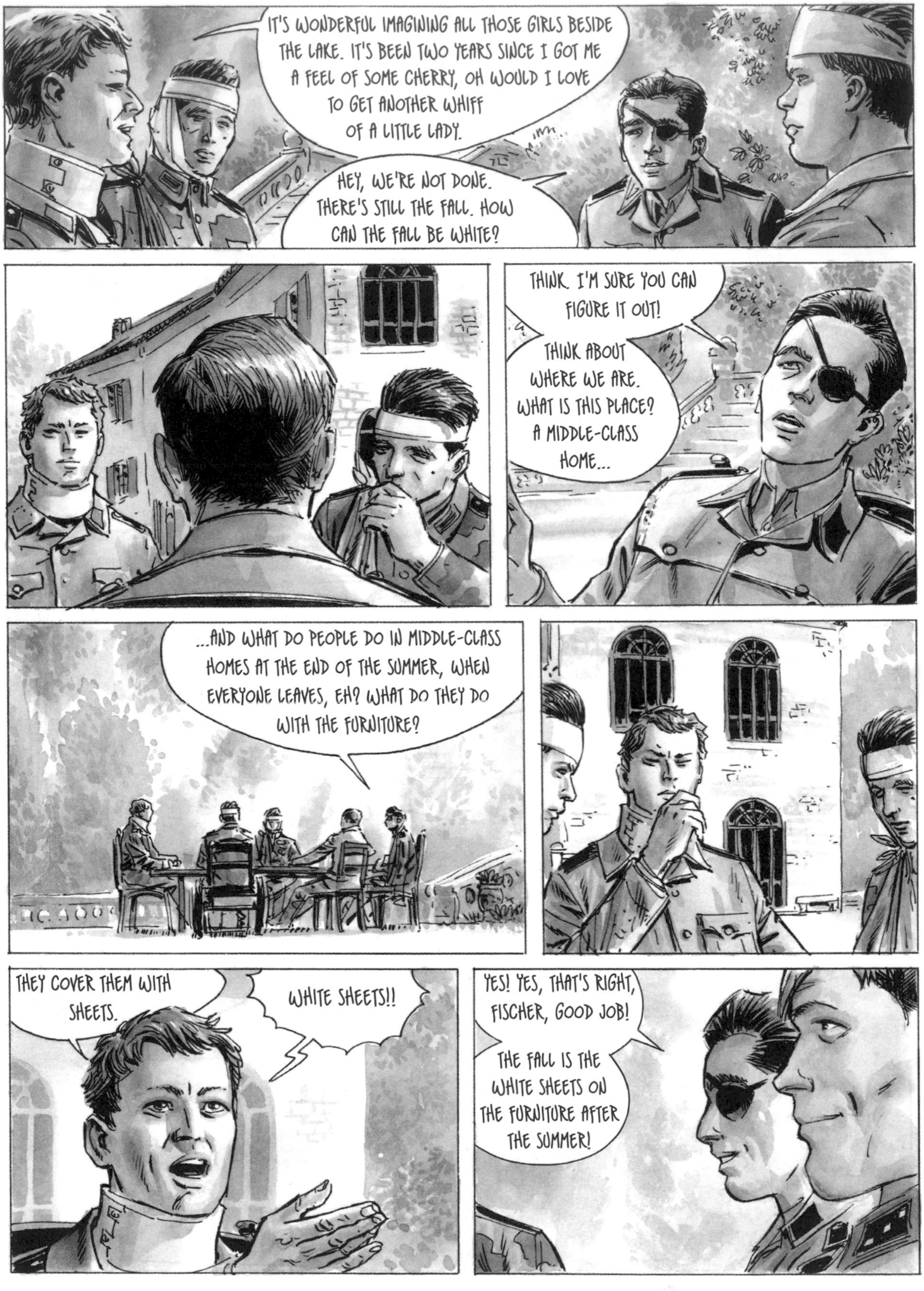

IT'S WONDERFUL IMAGINING ALL THOSE GIRLS BESIDE THE LAKE. IT'S BEEN TWO YEARS SINCE I GOT ME A FEEL OF SOME CHERRY, OH WOULD I LOVE TO GET ANOTHER WHIFF OF A LITTLE LADY.
HEY, WE'RE NOT DONE. THERE'S STILL THE FALL. HOW CAN THE FALL BE WHITE?
THINK. I'M SURE YOU CAN FIGURE IT OUT!
THINK ABOUT WHERE WE ARE. WHAT IS THIS PLACE? A MIDDLE-CLASS HOME...
...AND WHAT DO PEOPLE DO IN MIDDLE-CLASS HOMES AT THE END OF THE SUMMER, WHEN EVERYONE LEAVES, EH? WHAT DO THEY DO WITH THE FURNITURE?
THEY COVER THEM WITH SHEETS.
WHITE SHEETS!!
YES! YES, THAT'S RIGHT, FISCHER, GOOD JOB!
THE FALL IS THE WHITE SHEETS ON THE FURNITURE AFTER THE SUMMER!

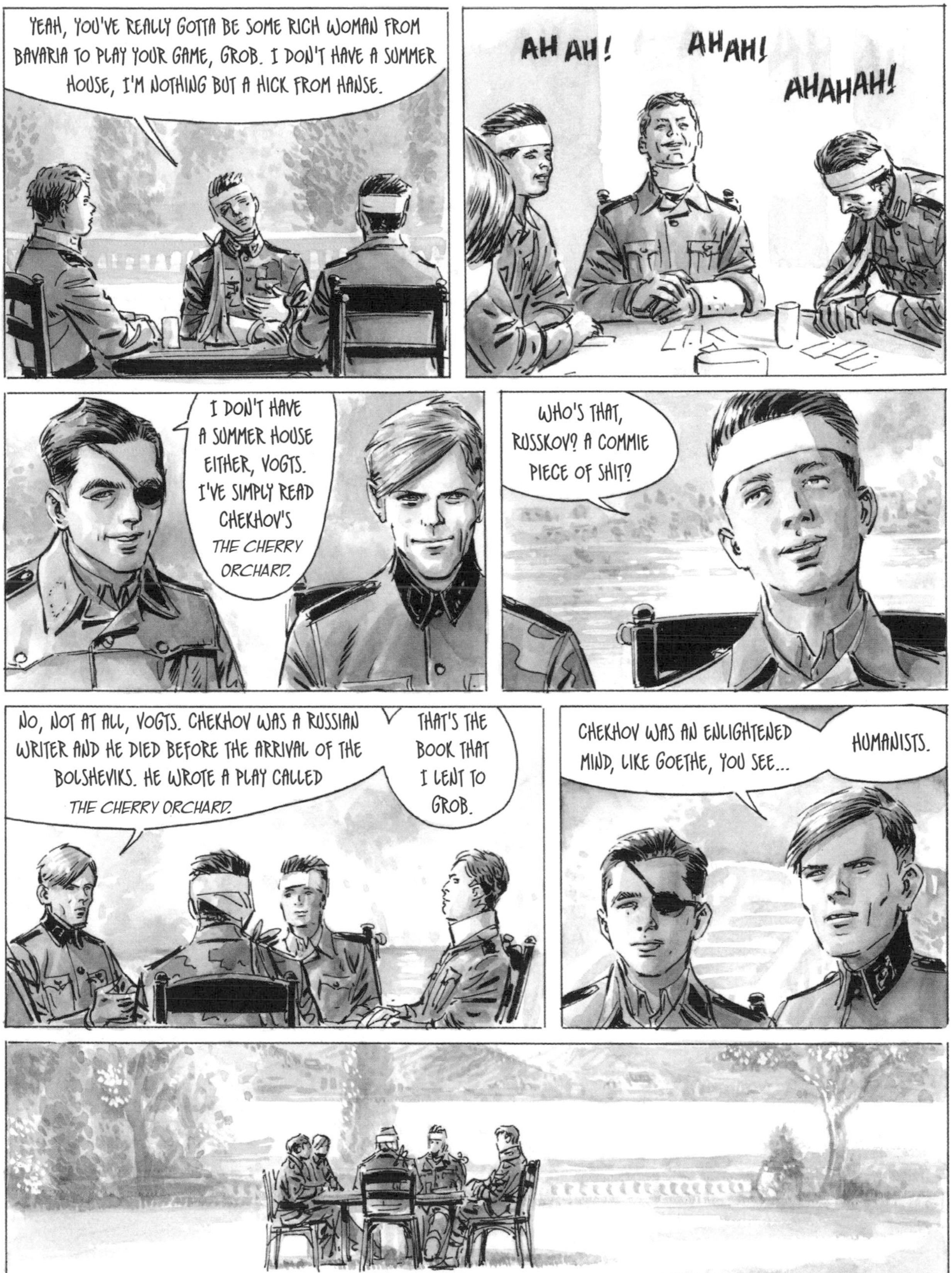
YEAH, YOU'VE REALLY GOTTA BE SOME RICH WOMAN FROM BAVARIA TO PLAY YOUR GAME, GROB. I DON'T HAVE A SUMMER HOUSE, I'M NOTHING BUT A HICK FROM HANSE.
AH AH!
AHAH!
AHAHAH!
I DON'T HAVE A SUMMER HOUSE EITHER, VOGTS. I'VE SIMPLY READ CHEKHOV'S *THE CHERRY ORCHARD*.
WHO'S THAT, RUSSKOV? A COMMIE PIECE OF SHIT?
NO, NOT AT ALL, VOGTS. CHEKHOV WAS A RUSSIAN WRITER AND HE DIED BEFORE THE ARRIVAL OF THE BOLSHEVIKS. HE WROTE A PLAY CALLED *THE CHERRY ORCHARD*.
THAT'S THE BOOK THAT I LENT TO GROB.
CHEKHOV WAS AN ENLIGHTENED MIND, LIKE GOETHE, YOU SEE...
HUMANISTS.

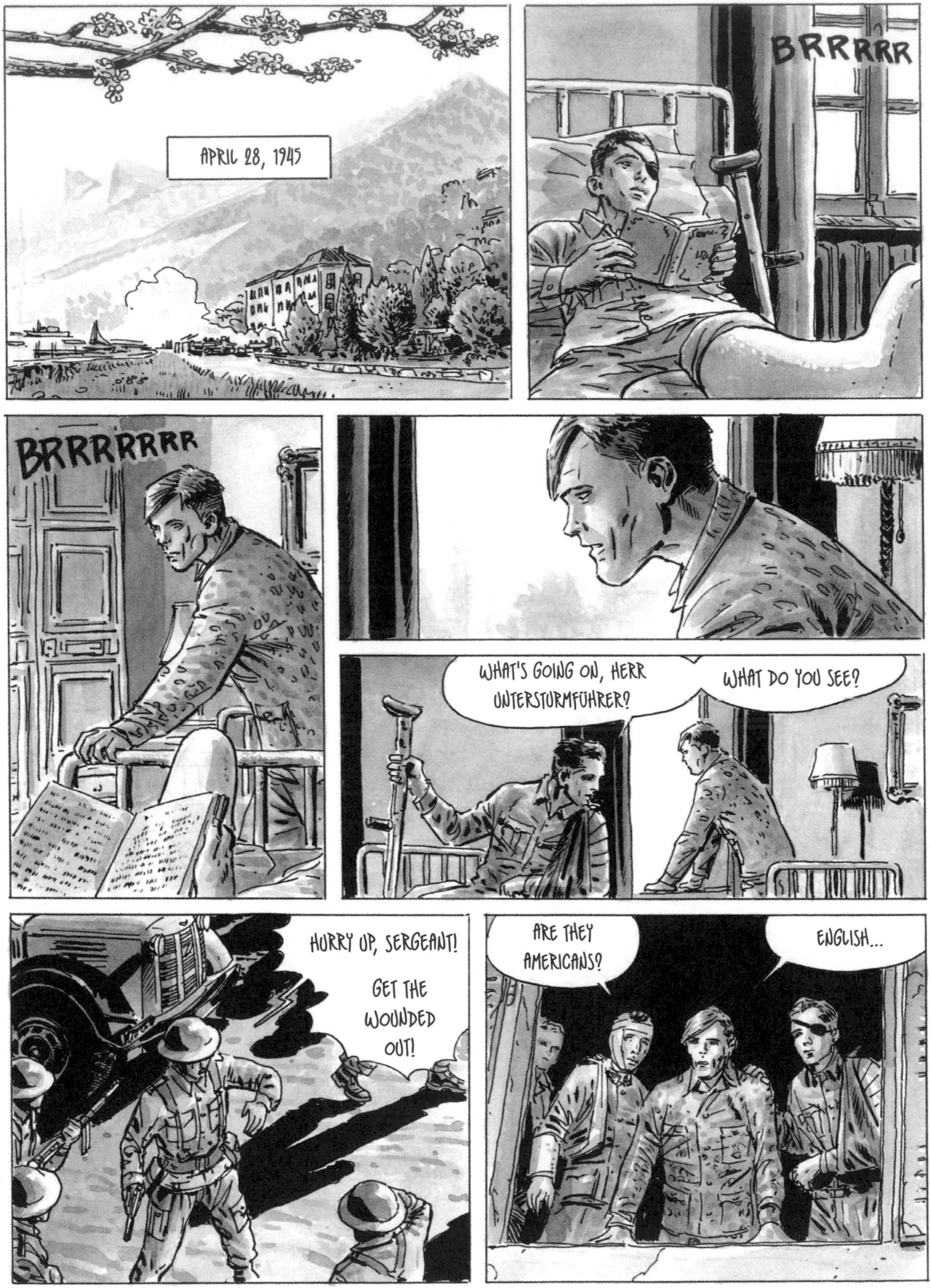
APRIL 28, 1945
BRRRRRR
BRRRRRRR
WHAT'S GOING ON, HERR UNTERSTURMFÜHRER?
WHAT DO YOU SEE?
HURRY UP, SERGEANT!
GET THE WOUNDED OUT!
ARE THEY AMERICANS?
ENGLISH...

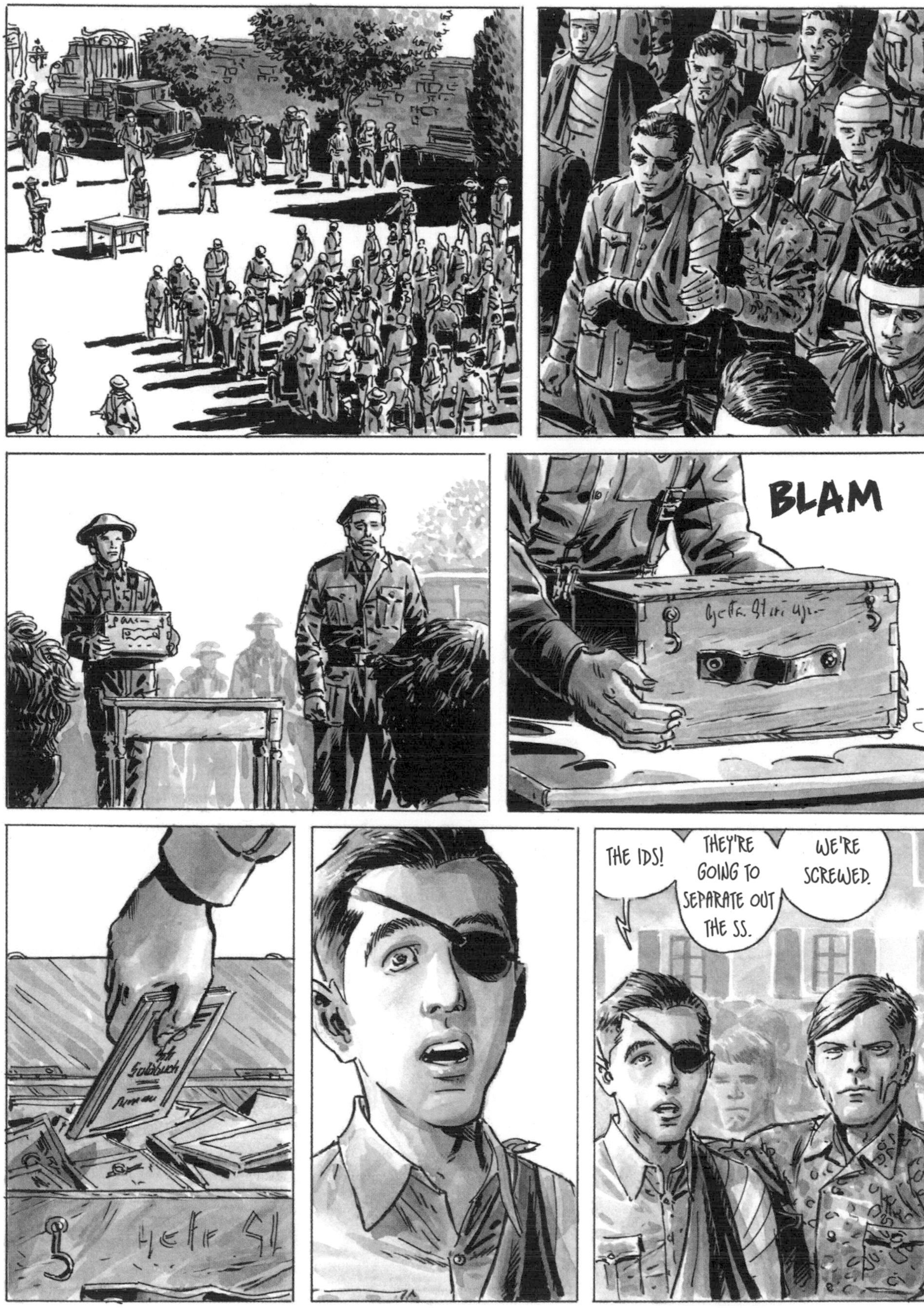
BLAM
THE IDS!
THEY'RE GOING TO SEPARATE OUT THE SS.
WE'RE SCREWED.

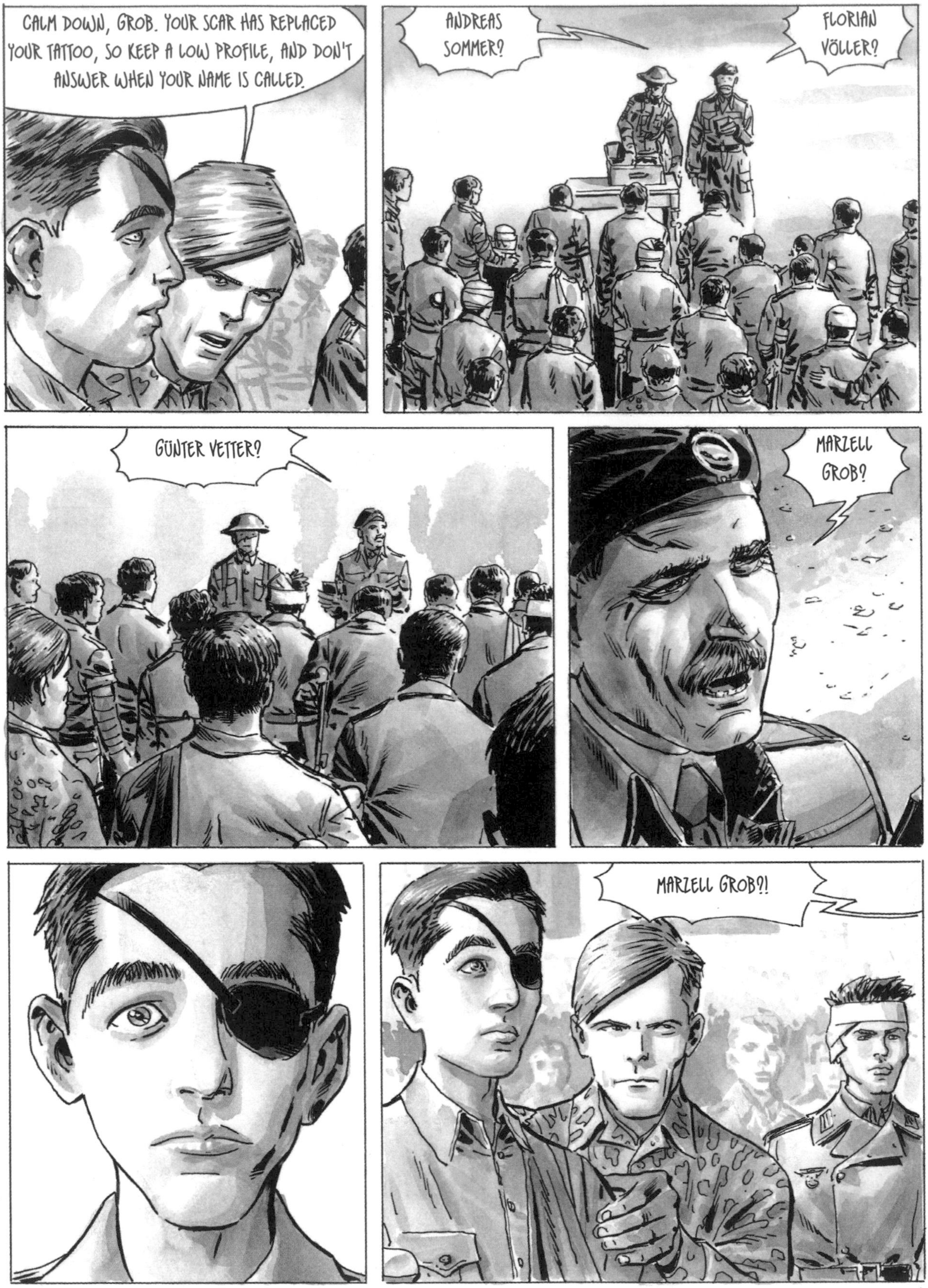
CALM DOWN, GROB. YOUR SCAR HAS REPLACED YOUR TATTOO, SO KEEP A LOW PROFILE, AND DON'T ANSWER WHEN YOUR NAME IS CALLED.
ANDREAS SOMMER?
FLORIAN VÖLLER?
GÜNTER VETTER?
MARZELL GROB?
MARZELL GROB?!

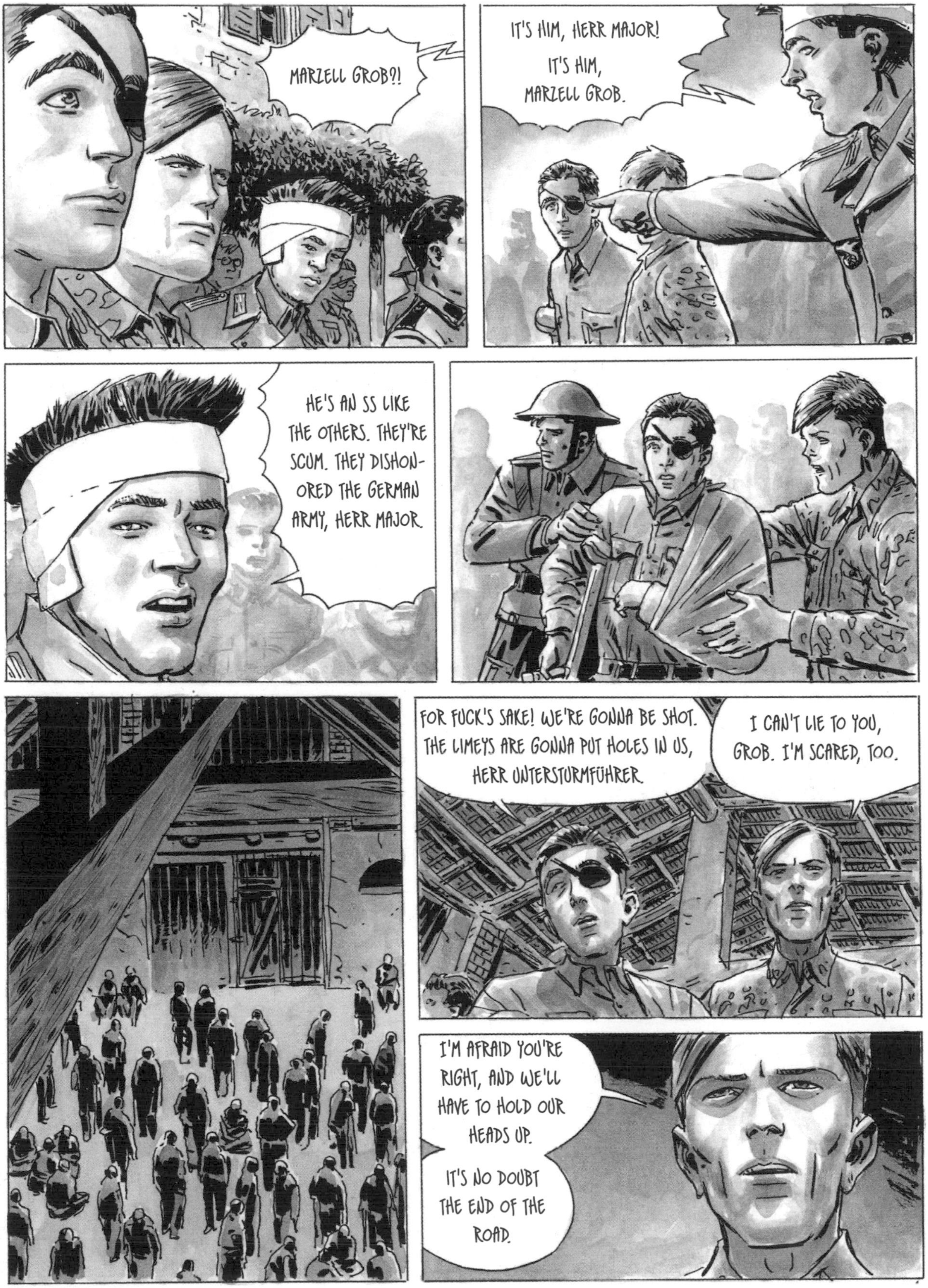
MARZELL GROB?!
IT'S HIM, HERR MAJOR!
IT'S HIM, MARZELL GROB.
HE'S AN SS LIKE THE OTHERS. THEY'RE SCUM. THEY DISHON-ORED THE GERMAN ARMY, HERR MAJOR.
FOR FUCK'S SAKE! WE'RE GONNA BE SHOT. THE LIMEYS ARE GONNA PUT HOLES IN US, HERR UNTERSTURMFÜHRER.
I CAN'T LIE TO YOU, GROB. I'M SCARED, TOO.
I'M AFRAID YOU'RE RIGHT, AND WE'LL HAVE TO HOLD OUR HEADS UP.
IT'S NO DOUBT THE END OF THE ROAD.

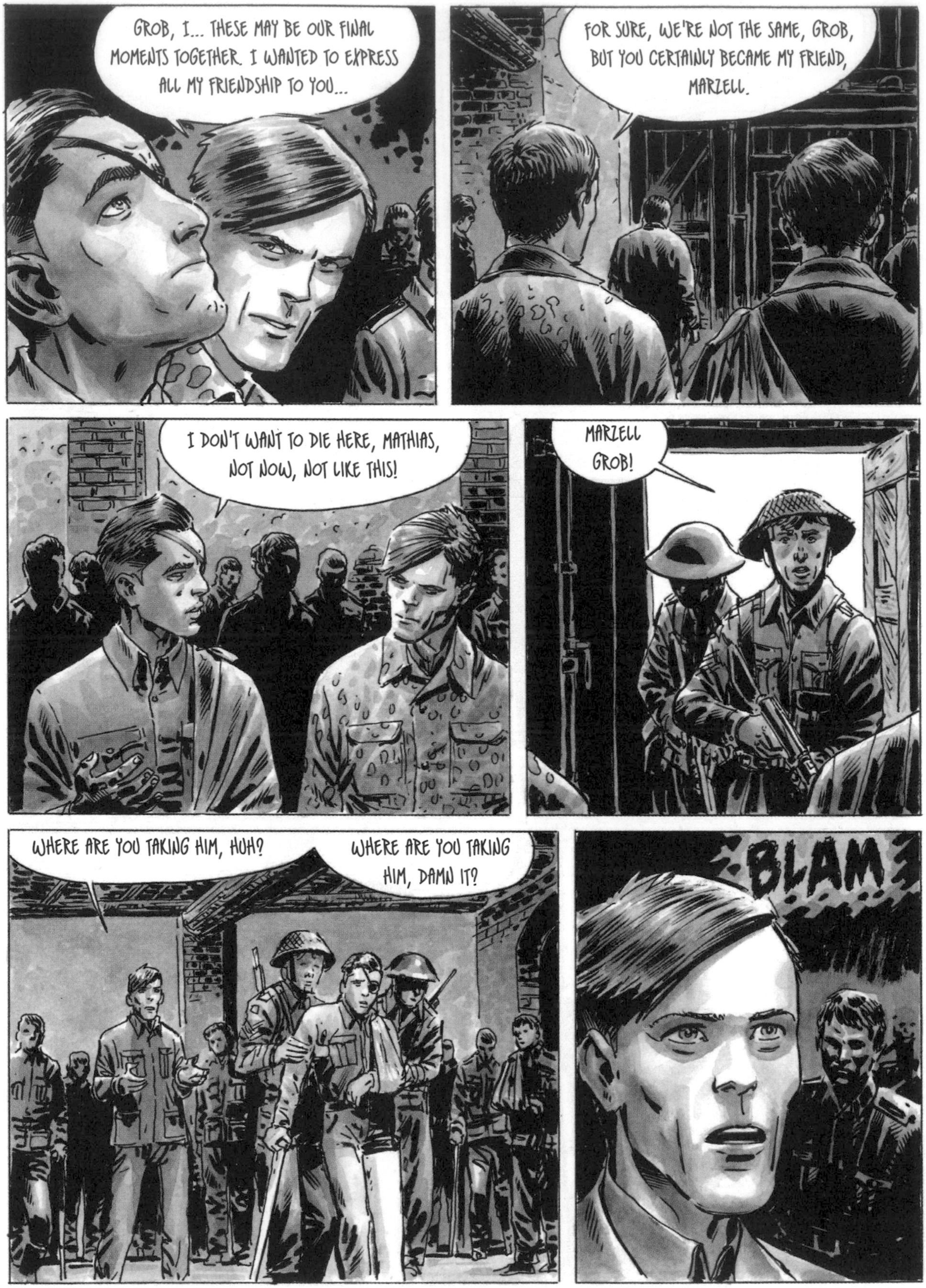
GROB, I... THESE MAY BE OUR FINAL MOMENTS TOGETHER. I WANTED TO EXPRESS ALL MY FRIENDSHIP TO YOU...
FOR SURE, WE'RE NOT THE SAME, GROB, BUT YOU CERTAINLY BECAME MY FRIEND, MARZELL.
I DON'T WANT TO DIE HERE, MATHIAS, NOT NOW, NOT LIKE THIS!
MARZELL GROB!
WHERE ARE YOU TAKING HIM, HUH?
WHERE ARE YOU TAKING HIM, DAMN IT?
BLAM

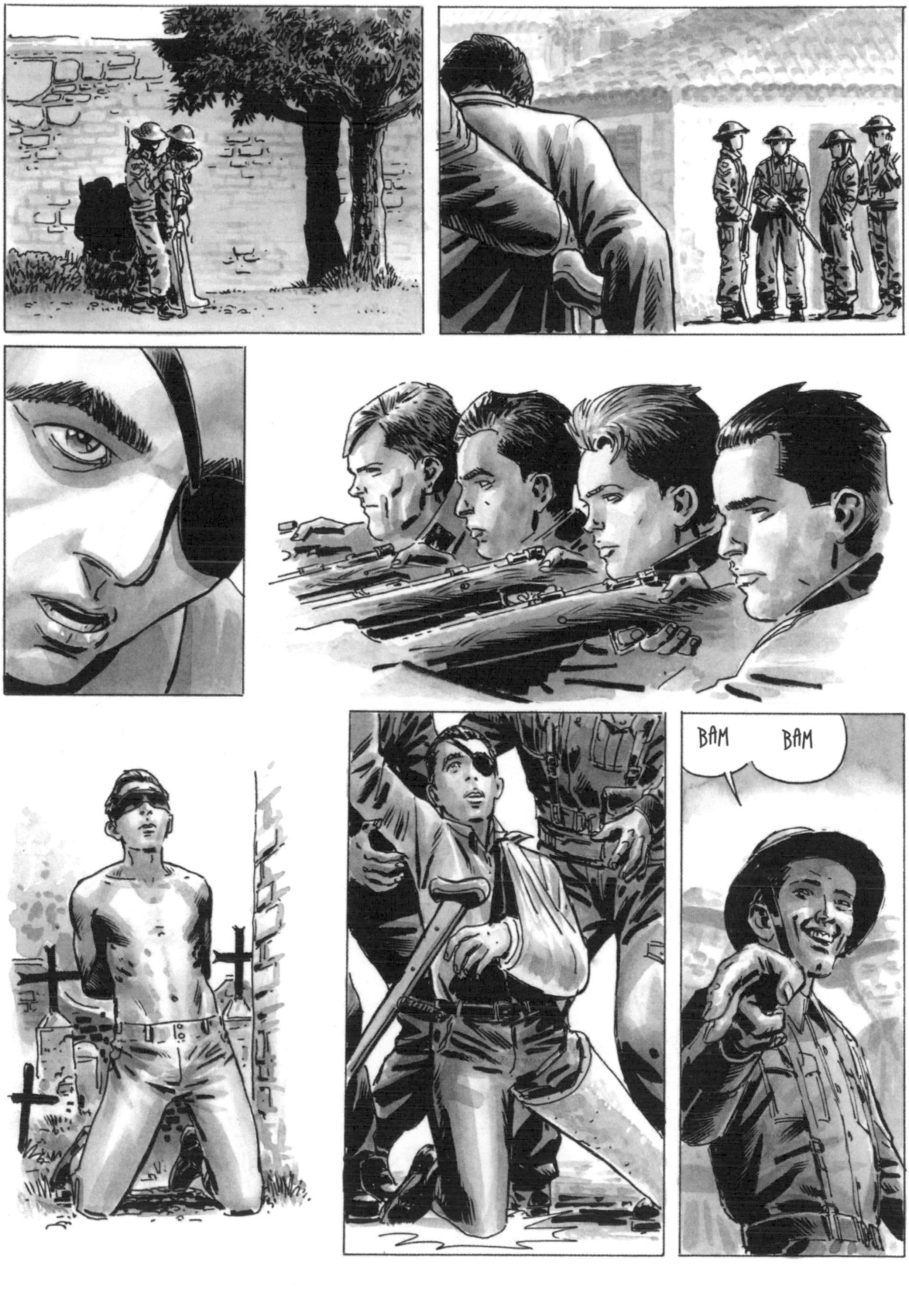
BAM
BAM

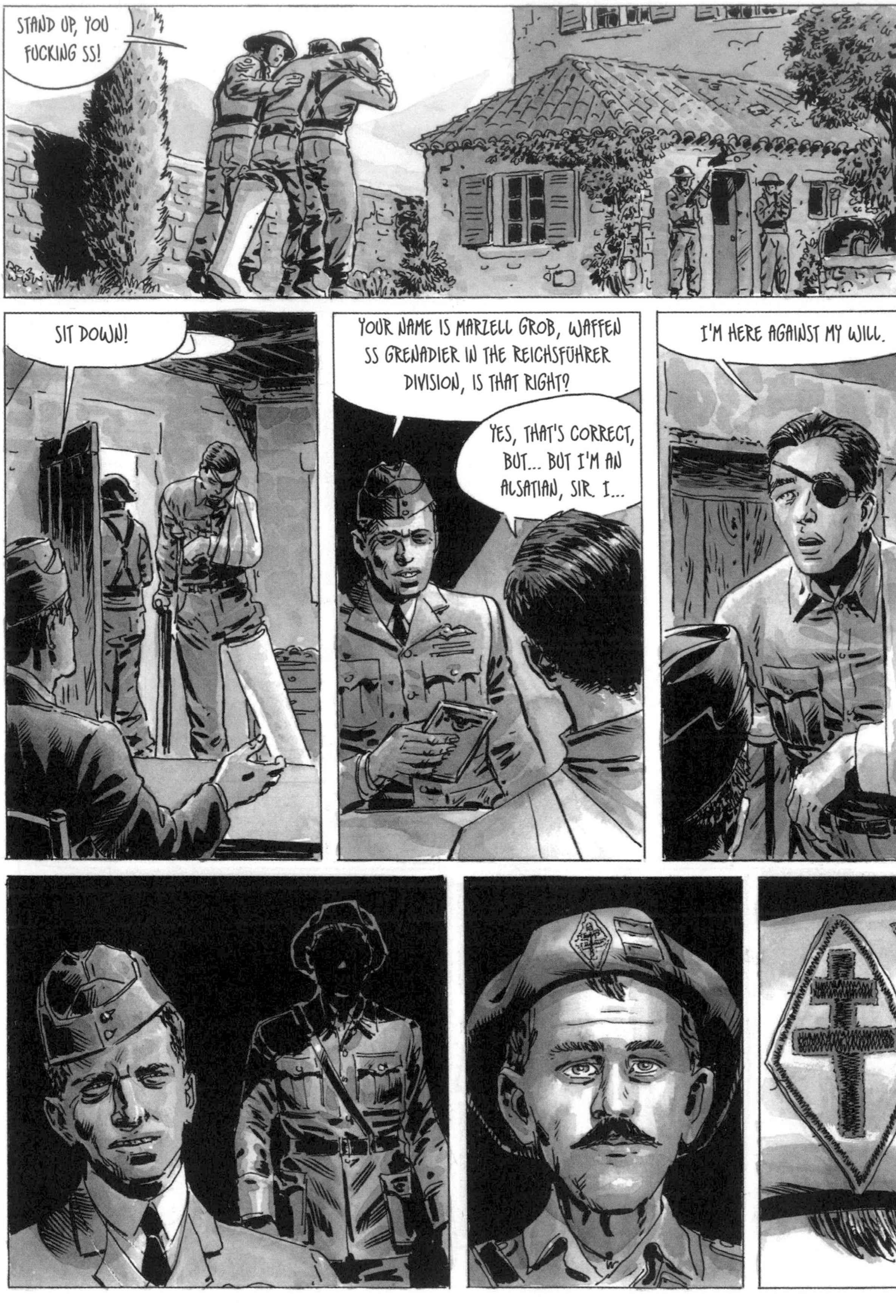
STAND UP, YOU FUCKING SS!
SIT DOWN!
YOUR NAME IS MARZELL GROB, WAFFEN SS GRENADIER IN THE REICHSFÜHRER DIVISION, IS THAT RIGHT?
YES, THAT'S CORRECT, BUT... BUT I'M AN ALSATIAN, SIR. I...
I'M HERE AGAINST MY WILL.

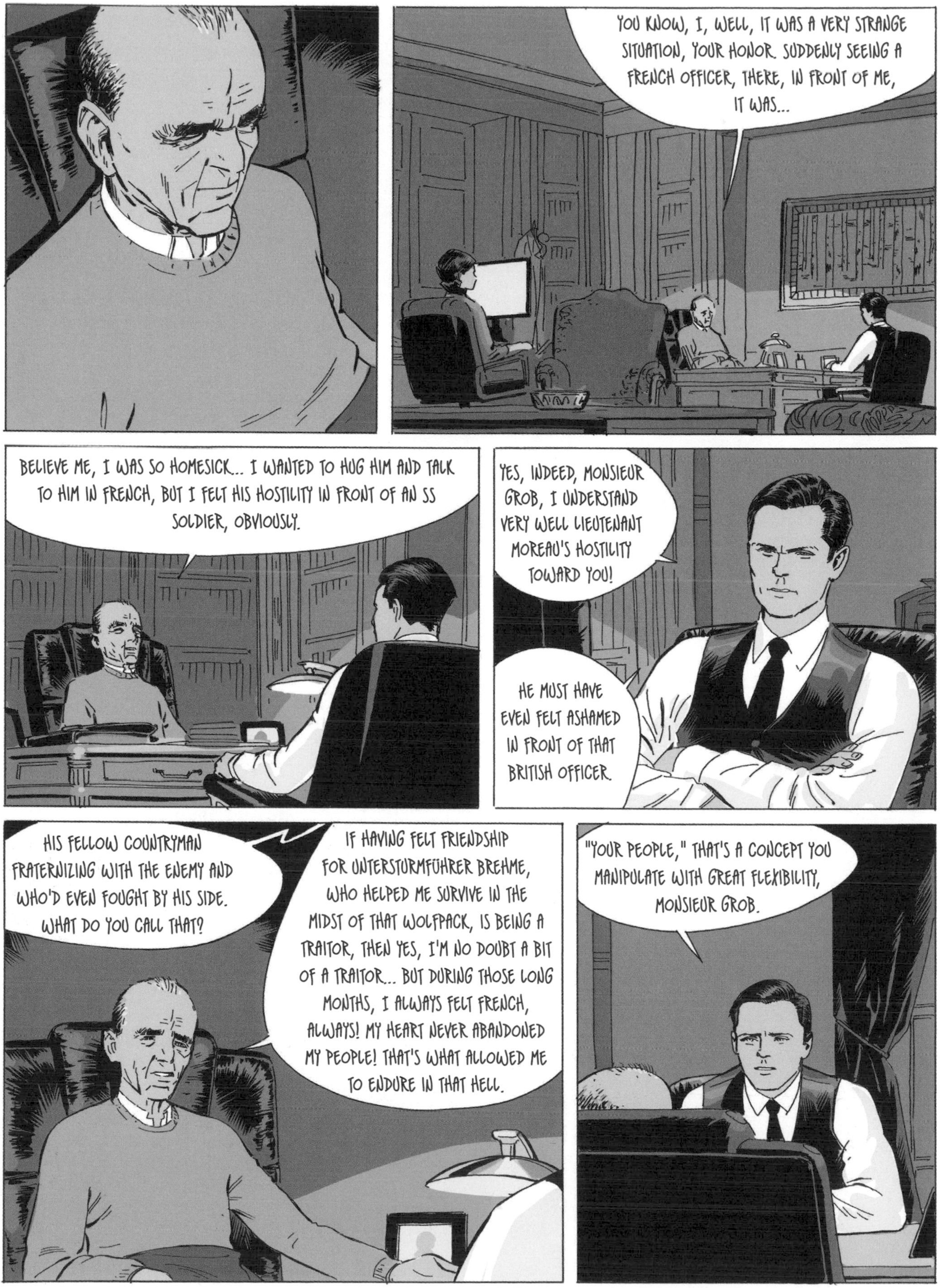

YOU KNOW, I, WELL, IT WAS A VERY STRANGE SITUATION, YOUR HONOR. SUDDENLY SEEING A FRENCH OFFICER, THERE, IN FRONT OF ME, IT WAS...
BELIEVE ME, I WAS SO HOMESICK... I WANTED TO HUG HIM AND TALK TO HIM IN FRENCH, BUT I FELT HIS HOSTILITY IN FRONT OF AN SS SOLDIER, OBVIOUSLY.
YES, INDEED, MONSIEUR GROB, I UNDERSTAND VERY WELL LIEUTENANT MOREAU'S HOSTILITY TOWARD YOU!
HE MUST HAVE EVEN FELT ASHAMED IN FRONT OF THAT BRITISH OFFICER.
HIS FELLOW COUNTRYMAN FRATERNIZING WITH THE ENEMY AND WHO'D EVEN FOUGHT BY HIS SIDE. WHAT DO YOU CALL THAT?
IF HAVING FELT FRIENDSHIP FOR UNTERSTURMFÜHRER BREHME, WHO HELPED ME SURVIVE IN THE MIDST OF THAT WOLFPACK, IS BEING A TRAITOR, THEN YES, I'M NO DOUBT A BIT OF A TRAITOR... BUT DURING THOSE LONG MONTHS, I ALWAYS FELT FRENCH, ALWAYS! MY HEART NEVER ABANDONED MY PEOPLE! THAT'S WHAT ALLOWED ME TO ENDURE IN THAT HELL.
"YOUR PEOPLE," THAT'S A CONCEPT YOU MANIPULATE WITH GREAT FLEXIBILITY, MONSIEUR GROB.

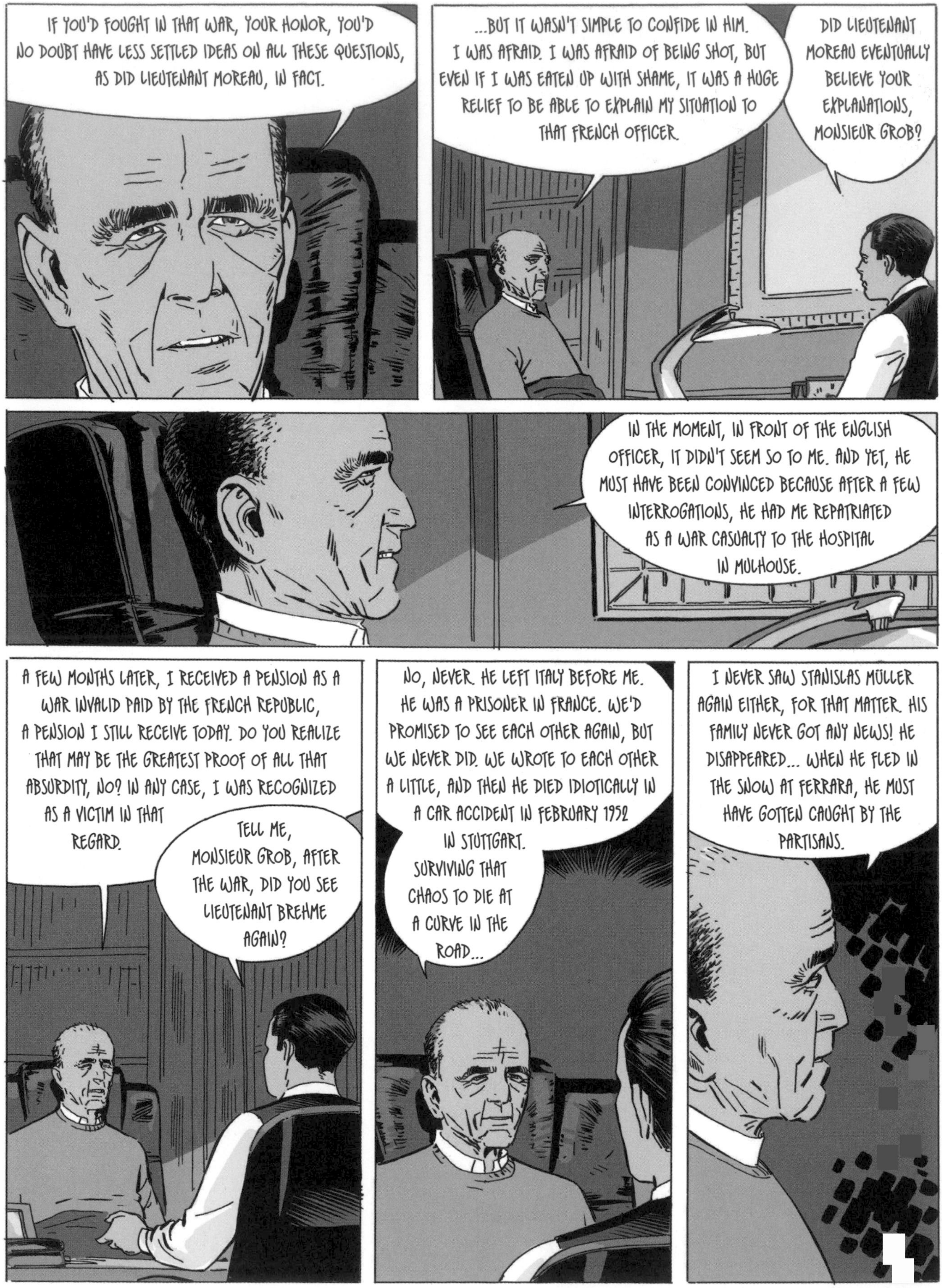
IF YOU'D FOUGHT IN THAT WAR, YOUR HONOR, YOU'D NO DOUBT HAVE LESS SETTLED IDEAS ON ALL THESE QUESTIONS, AS DID LIEUTENANT MOREAU, IN FACT.
...BUT IT WASN'T SIMPLE TO CONFIDE IN HIM. I WAS AFRAID. I WAS AFRAID OF BEING SHOT, BUT EVEN IF I WAS EATEN UP WITH SHAME, IT WAS A HUGE RELIEF TO BE ABLE TO EXPLAIN MY SITUATION TO THAT FRENCH OFFICER.
DID LIEUTENANT MOREAU EVENTUALLY BELIEVE YOUR EXPLANATIONS, MONSIEUR GROB?
IN THE MOMENT, IN FRONT OF THE ENGLISH OFFICER, IT DIDN'T SEEM SO TO ME. AND YET, HE MUST HAVE BEEN CONVINCED BECAUSE AFTER A FEW INTERROGATIONS, HE HAD ME REPATRIATED AS A WAR CASUALTY TO THE HOSPITAL IN MULHOUSE.
A FEW MONTHS LATER, I RECEIVED A PENSION AS A WAR INVALID PAID BY THE FRENCH REPUBLIC, A PENSION I STILL RECEIVE TODAY. DO YOU REALIZE THAT MAY BE THE GREATEST PROOF OF ALL THAT ABSURDITY, NO? IN ANY CASE, I WAS RECOGNIZED AS A VICTIM IN THAT REGARD.
TELL ME, MONSIEUR GROB, AFTER THE WAR, DID YOU SEE LIEUTENANT BREHME AGAIN?
NO, NEVER. HE LEFT ITALY BEFORE ME. HE WAS A PRISONER IN FRANCE. WE'D PROMISED TO SEE EACH OTHER AGAIN, BUT WE NEVER DID. WE WROTE TO EACH OTHER A LITTLE, AND THEN HE DIED IDIOTICALLY IN A CAR ACCIDENT IN FEBRUARY 1952 IN STUTTGART.
SURVIVING THAT CHAOS TO DIE AT A CURVE IN THE ROAD...
I NEVER SAW STANISLAS MÜLLER AGAIN EITHER, FOR THAT MATTER. HIS FAMILY NEVER GOT ANY NEWS! HE DISAPPEARED... WHEN HE FLED IN THE SNOW AT FERRARA, HE MUST HAVE GOTTEN CAUGHT BY THE PARTISANS.

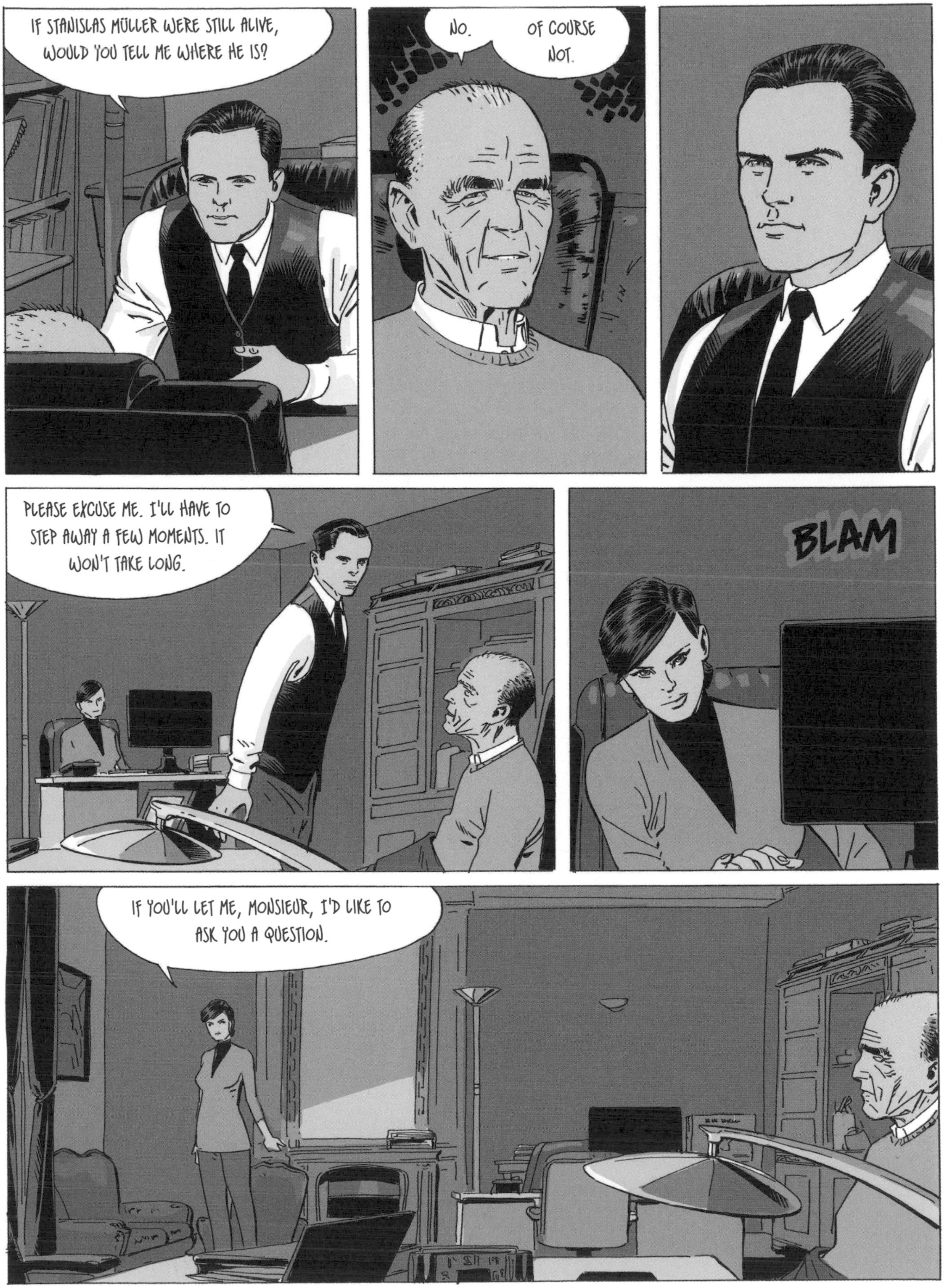

IF STANISLAS MÜLLER WERE STILL ALIVE, WOULD YOU TELL ME WHERE HE IS?
NO.
OF COURSE NOT.
PLEASE EXCUSE ME. I'LL HAVE TO STEP AWAY A FEW MOMENTS. IT WON'T TAKE LONG.
BLAM
IF YOU'LL LET ME, MONSIEUR, I'D LIKE TO ASK YOU A QUESTION.

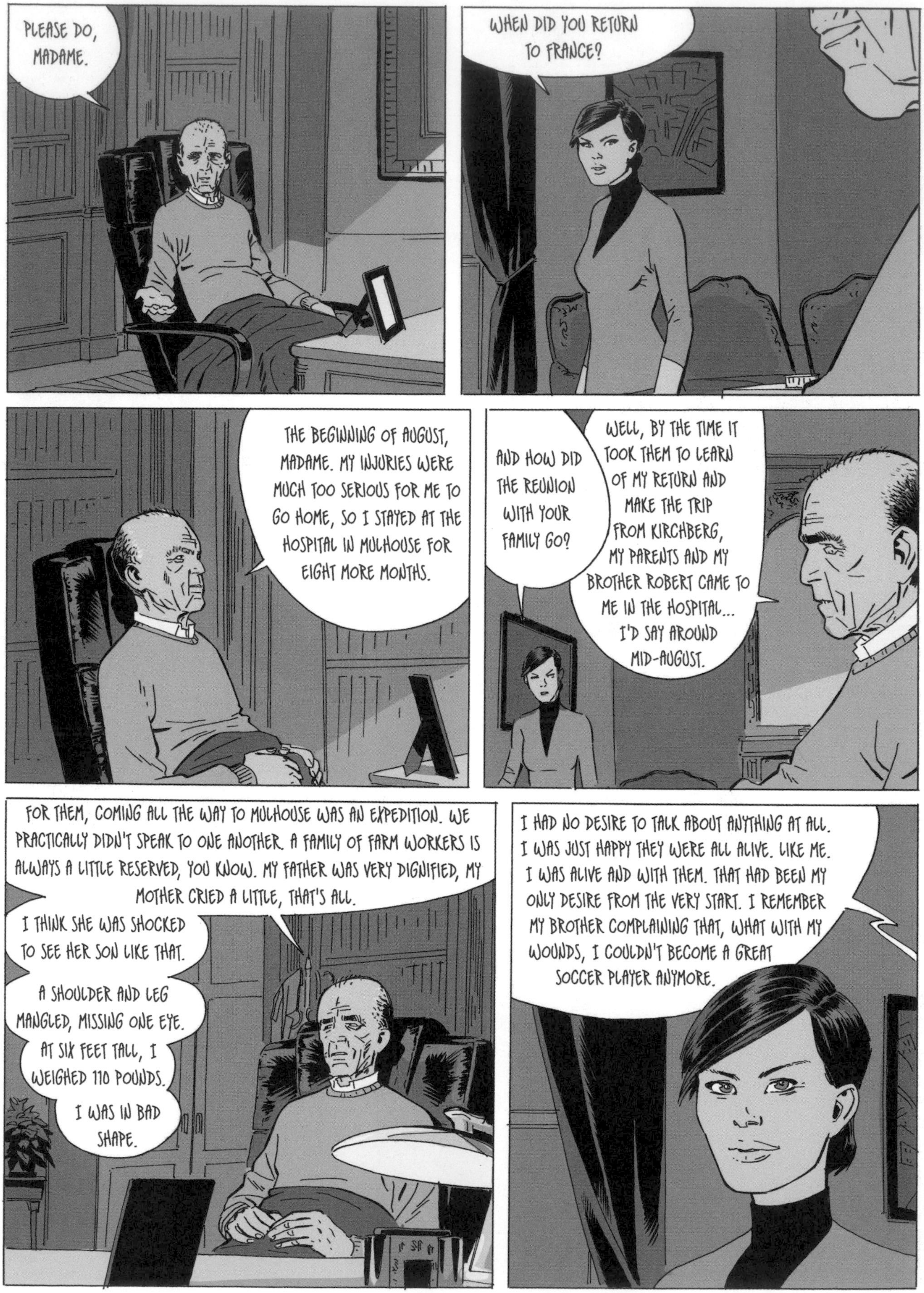
PLEASE DO, MADAME.
WHEN DID YOU RETURN TO FRANCE?
THE BEGINNING OF AUGUST, MADAME. MY INJURIES WERE MUCH TOO SERIOUS FOR ME TO GO HOME, SO I STAYED AT THE HOSPITAL IN MULHOUSE FOR EIGHT MORE MONTHS.
AND HOW DID THE REUNION WITH YOUR FAMILY GO?
WELL, BY THE TIME IT TOOK THEM TO LEARN OF MY RETURN AND MAKE THE TRIP FROM KIRCHBERG, MY PARENTS AND MY BROTHER ROBERT CAME TO ME IN THE HOSPITAL... I'D SAY AROUND MID-AUGUST.
FOR THEM, COMING ALL THE WAY TO MULHOUSE WAS AN EXPEDITION. WE PRACTICALLY DIDN'T SPEAK TO ONE ANOTHER. A FAMILY OF FARM WORKERS IS ALWAYS A LITTLE RESERVED, YOU KNOW. MY FATHER WAS VERY DIGNIFIED, MY MOTHER CRIED A LITTLE, THAT'S ALL.
I THINK SHE WAS SHOCKED TO SEE HER SON LIKE THAT.
A SHOULDER AND LEG MANGLED, MISSING ONE EYE.
AT SIX FEET TALL, I WEIGHED 110 POUNDS.
I WAS IN BAD SHAPE.
I HAD NO DESIRE TO TALK ABOUT ANYTHING AT ALL. I WAS JUST HAPPY THEY WERE ALL ALIVE. LIKE ME. I WAS ALIVE AND WITH THEM. THAT HAD BEEN MY ONLY DESIRE FROM THE VERY START. I REMEMBER MY BROTHER COMPLAINING THAT, WHAT WITH MY WOUNDS, I COULDN'T BECOME A GREAT SOCCER PLAYER ANYMORE.

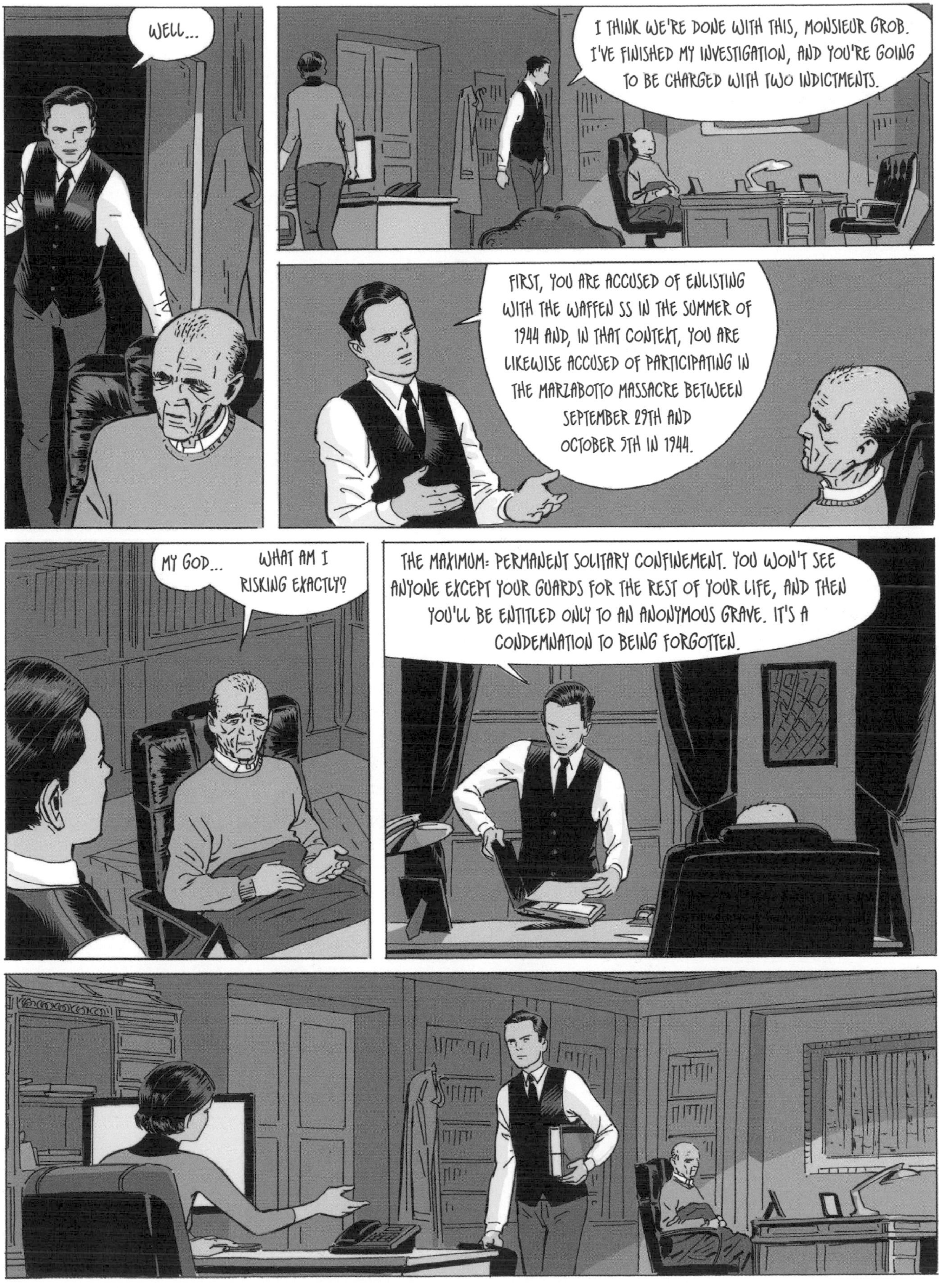
WELL...
I THINK WE'RE DONE WITH THIS, MONSIEUR GROB. I'VE FINISHED MY INVESTIGATION, AND YOU'RE GOING TO BE CHARGED WITH TWO INDICTMENTS.
FIRST, YOU ARE ACCUSED OF ENLISTING WITH THE WAFFEN SS IN THE SUMMER OF 1944 AND, IN THAT CONTEXT, YOU ARE LIKEWISE ACCUSED OF PARTICIPATING IN THE MARZABOTTO MASSACRE BETWEEN SEPTEMBER 29TH AND OCTOBER 5TH IN 1944.
MY GOD...
WHAT AM I RISKING EXACTLY?
THE MAXIMUM: PERMANENT SOLITARY CONFINEMENT. YOU WON'T SEE ANYONE EXCEPT YOUR GUARDS FOR THE REST OF YOUR LIFE, AND THEN YOU'LL BE ENTITLED ONLY TO AN ANONYMOUS GRAVE. IT'S A CONDEMNATION TO BEING FORGOTTEN.

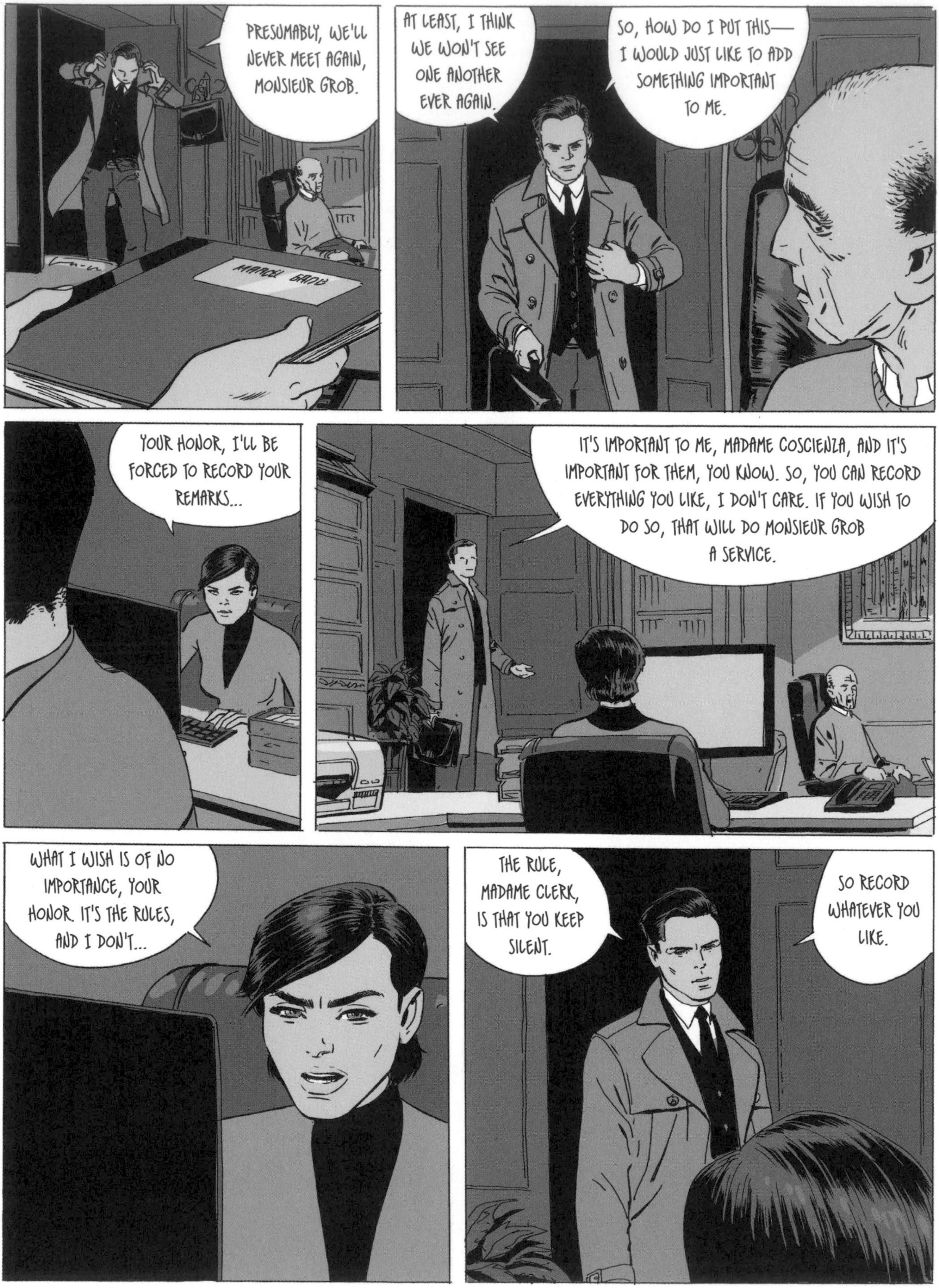
PRESUMABLY, WE'LL NEVER MEET AGAIN, MONSIEUR GROB.
AT LEAST, I THINK WE WON'T SEE ONE ANOTHER EVER AGAIN.
SO, HOW DO I PUT THIS— I WOULD JUST LIKE TO ADD SOMETHING IMPORTANT TO ME.
YOUR HONOR, I'LL BE FORCED TO RECORD YOUR REMARKS...
IT'S IMPORTANT TO ME, MADAME COSCIENZA, AND IT'S IMPORTANT FOR THEM, YOU KNOW. SO, YOU CAN RECORD EVERYTHING YOU LIKE, I DON'T CARE. IF YOU WISH TO DO SO, THAT WILL DO MONSIEUR GROB A SERVICE.
WHAT I WISH IS OF NO IMPORTANCE, YOUR HONOR. IT'S THE RULES, AND I DON'T...
THE RULE, MADAME CLERK, IS THAT YOU KEEP SILENT.
SO RECORD WHATEVER YOU LIKE.

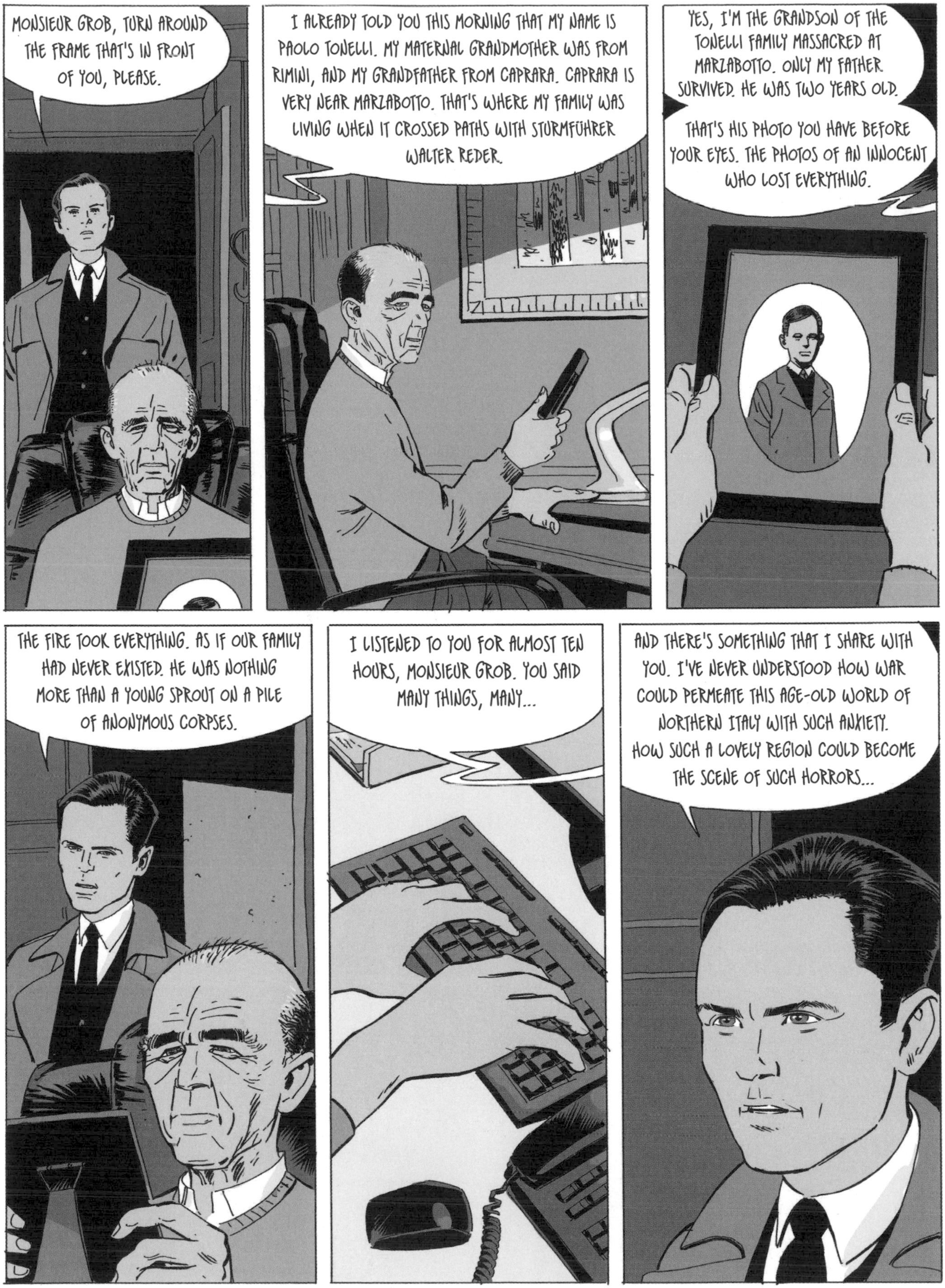
MONSIEUR GROB, TURN AROUND THE FRAME THAT'S IN FRONT OF YOU, PLEASE.
I ALREADY TOLD YOU THIS MORNING THAT MY NAME IS PAOLO TONELLI. MY MATERNAL GRANDMOTHER WAS FROM RIMINI, AND MY GRANDFATHER FROM CAPRARA. CAPRARA IS VERY NEAR MARZABOTTO. THAT'S WHERE MY FAMILY WAS LIVING WHEN IT CROSSED PATHS WITH STURMFÜHRER WALTER REDER.
YES, I'M THE GRANDSON OF THE TONELLI FAMILY MASSACRED AT MARZABOTTO. ONLY MY FATHER SURVIVED. HE WAS TWO YEARS OLD.
THAT'S HIS PHOTO YOU HAVE BEFORE YOUR EYES. THE PHOTOS OF AN INNOCENT WHO LOST EVERYTHING.
THE FIRE TOOK EVERYTHING. AS IF OUR FAMILY HAD NEVER EXISTED. HE WAS NOTHING MORE THAN A YOUNG SPROUT ON A PILE OF ANONYMOUS CORPSES.
I LISTENED TO YOU FOR ALMOST TEN HOURS, MONSIEUR GROB. YOU SAID MANY THINGS, MANY...
AND THERE'S SOMETHING THAT I SHARE WITH YOU. I'VE NEVER UNDERSTOOD HOW WAR COULD PERMEATE THIS AGE-OLD WORLD OF NORTHERN ITALY WITH SUCH ANXIETY. HOW SUCH A LOVELY REGION COULD BECOME THE SCENE OF SUCH HORRORS...

IN ALL GOOD CONSCIENCE, I MUST ADMIT, MONSIEUR GROB, THAT I COULDN'T MANAGE TO FIND THE TRUTH IN YOUR STORY. I'M NEVERTHELESS GOING TO INFORM THE JUDGES OF MY CONCLUSIONS AND OF MY PERSONAL BELIEF CONCERNING YOUR REMARKS.

YOUR HEARING IS SCHEDULED FOR 7:00PM IN THE TRIBUNAL'S COURTROOM. I'M CHARGING YOU IN THE SESSION OF THE CORTE VERITÀ, AND WE'LL SEE WHAT FATE AWAITS YOU.

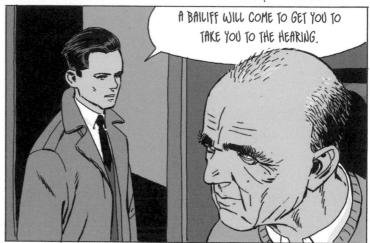

A BAILIFF WILL COME TO GET YOU TO TAKE YOU TO THE HEARING.

DON'T SAY ANYTHING ELSE, PLEASE.

I DON'T WANT TO HEAR YOU ANYMORE.

BLAM

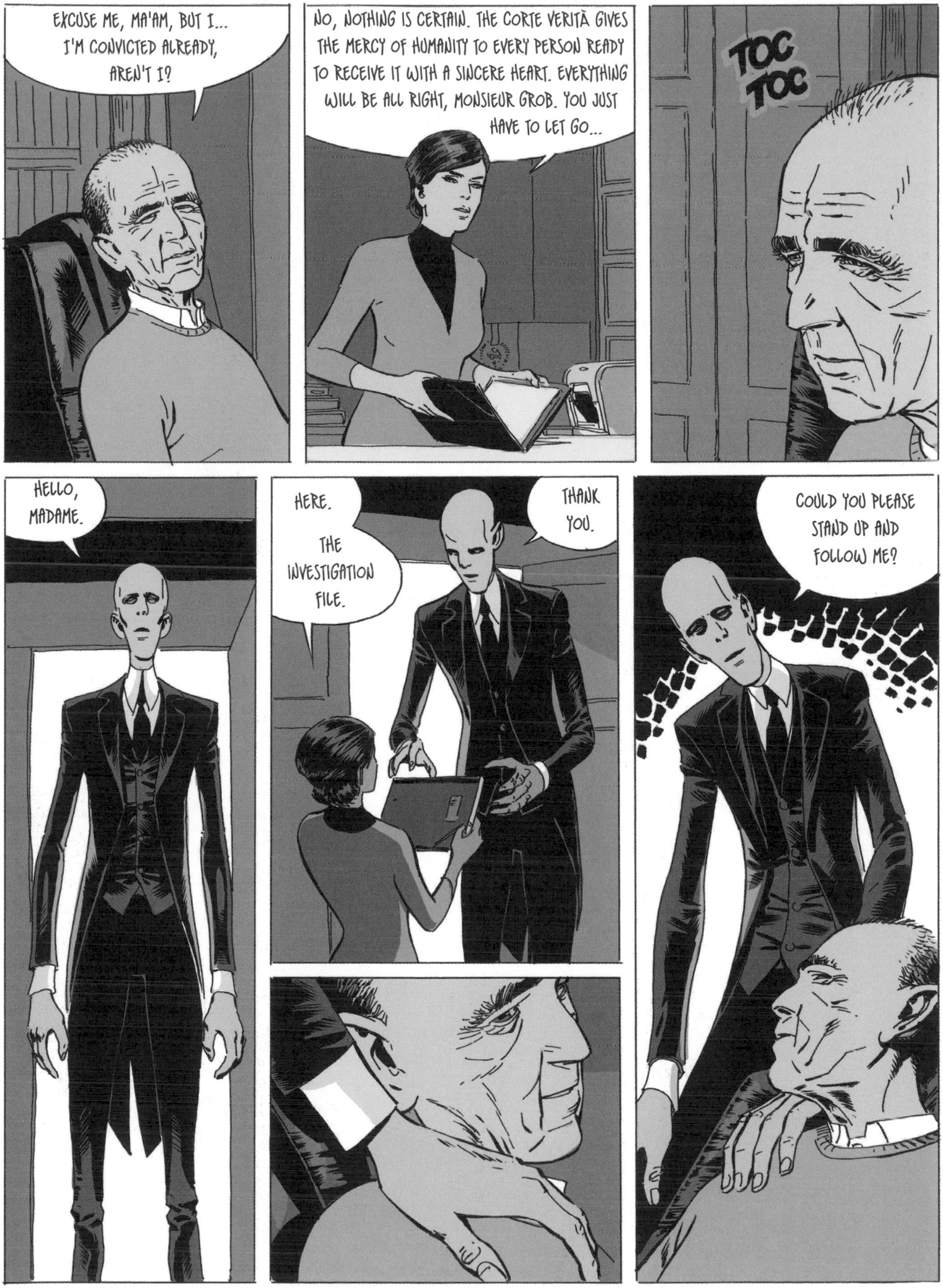

EXCUSE ME, MA'AM, BUT I... I'M CONVICTED ALREADY, AREN'T I?
NO, NOTHING IS CERTAIN. THE CORTE VERITÀ GIVES THE MERCY OF HUMANITY TO EVERY PERSON READY TO RECEIVE IT WITH A SINCERE HEART. EVERYTHING WILL BE ALL RIGHT, MONSIEUR GROB. YOU JUST HAVE TO LET GO...
TOC TOC
HELLO, MADAME.
HERE.
THE INVESTIGATION FILE.
THANK YOU.
COULD YOU PLEASE STAND UP AND FOLLOW ME?

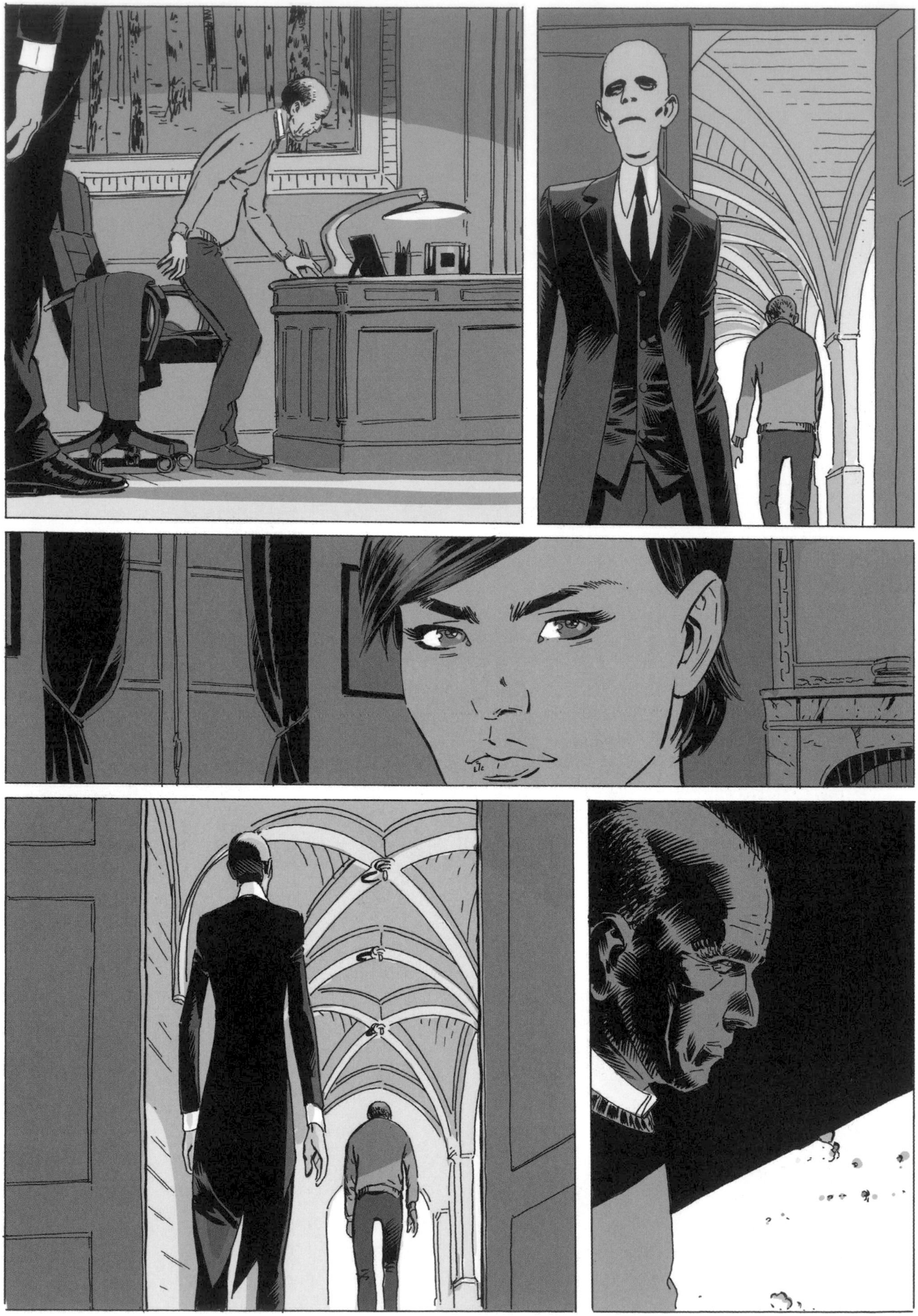

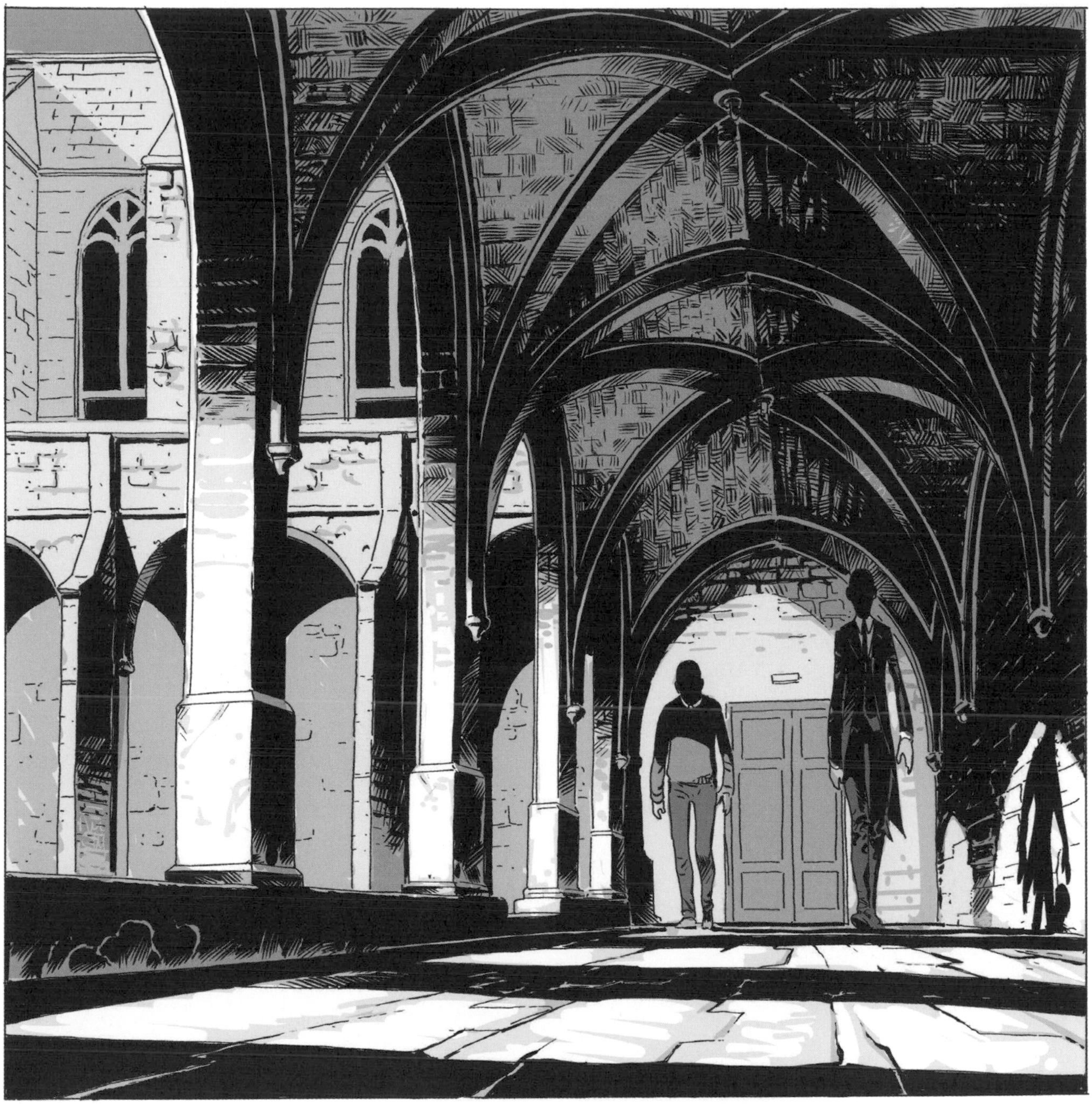

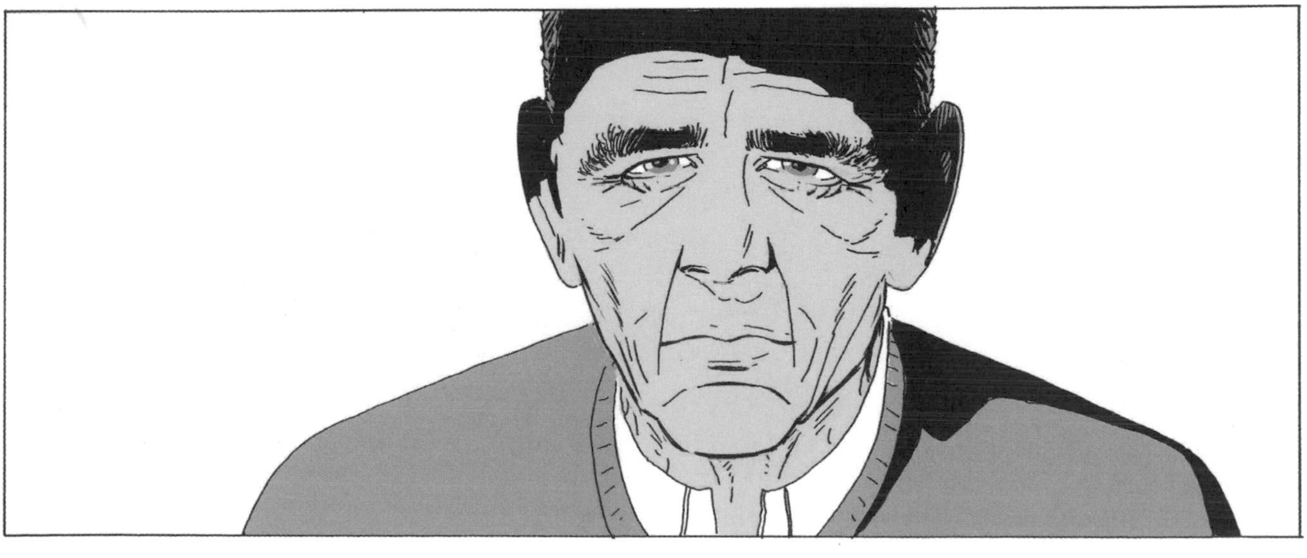

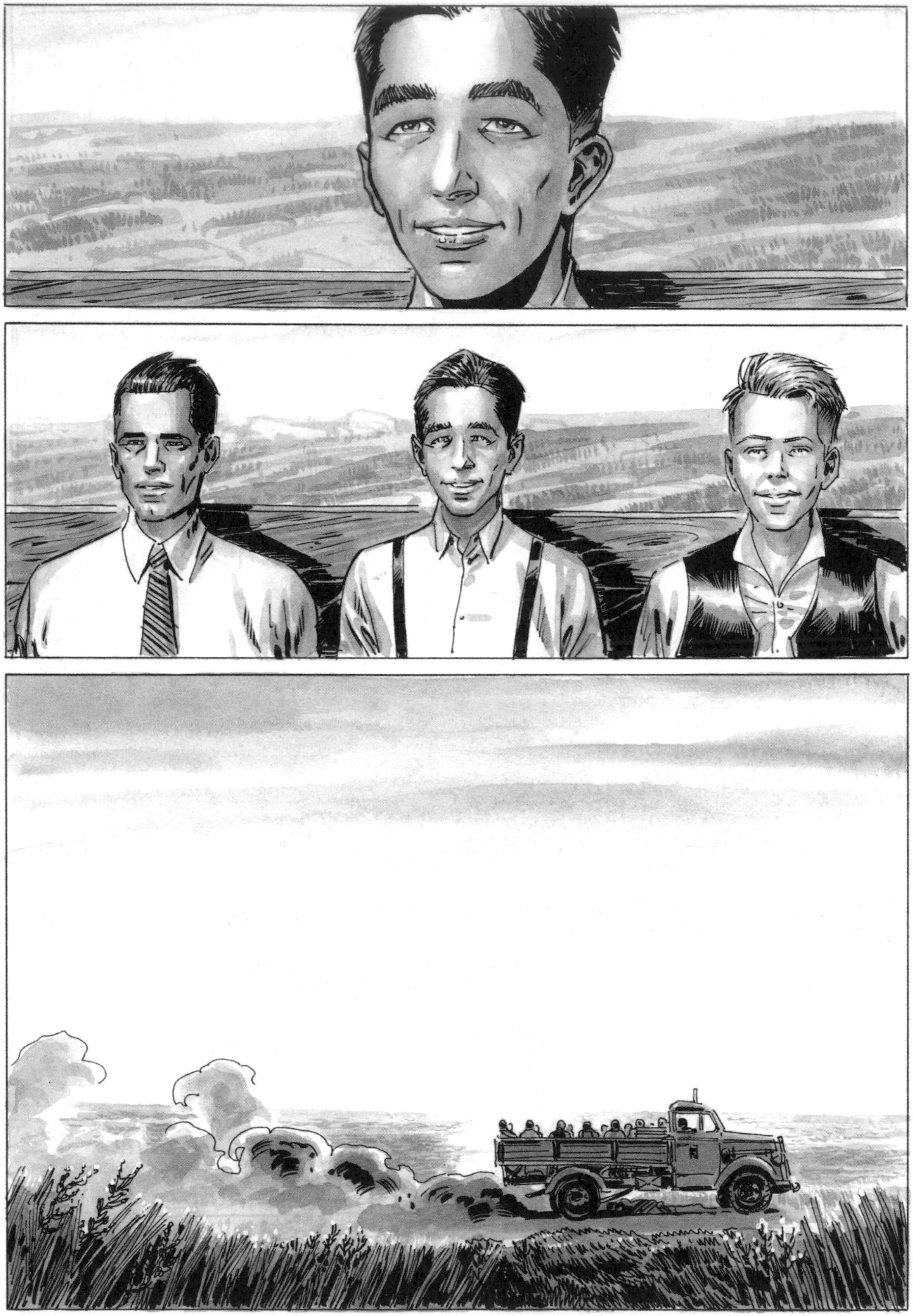

OCTOBER 12, 2009. 4:45AM.

BELIEVE ME, IT'LL ALL BE FINE, MARCEL. IT'LL BE OKAY.

DON'T RESIST, MY LOVE. STOP FIGHTING. YOU HAVE TO LET GO.

I'LL JOIN YOU SOON.

IT'S OVER, MADAME. I'M SORRY.

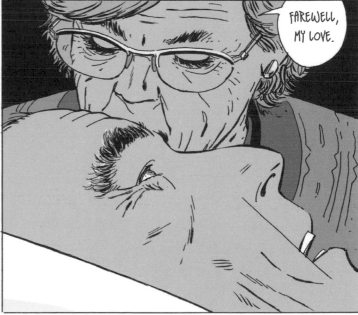

FAREWELL, MY LOVE.

179

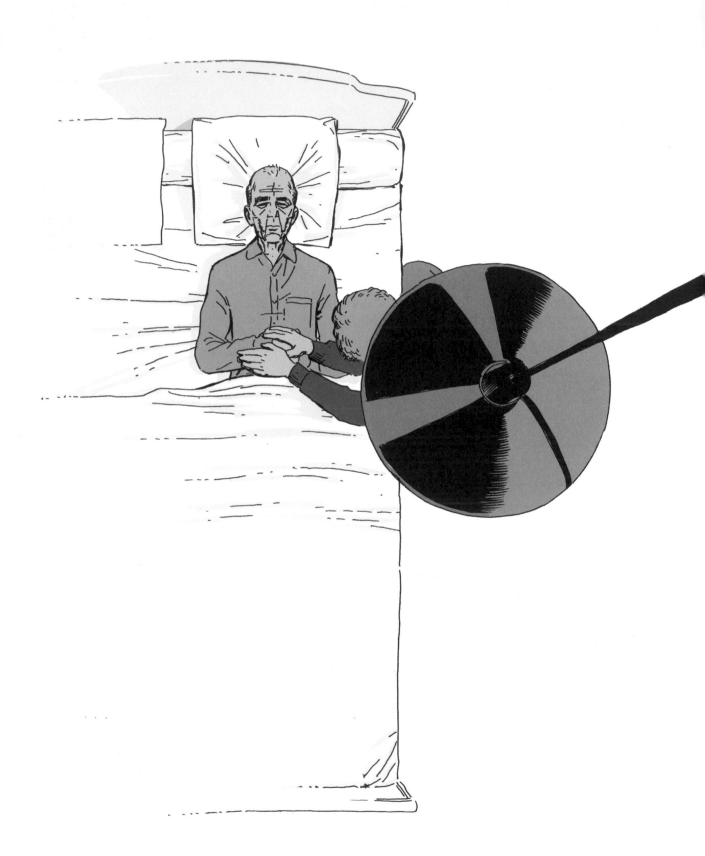

Nazi Germany in 1944
Axis Countries, satellites of Germany
Countries occupied by Germany
Neutral countries aligned with Germany
Neutral countries
Allied combatant countries and conquered land
Journey of Marcel Grob
NORWAY
SWEDEN
ESTONIA
USSR
IRELAND
UNITED KINGDOM
NORTHERN SEA
DENMARK
BALTIC SEA
LITHUANIA
BELARUS
NETHERLANDS
ENGLISH CHANNEL
landing June 6, 1944
BELGIUM
LUXEMBOURG
GERMANY
UKRAINE
ATLANTIC OCEAN
FRANCE
SLOVAKIA
HUNGARY
SWITZERLAND
RUMANIA
CROATIA
SERBIA
MONTENEGRO
BULGARIA
PORTUGAL
ANDORRA
SPAIN
ITALY
ADRIATIC SEA
BLACK SEA
ALBANIA
SARDINIA
TURKEY
GREECE
MEDITERRANEAN SEA
AEGEAN SEA
SICILY
IONIAN SEA
MOROCCO
ALGERIA
TUNISIA
300 km

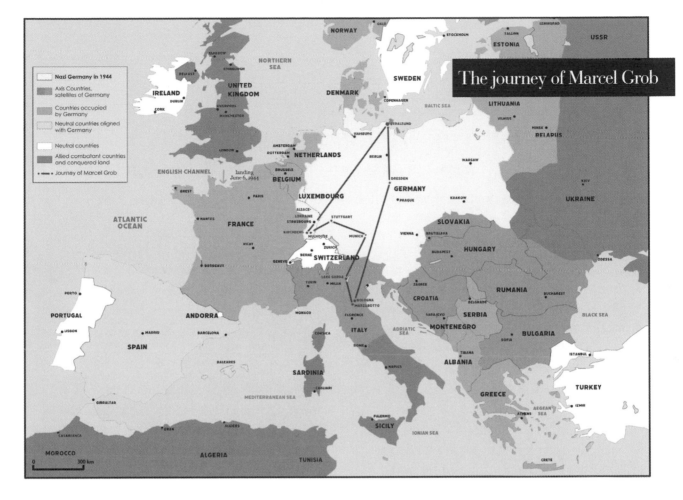

The journey of Marcel Grob

The Tragedy of the *Malgré-nous* Conscripted into the Waffen SS

—A HISTORICAL RECORD BY CHRISTIAN INGRAO

Christian Ingrao was born in 1970. He is the director of research at the Institut d'Histoire du Temps présent (IHTP, the Institute of History of Present Times) and teaches at the Université Catholique de l'Ouest in Angers. He is considered to be one of the foremost French experts on the history of Nazism and war violence. The translation of his latest work, *The Promise of the East: Nazi Hopes and Genocide, 1939–1943*, appeared in 2019 with Polity Press.

1942–1944

THE *MALGRÉ-NOUS*
MEN FROM ALSACE AND LORRAINE CONSCRIPTED "AGAINST THEIR WILL" INTO THE WEHRMACHT

The experience of war for Alsace and Alsatians in the twentieth century is very specific: on the one hand, because the territory and its inhabitants constituted a matter of high stakes in two worldwide conflicts and, on the other, because Alsatians born between 1870 and 1918 were of German nationality, whereas those born before or after that period were of French nationality, at least until 1942.

In fact, beginning in the summer of 1942 pressures exerted by the armed forces to introduce conscription in Alsace-Moselle resulted in the establishment of compulsory military service, along with the use of intimidation measures aiming to prevent desertions and decreeing citizenship in the Reich for enlistees.

Enlistments began in November 1942 and, throughout the German occupation, affected more than 100,000 Alsatians and 30,000 Lorrainers born between 1909 and 1926.

For the most part, the conscripts were placed in the infantry (the Heer); beginning in November 1943, however, the Waffen SS managed to grab a growing number of recruits who were not transferred there on a voluntary basis.

Alsatians and Mosellans fought primarily on the Eastern Front, where thousands were taken prisoner and imprisoned in very difficult conditions in the Tambov camp, but they also fought on the Western Front in Normandy and in Italy, as well as the French hinterlands in 1944.

It is rather difficult to calculate the human toll of this assimilation. Historians estimate about 35,000 men were killed or missing in action but differ on the categories taken into account. To that must be added the wounded and disabled. These figures suffice to single out the Alsatian situation and to make a special case of its war experience, more akin to that of a German Gau (region or shire) than a French region, while being fundamentally set apart by the very deep mistrust that German military authorities felt for Alsatians and Mosellans, whose loyalty was suspect and whose "racial purity" was untested.

The SS

The SS (*Schutzstaffel*) was created in 1925 as bodyguards for Hitler. The first years of its history coincide with those of the SA (*Sturmabteilung*, also known as Brownshirts). In 1929 the nomination of the third head of the SS for the Reich (Reichsführer), Heinrich Himmler, marked a fundamental change. Himmler immediately launched a policy of systematic expansion by employing intensive recruitment while still maintaining the organization's elite character. In 1932 the SS was already powerful, 52,000 men strong, and its numbers quadrupled the following year. Starting with Hitler's seizure of power, the SS began an unrelenting rise, freeing itself of all constraint other than that of Himmler, and granting itself ever-increasing operational fields. As the regime's elite ideological corps, it became a reservoir for leaders and a laboratory for ideas and took the lead in the three essential axes of the Nazi project.

First, the SS was the instrument of a dual conquest, that of power in Germany and of the empire in Europe. Next, between 1939 and 1943, it was one of the main tools of administration and operational policies in the occupied territories. Lastly, between 1941 and 1944, it was the nearly unique performer in the policies of repression and extermination that constitute the heart of the Nazi practice.

However, from 1929 to 1932 the SS was nothing more than a subordinate battalion of the SA. It was the latter, a mass movement associated as much with controlling streets as influencing the ballot box, that paraded by torchlight in the Berlin of January 30, 1933. For its part, the SS seemed to be relegated to secondary roles. However, after Himmler had been named chief of police in Munich with no portfolio, he used this position to take control of all German police forces and compete with the SA. On June 30, 1934, the SA, which constituted a force of instability in a Germany aspiring for calm after the "revolutionary period" of the first year of Nazi power, was eliminated.

The SS was the main actor in that: it took charge of executing the SA's leadership as well as targeted assassinations of conservative figures. As a result of this crisis, it obtained status as a body independent of the party, and Himmler, named chief of the political police of Prussia, could finally openly take control of all German police forces. After the elimination of the SA, Himmler set out to reorganize the SS by dividing it into paramilitary units named *Verfügungstruppen* (SS Dispositional Troops, SS-VT) and "Death's Head," or *Totenkopf*, units, charged with the administration of concentration camps. The heart of the SS' power, founded on elite paramilitary units that were still embryonic with respect to manpower, on the monopoly over policing and on intelligence services was thus put into place after successfully facing its first test.

In 1936, when Himmler finally assumed control of all German police forces, he named Paul Hausser inspector of the SS-VT, charging him with militarizing these units. Put to intensive military training, the three regiments of the SS-VT took part in the invasions of Austria, the Sudetenland, and Bohemia-Moravia. In 1939 the Waffen SS was created; its use in the campaign in Poland marked the beginning of an unprecedented expansion of the SS armed forces.

Between 1929 and 1939, Himmler laid the foundations of what would become the most powerful organizations of the Third Reich: the police and the Waffen SS. For conquest abroad inaugurated, in Hitler's eyes as in those of the Reichsführer SS, a new era. Germanization and exploitation would follow. ■

The WAFFEN SS

The existence of SS formations in barracks, ready for use and at the disposal of authorities (SS-*Verfügungstruppe*, SS-VT), dates back to March 1933. In June 1934 these formations with a still-obscure role had proven their effectiveness in the elimination of the SA during what was called the "Night of Long Knives" (June 30, 1934). Along with the "Death's Head" SS formations (SS *Totenkopfverbände*, SS-TV), themselves put in barracks and assigned to administer concentration camps, the SS-VT constituted a rapidly expanding institution whose independence in relation to the army and the police was recognized by Hitler on August 17, 1938. Thereafter and entirely independent of the Wehrmacht, Himmler—already the head of all German police forces and grand master of the concentration camps—had at his disposal the beginnings of a strong, parallel army numbering some 14,000 men at that time.

The invasion of Poland, the first real armed conflict of the Third Reich, was also that in which the SS-VT were engaged for the first time in their entirety. In September 1939 they handled missions securing the invasion troops' rear and brought attention to themselves for attacks upon civilians. On the evening of September 19, 1939, Hitler ordered Himmler to create a *Totenkopf* Division out of concentration camp guard units. At the same time, the SS-VT was increasingly supplied with heavy weapons, cannons, and antitank weapons. The militarization of these partisan and repression units into forces used in wartime indicated that a new form of troops was coming into being, something akin to a "political soldier." Ambiguous missions at the edges of the military role, that of policemen or militiamen— missions already characterized by great violence— were answered by the partisan, paramilitary, militant character of the SS-VT. In Himmler's view, the creation of the *Totenkopf* Division and the growing integration of the SS-VT into operations were beyond the scope of the Wehrmacht. It is with that in mind that, on December 1, 1939, Himmler decided to create a new organization, the Waffen SS, which would thereafter group together existing and future armed formations of the SS as well as their administrative systems.

Beginning with the creation of the Waffen SS, Himmler conducted a policy based on the tactical and operative subordination of active units to the Wehrmacht and an intensive recruitment campaign that, in December 1940, raised the Waffen SS' manpower to some 60,000 men, with almost 27,000 additional men enlisted in the *Totenkopf* regiments. In under two years, these groups' manpower had thereby sextupled.

Begun in June 1941, the war in the Soviet Union entered a new phase, with increasingly brutal behaviors as well as an institutional expansion. Eighteen months later, in December 1942, SS units—perfectly integrated into the active and operational reserve armed groups that Himmler held back, safe and sound—then counted 246,000 men, divided into eight divisions and two brigades. In December, Hitler declared that the Waffen SS would be the fourth branch of the Wehrmacht, on par with the Kriegsmarine, the Luftwaffe, and the Heer (the army). The year 1943 was marked by the most intensive recruitment campaigns: some 255,000 men were enrolled into the units of the dark order, with a fundamental reorientation toward recruitment of foreign volunteers. Whereas in 1940 the proportion of SS members born outside the Reich's borders did not exceed 1 percent of total troops, the formation of a division comprising ethnic German troops coming from the Croatian minority, the "Prinz Eugen," demonstrated a reorientation that opened recruitment to *Volkdeutsche* meeting criteria of neither "racial excellence" nor physical acuity. A breach was opening that would increase the ratio of Germans born outside the Reich's borders from an initial 1 percent to nearly 27 percent.

VOLUNTARY SERVICE, CONSCRIPTION, AND ENLISTMENT IN THE WAFFEN SS

The Waffen SS was an outgrowth of the SS, a paramilitary organization; initially, the rule was recruitment on a strictly voluntary basis among the pool of SS militants and of the *Verfügunstruppen*, those SS troops in barracks. They were, therefore, hardcore Nazis dead set in their commitment.

Their selection met the criterion of "racial excellence," which the candidates were required to establish by providing a family tree and by filling out an exhaustive questionnaire on the medical and clinical history of their family, in order to allow racialist physicians and selection committees to recruit only the best elements of what one could call the racially conscious vanguard of the Third Reich.

The fact remains that, by 1939, the elitism of the SS found itself in complete contradiction with the objective affirmed by Himmler to possess his own army: to have an army, it was necessary to open recruitment widely, to the detriment of the physical ideal and the ideology of the selective and numerically restricted elite. From December 1, 1939, the date of the official creation of the Waffen SS, through December 1940, there were no fewer than 70,000 carefully selected men placed in Waffen SS units and the *Totenkopf* Division. These numbers constituted a core selected with great rigor simultaneously for its physical fitness, its racial and esthetic pseudo-qualities, and the firmness of its ideological convictions.

Recruitment continued along these lines in 1941 and 1942, but losses occasioned by Operation Barbarossa and the expansion of the war to the east and in the Balkans made the need for recruits increasingly critical. In the summer of 1942, influxes of German volunteers sufficed to refill the ranks of SS line divisions, but in the view of the SS parties responsible for recruitment, the situation was rapidly getting worse.

Himmler then decided to introduce a universal draft for all citizens of Eastern Europe considered part of German culture—those called the *Volksdeutsche*, "ethnic Germans." Romanian, Baltic, Hungarian, and Serbian nationals, all of whom shared the German language and, at least partially, German culture and whom the Nazis had repatriated into the Reich beginning in 1939 or encountered during their conquests. The incorporation of ethnic Germans was, therefore, theoretically mandatory beginning in the summer of 1942, but its implementation happened progressively, and only at the end of 1943 and the beginning of 1944 did it truly become dangerous to try to avoid being drafted into the Waffen SS.

As far as the Reich was concerned, whether within the borders of 1938 or those of 1941 (thus including Alsace and Larraine and the territories incorporated to the East), the designation of eligible ethnic Germans was a complex and shifting issue that evolved at the pace of the creation of divisions. Until the winter of 1942, voluntary service had supplied sufficient quotas of troops, even though it had been necessary to expand recruitment to seventeen-year-old volunteers for whom parental consent was no longer required. Since 1939 SS recruiters had been conducting a slow, methodical campaign of brainwashing and propaganda in the camps of the *Reichsarbeitsdienst* (RAD), the national work service to which all boys were forcibly sent for one year and whose duration was extended by six months during the war. The RAD camps had become the Waffen SS' main breeding ground. Seventeen-year-old volunteers were first incorporated in January 1943, when the constraints on levying new divisions led recruiters to use coercion more frequently. In October 1943 the 16th SS Panzer Division Reichsführer SS, the main party responsible for the massacres in the Apennine Mountains, was created. At that moment, the SS had assured itself the recruitment of 25,000 volunteers coming from the RAD camps. This manpower, however, was insufficient for its needs, and the Waffen SS recruiters sought new sources for conscripts. Alsace was the first choice: conscription had been introduced there only in November 1942, and, beginning at the end of August 1943, the SS pursued negotiations with the civilian administration to send selection committees into RAD camps located in Alsace. Four thousand young Alsatians of the class of 1926–Marcel Grob's class–were made eligible for conscription into the Waffen SS beginning in November 1943. ■

THE EQUIPMENT OF THE WAFFEN SS FOOT SOLDIER

Enlisted upon exiting the Reich's Labor Service camps, Alsatian conscripts founds themselves declared fit for duty and issued an SS-*Soldbuch*–the military ID that is one of the key pieces of evidence used against Marcel Grob and that, by serving as an identifying document, recorded the different postings and stints of the conscript, as well as his leave and possible rewards, promotions, and decorations awarded to him.

Recruits were issued a uniform comprising a steel helmet (*Stahlhelm*), boots, underclothing, one set of combat pants, and a jacket marked on the collar by two SS symbols and indicating the foot soldier's possible rank on the left sleeve. Next, he was issued a belt equipped with a canteen, a mess kit, a gasmask holder, and a sabretache, a satchel allowing one to carry documents on the belt. Finally, cases were attached to the belt to hold cartridges and magazines, as well as stick grenades.

The young recruit was then issued personal weaponry consisting of stick grenades, a knife, and a 98k repeating rifle, issued with 7.92-millimeter caliber rounds, a large-caliber ammunition with a 500-meter operating range, or an MP 38 sub-machine gun whose lower caliber and more limited range were compensated by automatic fire at a rate of eight to nine shots per second.

Marcel Grob and his comrades were inducted into a division of mechanized, armored grenadiers: their job was to accompany the advance of tanks during offensives and exploit openings made by them. To do so, they were given more weaponry than conventional infantry regiments, notably light and heavy machine guns, and, at the end of the war, assault rifles. ■

BETWEEN COMBAT AND WAR CRIMES: THE WEHRMACHT AND SS BETWEEN THE EASTERN AND WESTERN FRONTS

There is a black legend concerning the Waffen SS–that of fanatical, cruel combatants who would fight to the last man; that of "political soldiers" who would never refrain from attacking civilians or from committing the worst atrocities at the front. Both developed and battled in the postwar period–one part of an amnesiac Germany seeking, during the 1960s, to pass them off as "soldiers like the others." This legend had several functions. On the one hand, it was about contrasting fanatical militants with a "clean" Wehrmacht and, on the other, about shifting the unfathomable violence that Nazism had mobilized between 1939 and 1945 into the order of simplistic fanaticism. Everything about this legend, however, must be rehashed except, quite obviously, the uncontrolled violence that the Germans deployed during World War II.

The first affirmation to debate, one often advanced by revisionists and veterans of the Waffen SS: the high value of Waffen SS combat troops. Certainly, Waffen SS units used as strategic reserves would come to shore up breaches in the Eastern fronts and then, beginning in the summer of 1944, in the Western ones. They had the reputation of units fit for emergency situations, but historians have also shown that the SS would take very special care, at every command level, to use units sparingly and to remove them from the front as often as possible. Second, in equal tactical situations, the SS infantry units did not prevail against "ordinary" Allied troops. They were, therefore, hardly the epitome of combat excellence, though certain units might have characterized themselves as possessing great intensity and remarkable tenacity.

The second affirmation: the Wehrmacht and the SS behaved radically differently with regard to civilians, with the army's units being perceived as noticeably less criminal than those of the SS. However, the Waffen SS, beginning with the campaign in Poland and in the Soviet Union, developed, like units in the Wehrmacht, incomparably radical practices of aggression against civilians. One might also argue that no unit of the Waffen SS was as engaged in the systematic extermination of Jews as was the 707th Infantry Division of the Wehrmacht, while SS units, like the special Dirlewanger Brigade of the *Kampfgrupper* Von Gottberg, displayed incredible brutality and decimated the rural Belarusian population. Units of Waffen SS also participated in innumerable Nazi acts of violence and were even the principal performer of them on the Western Front beginning in 1943.

Indeed, if German armed forces were guilty of continuous acts of violence on the entirety of the Eastern fronts, it can be observed that that was practically not the case on the Western one before 1944. From 1939 to 1944, a crescendo of violence could be observed in Poland, the Balkans, and the Soviet Union which transformed those sectors into a hell. In Belarus, for example, more than 650 villages were destroyed and burned and their populations exterminated during the three years of occupation. In that whirlwind of violence, SS units displayed enormous brutality. While the Waffen SS units, used as strategic reserves, participated in only a minor way in these crimes during the occupation phase, they were part of them during the invasion phase and during periods of evacuations and retreats; the porousness between security apparatus command structures and the Waffen SS units resulted in a circulation of leaders who brought the violent propensities of the rear units to those of the forward ones.

It is this ensemble of phenomena, coupled with a dynamic of radicalization of violent practices due to the return of combat in the West, that explains how Waffen SS units committed crimes such as those at Oradour-sur-Glane or Marzabotto. At Oradour, for example, the general commanding the SS Division Das Reich was the former executive officer of the general staff for the fight against partisans and is responsible for the systematic burning of Belarusian villages.

Beginning in January 1944 during the widespread retreat of the Wehrmacht and its allies from east to west, Europe experienced an unprecedented wave of massacres of civilians committed by Nazi troops in which the Waffen SS was very deeply implicated. In Italy, the wave of massacres took off north of the Gothic Line beginning in April 1944. ∎

THE 16TH SS PANZER GRENADIER "REICHSFÜHRER-SS"

The 16th SS Panzer Grenadier "Reichsführer-SS" was created in the fall of 1943 out of existing SS units; they were, in fact, escort detachments from the command general staff of Heinrich Himmler, the head of the SS (*Reichsführer SS*), as well as elements from the 3rd Armored SS "Death's Head" Division (*SS-Totenkopfverbände*), which constituted the original core. The founding of this division was not innocent: the units from the command staff played a considerable role in the radicalization of SS practices and in their transformation, during the summer of 1941, into genocidal practices against Jewish populations. In 1942 those elements that were to assure the personal protection of the head of the SS had been engaged in counterinsurgency operations against partisans and made themselves noteworthy by their involvement in multiple burnings of villages and in massacres of populations. The elements of the *Totenkopf* Division had historically come from units in charge of administering concentration camps. Brought together in Brittany at the end of 1942, they had been raised to the level of assault brigade; the leaders of the unit were thereafter safeguarded by officers reassigned from the *Totenkopf* Division.

Sent to Italy in July 1943, the brigade was then used in Corsica, where it fought against local resistance fighters beginning in August. After that two-month campaign, it returned to the mainland and fought in Italy. Simultaneously, an order by Hitler transformed the brigade into a division. That transformation proved to be difficult, considering the demographic situation of the SS in the fourth year of the war.

Dispersed between Slovenia and the area of Ljubljana on the one hand, and the area of Lucca and Benito Mussolini's residence on the other, the unit included two armored regiments of SS grenadiers in three battalions as well as a command company and three regimental units (artillery, machine-gun units, engineers, reconnaissance/intelligence, etc.). At the divisional level, this arrangement was completed by a regiment of artillery, an armored reconnaissance squadron, an armored squadron, engineering, transmission, an anti-aircraft defense, and logistical/transportation units.

So it was in fall 1943 that, with many difficulties and delays, the different units of the division incorporated the recruits as reinforcements. Between mid-October and mid-December, no fewer than 5,500 of the recruits were assigned to the 16th Division by the personnel staff of Waffen SS command. Among them were some 3,000 young recruits from the class of 1926—that of Marcel Grob—who filled the regiments of grenadiers but also the engineering, artillery, and transmission units. In addition, 2,500 more experienced grenadiers and artilleryman, graduates of the classes 1902 to 1922, were added.

The unit was therefore composed of experienced officers and leaders coming from the most militant units of the Waffen SS, which, moreover, had gained combat and occupation experience that, in the east, had played a large part in extremely brutal acts of aggression against civilian populations. As regards these troops, they comprised nearly 45 percent of experienced Waffen SS, who were no doubt volunteers and had also experienced those fever-pitched schools that are the Eastern fronts, and 55 percent of underaged, inexperienced conscripts.

Although its transformation constituted a success for the head of the SS, the 16th Division was suffering from the strategic and demographic situation of the Reich: its supplying was incomplete, the lack of means of transportation and of heavy arms was obvious, and the training of units did not allow the formation of squadrons and coherent, cohesive sections. Such a situation for the leadership, originating mainly from the

SS-Totenkopf Division, the elite of the elite corps that was the SS, constituted a frustrating sense of demotion.

The division entered Italy in those conditions. From the outset, the battles against U.S. forces were extremely taxing: at the end of two months of presence at the front, nearly 3,500 men were out of action. While three thousand soldiers were wounded or dead, the loss of officers was also quite considerable: three battalion commanders, twenty-six company commanders, and eighteen section heads were missing.

It was in that context, in July 1944, that the division was withdrawn from the front and engaged in counterinsurgency efforts against partisans. It destroyed villages and massacred populations. ∎

THE MASSACRE OF MARZABOTTO

Beginning on July 20, 1944, an escalation of attacks upon civilians could be observed in the 16th SS Division's operational sector located between the Arno and Magra rivers, south of the city of La Spezia, and north of Pisa up to the ridgeline of the Apennines. The region's security situation had slowly deteriorated in the eyes of the Nazis since the beginning of 1944 and, since June, numerous groups of partisans had been attacking the depots of the *Organisation Todt* (OT) and German supply lines.

The 16th Division was operating in a difficult situation and practiced a mixture of tracking partisans and controlling civilian populations. In August alone, some 10,190 men were selected to be sent to forced labor, provoking a massive flight of adult men who, seeking to escape the division, overwhelmingly joined the partisan movements.

The division withdrew into the Apennines in September 1944 and carried out tracking operations there. During the entire month of September, partisan harassment was persistent but without being truly worrisome in the eyes of leadership. On September 25, 1944, however, in the region of Monte Sole/Marzabotto, an attack led the 1st Parachute Corps to plan a search operation of the region of Marzabotto. The operations and their implementation were assigned to the 16th Armored Division of grenadiers, notably to the armored scouting company, accompanied by many elements from other units of the division (including the 35th Armored Regiment of grenadiers and a Russian battalion from the Wehrmacht infantry division). The third staff officer, Helmut Looß, a specialist in matters of intelligence and security (named lieutenant colonel in the order of battle) along with the head of the armored scout company, circulated the orders detailing the tactical conduct of the operation. Before being transferred to Italy as an intelligence officer, Looß, a *Sturmbannführer-SS*, had commanded an *Einsatzkommando* unit in Belarus from June 1943 to June 1944. He was therefore perfectly capable of importing the violent propensities developed by the SS in then-blood-soaked areas. With his commando unit, Looß had emptied prisons there by massacring their occupants regardless of age or sex and burned entire villages, women and children included. On the evening of September 28, he transmitted orders for the mission the next day to Walter Reder, commander of the reconnaissance battalion. During the night, his companies took their positions. What exactly was contained in the intervention orders is unknown. The officers in charge specify that nowhere was there any suggestion of massacring civilians.

The companies advanced and attacked at 6:00 a.m. on the 29th. Two kilometers to the north of the front line, around Gardeletta and Cadotto, the fighting began— as did the massacres.

The general movement of the operation consisted of scouring the massif of Monte Sole in a south-north direction, from departure positions along the road linking Rioveggio to Montazze to the little village of Marzabotto. For five days, the companies of the reconnaissance battalion fought rather hard battles, but above all systematically massacred the populations of the sector, notably with the help of light and heavy machine guns. At Casaglia, the SS made the populace exit the church where they had taken refuge, killed the young priest who could not give intelligence on the partisan movements, and then, in the cemetery, shot the gathered residents, mainly women, children, and the elderly.

The final mission report mentions 718 dead, including 497 "bandits" and 221 "accomplices of bandits," as well as 456 male civilians rounded up for forced labor. For a long time, estimations had calculated a much higher number of killings, close to 1,830 people, but the figure now established is 770 dead.

Operations around Marzabotto and Monte Sole resembled the tragic norm for the rural populations in the Soviet Union after the 1941 invasion: the annihilation of populations considered unfit for work by the Nazis, the predation of human and economic resources, and the hunt for partisans. German officers, militant Nazis or not, having gone through the unfettered experience in the east, ordered conscripts from throughout the Nazi empire to kill indiscriminately in western and southern Europe. Marzabotto is a tragic, characteristic example of such. One must not think that this was simply an excess of violence; studies show that these efforts were controlled and that there was nothing mechanical about their transposition from the east to the west. It was the result of a rational decisionmaking process. ■

FROM NUREMBERG TO LÜNEBERG: PUNISHING NAZI CRIMES, 1946–2015

The crimes committed at Monte Sole were the object of investigations after the liberation of northern Italy. The commander of the division, General Max Simon, and Walter Reder, the commander of the reconnaissance battalion that was responsible for the majority of executions, were sentenced, the former in spring 1947 in Padua, the latter in May 1948 in Bologna. Simon was condemned to death, while Reder was sentenced to life imprisonment. Their two sentences were commuted, and both were freed, the first in 1954, the second in 1985. In 2007 a group of conscripts into the Waffen SS who had been identified as murderers were indicted and sentenced in absentia before the Tribunal of La Spezia.

The chronology of investigations marks a long movement of remembering the occupation and Nazi crimes, which illustrates the consequences of this tragic part of European history.

First, the punishment of Nazi crimes resulted from a desire expressed by the Allies in the "Declaration on Atrocities" signed during the Moscow Conference in 1943. For the crimes whose context was defined nationally, the judgment was to occur on the spot and, preferably, by the people who had been the victim of them; Allied tribunals would take charge of crimes on the European scale. That is how, after 1943, investigative proceedings were put in place on all these levels with Soviet investigatory commissions, which worked in the course of the liberation of territory and the discovery of criminal atrocities committed during the occupation and which resulted in the first trials of Krasnodar in July 1943 and Kharkov in December 1943.

Following the unconditional surrender of the Germans in May 1945, the Allies prepared for a big trial of Nazi war criminals before an International Military Tribunal in Nuremberg, which judged and condemned those who had been identified as the greatest Nazi criminals. Of the twenty-four indicted, twenty-three were found guilty; twelve were condemned to death, and eleven were executed (Hermann Goering committed suicide before his execution). One man was acquitted, and there was one non-decision, that of Robert Ley, who committed suicide during the trial. In parallel, the United States began another series of trials, at the conclusion of which a very large number of death penalties were imposed. But those trials were much influenced by the vagaries of European political events, notably the Cold War, which prompted the Americans to impose less severe sentences.

At the end of the 1950s, new waves of trials occurred in succession, fragmenting the history of punishment for Nazi crimes into a multitude of sequences reflected in national frameworks for remembering the war. In Germany, the country that undertook by far the largest number of investigations, thousands of investigations were ordered and hundreds appeared in courts, contributing, through prominent symbolic trials, to the realization by European populations of the extent of Nazi criminal conduct.

The final person indicted in these trials, Oskar Groening—born in 1922, a volunteer in the SS, and an employee in the administration of Auschwitz—was condemned in 2015 to four years of imprisonment as an accessory to murder. His appeal was denied in 2016, and he died at the beginning of 2019 before his sentence in a German penitentiary could begin. That was the last case likely to be adjudicated in Germany. In Ludwigsburg, however, the *Zentralstelle der Landesjustizverwaltungen* is continuing to conduct about ten inquiries—proof that there are still investigators, through investigations and recourse to law, willing to keep alive the memory of victims of Nazi crimes. ■

BIBLIOGRAPHY AND FILMOGRAPHY

General Works on World War II

Ingrao, Christian. *Believe and Destroy: Intellectuals in the SS War Machine.* Translated by Andrew Brown. Cambridge, UK: Polity Press, 2013.

Leleu, Jean-Luc. *La Waffen-SS.* 2 vols. Paris: Tempus Perrin, 2014.

Littell, Jonathan. *The Kindly Ones.* New York: Harper, 2009.

Masson, Philippe. *Histoire de l'armée allemande: 1913–1945.* Paris: Tempus Perrin, 1997.

Works and Articles on the Conscription of Alsatians

Riedweg, Eugène. *Les Malgré nous. Histoire de l'incorporation de force des Alsaciens-Mosellans dans l'armée allemande.* Strasbourg, France: Éditions du Rhin, 1995.

Wagner, Robert and Marie-Joseph Bopp. "L'enrôlement de force des Alsaciens dans la Wehrmacht et la SS." *La revue d'Histoire de la Seconde Guerre mondiale* 5, no. 20 (1955): 33–42.

Articles on the Waffen SS in Italy

Gentile, Carlo. "Politische Soldaten. Die 16. SS-Panzer-Grenadier-Division 'Reichsführer-SS' in Italien 1944." *Quellen und Forschungen aus italienischen Archiven und Bibliotheken* 81 (2001): 529–61.

Prauser, Steffen. "Les crimes de guerre allemands en Italie, 1943–1945." *Occupation et répression militaire allemandes*, edited by Gaël Eismann and Steffen Prauser. Paris: Autrement, 2006.

Primary Source

Grob, Marcel. "SS Soldbuch," Panzer Grenadier of the Das Reichsführer Division, 1944–1945.

Filmography

Diritti, Giorgio, dir. *The Man Who Will Come.* 2010.

Dmytryk, Edward, dir. *Hitler's Children.* 1943.

Enrico, Robert, dir. *The Old Gun.* 1975.

Klimov, Elem, dir. *Come and See.* 1985.

Lee, Spike, dir. *Miracle at St. Anna.* 2008.

Prazan, Michael, dir. *Hitler's Death Army: Das Reich.* 2015.

Rossellini, Roberto, dir. *General Della Rovere.* 1959.

Rossif, Frédéric, dir. *De Nuremberg à Nuremberg.* 1989.

Sirk, Douglas, dir. *A Time to Love and a Time to Die.* 1958.

■

THE AUTHORS THANK

Sébastien Gnaedig, our editor, for his trust, his advice, and his presence throughout the creation of this volume. Frédéric Schwamberger and the entire Futuropolis editions team, especially Anne-Gaëlle Fontaine and Carole Tissier, as well as Didier Gonord, Virginie Migeotte, and Katell Daveau for their effectiveness on the ground. Christian Ingrao, a historian of Nazism and our volume's scientific expert. Victoire Fauche and Klara Fröhlich, for their research work. Thibaud Soubeyran, an investigating judge, who enlightened us about his experience. ■

PHILIPPE COLLIN THANKS

Marcel Grob, my Alsatian great-uncle, a good-natured soul to the end. May he rest in peace. Fernande Grob, my great-aunt, for her generosity and our discussions. Muriel Maynard, Frédéric Bonnaud, Clément Léotard, Henri-Marc Mutel, Laurent Bon, Pascale Clark, Candice Marchal, and Sarah Hirsch, my valued friends. Olivier Guez, a wonderful companion on my path. The AGAT Films company, which financed and realized the creation with Clément Léotard of an audiovisual trailer for this volume, and the entire film crew for that trailer. Laurence Bloch, for her unfailing support. Vincent Meslet, for his sound advice. Evelyne Colas, who led me to Futuropolis editions. Anne-Julie Bémont, for her kindness and stubbornness. Benoist de Changy, he knows why. Sébastien Goethals, for his humanity and talent. Thank you, Sébastien. Joy Raffin, my soulmate, without whom none of this would have existed. ■

SÉBASTIEN GOETHALS THANKS

Gom, for his kindly help with coloring and his talent, which he shares with such kindness and patience. Paul, Magali, and Julien for that salutary brainstorming about cover sketches. Everybody at the "Mine" studio who encouraged, sustained, and supported me. Marion Holweck, my lovely Alsatian, for the comprehensiveness of her work. Josépha, for all those evenings when you tore me from the clutches of the Nazis by making me laugh. Philippe Collin, for having shared such a dear, personal story with me with such great humility and infinite trust, which he'd kept inside himself for so long. Thank you, my friend. ■

Published by Dead Reckoning
291 Wood Road
Annapolis, MD 21402

Library of Congress Cataloging-in-Publication Data
Names: Colin, Philippe, 1975- author. | Goethals, Sébastien, 1970- illustrator. | Johnson, E. Joe (Edward Joe), translator. | Mitchell, T. Perran, letterer.
Title: The journey of Marcel Grob / a story by Philippe Colin and Sébastien Goethals ; based upon Philippe Colin's original idea ; art and color by Sébastien Goethals ; lettering by T. Perran Mitchell ; translation by Joe Johnson ; lettering, T. Perran Mitchell.
Other titles: Voyage de Marcel Grob. English
Description: Annapolis, MD : Dead Reckoning, [2022] | Includes bibliographical references.
Identifiers: LCCN 2022021529 (print) | LCCN 2022021530 (ebook) | ISBN 9781682478219 (paperback ; alk. paper) | ISBN 9781682478226 (ebook)
Subjects: LCSH: World War, 1939-1945–Comic books, strips, etc. | Waffen-SS–Recruiting, enlistment, etc.–Comic books, strips, etc. | Soldiers–France–Alsace–Comic books, strips, etc. | Marzabotto Massacre, 1944–Comic books, strips, etc. | BISAC: COMICS & GRAPHIC NOVELS / Historical Fiction | COMICS & GRAPHIC NOVELS / Literary |
LCGFT: Historical comics. | Graphic novels.
Classification: LCC PN6747.C57 V6913 2022 (print) | LCC PN6747.C57 (ebook) | DDC 741.5/944–dc23/eng/20220607
LC record available at https://lccn.loc.gov/2022021529
LC ebook record available at https://lccn.loc.gov/2022021530

♾ Print editions meet the requirements of ANSI/NISO z39.48-1992 (Permanence of Paper).
Printed in the United States of America.

30 29 28 27 26 25 24 23 22 9 8 7 6 5 4 3 2 1
First printing

Author: Philippe Collin
Illustrator: Sébastien Goethals
Translation: Joe Johnson
Lettering: T. Perran Mitchell

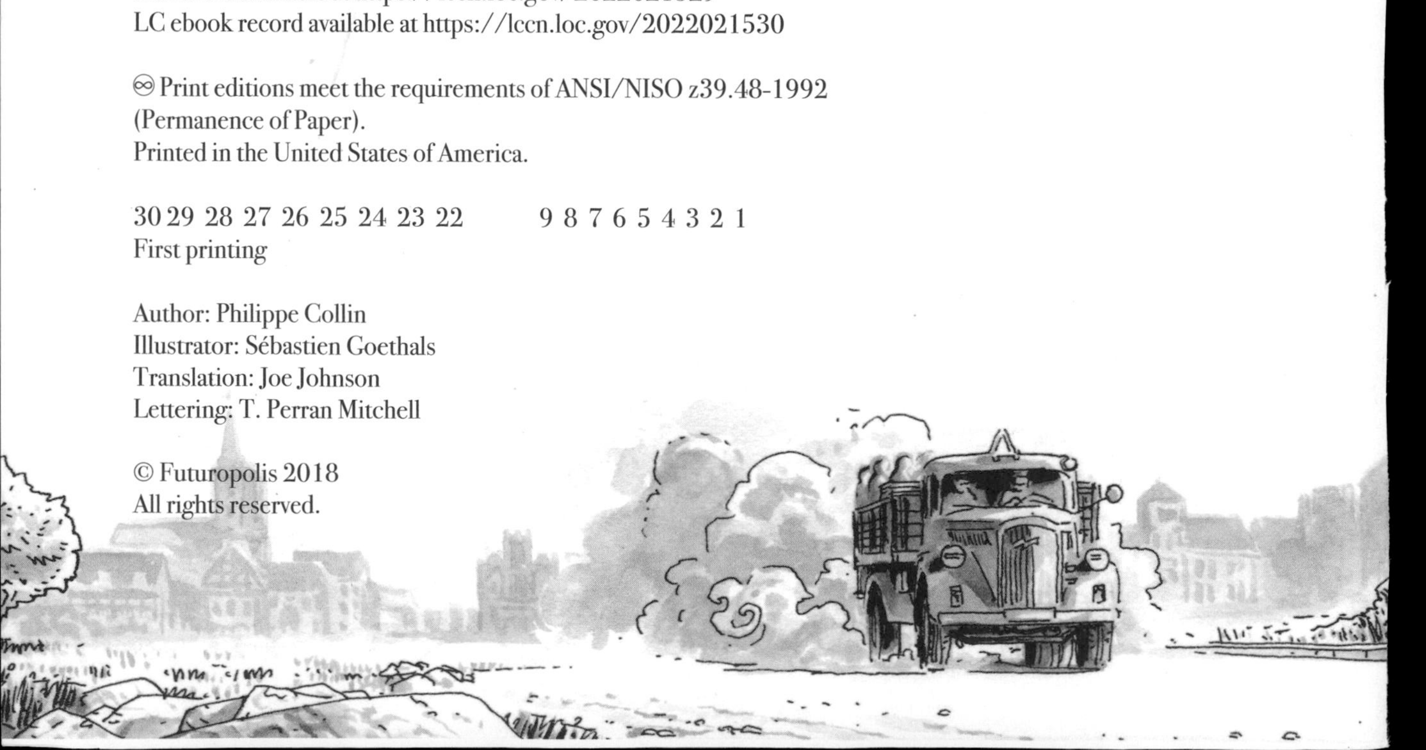